JESUS' DEATH AS SAVING EVENT

THE BACKGROUND AND ORIGIN OF A CONCEPT

by

Sam K. Williams

Published by

SCHOLARS PRESS

for

Harvard Theological Review

Distributed by

SCHOLARS PRESS
University of Montana
Missoula, Montana  59801

JESUS' DEATH AS SAVING EVENT
THE BACKGROUND AND ORIGIN OF A CONCEPT

by

Sam K. Williams
Department of Religion
The Colorado College
Colorado Springs, Colorado  80903

Library of Congress Cataloging in Publication Data

Williams, Sam K
  Jesus' death as saving event.

    (Harvard dissertations in religion ; no. 2)
    Originally presented as the author's thesis, Harvard,
1972.
    Bibliography: p.
    1.  Salvation--History of doctrines.  2.  Jesus Christ
--Crucifixion.  3.  Martyrdom.  4.  Suffering.  5.  Death.
I.  Title.  II.  Series.
BT752.W54  1975        234          75-28341
ISBN 0-89130-029-5

Printed in the United States of America

Printing Department
University of Montana
Missoula, Montana  59801

JESUS' DEATH AS SAVING EVENT

THE BACKGROUND AND ORIGIN OF A CONCEPT

HARVARD THEOLOGICAL REVIEW

HARVARD DISSERTATIONS IN RELIGION

edited by

Caroline Bynum

and

George Rupp

Number 2

JESUS' DEATH AS SAVING EVENT

THE BACKGROUND AND ORIGIN OF A CONCEPT

by

Sam K. Williams

---

SCHOLARS PRESS
Missoula, Montana

TABLE OF CONTENTS

FOR BILLIE ANN

who made it possible

## ABBREVIATIONS

AP        The Apocrypha and Pseudepigrapha of the Old
          Testament in English.  Edited by R. H. Charles.
          2 vols.  Oxford:  At the Clarendon Press, 1913.

BASOR     Bulletin of the American Schools of Oriental
          Research

BZ        Biblische Zeitschrift

CBQ       Catholic Biblical Quarterly

CIG       Corpus Inscriptionarum Graecarum

ET        Expository Times

EvTh      Evangelische Theologie

FRLANT    Forschungen zur Religion und Literatur des Alten
          und Neuen Testaments

Grimm     Carl L. Wilibald Grimm.  Kurzgefasstes exegetisches
          Handbuch zu den Apokryphen des Alten Testamentes.
          Vol. IV.  Leipzig:  Verlag von S. Hirzel, 1857.

HNT       Handbuch zum Neuen Testament

HTR       Harvard Theological Review

JBL       Journal of Biblical Literature

JBR       Journal of Bible and Religion

JJS       Journal of Jewish Studies

JTS       Journal of Theological Studies

Kautzsch  Die Apokryphen und Pseudepigraphen des Alten
          Testaments.  Edited by E. Kautzsch.  2 vols.
          Tübingen:  Verlag von J. C. B. Mohr (Paul Siebeck),
          1900.

LCL       The Loeb Classical Library

Meyer     Kritisch-Exegetischer Kommentar über das Neue
          Testament, founded by H. A. W. Meyer

MPL       J.-P. Migne, Patrologia Latina

NTS       New Testament Studies

RGG       Die Religion in Geschichte und Gegenwart.  6 vols.
          and index vol.  3rd ed.  Tübingen:  J. C. B. Mohr
          (Paul Siebeck), 1957-62, 1965.

| | |
|---|---|
| TDNT | Theological Dictionary of the New Testament. Edited by Gerhard Kittel. 9 vols. Translated by Geoffrey W. Bromiley. Grand Rapids, Mich.: Wm. B. Eerdmans Publishing Company, 1964-68. |
| ThBl | Theologische Blätter |
| TLZ | Theologische Literaturzeitung |
| TZ | Theologische Zeitschrift |
| VT | Vetus Testamentum |
| WMANT | Wissenschaftliche Monographien zum Alten und Neuen Testament |
| ZNW | Zeitschrift für die neutestamentliche Wissenschaft und die Kunde der älteren Kirche |
| ZTK | Zeitschrift für Theologie und Kirche |

PREFACE

In November, 1971, I defended <u>Jesus' Death as Saving</u> <u>Event</u> before a committee consisting of Professors Helmut Koester, John Strugnell, Dieter Georgi, Paul D. Hanson and Zeph Stewart. The dissertation is presented here substantially as they approved it. My most ambitious changes have been the rewriting or modification of several paragraphs (pp. 109-110 and 212) and the addition of a parallel between Hebrews and IV Maccabees (p. 240).

This preface gives me the welcome opportunity to express my appreciation to my thesis adviser, Helmut Koester, who suggested the topic from which this study developed, and to John Strugnell, who, in the summer weeks prior to my departure from Cambridge, carefully read several sections of the thesis. I feel a special debt of gratitude to Dieter Georgi, whose steady encouragement through the spring of 1971 was a crucial factor in my completing the thesis before I left Harvard to begin a teaching career.

I am also grateful to The Colorado College for a Study/ Research Grant which defrayed the cost of having the thesis retyped in order to meet the specifications of Harvard Dissertations in Religion and Scholars' Press.

xi

The purpose of this thesis is to investigate the
background, source and origin of an early Christian concept
which was destined to play a crucial role in the history of
Christian doctrine and liturgy:  the idea that Jesus' death
was a saving event because it effects expiation of sin.

It can be said at once that this study yields results
which find themselves at odds with a significant segment of
contemporary scholarship.  That this is the case is due in
large measure to my uneasiness with regard to several revered
presuppositions which frequently govern investigations of
early Christian soteriology; for example, that for first
century Jews the death of a worthy man could quite naturally
have been interpreted in terms of vicarious expiation; that it
would have been an easy step from the sacrificial offering of
animals to such an interpretation of a human death; that Isaiah
53 and its doctrine of vicarious suffering exerted widespread
and pervasive influence in the early church; or that, in fact,
the concept of the vicarious expiatory death of a righteous
man was a familiar theologumenon in first century Judaism.
These assumptions have not been adopted here as presuppositions
but as potentially useful opinions which first had to be tested
anew.  When analysis has rendered them untenable I have felt
at liberty to abandon them completely and to search for alternatives.

The customary way to go about answering the question
of the sources of the concept under discussion is to turn
immediately to the Old Testament on the one hand and to rabbinic texts on the other.  Both approaches may be useful.  However,
the pre-Pauline formulation at Rom. 3: 24-26, which the thesis
takes as its point of departure, suggests that one's initial
step be in another direction.  The word ἱλαστήριον finds a
striking parallel in IV Maccabees (17:22), a writing in which
the deaths of the Jewish martyrs at the hands of Antiochus
Epiphanes can also be described with the language of purification (1:11, 6:29, 17:21), ransom (ἀντίψυχον:  6:29; 17:21:
τῆς ἁμαρτίας !) and possibly propitiation (ἀρκεσθείς . . .

2

ὑπὲρ αὐτῶν: 6:28). That a writing earlier than or contemporary with primitive Christianity[1] exhibits language so
reminiscent of the interpretation of Jesus' death in early
Christian literature[2] suggests that an analysis of certain
aspects of IV Maccabees might be a fruitful approach to the
question of the sources of the concept of Jesus' death as
saving event.

A great deal, then, rests on the proposed analysis of
IV Maccabees--so much, in fact, that I have judged it necessary
to examine this writing in a broader context lest its own
theology of martyrdom be distorted by a superficial reading.
Thus, as one step into the background of IV Maccabees, the
thesis inquires into the tradition of the Maccabean martyrs
from Daniel to II Maccabees and Josephus (Chapter II).

Chapter II shows that in the tradition prior to IV
Maccabees one finds no interpretation of the martyrs' deaths
corresponding to that reflected in IV Mac. 1:11, 6:28-29,
17:21-22 and in other statements throughout the writing.
Therefore a new and pressing question is raised: What is the
probable background and source of IV Maccabees' interpretation
of the martyrs' deaths? This question necessitates two further
steps into the thought world of the first century. Chapter III
examines the understanding of suffering and death in the Old
Testament and other Jewish literature; Chapter IV provides a
look at various ways of viewing suffering and death in Greek
and Hellenistic literature. Against this background the
question of the context, sources, and origin of the interpretation of the martyrs' deaths in IV Maccabees is explored in
some detail (Chapter V).

From the standpoint of structure, Chapters II through
V constitute a unit that is bracketed by Chapter I, by which
it is made necessary, and by Chapter VI, for which it prepares
the way. The results of Chapter I and the insights gained

---

[1]For support of this position cf. infra, pp. 197-202.

[2]Mark 10:45; 14:22-25 par., I Cor. 11:23-25; Rom.
4:25; I Cor. 15:3; John 1:29, 6:51; I John 1:7, 2:2, 12;
3:5‾6, 4:10; Rev. 1:5, 5:8-9, 7:14, 12:11; I Peter 1:2, 19;
2:21-24; 3:18; Hebrews passim; I Clement 7:4, 16:7, 21:6,
49:6; Barnabas 5:1, 7:2ff.

from Chapters II through V into the meaning of precipitous human death in first century Judaism provide the perspective from which the central problem of the thesis is dealt with in Chapter VI. There the question of the origin of the concept of Jesus' death as saving event is asked in view of the four hypothetical models of event interpretation suggested in an Excursus at the end of Chapter I. The answers provided by three of these models are rejected as improbable. An hypothesis suggested by the present study is then proposed in terms of the fourth model.

CHAPTER I

THE MEANING OF JESUS' DEATH IN ROMANS 3:24-26

The thesis begins with an analysis of the pre-Pauline
formulation preserved at Rom. 3:24-26. Several factors render
this text ideal as a focal point for the study proposed. As
a pre-Pauline formulation it is one of our earliest pieces of
evidence for the concept in question. Unlike other pre-Pauline
texts (e.g., I Cor. 11:23-25 or 15:3-5) the formulation at
Rom. 3:24-26 does not appear to be the end product of a process
of liturgical development. Furthermore, it is a substantial
text and, in contrast to Rom. 4:25 or I Cor. 15:3-5, it is
exclusively concerned with the meaning of Jesus' death (i.e.,
not his resurrection as well). Even more significantly, the
peculiar language employed here provides scholars with an
extraordinary opportunity for an investigation of the origin
of the idea that Jesus' death has saving power.

Before attempting to understand the theology reflected
by the pre-Pauline formulation, it is necessary to justify the
contention that vv. 24-26 do include a quotation and to determine its extent.

I. The Pre-Pauline Formulation at Romans 3:24-26

Modern exegetes give Rudolf Bultmann credit for the
suggestion that in Rom. 3:24f. Paul is dependent on a traditional formulation. Bultmann's suggestion rests on three
observations: 1) only here in Paul is Christ designated as
ἱλαστήριον; 2) Paul typically speaks of the cross, mentioning
the blood of Christ elsewhere only when following tradition;
3) foreign to Paul is the idea of the divine righteousness
demanding expiation for former sins.[1]

E. Käsemann has attempted to refine and strengthen
Bultmann's suggestion.[2] He argues that the sentence construction of v. 23 is not continued and he notes terminology in

---

[1]Theology of the New Testament (New York, 1951) I, p. 46.

[2]"Zum Verständnis von Römer 3 24-26," ZNW 43(1950-51),
150-54.

6

vv. 24-25 that is not characteristic of Paul: πάρεσις, προγεγο-
νότα ἁμαρτήματα, προτίθεσθαι (in the sense of "to manifest"),
δικαιοσύνη as a divine attribute, and ἀπολύτρωσις as a designation of salvation already attained. Furthermore, the ornate
style of v. 25--with its genitival constructions and prepositional associations--is reminiscent of the Deutero-Pauline
epistles and comes, as does their distinctive style, out of the
hymnic-liturgical tradition of the Near East.[3] The argument
that Käsemann himself seems to consider most persuasive, however,
is theological: v. 25 simply cannot be reconciled with Paul's
thought. Whereas δικαιοσύνη in v. 26 has its usual Pauline
meaning (i.e., God's eschatological activity), in v. 25 it is
merely a divine attribute. In addition, vv. 24-25 describe the
effect of Christ's death as the restoration of the old covenant,
which had been broken by man's sin; Paul, however, understands
the new covenant not as restoration but as antithesis of the
old.

Since the appearance of Käsemann's essay, numerous
scholars have adopted the idea that Rom. 3:24-25 includes a
pre-Pauline formulation, among them G. Bornkamm, J. Jeremias,
A. M. Hunter, and E. Schweizer.[4]

In 1966, however, two articles appeared which argue,
on very different grounds, that the verses concerned contain a
non-Pauline fragment which was inserted subsequent to the
composition of Romans by someone other than Paul.[5] The
arguments central to these two articles must be examined
carefully; if they prove to be valid, the Bultmann-Käsemann
theory of a pre-Pauline formulation at Rom. 3:24-25 will have
to be abandoned.

Charles Talbert argues that the fragment begins not
with the participle of v. 24 but with the relative pronoun of
v. 25. With the exception of διὰ πίστεως (v. 25), ἐν τῷ νῦν

_____

[3]Ibid., 151--citing E. Percy, Die Probleme der Kolosser-
und Epheserbrief (Lund, 1946), pp. 191, 213.

[4]Cf. the enumeration, with literature cited, in D.
Zeller, "Sühne und Langmut," Theologie und Philosophie 43
(1968), 52, n. 10.

[5]Charles H. Talbert, "A Non-Pauline Fragment at Romans
3 24-26?" JBL 85(1966), 287-96; Gottfried Fitzer, "Der Ort
der Versöhnung nach Paulus," TZ 22(1966), 161-83.

καιρῷ and τὸν ἐκ πίστεως 'Ιησοῦ (v. 26) the fragment includes all of vv. 25-26 and these verses exhibit a very balanced formal structure.[6] If these two verses be detached from the present text and a period be placed after τῆς δόξης τοῦ θεοῦ (v. 23), the next sentence, which begins with δικαιούμενοι, continues smoothly at 3:27: ποῦ οὖν ἡ καύχησις. According to Talbert, then, the sentence as Paul wrote it should be translated: "Since we are justified freely by his grace through the redemption which is in Christ Jesus, where then is our boasting? It is excluded."[7] Rom. 3:25-26 should be considered a later non-Pauline interpolation into the middle of a Pauline sentence. Are there any parallels to such a phenomenon? Talbert thinks there are. Citing Bultmann's essay on glosses in Romans[8] he refers to Rom. 6:17b as a direct parallel; another is I Cor. 12:31b-14:1a.[9] Partial parallels ("partial" because the insertions were written by Paul himself) are said to be II Cor. 6:14-7:1 and Phil. 3:1b-4:3. But why would such an interpolation have been added in Romans 3? Talbert answers: "By the addition of διὰ πίστεως (3 25; cf. 3 22a), τὸν ἐκ πίστεως 'Ιησοῦ (3 26; cf. 3 22b), and ἐν τῷ νῦν καιρῷ (3 26; cf. 3 21), the editor causes the fragment to sum up all of the major themes of the previous section."[10]

Talbert's theory, persuasive at first glance, collapses under more careful scrutiny. Of several weaknesses, only two of the most serious ones can be considered here. In the first place none of the alleged parallels to which Talbert appeals is a genuine parallel. He equates Rom. 3:25-26 with Bultmann's "summarizing insertions," but none of these (7:25b, 8:1, 10:17, 2:1, 13:5) interrupts an otherwise well-balanced sentence. Only Bultmann's "genuine interpolations" (2:16 and 6:16b)-- which supposedly make explicit what the redactor thought to be implicit in Paul's words--so interrupt a sentence. But the purpose of 3:25-26 can hardly be to "make explicit": in the

---

[6]Talbert, op. cit., 288-89.    [7]Ibid., 291.

[8]"Glossen im Römerbrief," TLZ 72(1947), 197-202.

[9]Following E. L. Titus, "Did Paul Write I Corinthians 13?" JBR 27(1959), 299-302, who asserts that I Cor. 13 was not written by Paul.

[10]Talbert, op. cit., 295.

8

preceding paragraphs Paul has already been as explicit as he could be! The passages cited in II Cor. and Phil. are hardly parallels, for in each case the situation (of redaction) is quite different from that which Talbert proposes regarding Romans 3; and Titus is clearly wrong in calling I Cor. 13 a later, non-Pauline interpolation. Furthermore, none of the possible interpolations that Talbert cites as parallels looks like the confessional-liturgical type of statement at Rom. 3:25, and certainly none of them attaches to a preceding noun with a relative pronoun. Paul himself, however, does exactly this sort of thing at Rom. 4:25 and Phil. 2:6 (cf. also Col. 1:15, I Tim. 3:16, Tit. 2:14), as Talbert also recognizes.

A second major counterargument to Talbert's theory is this: from the standpoint of syntax his reconstructed Pauline sentence has no parallel in Paul or in the rest of the New Testament. The major syntactical elements of the reconstructed sentence are a (present middle-passive) participle, nominative case, plus a clause--if we assume the implicit copula--introduced by an interrogative adverb; the subject of this clause (ἡ καύχησις) is not identical with the subject of the preceding participle. Paul never uses a participle and an interrogative adverb together in this way.[11] Often both ποῦ and πῶς are joined with an if-clause but never with a participle whose subject is not identical with the subject of the ποῦ or πῶς clause.[12] The reason for this state of affairs, as clear as it is simple, is apparent from any reliable Greek grammar-- Smyth, for example: "The subject of the participle is identical with the noun or pronoun subject or object of the leading verb, and agrees with it in gender, number, and case."[13] The exceptions to this "rule," of course, are the genitive absolute and the accusative absolute, but neither of these is to be found at Rom. 3:24, 27. The attempt to find parallels in

_____

[11]For ποῦ see I Cor. 12:17, 19; Gal. 4:15; also OT quotes at I Cor. 1:20, 15:55; cf. also I Pet. 4:18, II Pet. 3:4. For πῶς see Rom. 4:10, 6:2, 10:14; I Cor. 15:12, 14:7, 9, 16; Gal. 4:9, 2:14.

[12]Therefore Gal. 4:9 is not a parallel because "you" is the subject of participle and πῶς clause.

[13]H. W. Smyth, Greek Grammar (Cambridge, Mass., 1963), par. 2056.

texts where a finite verb must be supplied or where the
participle is used in the place of a finite verb (e.g., Rom.
5:11, 12:6, 13:11) does not at all meet the grammatical point
at issue. These observations are not proof that Rom. 3:25-26 is
not a post-Pauline interpolation. They do, however, sufficiently refute the particular arguments on which Talbert con-
structs that theory.

G. Fitzer mounts a double attack on the Bultmann-
Käsemann thesis. He sees v. 25b-26a as a post-Pauline gloss.
A primitive questioner evidently asked, in regard to v. 26:
What about those sins committed prior to Christ? and then
formulated his own answer according to Rom. 2:4.[14] The
remainder of vv. 24-26 Fitzer considers to be genuinely Pauline,
by no means a pre-Pauline formulation.

In spite of some perceptive observations, several
weaknesses vitiate Fitzer's theory. For example, he notes
(correctly) the formal parallelism of vv. 25b and 26 and the
additional fact that they are not joined together by any
connecting word--a situation unusual for Paul, who is fond of
using particles freely. This situation makes Fitzer suspicious
of one of these two phrases. He decides that it is 25b which
did not originally belong here; his reasoning is that the
repetition of τοῦ θεοῦ (instead of αὐτοῦ) with ἀνοχή is
"improbable."[15] But why is the repetition of τοῦ θεοῦ any less
improbable in the comment of a "primitive questioner" than in
a community formulation or a Pauline statement? Furthermore,
Fitzer completely overlooks the fact that in stylized passages
the subject is sometimes repeated where one would expect the
personal pronoun, for example at I Cor. 1:4, II Cor. 1:4, 4:6[16]

Fitzer maintains that Rom. 3:25a is completely understandable as a genuinely Pauline statement. Noting "a certain
preference for the prefix προ-" on Paul's part, Fitzer draws
this questionable conclusion regarding προτίθεσθαι: "Die
Häufigkeit dieser Wendungen mit προ- macht wahrscheinlich,
dass προτίθεσθαι in Rom. 3, 25 paulinischem Sprachgebrauch

---

[14] Fitzer, op. cit., 164.

[15] Ibid., 163.    [16] D. Zeller, op. cit., 53 n. 12.

zuzurechnen ist."[17] Ἰλαστήριον, too, is best understood as a Pauline term. Regarding this important term Fitzer writes:

> Weder von der LXX noch von Philo her ist Hilasterion Sühnopfer oder Sühnmittel, sondern der Ort der Gegenwart Gottes, der Gnade Gottes, an welchem durch die Manipulationen des Priesters, nämlich durch die kultischen Heiligungsriten, die Gnade Gottes zur Wirklichkeit wird.
> In dem Ausdruck Rom. 3, 25 ὃν προέθετο ὁ θεὸς ἱλαστήριον wird nun Jesus gerade nicht mit den Manipulationen des Priesters verglichen, sondern ist gewissermassen selbst schon die Gnade Gottes darstellende Ort der Gegenwart Gottes.[18]

And this view, according to Fitzer, is completely consistent with Paul's understanding of God's act in Christ.[19]

Fitzer supports this interpretation of the meaning of ἱλαστήριον by appealing to selected portions of Deissmann's classical work.[20] But although his own interpretation is strikingly similar to that of T. W. Manson,[21] Fitzer does not refer to Manson's work or to criticism that has been leveled against it.[22] He also ignores C. H. Dodd's important essay on ἱλάσκεσθαι in the LXX.[23] Even more puzzling is the omission of any reference to the text most often cited in discussions of ἱλαστήριον--i.e., IV Maccabees 17:22. Such oversights, whether deliberate [24] or accidental, are sufficient to cast doubt, a priori, upon Fitzer's "conclusions."

---

[17]Fitzer, op. cit., 166.      [18]Ibid., 171.

[19]Ibid., 174ff. Fitzer calls special attention to Rom. 11:33ff., I Cor. 15:28; Rom. 1:27, 3:21, 1:18; Gal. 4:4; Rom. 8:3; II Cor. 5:19, 21; Rom. 1:16; I Cor. 1:18 and draws this conclusion: "Dementsprechend gilt: Gott hat Jesus Christus in zuvorkommenden Handeln zum Hilasterion gesetzt" (174).

[20]A. Deissmann, "ΙΛΑCΤΗΡΙΟC und ΙΛΑCΤΗΡΙΟΝ," ZNW 4 (1903), 193-212.

[21]T. W. Manson, "ΙΛΑΣΤΗΡΙΟΝ," JTS 46(1945), 1-10.

[22]E.g., L. Morris, "The Meaning of ʹΙΛΑΣΤΗΡΙΟΝ in Romans III. 25," NTS 2(1955-56), esp. 36-37, 39-43.

[23]C. H. Dodd, "ΙΛΑΣΚΕΣΘΑΙ, Its Cognates, Derivatives, and Synonyms, in the Septuagint," JTS 32(1931), 352-60.

[24]Cf. his statement of purpose (op. cit., 161): to demonstrate that Paul did not understand the death of Jesus as expiatory sacrifice. Although that thesis may well be correct, Fitzer's selective oversight and circular reasoning suggest that his judgment is often tendentious.

11

The attempts of Talbert and Fitzer to demonstrate that
Rom. 3:25-26 and 3:25b, respectively, are post-Pauline glosses
are unsuccessful. To make this judgment is not to prove that
these verses contain a pre-Pauline formulation. Nevertheless,
the striking concentration in these verses of terms and phrases
which either are not found elsewhere in Paul or are not characteristic of Paul[25] points to the overwhelming probability that
vv. 24-26 contain a non-Pauline formula. Since no valid arguments have been given for considering this formula a post-
Pauline interpolation and since scholars recognize that Paul
himself does sometimes quote or paraphrase church traditions,
the present study will proceed on the assumption that Rom.
3:24-26 contains a traditional pre-Pauline fragment.

Given this assumption, the next step is to determine
the extent of the traditional unit. Without justification or
explanation Bultmann suggested that it begins with the participle δικαιούμενοι in v. 24.[26] Käsemann supported this
suggestion with the comment that "die Satzkonstruktion von
v. 23 in v. 24 nicht fortgeführt wird. Insbesondere bleibt das
betonte πάντες ohne jene Entsprechung in v. 24, welche die
Antithese eigentlich erfordern würde."[27] Two observations may
be pertinent by way of immediate response. First, it is by no
means clear that the "antithetical" statement (v. 24) would
require any equivalent to the πάντες of v. 23. Furthermore,
if such were required for logic or clarity, why did Paul not
alter that deficiency; after all, according to Bultmann and
Käsemann, Paul felt perfectly free to clarify the traditional
statement with several other additions (although of a different
type, admittedly).

Such questions have not been entertained by many recent

---

[25]Προτίθεσθαι, ἱλαστήριον (through faith) in his blood,
πάρεσις, προγίνεσθαι and the plural "sins."

[26]Loc. cit.

[27]Op. cit., 150

12

exegetes, who trustingly adopt Käsemann's view that the traditional unit begins with δικαιούμενοι.[28]

Several additional observations can be made in response
to this view. 1) Although participial constructions are
sometimes signs of traditional formulations, none of those
texts frequently considered to be traditional formulations
begins with a participle which refers to someone other than
Jesus (or God). Most confessional or liturgical fragments
begin either with "Christ" (or αὐτός)[29] or with the relative
pronoun ὅς;[30] the formulations in the Romans and Galatians
prescripts begin with articular participles but the participles
connect with and modify Jesus (or God). If NT parallels are
any argument, then, the relative pronoun (attaching to "Christ
Jesus") has a better claim than δικαιούμενοι to mark the beginning of the pre-Pauline statement.[31]

2) With one exception, those terms in 3:24-26 which
Käsemann and others recognize as unusual for Paul are restricted to v. 25; only ἀπολύτρωσις is found in v. 24.

3) Käsemann himself, following Bultmann, would strike
δωρεὰν τῇ αὐτοῦ χάριτι from the original pre-Pauline statement.
That deletion would leave, in v. 24, only δικαιούμενοι διὰ τῆς
ἀπολυτρώσεως τῆς ἐν Χριστῷ ᾽Ιησοῦ. Eduard Lohse, however,
makes the interesting point that ἐν Χριστῷ ᾽Ιησοῦ is just as

---

[28] E.g., A. M. Hunter, Paul and His Predecessors
(London, ²1961), p. 120, comments on the "syntactical incon-
cinnity of the opening δικαιούμενοι." J. Reumann, "The Gospel
of the Righteousness of God," Interpretation 20(1966), 435,
argues that v. 24 does not continue v. 23; instead of an expected indicative form, perhaps with δέ, there is a participle
and no conjunction at all. Zeller, op. cit., 51, writes:
"Der Nominativ δικαιούμενοι lässt sich nicht glatt an V. 23
anschliessen . . . ." Although he disagrees with Käsemann's
analysis, Talbert too thinks δικαιούμενοι is "awkward" if
taken with v. 23 (op. cit., 287, 292). See also: H. Thyen,
Studien zur Sündenvergebung (Göttingen, 1970), p. 164.

[29] E.g., I Cor. 15:3; Eph. 2:14.

[30] Rom. 4:25, Phil. 2:6, Col. 1:15, I Tim. 3:16.

[31] So Talbert, op. cit., 288-89. That we have in Rom.
3:25 the acc. ὅν instead of the normal nom. ὅς does not in any
way argue against this view; the acc. can be explained by the
simple fact that in the traditional formula God is the acting
subject.

likely a Pauline addition as is δωρεὰν τῇ αὐτοῦ χάριτι.[32] The
phrase cannot be documented prior to Paul and Paul was probably
its creator.[33] In support of Lohse, it should be noted that
outside the Pauline "school" (i.e., Paul, Deutero-Paulines,
Pastorals) the phrase ἐν Χριστῷ ('Ιησοῦ) or the equivalent
ἐν αὐτῷ appears in only two NT writings: I Peter (3:16, 5:10,
5:14) and I John (5:20). The probability that ἐν Χριστῷ is a
Pauline creation makes a shambles of Käsemann's thesis regarding
v. 24 as a part of the formal traditional unit, for it leaves
nothing in v. 24 to which the relative pronoun in v. 25 could
have been attached.[34] If it were a part of a pre-Pauline
formula, then, v. 24 consisted only of δικαιούμενοι διὰ τῆς
ἀπολυτρώσεως. Now, aside from the fact that the direct juxtaposition "justified through redemption" is rather jarring conceptually, there are no a priori grounds for assigning a word
which Paul uses frequently (δικαιοῦν) to a pre-Pauline formula.
This is not to say that the concept of God justifying through
Jesus was not an element in Christian theologizing prior to
Paul; indeed, 3:26c, if it were a part of the original formulation, would prove that Paul did not create this concept. But
the point at issue here is not the concept embodied in δικαιοῦν
and the question whether it is pre-Pauline or not but rather
the boundary of a fixed, formal unit. Since the word δικαιοῦν
is, at best, inconclusive evidence, all that remains is the
syntactical argument: in view of the content and structure
of v. 23 (especially πάντες and finite verbs) the participial
form (δικαιούμενοι) seems inappropriate and awkward. But in

---

[32] E. Lohse, Märtyrer und Gottesknecht (Göttingen,
1955), p. 150 in the note beginning on the previous page.

[33] The counterargument that ἐν Χριστῷ 'Ιησοῦ is instrumental in v. 24 is no argument at all: (a) it is often instrumental in Paul also, and (b) it does not appear outside
the writings mentioned above even in an instrumental sense.

[34] Reumann's attempt (op. cit., 441-42) to wriggle out
of this difficulty is hardly convincing.

14

the context of an alternate exegesis (see below), this difficulty also disappears.[35]

And what about ἀπολύτρωσις? The word is found in only
two other Pauline texts: Rom. 8:23 and I Cor. 1:30 (in the
Deutero-Pauline epistles: Col. 1:14, Eph. 1:7, 14; 4:30).
Käsemann[36] observes that in Rom. 3:24 the term points to
salvation already attained, compares this to the same connotation "in der geprägten Formel" at I Cor. 1:30, and, by omitting
reference to Rom. 8:23 (where the meaning is eschatological-
future), implies that Rom. 8:23 reflects Paul's own thinking
whereas ἀπολύτρωσις in Rom. 3:24 mirrors the meaning of the
term in the pre-Pauline tradition. What is not at all certain,
however, is that Rom. 3:24 should be taken as the typical non-
and pre-Pauline usage of ἀπολύτρωσις, as Käsemann strongly
implies with his talk about a "geprägte Formel" at I Cor. 1:30.
Furthermore it can be questioned whether ἀπολύτρωσις in Rom.
3:24 is accurately characterized as "Bezeichnung der bereits
erfolgten Erlösung." It could be argued that ἀπολύτρωσις here
is just as "timeless" as is δικαιούμενοι! Nevertheless, it is
clear that this term is not "Pauline"; that is, it does not
belong to that normal theological vocabulary upon which Paul
draws frequently. It is quite probable that the apostle adopts
this word from the same fixed tradition from which he begins
to quote exactly in v. 25. It does not follow that the whole
of v. 24 therefore belongs to the pre-Pauline formula.

4) To the charge that δικαιούμενοι is awkward and
inappropriate and does not continue v. 23, the observation can
be offered that in several NT passages participles function
syntactically just as δικαιούμενοι does in Rom. 3:24. The
example closest to hand is Rom. 3:21: μαρτυρουμένη--a present

---

[35]Reumann (op. cit., 440) observes that the present
passive participle is not characteristic of Paul, that a past
tense is normal for the apostle. The exegesis to be offered
in the present study, however, shows that Paul used the present
passive participle in 3:24 for a very specific reason: because
it expressed precisely what he meant! At this point it need
only be observed, regarding the texts that Reumann cites, that
when Paul uses the aorist passive participle (Rom. 5:1, 9) or
verb (I Cor. 6:11) the subject of the participle is "we" or
"you" and the participle describes a reality that has already
been experienced by those concrete persons within the church;
but that is not the case in 3:24, where the subject is πάντες.

[36]Käsemann, op. cit., 150.

middle-passive participle, nominative case, without accompanying
particle--is used attributively to modify the subject of the
preceding clause. Cf. also δεόμενος at Rom. 1:10; ἀποθανόντες
at Rom. 7:6; μὴ ἔχων at Phil. 3:9; διδούς in the OT quotation
at Heb. 8:10 (=10:16); ποιῶν at Heb. 13:21; and compare
ἀρκεσθείς at IV Mac. 6:28.

5) In light of an alternative interpretation, δικαιούμενοι appears to be neither awkward nor otherwise inappropriate.
Given Paul's purpose, it can be understood as a very precise
theological statement. The key to this understanding is the
recognition that δικαιούμενοι is not intended to function as a
circumstantial participle; that is, its function is not adverb-
ial but adjectival.[37] Δικαιούμενοι and v. 24 point back to
πάντες and make a further statement about all men, who sinned
and fall short of God's glory. Paul does not use the aorist
participle because he is not speaking of actual persons who
have experienced God's justifying act. He is speaking rather
about "everyman"; in other words, he is stating a principle.[38]
Thus he uses the present participle. Paul uses the participle
rather than the finite verb because it is not his aim in this
particular sentence to emphasize the concept δικαιοῦσθαι.
Rather he wants the accent to fall on what follows the participle. If the emphasis in v. 23 is upon the all-inclusiveness
of human sin (πάντες), the stress in v. 24 is upon the way in
which God justifies all men (δωρεάν, τῇ αὐτοῦ χάριτι)--not on
the bare fact of justification itself.

In Rom. 3:21ff., then, Paul is affirming that the righteousness of God has been revealed to all who believe; for it is
illegitimate to make any distinction: all have sinned and are
constantly falling short of God's glory--justified (a
present participle, describing "all" and stating a principle:
if and when men are justified or declared righteous, it can

---

[37]It might be objected that δικαιούμενοι does not fit
into the grammarians' classification of the attributive participle, because more or less immediate proximity is considered
essential for an attributive participle. But such proximity
is not possible in Rom. 3:24 or 3:21 because intrinsic to the
meaning of the passive participle are the accompanying modifi-
ers: ὑπό . . . (3:21), δωρεάν and τῇ αὐτοῦ χάριτι (3:24).
Unfortunately, neither Robertson, Moulton, nor Blass-Debrunner
discusses the participle at Rom. 3:21 or 3:24.

[38]This principle is stated even more explicitly at Rom.
3:28: λογιζόμεθα γὰρ δικαιοῦσθαι πίστει ἄνθρωπον χωρὶς ἔργων
νόμου. Cf. also Gal. 2:16: οὐ δικαιοῦνται ἄνθρωπος ἐξ ἔργων
νόμου . . . .

only be in this manner, on these terms:) as a gift ("for nothing"), i.e., by His grace (which is manifested:) by means of redemption through Christ Jesus.

In view of the foregoing observations, it seems almost certain that it is not until v. 25 (ὄν) that Paul begins to quote from a fixed, traditional formulation. Still remaining is the question of where this formulation ends. Zeller finds in the feature of parallelismus membrorum a positive indication that v. 26b does belong to the quoted formulation.[39] It is dangerous to rely on any sort of strophic arrangement of the text as the decisive criterion, however. The very diverse schemata that different scholars have proposed suggests that this method of determining the extent of the original formulation is prone to the charge of excessive subjectivity.[40] A. Debrunner's remark that "alle Kolometrie an gegebenen Texten ist subjektiv"[41] points to the desirability of alternate criteria if they are available.

Several scholars (e.g., Zahn, Kuss, Fitzer, Zeller) have noted that the direct juxtaposition of vv. 25-26a and v. 26b--without the aid of a particle--is very un-Pauline. In Fitzer's words:

Das ist für den partikelfreudigen Paulus ungewöhnlich. Er verbindet mit καί, δέ, γάρ, οὖν. In Aufzählungen werden um der rhetorischen Wirkung willen Fragesätze unverbunden nebeneinander gestellt (vgl. Röm. 2, 21f.); aber hier geht es nicht um Aufzählung, sondern um einen Gegensatz. Hier hilft die These Käsemanns nichts. Denn wenn Paulus einen (übernommenen) Gedanken korrigiert, hätte er sicher mindestens ein δέ eingefügt--oder gar ein τὸ λοιπόν oder πλήν₂(vgl. Phil. 3, 1; 4, 8; 1. Thess. 4, 1; 2. Kor. 13, 11).[42]

---

[39]Op. cit., 73.

[40]Cf., for example, the arrangements of Talbert, Zeller and Alfons Pluta (Gottes Bundestreue, 1969). Pluta, referring to the work of R. Schutz ("Die Bedeutung der Kolometrie für das Neue Testament," ZNW 21[1922], 161-84), lays special weight upon cola length (determined strictly by count of accented syllables) as the decisive criterion. It is not necessary to disagree with Schutz ("In der griechischen Sprache ist es der akzentuierende Ton, der wirklich Musik macht. . . ."--p. 182) to question whether Pluta's syllable count is a trustworthy criterion. Cf. G. Schille's review in TLZ 92(1967), 35-37, of J. Schattenmann's Studien zum neutestamentlichen Prosahymnus (Munich, 1965).

[41]A. Debrunner, "Grundsätzliches über Kolometrie im Neuen Testament," ThBl 5(1926), 231-33.

[42]Fitzer, op. cit., 163.

If, however, one does not take 26b as a Gegensatz and does not
assume that here Paul is correcting the traditional formulation,
there are no obvious reasons why a particle is necessary. The
πρός phrase would appear to be unusually repetitive and cumbersome as a part of the traditional unit. Moreover, ἐν τῷ νῦν
καιρῷ very likely is Paul's own phrase (cf. Rom. 8:18, 11:5;
II Cor. 8:14). Thus πρός . . . αὐτοῦ can best be taken as a
Pauline restatement of 25b--repeated as a rhetorical base for
his emphatic and clarifying addition, "at the present time."[42a]

The situation is different in 26c (εἰς τὸ . . .).
Several terms or expressions here are not characteristic of
Paul. 1) Zeller observes that the adjective δίκαιος appears
in the Pauline corpus as a divine attribute only at II Tim.
4:8.[43] 2) The phrase πίστις Ἰησοῦ is not found elsewhere in
Paul in spite of the fact that in other connections Paul does
speak of "Jesus" (i.e., not in conjunction with "Christ" and/or
"our Lord") and πίστις Χριστοῦ / Χριστοῦ Ἰησοῦ or Ἰησοῦ / υἱοῦ
τοῦ θεοῦ, etc. 3) The more inclusive phrase τὸν ἐκ πίστεως
Ἰησοῦ seems unusual when compared with Pauline usage elsewhere.
Several times Paul uses phrases such as οἱ ἐκ πίστεως to refer
to particular groupings of people (Gal. 3:7 and 9; possibly
Rom. 4:14; cf. also Gal. 2:12 and Rom. 3:19), but the phrase
at Rom. 3:26 diverges from the pattern of these other instances
at two significant points: a) at Rom. 3:26 the article is
singular whereas in the other instances it is plural.[44] b) In
the parallel instances of οἱ ἐκ πίστεως no supplementary noun
follows πίστις. In these instances ἐκ πίστεως appears to
designate a general religious principle. At Rom. 3:26, however,
Ἰησοῦ adds a note of particularity that prevents (ὁ) ἐκ πίστεως Ἰησοῦ from being the precise equivalent of (οἱ) ἐκ
πίστεως. 4) A final observation can be made regarding

---

[42a]If Paul had been using modern punctuation he might
well have set a dash before πρός. Just as in the last sentence
preceding this note the dash makes unnecessary a conjunction
with "repeated," so Paul did not need a particle to express
his intent in 3:26b.

[43]Op. cit., 73.

[44]Against O. Michel, Der Brief an die Römer (Göttingen,
12 1963), p. 110, the two τῷ ἐκ . . . phrases at Rom. 4:16 are
not parallels to that at Rom. 3:26; in both cases τῷ represents
τῷ σπέρματι in the preceding clause. Cf. Smyth, op. cit.,
par. 1145.

18

δικαιοῦντα τὸν ἐκ πίστεως 'Ιησοῦ. According to the parallels
to τὸν ἐκ πίστεως adduced above, ἐκ at Rom. 3:26 has to be
read in a partitive/partisan sense (i.e., "the man of faith").
However, in all other instances in Paul where ἐκ (or διὰ)
πίστεως is found in conjunction with the verb δικαιοῦν (active
or passive voice), ἐκ clearly has an instrumental meaning (i.e.,
"by faith": Rom. 3:30; 5:1; Gal. 2:16; 3:8, 24; "by works":
Rom. 3:20, 4:2; cf. also Matt. 12:37 and James 2:21, 24, 25!).
Thus the last (participial) phrase in Rom. 3:26 has no genuine
Pauline parallel.[45]

45
In his brief but extremely influential essay on Rom.
3:24-26, Käsemann has taken into account none of the considerations mentioned above. As suggestive as it is, Käsemann's
essay can be faulted for undocumented assumptions. Among the
questions that might be raised are these:
1) Referring to IV Ezra 8:36 Käsemann asserts that
"Gerechtigkeit ist hier die Eigenschaft der Bundestreue
und darum mit Güte und Barmherzigkeit fast synonym.
Gott hält an seinem Bunde fest, selbst wenn die Menschen
übertretend daraus fallen, und erweist sich darin als
zugleich gerecht, gütig and langmütig" (152-53).
But where is the evidence that righteousness here is the
characteristic of covenant loyalty--that is, in any sense
other than the very general one that most statements about
God in Jewish literature are set in a broad covenant context?
Käsemann's assertion also seems to overlook the irony of the
divine reply in IV Ezra 8:37-40. In any case, IV Ezra 8:36
is a small base upon which to conclude that δικαιούμενοι
characterizes "those who stand in the reestablished covenant"
and that v. 24 "centers around the motif of the renewed
covenant" (153).

2) Käsemann writes: "Nur auf der Basis eines Sühne-
mittels [= ἱλαστήριον] kann dieser Bund neu statuiert werden"
(153). Is this an acceptable statement in the context of
Hebrew-Jewish theology? Where in the OT or other Jewish
literature is any covenant established or renewed "only on
the basis of a means of expiation"? Where is covenant making
or renewal connected directly with expiation at all? To be
sure, covenant-making in Israel creates the context or relationship in which expiation of sin is possible; one aspect of the
covenant relationship is the divine provision of the means of
expiation. But this fact does not justify Käsemann's assertion.
It is also true, of course, that in the Semitic sphere the
slaughter of an animal was an integral part of "cutting" a
covenant. But this killing of an animal should be seen as an
acted-out threat or curse rather than an expiatory sacrifice.
Cf. Dennis J. McCarthy, Treaty and Covenant (Rome, 1963),
pp. 51-57.

3) Käsemann speaks of "another meaning of δικαιοσύνη
in v. 26" (as compared with v. 25). Furthermore, he asserts,
"Gottes Gerechtigkeit ist für ihn [Paul] eben nicht primär
Restitution des alten Bundes. . . . So distanziert das ἐν

19

Standing alone, none of these considerations is conclusive; taken together, however, they constitute strong evidence
that, like v. 25, Rom. 3:26c--or, more accurately, at least the
adjective δίκαιος and the phrase δικαιοῦν (or the clause
δίκαιος . . .?) τὸν ἐκ πίστεως 'Ιησοῦ--was a part of the
traditional pre-Pauline formulation.


II. The Meaning of Jesus' Death in the Pre-Pauline Formulation

In my view the πάρεσις-ἀνοχή statement in the formulation of Rom. 3:25-26 provides the most significant clue to the
meaning of the quotation and the situation out of which it
came. Therefore I begin this section with a consideration of
that statement, proceeding then to the main clause of the
formula and, finally, to the phrases about God's righteousness.

A. Διὰ τὴν πάρεσιν τῶν προγεγονότων ἁμαρτημάτων ἐν τῇ ἀνοχῇ
τοῦ θεοῦ

The major problems to be considered here are:  the
most appropriate rendering of διά plus accusative, the meaning
of πάρεσις, and the connotation intended for ἀνοχή.

It need not be demonstrated that in classical and
Hellenistic Greek διά with accusative normally has a causal
meaning:  "because of, on account of."  Very rarely can this
construction be understood in the sense of "for the sake of,
with a view to."  The texts often cited as evidence of this
alternate meaning are:  Thucydides 2.87, 4.40, 4.102, and 5.53.

τῷ νῦν καιρῷ viel schärfer von der Vergangenheit, als
v. 25 es tat.  Nicht die von Moses eingeleitete Heils-
geschichte Israels, sondern die Welt des gefallenen und
unter dem Gotteszorn befindlichen Adam ist für Paulus
das Gegenüber des gegenwärtigen Kairos, der darum die
Zeit des weltweiten Christusleibes und der Heidenmission
ist" (154).
Perhaps.  These assertions may be a suggestive summary of
Pauline theology, but they are not founded upon Rom. 3:24-26;
one can question whether they are even supported by Rom. 3:24-
26.  Their sole supporting datum, after all, is the phrase
ἐν τῷ νῦν καιρῷ.

H. G. Meecham notes, however, that 4.40 and 4.102 may be
adscripts attributable to late idiom.[46] In Aristotle, Ethics
4.3.31, the causal sense is quite as possible as the prospective. The prospective meaning is more certain, however, in
Plato, Republic 524C. Twice in Polybius (2.56, 12) the same
meaning is clear, but the LXX and papyri provide no additional
examples of the prospective use of διά plus accusative.[47] Even
so, Meecham recognizes that

> The prepositions in Hellenistic Greek are noticeably
> fluid. The notion of ground ('because of') easily
> blends with aim ('for the sake of'). In Attic
> inscriptions, according to Meisterhans, διά c. acc.
> gradually encroaches on ἕνεκα. [Meecham points to II
> Mac. 8:15; cf. also Gen. 18:24, 26; Mark 2:27, John
> 12:30, I Cor. 11:9.] . . . It is no distant step from
> 'for the sake of' to 'with a view to'.

The available evidence leads Meecham to the following conclusion:

> It would seem, therefore, that διά may approximate to
> a prospective sense, but, as Winer held, does not
> directly denote purpose. The evidence suggests that
> the development was sporadic. In view of the over-
> whelming use of διά c. acc. in a causal and retrospec-
> tive sense in the classical and Hellenistic language
> it is precarious to depart from that sense in these
> two Pauline passages, and still more so to support
> exegetical conclusions on so rare a meaning of the
> preposition.[48]

Some confirmation of this position can be seen from
the fact that, whereas in Hellenistic usage διά τό with
infinitive can be the equivalent of ἵνα with subjunctive, in
twenty-eight NT instances of διά τό with infinitive the
purposive sense is never possible.[49]

On the basis of Meecham's observations I propose the
following criterion for the translation of διά with accusative:
In those instances in which the connotation of "because of/on
account of" shades into "for the sake of" or "with a view to"
one of the latter phrases can be considered a satisfactory

---

[46]H. G. Meecham, "Romans iii. 25f., iv. 25--the meaning
of διά c. acc.," ET 50(1938-39), 564.

[47]Ibid.

[48]Ibid.

[49]Ibid.

rendering of the Greek. Examples are: Mark 2:27, John 12:30, Rom. 4:23, 24, 25; I Cor. 11:9. On the other hand, in those instances where additional factors (e.g., a temporal element) make necessary a sharp distinction between the ideas of cause and purpose, διά with accusative should be rendered "because of" because this is its meaning in the overwhelmingly preponderant majority of cases--that is, unless this translation is nonsensical for the given text. A few examples are: Matt. 10:22; 13:21, 58; Luke 5:19; 8:19; 23:25; Rom. 15:15; Gal. 4:13; Phil. 1:15; Eph. 2:4.

At Rom. 3:25 the attributive participle προγεγονότες introduces a temporal factor which drives a wedge between causal and purposive meanings. Therefore, according to the criterion proposed, διά τήν at Rom. 3:25 should be rendered "because of" (reason) rather than "with a view to" (purpose).

H. Lietzmann,[50] while proposing "entsprechend, im Hinblick auf" as the proper translation of διά at Rom. 3:25, goes on to suggest that "es grenzt schon an die Bedeutung 'durch'. . . ." Hellenistic and patristic texts are cited in support. W. G. Kümmel abandons Lietzmann's caution ("es grenzt . . .") and translates διά at Rom. 3:25 as "through" on the grounds that

> There is indeed no doubt that διά with the accusative frequently came to have an instrumental sense in the Hellenistic period, and that the New Testament is clearly familiar with this usage (Jn. 6:57; Rev. 12:11; 13:14).[51]

(Lietzmann also cites Rom. 8:20 and "probably" 8:10.) But a possible translation is not necessarily the correct one. Why then does Kümmel insist on "through"? The answer to this query is to be found in the following statement: ". . . if πάρεσις has the meaning 'remission' here [i.e., in Rom. 3:25], it only makes sense if one renders διά τήν πάρεσιν with 'through the remission.'"[52] This statement is impeccable in its logic but faulty in its basic premise, for Kümmel fails to

[50]H. Lietzmann, An die Römer (Tübingen, [4]1933), p. 51.

[51]W. G. Kümmel, "Πάρεσις and Ἔνδειξις," Journal for Theology and the Church, vol. 3 (Tübingen and New York, 1967), p. 10.

[52]Ibid.

demonstrate that πάρεσις means remission or pardon in Rom.
3:25.[53] Consequently his sole reason for rendering διά with
accusative by the word "through" evaporates.  Thus the texts
adduced to show that διά with accusative can mean "through,"
while interesting and instructive, are irrelevant.

In view of Kümmel's claims, however, a modified version
of the criterion proposed earlier is necessary:  In those cases
in which the idea involved neither demands nor allows a clear
distinction between cause and means, διά with accusative can
legitimately be rendered "through."  A clear case is Rev. 4:11:
σὺ ἔκτισας τὰ πάντα, καὶ διὰ τὸ θέλημά σου ἦσαν καὶ ἐκτίσθησαν.
Here the translation "through" is by no means required because
a causal intent cannot be completely eliminated.  On the other
hand, where additional factors make a distinction between
cause and means necessary, διά with accusative must be translated "because of" simply because this is its ordinary meaning
--unless the causal meaning makes nonsense of the given text.

If the texts cited by Lietzmann and Kümmel be viewed
in light of this criterion, three of them require no sharp
distinction between cause and means; at John 6:57, Rom. 8:10
and 8:20 διά could be translated "through" but the causal note
certainly cannot be dismissed.  There is, in fact, no good
reason to abandon the translation "because/on account of" in
any one of these three texts.  The situation is somewhat
different in Rev. 12:11 and 13:14.  In Rev. 12:11 "by means of"
is preferable for both occurrences of διά but the idea of
ultimate cause is by no means absent in the first instance.
In other words, διὰ τὸ αἷμα does not mean that the brethren
employ the blood of the lamb in apotropaic fashion against
Satan; rather it is because Christ died that Satan is defeated.
However, διὰ τὸν λόγον can hardly be rendered any other way
than "by means of their testimony."  In Rev. 13:14, too, διὰ
τὰ σημεῖα can only mean "by means of the signs"; the sense of
the statement here demands that διά function instrumentally.
(The question raised by πλανᾷ is not Why? but How?  Therefore
the translation is "by means of" rather than "because of.")

---

[53]Cf. the following critical reaction and an alternate
interpretation.

But what about διά in Rom. 3:25? Does the sense of the
statement there either demand or allow διά to mean "by means
of"? The first point to be noted is that in this verse it
makes a great deal of difference whether one translates "through"
or "because of"; cause and means are in this case mutually
exclusive. At stake is the "when" of πάρεσις. "Through" makes
πάρεσις a present act (i.e., possible only since Christ)
whereas "because of" requires that πάρεσις be taken as a past
(pre-Christ) act. According to the proposed criterion, then
(a distinction between cause and means is necessary and, unlike
Rev. 13:14, the causal meaning does not make nonsense of the
text),[54] it is necessary to disagree with Lietzmann's suggestion
and Kümmel's assertion. Διά with accusative in Rom. 3:25
should not be translated "through"; the intent of the preposition in this instance--as normally--is causal and a proper
translation must reflect that causal intention. Διὰ τὴν
πάρεσιν must be rendered "because of the πάρεσις."

Πάρεσις does not occur elsewhere in the NT or LXX, so
it is necessary to turn to extra-biblical texts for clues to
its possible meanings. The texts usually cited are these:

Plutarch, Comp. Dion. Brut. 2: πάρεσις ἐκ Συρακουσιῶν.
According to Liddell and Scott here the word means "letting go,
dismissal"; Kümmel prefers "letting go, liberation." (This
text is not cited by Bauer.)

Dionysius of Halicarnassus, Ant. Rom. 7.37.2: παρὰ δὲ
τῶν δημάρχων πολλὰ λιπαρήσαντες (οἱ ὕπατοι) τὴν μὲν ὁλοσχερῆ
πάρεσιν οὐχ εὕροντο, τὴν δ'εἰς χρόνον ὅσον ἠξίουν ἀναβολὴν
ἔλαβον. Here Liddell and Scott render the word as "release";
Bauer suggests "Hingehenlassen, Ungestraftlassen"; Kümmel
thinks that the meaning "remission" is "absolutely certain";
J. M. Creed writes:[55]

> It is obvious that πάρεσις cannot here be used in the
> judicial sense of release or acquittal, for the point
> at issue is not whether Coriolanus shall be acquitted
> or condemned, but whether or not the trial itself shall
> be allowed to take place. The words ὁλοσχερῆ πάρεσιν
> . . . can only mean 'to let the whole matter drop'.

---

[54]It should be noted that this is precisely why Kümmel
wishes to avoid taking διά in a causal sense at Rom. 3:25: in
his view to translate "because of" is to make the text meaningless.

[55]J. M. Creed, "ΠΑΡΕΣΙΣ in Dionysius of Halicarnassus
and in St. Paul," JTS 41(1940), 29.

24

Creed further notes that elsewhere in the same narrative
Dionysius has several opportunities to speak of acquittal or
release and he consistently uses ἄφεσις and ἀφιέναι. Thus,
Creed concludes, ". . . in one of the very few places where
the word πάρεσις occurs it is certainly not the equivalent of
ἄφεσις."[56] Kümmel objects that, while πάρεσις here does refer
to the dismissal of a trial, it certainly does not mean "passing over."[57] Agreed! But just as surely it does not mean
"remission." Better is the translation: "dismissal"--in the
sense of leaving permanently in abeyance.[58]

From the foregoing it follows that: 1) The texts in
which the noun occurs are too few and too inconclusive to
yield a decisive clue as to "the" meaning of πάρεσις. Furthermore, in these texts neither "pardon" nor "passing over" seems
to be as appropriate a translation as "release" or "dismissal."
2) The experts disagree among themselves about the exact meaning of the noun in each of these texts. 3) The verb παριέναι
either can mean "pass over, leave unpunished, not regard" or
it can be used of the remission of debts or other obligations.

It is in view of this situation that Kümmel himself,
while insisting that the idea of remission is common for the
noun, admits that because the verb can mean "pass over," only
the context can decide the meaning of πάρεσις in Rom. 3:25.
This is a sensible proposal and is to be heartily endorsed.
Kümmel himself argues that if one reads "passing over" the
sentence must mean that God wanted to prove his righteousness
because it had been called into question due to his overlooking of previous sins; this idea, however, Kümmel considers

---

[56]Ibid., 30.

[57]Kümmel, op. cit., p. 4.

[58]Liddell and Scott and Kümmel are agreed that in
Phalaris, Ep. 81.1 (χρημάτων πάρεσις) πάρεσις refers to the
remission of debt. But regarding πάρεσις at BGU 624,21 and
Dio Chrys. 80(30).19, Bauer translates "Hingehenlassen, Ungestraftlassen" whereas Kümmel insists on "remission." On the
other hand, Kümmel does agree with Bauer (and Creed) regarding
the use of the verb παριέναι in extra-biblical texts. According to Kümmel it can mean both "to skip over, to intentionally
overlook" and "to remit, to abandon"; according to Bauer:
"strafloslassen" and "nachlassen" (of debts and other obligations).

highly problematic within the framework of Pauline theology.[59]
On neither count will Kümmel's argument hold.[60] Moreover, on
the basis of several statements made at the beginning of his
essay, it does not seem unfair to suggest that Kümmel is
writing to refute an interpretation of Rom. 3:25f. with which
he disagrees. Because he considers the equation πάρεσις =
"passing over" to be an essential ingredient in that interpretation, his refutation must demonstrate that πάρεσις means
"pardon, remission." Thus Kümmel appears to begin with a
preconceived notion of what πάρεσις has to mean.

The conclusion to be drawn from this critique of
Kümmel's argument is that he has not successfully demonstrated
that at Rom. 3:25 πάρεσις means "pardon" or "remission" or
"forgiveness." The connotation of this term in the pre-Pauline
fragment in Rom. 3 has yet to be determined. Does πάρεσις
mean "remission" as Kümmel believes (but for reasons other than
his!) or does it mean "passing over"?

Since the other occurrences of πάρεσις in Hellenistic
documents yield inconclusive evidence, Kümmel is certainly
correct in suggesting that the meaning of πάρεσις at Rom. 3:25
can be decided only on the basis of its present context. One
of the most significant terms in that context is ἀνοχή.

In Kümmel's view the phrase ἐν τῇ ἀνοχῇ τοῦ θεοῦ,
through its parallelism with ἐν τῷ νῦν καιρῷ (v. 26), designates a period of time:  the time of God's ἀνοχή.[61] In spite

---

[59] Kümmel, op. cit., p. 9.

[60] 1) The first point is based on a non sequitur. From
the opening paragraphs of the essay it is clear that Kümmel
has derived a very significant false premise (i.e., that if
πάρεσις means "passing over" it follows necessarily that
ἔνδειξις must mean "proof," that God's righteousness is en-
dangered and has to be proven as a fact, etc.) from his understanding of an interpretation of Rom. 3:24-26 which he sets
out to refute. It is by no means impossible, however, to
understand πάρεσις as "passing over" and still interpret
ἔνδειξις as a revelation event grounded in God's totally free
and sovereign will. Kümmel's faulty reasoning at this point
is due in part to his assumption that a sharp distinction can
be made between ἔνδειξις as rational demonstration of fact and
ἔνδειξις as revelation event. Such a distinction is questionable; one might note, for example, that Liddell and Scott give
no indication that ἔνδειξις had a specialized meaning such as
"logical proof," as Kümmel seems to imply. 2) In the second
place, if Rom. 3:25-26 (or 24-25) is considered a pre-Pauline
formulation, it is irrelevant that an idea expressed in v. 25
is problematic in the framework of Paul's own theology.

[61] Ibid., p. 9.

of Bauer's Wörterbuch this interpretation is unwarranted. It is not necessary to deny the presence of historical periodization in Paul[62] in order to insist that the interpretation of ἐν τῇ ἀνοχῇ τοῦ θεοῦ as the time of God's ἀνοχή has no basis in the text. The assumption that ἐν τῇ ἀνοχῇ τοῦ θεοῦ is conceptually (as distinct from stylistically) parallel to ἐν τῷ νῦν καιρῷ is unjustified. According to Kümmel's translation, ἐν τῇ ἀνοχῇ τοῦ θεοῦ has to be taken with the participle προγεγονότες: sins committed previously in the time of God's patience. But if that were the intention of the text a less ambiguous syntactical structure would be: τῶν ἁμαρτημάτων (τῶν) προγεγονότων ἐν τῇ ἀνοχῇ τοῦ θεοῦ. As the text stands, however, the ἐν phrase can most reasonably be understood as referring to πάρεσις; it describes the ground of the πάρεσις: πάρεσις due to (on account of) God's ἀνοχή. This interpretation is supported by a very similar (but Pauline) statement at Rom. 9:22 (ἤνεγκεν ἐν πολλῇ μακροθυμίᾳ σκεύη ὀργῆς), where πολλῇ is sufficient evidence that ἐν μακροθυμίᾳ cannot refer to the time of God's forbearance.[63]

How, then, shall one understand this term which provides an important clue to the meaning of πάρεσις in Rom. 3:25? According to Liddell and Scott ἀνοχή can mean "holding back, stopping," especially of hostilities, and is thus used, mostly in the plural, to mean "armistice, truce" (e.g., Xenophon, **Mem.** 4.4.17). In POxy. 1068.15 ἀνοχή means "a delay"; in Dio Cassius the plural noun designates "holidays" (cf. 39.30 and 55.26). According to Bauer, Epictetus (1.29.62) and a third century papyrus (PSI 632.13) use ἀνοχή in the sense of "clemency."

---

[62]**Ibid.**

[63]For ἐν as designating cause or reason see the texts given by Bauer at ἐν III. 3., especially I Mac. 16:3, I Cor. 7:14, Matt. 6:7, John 16:30; Eph. 4:2 could perhaps be included here. It is clear that in these instances the idea of cause or reason cannot be sharply distinguished from that of means, instrumentality. Special attention is due II Mac. 5:20: the Temple was forsaken ἐν τῇ τοῦ παντοκράτορος ὀργῇ, which is manifested passively--i.e., by divine indifference towards the Temple for a while (περὶ τὸν τόπον παρόρασις).

This is also the apparent connotation of ἀνοχή at Rom. 2:4, but in other instances of the word in Jewish and early Christian literature it can hardly mean "clemency" or "forbearance."
Ἀνοχή is found only once in the LXX, at I Mac. 12:25: καὶ ἀπῆρεν ἐξ Ιερουσαλημ καὶ ἀπήντησεν αὐτοῖς εἰς τὴν Αμαθῖτιν χώραν · οὐ γὰρ ἔδωκεν αὐτοῖς ἀνοχὴν τοῦ ἐμβατεῦσαι εἰς τὴν χώραν αὐτοῦ. Liddell and Scott here render ἀνοχή "opportunity," but overtones of a diminishing of military activity are very likely. In Josephus, War, 1.173 ἀνοχή appears in a genitive absolute construction: ἀνοχὴν τοῦ πολέμου διδόντος: "if the war would give an ἀνοχή" (="opportunity" but with the connotation of a pause in the fighting, a respite). Josephus, Ant., 6.72 reads: ἀνοχὴν δ'ἡμερῶν ἐπτὰ λαβεῖν ἠξίωσαν: "they requested an ἀνοχή of seven days"; here ἀνοχή is the delay of a threatened conflict to give opportunity for deciding whether to fight or surrender.[64]

Ἀνοχή occurs three times in the Similitudes of Hermas. At 6.3.1: ἐλυπούμην ἐπ' αὐτοῖς, ὅτι οὕτως ἐβασανίζοντο καὶ ἀνοχὴν ὅλως οὐκ εἶχον: "I grieved for them because they were tormented so and had no ἀνοχή at all" (= no respite, no break or pause in the torture; cf. 6.2.7: ἀνάπαυσιν αὐτοῖς οὐκ ἐδίδου). At 9.5.1: "And on that day the building was completed--all except the tower, for more was going to be added to it, and ἐγένετο ἀνοχὴ τῆς οἰκοδομῆς: there was an ἀνοχή in the building" (= a pause, delay, holding back completion; cf. the next clause: the builders are commanded to stop and rest). Similarly 9.14.2: τῆς οἰκοδομῆς ἀνοχὴ ἐγένετο.

Of the texts cited above, only in Rom. 2:4, Epictetus, and PSI 632,13 could ἀνοχή designate clemency or forbearance in the sense of mercy. Otherwise, when the context is an act or event already begun ἀνοχή refers to some sort of temporary cessation, that is, a pause or respite. When the context is an impending event (as at Jos. Ant., 6.72) ἀνοχή has the sense of "delay." Common to all these instances is a connotation of "holding back."

---

[64]The context is the narrative of I Sam. 11; what Josephus gives in indirect discourse, I Sam. 11:3 has in direct: καὶ λέγουσιν . . . ἄνες ἡμῖν ἐπτὰ ἡμέρας (LXX); MT: They said ימים שבעת לנו הרף (let us alone for seven days).

This connotation of the noun ἀνοχή is completely congenial with one of the uses of the verb ἀνέχειν in the LXX. Although the verb often means "to carry, bear, endure, tolerate" (usually in the middle voice; cf. Is. 1:13, 46:4; II Mac. 9:12; III Mac. 1:22; IV Mac. 13:27), the meaning "hold back, restrain, check" is obvious elsewhere (e.g., Gen. 45:1; III Kings 12:24 [in B], Job 6:11; Sir. 48:3; Amos 4:7; Hag. 1:10; IV Mac. 1:35; Is. 42:14, 63:15, 64:11).

The fact that ἀνέχειν frequently means "to hold back, restrain" in the LXX and that ἀνοχή customarily has a connotation of "pause, respite, holding back" in pagan, Jewish, and Christian texts suggests that in Rom. 3:25 ἀνοχή refers to God's forbearance in the sense of holding back or restraint. If this is the case, however, πάρεσις can no longer be understood as remission or forgiveness, because the sense of finality connoted by forgiveness is not compatible with God's "holding back." Thus the following translation of Rom. 3:25b-26a is called for: ". . . for a demonstration of his righteousness because of the passing over of previous sins due to God's restraint."

This translation-interpretation can claim these advantages: 1) It allows διά with accusative to retain its normal causal meaning. 2) It allows ἀνοχή to bear its typical connotation of "holding back." 3) It allows the meaning of πάρεσις that is most compatible with ἀνοχή = "holding back." 4) It explains why the standard early Christian expression for forgiveness of sins (i.e., ἄφεσις) is not used in the pre-Pauline formulation if forgiveness is really the idea intended.[65]

---

[65]Kümmel cannot explain satisfactorily why a hapax legomenon (in the NT) is used in Rom. 3:25 for "remission" when the technical expression for forgiveness of sins in the early church was ἄφεσις. His observation (op. cit., p. 10) that Pauline usage is too slight to be used as evidence--Paul speaks elsewhere of God's forgiveness only twice and on those occasions uses ἄφεσις (Col. 1:14) or ἀφιέναι (Rom. 4:7 = Ps. 32:1) --hardly meets the real point. The point is that the NT writers who do talk about forgiveness of sins customarily use ἄφεσις/ἀφιέναι. Zeller (op. cit., 72) suggests, in the form of a question, that ἄφεσις may have been deliberately avoided in the pre-Pauline formula because of its individualistic overtones, but this is a conjecture fathered by necessity. Would Zeller claim that all the instances of ἄφεσις and ἀφιέναι in the NT refer exclusively to forgiveness of individuals as individuals?

5) It demonstrates that 3:26 is not a superfluous re-presenta-
tion of 25b. V. 25b (διὰ τὴν πάρεσιν . . .) describes the
reason why the manifestation of God's righteousness now and in
this way (25a) was desirable in accord with His purpose; v. 26c
(εἰς τὸ εἶναι . . .) describes the effect of that act.

Further insight into the meaning of the διὰ . . . θεοῦ
phrase of the pre-Pauline formulation comes with the recognition
that the πάρεσις-ἀνοχή idea in Rom. 3:25 is not positive (i.e.,
God graciously forgave) nor even neutral (God simply disregarded sin) but negative. One of the bases for such a view is the
fact that already in the OT the ἀνοχή of God was confronted as
a problem! This problem finds clearest expression at Isaiah
64:10-12: "Your holy city Zion has become a wilderness,
Jerusalem has become like a desert, our holy temple is accursed
and the splendor which our fathers praised has been burned with
fire, and all that we esteemed suffered misfortune. And after
all these things you restrained yourself, Lord, and you kept
silent and humiliated us sorely (καὶ ἐπὶ πᾶσι τούτοις ἀνέσχου,
κύριε, καὶ ἐσιώπησας καὶ ἐταπείνωσας ἡμᾶς σφόδρα -LXX). It is
clear that in this passage God's "holding back" is his inactivity, his failure to act on behalf of his people. The temple
has been burned, the holy city is a rubble heap--and still God
restrains himself and does not act. Two further points:  in
Is. 64 the "objects," the beneficiaries, of God's ἀνοχή are
the enemies of Israel who have caused her to suffer. The wider
question underlying these statements is thus, rather obviously,
the problem of theodicy.

Similar currents run through two other passages in
Isaiah. At Is. 63:15 (LXX) God's ἀνέχειν is the failure to
manifest his zeal and power, his mercy and compassion:  "Where
is your zeal and your strength? Where is the wealth of your
mercy and your compassion that you have withheld yourself from
us (ὅτι ἀνέσχου ἡμῶν)?" In the context of the divine act of
vengeance against the foes of God and Israel, Second Isaiah has
God say: "I have been silent, but shall I be silent and restrain myself forever (μὴ καὶ ἀεὶ σιωπήσομαι καὶ ἀνέξομαι)?
I have been longsuffering (ἐκαρτέρησα), like a woman in child-
birth, but I shall turn things upside down and cause things to
wither (ἐκστήσω καὶ ξηρανῶ)" (Is. 42:14 LXX). In these
Isaianic passages, then, it is clear that 1) God's patience is
conceived negatively, and 2) God's patience refers to his
present attitude toward the nations who oppress Israel.

Another kind of support for the view that the πάρεσις-
ἀνοχή idea in Rom. 3:25 is a negative one comes from post-
biblical Jewish writings. In the Psalms of Solomon--which
writing also at several points struggles with the problem of
theodicy--one reads about God's chastening (παιδεία) or reproof
(ἐλεγμός) which is often contrasted directly with the fate of
unrepentant sinners, namely eternal destruction (7:3-5; 14:1-10;
16:11, cf. vv. 4-5). Of special interest are the following
statements: "Happy is the man whom the Lord has remembered by
reproving and has detoured from the way of evil with stripes,
that he might be cleansed from sin before it multiplies" (Ps.
Sol. 10:1; cf. vv. 2-5). "The pious man has been disturbed
(ἐταράχθη) because of his transgressions, lest he should be
carried away alongside the sinners . . ."(13:5). "The Lord
spares his devout ones and blots out their transgressions
through discipline (ἐν παιδείᾳ). For the life of the righteous
will be forever, but sinners will be taken away to destruction"
(13:10-11; v. 12 describes the fate of the righteous in terms
of God's mercy).

In none of these passages is it stated that God does
not also chasten the sinners, but this contrast to the present
experience of the righteous is certainly implied. Thus,
although the terminology itself is not used, one finds here
the idea of God "passing over" sin, allowing sinners to prosper
in the present, "holding back" their punishment until a future
date. Very likely, however, the "sinners" of Ps. Sol. are not
Gentiles but fellow Jews whom the author(s) consider(s)
apostates.

In IV Ezra and II Baruch one finds ideas similar to
those observed in Isaiah and Psalms of Solomon, but now set in
an apocalyptic framework and now, as in the Isaiah passages,
related explicitly to the Gentiles. In IV Ezra 3:30 the seer
complains that God has spared his enemies, the ungodly, but
has destroyed his own people (cf. 4:22-25, 5:23-30, 6:55-59).
The divine response is that the day is soon coming when the
sinners will pay the penalty for their evil (6:18-19; cf. 4:26,
6:27, 7:16).

II Baruch understands Israel's misfortune as the divine
chastisement which sanctifies those who suffer: God ". . .
had aforetime no mercy on His own sons, but afflicted them as
His enemies, because they sinned; then therefore were they
chastened that they might be sanctified." ". . . you have

now suffered those things for your good, that you may not finally be condemned and tormented."[66] On the other hand, the nations, now prosperous, can expect to be smitten (13:5-8): "For assuredly in its own season shall the (divine) wrath awake against thee, which now in long-suffering is held in as it were by reins" (12:4).[67] Again it is clear that God's longsuffering means that He allows the iniquities of the Gentiles to go unpunished until finally, at the end, He exacts due penalty.[68]

There are significant points of similarity between the foregoing texts and another which is even more important for present purposes: II Maccabees 6:14. The implications of this verse are clear only within the context of the larger unit, vv. 12-17. This passage can be translated as follows:

Thus I beseech those of you reading this book not to be downcast because of these disastrous events but to understand that the punishments (described previously) were not meant to destroy but to discipline (πρὸς παιδείαν) our people. For indeed it is a sign of great kindness for the impious (τοὺς δυσσεβοῦντας) not to be let alone for a long time but to be punished right away. For the Lord does not delay and hold back punishment (ἀναμένει μακροθυμῶν ὁ δεσπότης . . . κολάσαι) as he does in the case of other peoples--that is, until they have reached the full measure of sin. Rather, in our case, He decided for these things to happen (οὕτως καὶ ἐφ' ἡμῶν ἔκρινεν εἶναι) so that he might not [have to] take vengeance on us in the future when our sins had reached their height. Therefore [we can still affirm that] He never withdraws his mercy (τὸν ἔλεον) from us; although He disciplines (παιδεύων) them with misfortunes, He does not abandon his own people. However, I have mentioned these things as a reminder to ourselves, but now, after these few words [rendering δι' ὀλίγων δέ], I must return to my account.

_____

[66]Both quotations (13:9-10 and 78:6) follow the translation of R. H. Charles, AP, II. Cf. also 48:48-50, 52:5-7.

[67]Charles' translation from the Syriac. The Oxyrhynchus fragment of this text, which Charles reproduces from Grenfell and Hunt, has μακροθυμ[ ]. Cf. also 14:1-2, 82:3-83:3.

[68]A reflection of this same pattern of thought is to be found in the community Rule at Qumran. In 1QS 10.17-20 the sectary can say that he will initiate no act of judgment or retribution upon the ungodly until the (impending) day of vengeance, when God himself will judge. Here, as a son of light and therefore God's earthly representative, the sectary assumes the same stance toward the enemies which in II Baruch God himself assumes. However, in 1QS the enemies are not Gentiles but sinful Jews who stand beyond the pale of the chosen end-time community. On the "spirit of concealment" at Qumran see Krister Stendahl, "Hate, Non-Retaliation, and Love. IQS x, 17-20 and Rom. 12:19-21," HTR 55(1962), 349-350.

In this passage it is quite clear that God's long-suffering is not being thought of positively in terms of mercy and gracious compassion. Indeed, here μακροθυμῶν is almost precisely the reverse of mercy (ὁ ἔλεος: v. 16). The emphatically negative character of God's patience, his "holding back," is seen in its eventual result: the piling up of sins so that the punishment appropriate to them will likewise be multiplied. God's μακροθυμία is not an act of clemency nor the divine attribute of mercy. It is rather the divine inactivity, the failure to intervene, which allows sin to run its natural course until the day of judgment when finally God will indeed act. And from whom does God hold back punishment so that sins pile up? Again it is other nations, other peoples. To his own people God demonstrates his mercy by early chastisement, but the Gentiles he leaves alone until their sins have accumulated beyond the breaking point. Not Jews but Gentiles are the present beneficiaries of God's longsuffering in II Maccabees 6.

On the basis of the texts considered in the foregoing pages one is justified in speaking of a rather widespread tradition (Ps. Sol., 1QS, IV Ezra, II Baruch, II Mac.), rooted in the OT (Isaiah), in which God's longsuffering is conceived negatively as a self-restraint which allows sin to accumulate and thus assures a more severe retribution in the future.[69] This idea can be employed to describe the penalty in store for apostate Jews (Ps. Sol., 1QS). It can also be used with great effectiveness to account for the apparent fact that in the present God does not requite the Gentiles for their wickedness (IV Ezra, II Baruch, II Mac.).

It is my contention that 1) just such a tradition as this underlies the πάρεσις-ἀνοχή statement in the formulation from which Paul quotes; and 2) according to the formula it is the Gentiles whose previous sins God has "passed over" due to his patience/restraint.[70] Thus ἡ πάρεσις τῶν προγεγονότων

---

[69] I Cor. 11:32 points to the possibility that Paul was familiar with such a tradition: κρινόμενοι δὲ ὑπὸ τοῦ κυρίου παιδευόμεθα ἵνα μὴ σὺν τῷ κόσμῳ κατακριθῶμεν. Significantly, IV Maccabees, in the words of the fifth brother to Antiochus (11:3), reflects the same basic idea.

[70] I do not mean to imply that in Rom. 3 Paul is talking about Gentiles only. As 3:9 and 3:23 make clear, he is talking about all men (πάντες). In line with the interpretation of

ἁμαρτημάτων ἐν τῇ ἀνοχῇ τοῦ θεοῦ points to the "outsiders,"
that is, to the Gentiles and to their situation prior to God's
act in Christ. Those sins committed previously, before Christ,
by non-Jews God had not dealt with positively. With a view to
his eventual judgment, God had allowed sins to pile up; He had
"held back" and "passed over" the transgressions of those who
did not belong to his chosen people. It is due to this situation, insists the formula, that God "presents" Christ crucified
as an ἱλαστήριον for the sins of the Gentiles. For the first
time they too now have access to an ἱλαστήριον, as the Jews
had had for generations.

The argument that the πάρεσις-ἀνοχή clause in Rom. 3:25
refers to the Gentiles and to their situation prior to God's
recent act (προτίθεσθαι ἱλαστήριον) is supported by two Lucan
texts, both of which occur in "speeches" to Gentiles. Acts
14:16 reads: "In past ages God allowed all peoples (πάντα τὰ
ἔθνη) to go their own ways." According to Acts 17:30, "Although
God overlooked the times of ignorance, now He declares to all
men everywhere that they should repent . . . ." Since here
the time of God's ὑπεριδεῖν is contrasted with that of man's
μετανοεῖν, God's overlooking sin in the past can hardly be
interpreted as "forgiveness." Similar to the juxtaposition of
ὑπεριδεῖν and μετανοεῖν is the relationship of πάρεσις and
δικαιοῦν in Rom. 3:25-26. The primary difference is that in
Rom. 3:25-26 God is the subject of both acts. Just as ὑπεριδεῖν
refers to God's previous relationship to non-Jews, so in the
quotation does πάρεσις point to the Gentiles.

More importantly, the interpretation proposed is
supported, in my view, by the pre-Pauline formulation itself.
The statement προέθετο ὁ θεὸς ἱλαστήριον makes excellent sense
when understood as a reference to God's new relationship to the
Gentiles. It is not so intelligible if one assumes that the

---

the quotation at Rom. 3:25-26 proposed here, however, Paul
does not apply to the Gentiles a "Jewish Christian" formula
concerning the restoration of God's covenant with his people
through the blood of Christ. Rather, the discussion in which
the quotation is set suggests that Paul took a traditional
statement about how God now brings the Gentiles into his
saving purposes and interpreted God's new relationship to the
Jews in the same way! The movement from the tradition to Paul's
own theologizing therefore is not: as God deals with Israel
so will he now deal with the Gentiles; rather: as God now
justifies the Gentiles, so--on the same basis and on no other,
i.e., χωρὶς νόμου--will he henceforth deal with Israel.

quotation is talking about the Jews. Why? Because, according
to the OT, numerous means of expiation had for generations been
available to God's chosen people through the cultic institutions
of Israel (sacrifice, prayer and confession, the ritual of the
Day of Atonement).[71] By contrast, the Gentiles had had available no such means of expiation--unless, of course, they first
became Jews.

The pre-Pauline formulation quoted in Rom. 3:25-26
intends to say that whereas God had passed over the previous
sins of the Gentiles due to his restraint, He has now taken
positive action to deal with those sins. Precisely what it is
that God has done is expressed in the main clause of the formulation.

B.  Ὃν προέθετο ὁ θεὸς ἱλαστήριον

Sanday and Headlam prefer to translate προέθετο by
"set forth publicly" on the basis of several terms in the
immediate context which denote publicity πεφανέρωται, εἰς
and πρὸς ἔνδειξιν). "The Death of Christ is not only a manifestation of the righteousness of God, but a visible manifestation . . . ."[72] Other references imply that by "set forth
publicly" Sanday and Headlam have in mind the event of the
crucifixion itself.[73] That is clearly the position of O.
Michel: "Gott stellt das Kreuz Jesu als ein öffentliches
Ereignis heraus." "Pls denkt also doch wohl an eine öffent-
liche Herausstellung des geschichtlichen Ereignisses."[74] This
interpretation has little to commend it. Ἔνδειξις means a
demonstration or manifestation, but here it certainly does not

---

[71]An early Christian could argue, as the author of
Hebrews does (e.g., at 10:1-4), that cultic means of expiation
available to the Jews were but "shadows" of real salvation in
Christ. But such an argument would appear to be a theological
development subsequent to the tradition from which Paul quotes.
The quotation itself betrays no sign of that notion.

[72]William Sanday and Arthur C. Headlam, A Critical and
Exegetical Commentary on the Epistle to the Romans (Edinburgh,
1902), p. 87.

[73]Cf. their suggestion to compare Gal. 3:1 and their
view that ἱλαστήριον probably does not mean "mercy seat"
because the sprinkling of the mercy seat was the one rite which
was withdrawn from the sight of the people.

[74]Michel, op. cit., p. 107 and p. 107, n. 1.

point to a public spectacle, an event that could be observed by any passer-by! And no argument at all can be founded upon πεφανέρωται (v. 22) because the context cannot be relied upon to explain a pre-Pauline formula from which it must be distinguished; besides, that verb hardly refers to the empirical crucifixion event either.

Another possible translation is "proposed, planned, intended"; this is the meaning of the middle verb at Rom. 1:13 (προεθέμην ἐλθεῖν πρὸς ὑμᾶς). But this sentence exhibits a syntactical structure different from Rom. 3:25. In 1:13 the verb is augmented conceptually as well as grammatically by the infinitive. This construction--and the context--insure the meaning "I planned to come . . . ." In Eph. 1:9 (ἣν προέθετο ἐν αὐτῷ) the verb is not supplemented by an infinitive but by a direct object: ἣν (=εὐδοκίαν ). This construction is more nearly like Rom. 3:25, where the verb takes no infinitive but has double objects (ὅν, ἱλαστήριον). In Eph. 1:9 the translation "plan, propose, intend" is hardly possible; nor does the syntax (i.e., no infinitive) suggest this meaning at Rom. 3:25.

Dieter Zeller observes that at Eph. 1:9f., 3:9-11 and II Tim. 1:9f. προτίθεσθαι and πρόθεσις appear in stylized revelation contexts.[75] Προέθετο should therefore be understood in terms of God's predestining for the purpose of revelation. "Christus ist das von Ewigkeit her ausersehene, einmalige Sühnopfer, das erst im eschatologischen Jetzt offenbar wird, um die Sünden hinwegzutun."[76] The same idea Zeller finds reflected in I Pet. 1:19f., I John 3:5, John 1:29-31 and Heb. 9:26.

Zeller's interpretation is an attractive one and the most adequate thus far suggested. It must, however, be considered in light of the following observations: 1) In Eph. 1:9 it is God's εὐδοκία which he predestined (or "set forth")

---

[75]Zeller, op. cit., 57.

[76]Ibid., 58. Note that in making this statement Zeller seems to be overlooking the possibility that the eschatological emphasis (ἐν τῷ νῦν καιρῷ) may be a Pauline addition.

in Christ; in Eph. 1:11 it is Christians who have been predestined (προορισθέντες) according to God's πρόθεσις. Eph.
3:11 reads: "according to the eternal πρόθεσις which he
effected through Christ Jesus our Lord." In II Tim. 1:9
Christians are saved not according to their works but according
to God's own πρόθεσις and χάρις given to them in Christ.
Conclusion: there is no example in these texts of the idea
that God predestined Christ. Moreover, Christ seems to be
understood more as the means through which God effected his
πρόθεσις than as its object or content.

2) Paul's own "neutral" use of the word (Rom. 1:13)
clearly means "intend, plan." For Paul himself, then, προτίθεσθαι certainly is not a technical term which automatically
brings to mind the subject of God's predestination and revelation. 3) One cannot be certain that προέθετο in Eph. 1:9
means "intended, planned, proposed" (so Bauer); it could as
well mean "set forth" (so RSV). In the case of the latter
interpretation, reference would be to the Christ event, not a
pre-Christ act of God's predestination. 4) Zeller points to
I Pet. 1:19f. by way of support. But is it not significant
that the term used there is προγινώσκεσθαι, not προτίθεσθαι?
One notices also that the object of προορίζειν at I Cor. 2:7
is God's wisdom and that at Rom. 8:29-30 προγινώσκειν and
προορίζειν clearly refer to Christians. 5) Προτίθεσθαι
obviously can be used in a context of revelation (Eph. 1:9);
so can πρόθεσις. That is not surprising since God's plan and
purpose is naturally the subject in such a context. The
crucial question is: Is there anything in Rom. 3:25 other than
this word to suggest an act of God's predestining? Do other
NT uses of προτίθεσθαι compel this sense here? The answer to
both questions is: No. In regard to the first question, one
should note, by way of contrast, to Rom. 3:25-26, the accumula-
tion of words in Eph. 1:9-11 which refer to God's salvation
plan: μυστήριον, θέλημα, εὐδοκία, οἰκονομία, πλήρωμα τῶν
καιρῶν.

To this point Zeller's interpretation of προτίθεσθαι
appears to be possible but not compelling. Three further
considerations, however, tip the scales against his view. In
the first place, other scholars are not nearly so certain as

Israel (17:22). God is the active agent here. He it is who
purifies the land through the purifying (=expiatory) blood of
the martyrs. On the other hand overtones of the propitiation
of the divine anger are by no means absent in IV Maccabees.
According to 4:21, ἀγανακτήσασα ἡ θεία δίκη αὐτὸν αὐτοῖς τὸν
Ἀντίοχον ἐπολέμωσεν. Conversely, the departure of Antiochus,
one can assume, means that God is no longer angry, i.e., that
He has been propitiated (although this is never stated explicitly in IV Maccabees). Furthermore, Eleazar prays for God to
"be satisfied" (ἀρκεσθείς) by the martyrs' punishment, and this
participle may bear the connotation of God's being propitiated.
(Ἀντίψυχον [=ἐμὴ ψυχῆ] at 6:29 also suggests that Eleazar's
life may be understood as a propitiatory offering, but this
impression is counterbalanced by the different phraseology at
17:21: ἀντίψυχον τῆς τοῦ ἔθνους ἁμαρτίας.) In IV Maccabees,
then, ἱλαστήριος means "expiatory" but carries at the same
time connotations of propitiating God by removing that which
has aroused his anger.

The parallelism of ἱλαστήριον in Rom. 3:25 and ἱλαστήριος θάνατος in IV Mac. 17:22 has far greater implications for
the understanding of the pre-Pauline formulation than the
precise meaning of one term. Much more important than this
terminological parallel is the conceptual one: pre-Christian
Jewish literature provides no closer parallel to (Χριστὸν)
προέθετο ὁ θεὸς ἱλαστήριον than IV Mac. 17:22, especially when
the author's declaration is understood as the "answer" to
Eleazar's plea at 6:29: καθάρσιον αὐτῶν ποίησον τὸ ἐμὸν αἷμα
. . . . Eleazar prays that God will make his blood their
purification, that is, that He will accept it, regard it as
such. That, in different terminology, is exactly what the pre-
Pauline formulation says that God has done in response to the
death of Jesus: He has regarded Christ crucified as a (propitiating) means of expiation!

C. Διὰ πίστεως ἐν τῷ αὐτοῦ αἵματι

The main clause of the pre-Pauline formulation is modified by the immediately following phrase: διὰ πίστεως ἐν τῷ
αὐτοῦ αἵματι. Brief as it is, this phrase abounds with
problems. First off, there is the question of whether διὰ

reading of A is to be preferred, the article must be omitted,
and ἱλαστηρίου should be read as an adjective modifying "their
death."

42

πίστεως at Rom. 3:25 occurred in the Pauline autograph. This question is raised by the reading of A, which omits διὰ πίστεως altogether. Since the other MSS present the lectio difficilior, however, it is preferable to ascribe the absence of διὰ πίστεως in A to a copyist's omission.

A second question is: Did διὰ πίστεως belong to the formulation from which Paul quotes, or is the phrase a Pauline insertion? Rudolf Bultmann characterizes διὰ πίστεως in Rom. 3:25 as one of the "specifically Pauline expressions" which Paul adds to the quoted formula. Käsemann refers to Bultmann's theory, but without giving any additional reasons.[88] Subsequent to Käsemann's essay, numerous other scholars have asserted that διὰ πίστεως is a Pauline interpolation. Usually their evidence is the pronouncements of Käsemann and Bultmann! H. Conzelmann is one of the few who tries to support this assumption: "Dass dies ein Zusatz ist, geht daraus hervor, dass er im Satz nicht sinnvoll bezogen werden kann. Er markiert als eine Art Ausrufezeichen die Intentionen des Paulus."[89] In spite of such friendly support, can Bultmann's suggestion withstand scrutiny?

1) If Paul did indeed add διὰ πίστεως to the original formula he thereby created the resultant phrase διὰ πίστεως ἐν τῷ αὐτοῦ αἵματι. It is possible to maintain that Paul's readers would have understood quite naturally that ἐν τῷ αὐτοῦ αἵματι was to be taken with ἱλαστήριον in some such manner as this: ἱλαστήριον, through faith, by means of his blood.[90] But in the ancient continuous script it was impossible to make a separation of words by visual means such as commas. Would Paul not have recognized that ἐν τῷ αὐτοῦ αἵματι could

---

[88]R. Bultmann, op. cit., I, p. 46. E. Käsemann, op. cit., 150.

[89]Conzelmann, "Die Rechtfertigungslehre des Paulus: Theologie oder Anthropologie?" EvTh 28(1968), 396, n. 43. Regarding Conzelmann's first claim: How could Paul have done such a thing? Regarding the second statement: Why would Paul wish to emphasize his intention with a "kind of exclamation mark" which cannot meaningfully be related to the sentence?

[90]Many commentators translate: "ἱλαστήριον by/in his blood, through faith." By shifting the position of "through faith" these scholars tacitly recognize the difficulty of understanding Rom. 3:25 as "ἱλαστήριον through faith by his blood." That recognition, though tacit, is a rather significant concession.

be taken as well with πίστις as with ἱλαστήριον by his Roman readers? That possibility seems quite as real as the likelihood that Paul's readers would automatically associate ἐν τῷ αὐτοῦ αἵματι directly with ἱλαστήριον. In this connection, moreover, it should be noted that Paul never speaks of faith ἐν Jesus' blood (or cross, or death).[91] In fact, only twice does Paul use the expression πίστις ἐν . . . at all. I Cor. 2:5 reads: "that your faith may not be ἐν the wisdom of men but ἐν the power of God." And, according to the preferred reading, Gal. 3:26 has "through faith ἐν Christ Jesus." Thus if one assumes that Paul has altered a traditional formula by adding διὰ πίστεως, he is saying in effect that Paul created an expression ("through faith ἐν his blood") which is notably uncharacteristic of him.

2) Why would Paul have thought it useful to add διὰ πίστεως to a quoted formula? Not because such an addition was necessary, either to clarify his own position or to prevent misunderstanding. Already in the four preceding verses, especially v. 22, Paul has made it clear that faith is the only appropriate response to what God has done through Christ--to say nothing of 1:16-17. And if one can assume that Paul had in mind some idea of what he intended to say after quoting the formula, 3:27ff. supports the present objection.

3) Käsemann's followers insist that διὰ πίστεως is obviously a secondary insertion because it interrupts such a smooth and natural phrase: ἱλαστήριον ἐν τῷ αὐτοῦ αἵματι.[92] But if ἐν τῷ αὐτοῦ αἵματι is so integral to the idea of ἱλαστήριον involved here that the five words constitute a single thought unit, would this not have been obvious to Paul? Why would he split that phrase apart with διὰ πίστεως? The least that can be said is that if ἱλαστήριον and ἐν τῷ αὐτοῦ αἵματι originally belonged together, Paul chose a singularly inauspicious place to insert his "correction." Why would he not, rather, have added such a phrase at the end of the thought-line, i.e., after αἵματι?

---

[91] Whether ἐν should be read as "in" or "through" is inconsequential for the present discussion; the points to be made here are not dependent on a particular translation.

[92] Cf., e.g., Lohse, op. cit., p. 150.

4) Bultmann suggests that the "specifically Pauline expressions" can be bracketed as Paul's additions. This suggestion involves two unexamined assumptions: a) that what is "specifically Pauline" must be uniquely or exclusively Pauline as well, and b) that διὰ πίστεως is Paul's preferred expression for "by means of faith." Point a) cannot be disproved because we have so little pre-Pauline material to use as a control; the fact that διὰ πίστεως does not appear in what pre-Pauline material we do have is hardly proof that the phrase is uniquely Pauline, however. Furthermore, assumption a) is suspect at once in light of a phrase such as δικαιοσύνη θεοῦ. This phrase certainly must be considered a "specifically Pauline expression" --it is found outside Paul only at Matt. 6:33 and James 1:20 in the NT--but it cannot be considered uniquely Pauline. That Paul did not introduce this rubric into Christian thought is proved by Rom. 3:25. As for assumption b) one might observe that Paul uses the phrase ἐκ πίστεως fifteen times, διὰ πίστεως only eight times (although he can use these expressions interchangeably: Rom. 3:30, cf. Gal. 2:16); the dative πίστει he uses at least ten times.[93] Thus he appears to prefer ἐκ πίστεως to διὰ πίστεως. If one wishes to talk about a Pauline rubric, it would probably be more accurate to talk about ἐκ πίστεως than about διὰ πίστεως.[94]

Given these four considerations, the weightiest objection to the assertion that διὰ πίστεως is a Pauline addition is a negative one: the proponents of that view have failed to present adequate evidence for it. They come no closer to divulging that evidence than the remark of Conzelmann quoted above or Lohse's comment about the phrase διὰ πίστεως, "die die zusammengehörigen Wörter ἱλαστήριον ἐν τῷ αὐτοῦ αἵματι

---

[93] Ἐκ πίστεως: Rom. 1:17, 3:30, 4:16 (twice), 5:1, 9:30, 9:32, 10:6, 19:23 (twice); Gal. 3:8, 12, 22, 24; 5:5. Διὰ πίστεως: Rom. 3:22, 30, 31; II Cor. 5:7; Gal. 2:16; 3:14, 26; Phil. 3:9. This tabulation does not include the Habakkuk quotation at Rom. 1:17 and Gal. 3:11, the phrase οἱ ἐκ πίστεως (because in that case ἐκ is partitive/partisan, not instrumental), or the special use of διὰ . . . πίστεως with (συμ) παρακαλεσθαι (Rom. 1:12, I Thess. 3:7). For πίστει cf. Rom. 3:28, 4:19, 20; 5:2, 11:20, 14:1; I Cor. 16:13; II Cor. 1:24, 8:7; Phil. 1:27.

[94] That this preference for ἐκ πίστεως stems ultimately from ἐκ πίστεως in Hab. 2:4 is an interesting, if unprovable, possibility.

auseinanderreisst . . . ."[95] Lohse does not tell why we should
understand these words as belonging together, nor does he explain
why we should consider Paul's grasp of the syntax necessary for
clear communication less developed than that of the fellow
Christian(s) from whom this formulation derives. Lohse's
assertion that ἰλαστήριον and ἐν τῷ αὐτοῦ αἵματι "belong
together" is based upon a judgment about the apparent natural-
ness of the phrase ἰλαστήριον ἐν τῷ αὐτοῦ αἵματι. But what
sounds natural to the exegete is not necessarily what is correct
as a reconstruction of the original text.

The only conclusion appropriate to these observations
is that the proponents of Bultmann's suggestion (that διὰ
πίστεως is a Pauline interpolation) have not proved their case.
Therefore, in the absence of persuasive evidence to the contrary
and in view of the observations made above, διὰ πίστεως will
here be considered a part of the original pre-Pauline formula
at Rom. 3:25-26.

The question now becomes: What does (ἰλαστήριον) διὰ
πίστεως ἐν τῷ αὐτοῦ αἵματι mean in the context of the formulation? The major prerequisite of an adequate interpretation is
the recognition that the formula is not talking about faith
in Jesus' blood. That is, ἐν does not point to the object of
faith. This is not the way that any traditional formulation or
any NT writer speaks about the relationship between Jesus'
death and Christian faith (but cf. Ignatius to the Smyrnaeans
6:1:  . . . πιστεύσωσιν εἰς τὸ αἷμα Χριστοῦ).

Although numerous variations are possible, three basic
interpretations of this phrase appear to be preferable. In my
view none of the three is wholly satisfactory, nor am I acquainted with an interpretation which is not objectionable for
one reason or another.

The first interpretation is founded on three premises:
1) an adequate interpretation will be compatible with the
meaning of προέθετο suggested earlier; 2) the order of the
two prepositional phrases (διὰ . . ., ἐν . . .) actually facil-
itates the intended meaning; 3) because of the terminological-
conceptual ἰλαστήριον parallel, IV Maccabees can be taken
seriously as a potential source of illumination regarding the
meaning of διὰ . . . αἵματι.

---

[95]Lohse, op. cit., p. 150.

46

It was suggested earlier that προτίθεσθαι intends to say that God "regarded" Christ crucified in a certain way, that is, as a means of expiation. But did this divine decision rest upon Jesus' death qua death? Or is there another factor? To ask the question differently: Does the formulation at Rom. 3: 25 suggest why God "regarded" Christ crucified as ἱλαστήριον? Whether it does or not is largely dependent on how one understands the syntactical relationship between the two prepositional phrases and how one translates ἐν . . . αἵματι.

Rom. 3:25 can be set forth schematically in this way:

ὃν προέθετε ὁ θεὸς ἱλαστήριον
    διὰ πίστεως
      ἐν τῷ αὐτοῦ αἵματι
εἰς ἔνδειξιν τῆς δικαιοσύνης αὐτοῦ
    διὰ τὴν πάρεσιν . . .
      ἐν τῇ ἀνοχῇ τοῦ θεοῦ.

It is apparent that διὰ πίστεως and ἐν . . . αἵματι are structurally analogous to the two prepositional phrases in the ἔνδειξις statement; even the prepositions themselves are identical. In that statement, however διὰ . . . is dependent on the preceding phrase (εἰς ἔνδειξιν) whereas ἐν . . . refers directly to the noun (πάρεσις) in the διὰ phrase. Now, if the structural parallelism noted is taken seriously as a reflection of "liturgical balance" and as a clue to meaning, it would appear likely that διὰ πίστεως is dependent on προέθετο . . . ἱλαστήριον, while ἐν . . . αἵματι refers directly to πίστις. Accordingly one has: "God 'regarded' (Christ) as a means of expiation διὰ faith, faith ἐν his blood."

How shall ἐν be understood? The translation "in" (Christ's blood as the object of faith) has already been judged improbable. Another possibility is suggested by Nigel Turner; in my view this translation possibility should be given very serious consideration. Regarding ἐν at Rom. 3:25, 5:9 and Rev. 5:9, Turner writes: "A curious instrumental dative of price is found with ἐν, a distinctly Semitic construction literally rendering the beth pretii . . . ."[96] One can assume that "distinctly Semitic" does not mean that ἐν at Rom. 3:25 necessarily reflects the Greek translation of an Aramaic original, which in turn would mean that this formulation originated in (Palestinian) Aramaic-speaking Christianity.

---

[96] James Hope Moulton, A Grammar of New Testament Greek. Vol. 3: Syntax, by Nigel Turner (Edinburgh, 1963), p. 253.

The following instances of translation suggest that this particular sense of ἐν must have been familiar to Jews and Gentiles
whose Bible was the LXX: II Sam. 23:17: בנפשׁותם = ἐν ταῖς
ψυχαῖς αὐτῶν. Josh. 6:26: בבכרו = ἐν τῷ πρωτοτόκῳ αὐτοῦ and
ובצעירו = καὶ ἐν τῷ ἐλαχίστῳ αὐτοῦ. I Chron 12:20: בראשׁינו =
(12:19) ἐν ταῖς κεφαλαῖς τῶν ἀνδρῶν ἐκείνων. Num. 17:3:
החטאים האלה בנפשׁתם = αὐτῶν ἁμαρτωλῶν τούτων ἐν ταῖς ψυχαῖς
αὐτῶν. Cf. also II Sam. 3:14, 24:24, Lam. 5:9 and Ez. 14:19.

Read in light of this usage, the pertinent phrase in
Rom. 3:25 can be rendered: "διά faith, faith at the cost/price
of his blood." It is at this point that reference to IV Maccabees may again be helpful. In IV Maccabees neither the phrase
διὰ πίστεως nor ἐν αἵματι occurs. However, the whole tenor of
the writing leaves no doubt that it was by virtue of the martyrs'
endurance unto death that God responded favorably to Eleazar's
prayer (6:29: "make my blood their purification, accept my
life . . .") and through the martyrs' blood, their expiatory
death, delivered Israel (17:22). Interpreted in the light of
IV Maccabees, then,[97] Rom. 3:25 intends to say that God "regarded" Christ crucified as a means of expiation by virtue of
faith (i.e., his faith) at the cost of his blood.[98]

One drawback to this interpretation is the fact that
πίστις as Jesus' faith is not to be found in the NT (with the
possible exception of Rom. 3:25-26!).

This assertion holds also for the Pauline phrase πίστις
Χριστοῦ. Admittedly the phrase is ambiguous as Paul uses it.
Nevertheless it is clear that Paul does not mean faith in
Christ. 1) In several Pauline statements in which πίστις
Χριστοῦ occurs, an additional phrase appears which would be
somewhat superfluous if πίστις Χριστοῦ meant merely faith in

---

[97]That this approach is legitimate and appropriate is
one of the implications of the last section of this thesis;
cf. infra, pp. 233-254.

[98]For διά with genitive to denote occasion see Bauer,
s. v., III. e. and the texts given there: Rom. 12:3, Gal. 1:15,
3:18, 4:23, Philemon 22; (cf. other passages where διά with gen.
seems to have a special nuance when used with παρακαλῶ: Rom.
12:1, 15:30, I Cor. 1:10, II Cor. 10:1). This use could be
understood as a half-way house between a strictly instrumental
(write with pen) and causative use (so Bauer for Rom. 8:3).
In several NT texts διά with gen. is usually rendered "through"
(e.g., "through his blood" at Acts 20:28; cf. Rom. 5:10, Eph.
2:16) where it could perhaps be translated more properly "in
virtue of"--a translation which would prevent total eclipse of
the causal dimension.

48

Christ. Note, e.g., Rom. 3:22: διὰ πίστεως ('Ιησοῦ) Χριστοῦ
εἰς πάντας τοὺς πιστεύοντας. Gal. 2:16: ἡμεῖς εἰς Χριστὸν
'Ιησοῦν ἐπιστεύσαμεν, ἴνα δικαιωθῶμεν ἐκ πίστεως Χριστοῦ . . . .
Gal. 3:22: ἴνα ἡ ἐπαγγελία ἐκ πίστεως 'Ιησοῦ Χριστοῦ δοθῇ
τοῖς πιστεύουσιν. 2) In Rom. 3:21-22 Paul writes that the
righteousness of God has been revealed (note the perfect!) διὰ
πίστεως Χριστοῦ. He probably does not intend to say that God's
righteousness has been revealed through faith in Christ. 3)
In Gal. 3:23 πίστις is probably equivalent to πίστις 'Ιησοῦ
Χριστοῦ in the last clause of the preceding verse. But in v. 23
that faith is something which, from a past perspective, "was
going to be revealed." It is difficult to imagine that faith
in Christ is something which could be "revealed."

On the other hand πίστις Χριστοῦ in Paul cannot be
properly translated "Christ's faith" either. 1) The function
of πίστις Χριστοῦ in Paul's letters is too closely analogous
to that of πίστις (when it is obvious that πίστις is the
believer's faith) to allow one to understand that phrase as a
reference to Christ's own faith. Cf. Rom. 3:28: . . . δικαιοῦσθαι πίστει ἄνθρωπον χωρὶς ἔργων νόμου and Gal. 2:16: οὐ
δικαιοῦνται ἄνθρωπος ἐξ ἔργων νόμου ἐὰν μὴ διὰ πίστεως Χριστοῦ
'Ιησοῦ. Cf. Rom. 1:17: δικαιοσύνη θεοῦ . . . ἀποκαλύπτεται ἐκ
πίστεως . . . and Rom. 3:21-22: δικαιοσύνη θεοῦ πεφανέρωται
. . . διὰ πίστεως ('Ιησοῦ) Χριστοῦ. 2) The juxtaposition of
πίστις Χριστοῦ and ἔργα νόμου in Gal. 2:16 suggests that πίστις
Χριστοῦ is something that man "does" or "participates in"; thus
it cannot be simply Christ's own faith.

The problems involved in translating πίστις Χριστοῦ
as "faith in Christ" or "Christ's faith" can be avoided if one
abandons the notion that Χριστοῦ has to be taken either as an
"objective genitive" or as a "subjective genitive." Gal. 3:22-
25 encourages one to see beyond this either-or choice. According to v. 22 "the scripture confined/imprisoned all things
under sin in order that the promise (i.e., what was promised)
might be given (by God) ἐκ πίστεως 'Ιησοῦ Χριστοῦ to those who
believe." In the following verses (23-25) Paul says that:
      before faith came -- we were always guarded by the Law
      until the coming
         faith was to be
         revealed         -- we were used to being confined
      until Christ        -- the Law was our guardian
      since faith         -- we are no longer under a guardian.

In these verses it would appear that "Christ" and "faith" are
being identified in the closest possible manner. "Faith" and
"Christ," in fact, seem to be designations of the same "event."
(Cf. Gal. 3:14 where ἐν 'Ιησοῦ Χριστῷ and διὰ τῆς πίστεως, in
adjoining ἴνα clauses, appear to be very closely related conceptually.) The "coming" of faith seems to be bound up with,
dependent on, the coming of Christ. Thus he is the source of
that faith which "comes" with him. In that sense it is "his"
faith, πίστις Χριστοῦ, "Christ-faith." When Paul speaks about
πίστις Χριστοῦ, then, he apparently intends to emphasize that
he is not talking about faith as a general principle, a natural
human possibility. Rather he means specifically that faith
which Christ brought.

Paul's understanding of the "given" or objective dimension of Christ-faith is indicated clearly by Phil. 3:9-10: ἔχων . . . τὴν (δικαιοσύνην) διὰ πίστεως Χριστοῦ, τὴν ἐκ θεοῦ δικαιοσύνην ἐπὶ τῇ πίστει. On the one hand the righteousness which has God as its source has become manifest to man by means of Christ-faith. On the other hand, it has to be appropriated "on the basis of faith."

But if the NT includes no instance of the term πίστις used with unambiguous reference to the faith of Jesus, there are several statements emphasizing his obedience or the fact that he was faithful. These statements cannot be considered irrelevant, since frequently in Judaism and in the NT the word πίστις has connotations of faithfulness and obedience as well as of belief and trust.[99] In the Christ-hymn which Paul quotes in Phil. 2 Jesus is exalted by God precisely because he was ὑπήκοος μέχρι θανάτου (Phil. 2:8). At Rom. 5:19 Paul (again dependent on tradition?) explicitly contrasts the παρακοή of Adam with the ὑπακοή of Christ, while the phrase ὑπακοὴ πίστεως (Rom. 1:5, 16:26) shows how nearly synonymous the two terms could be conceived. The intriguing passage at Hebrews 5:7-10 preserves a tradition which mentions that "he learned obedience by means of what he suffered." It is also in Hebrews that through his suffering and death Jesus becomes the "faithful (πιστός) high priest," in order to make expiation for the sins of the people (Heb. 2:17). Similarly, at Heb. 3:2, Jesus is said to be πιστός to Him who appointed him, as was Moses (cf. also vv. 5-6). That Jesus' faithfulness precedes his exaltation and therefore refers to faithfulness in suffering is suggested by 3:3. At Heb. 12:2 Jesus is ὁ τῆς πίστεως ἀρχηγὸς καὶ τελειωτής, who endured the cross. In my view, the author of Hebrews considers it appropriate and necessary for the Christian, as he runs, to look to Jesus precisely because Jesus also had faith and endured unto death. That is why, for the Christian, Jesus is "the originator and perfector of faith." At Rev. 1:5 and 3:14 the now-exalted Jesus is called ὁ μάρτυς ὁ πιστός (cf. 19:11), and 1:5 suggests that he was πιστός prior to his resurrection, i.e., in death.[100]

---

[99] Cf. R. Bultmann, "πιστεύω, κτλ." TDNT, VI, pp. 197-208.

[100] In IV Maccabees the mother's capacity to watch the execution of her seven sons is attributed to ἡ πίστις πρὸς θεόν (15:24). Before their death she had reminded them of former heroes of their people and had exhorted them: καὶ ὑμεῖς

50

More important than these texts, perhaps, is the fact
that, in spite of his high Christology, Ignatius of Antioch
could speak almost casually about Jesus' πίστις. Towards the
end of his letter to the Ephesians (20:1) he promises to write
a "second book." In it, he writes, προσδηλώσω ὑμῖν, ἧς ἠρξάμην
οἰκονομίας εἰς τὸν καινὸν ἄνθρωπον Ἰησοῦν Χριστόν, ἐν τῇ αὐτοῦ
πίστει καὶ ἐν τῇ αὐτοῦ ἀγάπῃ, ἐν πάθει αὐτοῦ καὶ ἀναστάσει.
That Jesus' faith and love, along with his suffering and resurrection, were important enough subjects to warrant attention in
another writing suggests that Ignatius was familiar with a
tradition which referred to Jesus' faith.

There is scattered evidence, therefore, that in early
Christianity the idea of Jesus' own faith, particularly his
faith in suffering, was not unfamiliar. Accordingly, it is
possible--the evidence will not permit a stronger adjective--
that πίστις in the pre-Pauline formulation in Rom. 3:25 is
intended as a reference to Jesus' faith. The resulting sense
would be: "whom God 'regarded' as a means of expiation by
virtue of (Jesus') faith at the cost of his blood."

Another objection to the preceding interpretation of
διὰ πίστεως ἐν τῷ αὐτοῦ αἵματι is that the meaning of ἐν upon
which it depends, although documented in the LXX, would have
been less familiar (and is therefore less likely at Rom. 3:25)
than an instrumental connotation would have been. This objection, however, should be balanced by the following observation:
it is not clear that in other NT occurrences of ἐν τῷ αὐτοῦ
αἵματι (or equivalent) ἐν always has an instrumental sense. In
Rev. 1:5 and 5:9, and perhaps in Rom. 5:9 (as Turner suggests),
the meaning "at the price of" is possible; this meaning is not
even excluded for Luke 22:20 and I Cor. 11:25. Nevertheless,
this objection suggests another interpretation of διὰ πίστεως
ἐν τῷ αὐτοῦ αἵματι.

A second interpretation of the phrase under discussion
surrenders the premise that ἐν τῷ αὐτοῦ αἵματι relates directly

---

οὖν τὴν αὐτὴν πίστιν πρὸς τὸν θεὸν ἔχοντες μὴ χαλεραίνετε
(16:22). The author of IV Mac. declares in admiration that by
her steadfastness and her virtual suicide (so no one might
violate her body) the mother demonstrated "the nobility of
faith" (17:2). Nor is it without relevance that Philo could
call πίστις a "blameless and superior sacrifice" offered unto
God (de Cher. 85).

to πίστις. It does presuppose, however, that the order of the prepositional phrases does not interfere with the intended meaning. According to this second view, διὰ πίστεως is still taken to refer to Jesus' faith but ἐν is understood in the sense "on account of" as at LXX Zech. 9:11 (ἐν αἵματι διαθήκης) and possibly Heb. 13:20 (. . . ὁ ἀναγαγὼν ἐκ νεκρῶν τὸν ποιμένα τῶν προβάτων τὸν μέγαν ἐν αἵματι διαθήκης αἰωνίου. . .) and Heb. 10:19 (ἔχοντες παρρησίαν εἰς τὴν εἴσοδον τῶν ἁγίων ἐν τῷ αἵματι 'Ιησοῦ). In this case Rom. 3:25 would mean: "whom God 'regarded' as a means of expiation due to (his) faith, on account of his blood."

Still a third type of interpretation surrenders the view that διὰ πίστεως refers to Jesus' faith. Accordingly διὰ πίστεως, related directly to ἱλαστήριον, points to the fact that expiation is not automatic. The means of expiation made available by God has to be appropriated or actualized by the believer's response of faith. Thus the meaning: "a means of expiation (effectuated) through faith." To harmonize with this view, ἐν τῷ αὐτοῦ αἵματι can be taken a) with προέθετο (through Jesus' blood/death God acted to make Jesus a means of expiation), or b) with ἱλαστήριον (the means of expiation is explicitly by means of his death), or c) with πίστεως (ἐν is instrumental; the Christian's faith is by means of, made possible by, his death). Of these three possibilities a) is not altogether compatible with the interpretation of προέθετο suggested previously; c) strikes one as strange in the framework of early Christian theology and can therefore be judged improbable. Preferable is b): the means of expiation is by faith, through his blood/death. But even this interpretation is not without its problems because it would appear that if both prepositional phrases refer directly to ἱλαστήριον, the smoother, more appropriate order would have been (ἱλαστήριον) ἐν τῷ αὐτοῦ αἵματι διὰ πίστεως: a means of expiation through his blood, (appropriated) by faith. One might note that the awkwardness of διὰ πίστεως in its position between ἱλαστήριον and ἐν . . . αἵματι is one of the considerations which leads scholars such as Bultmann and Käsemann to excise διὰ πίστεως from the pre-Pauline formula (without, however, explaining why Paul would have inserted it there!).

52

D. Εἰς ἔνδειξιν τῆς δικαιοσύνης αὐτοῦ / δίκαιος καὶ δικαιοῦν τὸν ἐκ πίστεως ᾿Ιησοῦ

The context within which one attempts to discover the meaning of δικαιοσύνη αὐτοῦ in Rom. 3:25-26 should be the pre-Pauline formulation itself rather than the Pauline understanding of δικαιοσύνη θεοῦ.[101] 1) The quotation says, in the first place, that the righteousness of God is "demonstrable"--and that by God himself: ὁ θεὸς . . . εἰς ἔνδειξιν . . . .[102] 2)"For a demonstration of his righteousness" explains the purpose and intention of God's act ("decision") προτίθεσθαι (Χριστὸν ᾿Ιησοῦν) ἱλαστήριον, that is, to make available for the Gentiles a means of expiation before Him. 3) The "reason" that God saw fit προτίθεσθαι ἱλαστήριον . . . εἰς ἔνδειξιν τῆς δικαιοσύνης αὐτοῦ was his own previous response (of inactivity, "passing over") to sins (of the Gentiles!) committed previously: διὰ τὴν πάρεσιν τῶν προγεγονότων ἁμαρτημάτων ἐν τῇ ἀνοχῇ τοῦ θεοῦ.

---

[101]From the vast literature on "righteousness of God" in Paul see especially A. Oepke, ΔΙΚΑΙΟΣΥΝΗ ΘΕΟΥ bei Paulus in neuer Beleuchtung," TLZ 78(1953), 257-64; E. Käsemann,"God's Righteousness in Paul," Journal for Theology and the Church, vol. 1 (Tübingen and New York, 1965), pp. 100-10; R. Bultmann, "ΔΙΚΑΙΟΣΥΝΗ ΘΕΟΥ," JBL 83(1964), 12-16; P. Stuhlmacher, Gerechtigkeit Gottes bei Paulus (Göttingen, 1965), pp. 74-101; O. Kuss, Der Römerbrief (Regensberg, 1963), pp. 115-21.
On the righteousness of God in the OT cf. von Rad, op. cit., I, pp. 370-80 (literature: p. 370, n. 1). Von Rad stresses that "Jahweh's righteousness was not a norm, but acts, and it was these acts which bestow salvation" (p. 373). Cf. also the study by H. H. Schmid, Gerechtigkeit als Weltordnung (Tübingen, 1968) (literature: n. 1); Stuhlmacher, op. cit., pp. 106-84 (righteousness of God in OT and other Jewish writings); Stuhlmacher's work should be evaluated in light of Schmid's study and in view of the specific criticism of H. Thyen, op. cit., pp. 57-60.

[102]Michel, op. cit., p. 107, n. 2, considers εἰς ἔνδειξιν (or equivalent) a "fixed Hellenistic formula." That may be the case, but in the texts cited by Michel it appears to have no constant, technical meaning. Usually it simply means "to demonstrate, show, make clear," although more precise connotations are present at times; e.g., Josephus, Ant. 14.159: the connotation is "to show off"; in Philo, op. mund. 87 there are overtones of proving as a fact. In II Cor. 8:24 Paul uses ἔνδειξις to mean "evidence" in the non-technical sense of demonstration, indication; in Phil. 1:28 the term can be translated "sign" or "omen" (so Bauer, s. v.).

Earlier in this study I argued that the δίκαιος καὶ δικαιοῦν statement at v. 26c belonged, in some form, to the pre-Pauline formulation. Whether it had its present form (i.e., εἰς τὸ εἶναι . . .) is a question difficult to decide. On the one hand one might note that Paul is particularly fond of εἰς τό plus infinitive phrase or infinitive; in Romans alone this construction is found at 1:11, 20; 4:11 (twice), 16, 18; 6:12; 7:4, 5; 8:29; 11:11; 12:2, 3; 15:8, 13, 16. This style also strikes one as somewhat incongruous beside the prepositional style of v. 25. On the other hand, Eph. 1:12 shows that εἰς τὸ εἶναι . . . can occur in a liturgical passage whose prepositional style resembles Rom. 3:25. In spite of this fact, it seems probable that Paul has adopted a statement (. . . δίκαιος καὶ δικαιοῦν τὸν ἐκ πίστεως 'Ιησοῦ) from the traditional formulation from which he also takes the term ἀπολύτρωσις in v. 24 but from which he quotes precisely in v. 25(-26a); this statement he has introduced with εἰς τὸ εἶναι.

If this is indeed the case, one cannot be absolutely certain about the exact relationship between δικαιοσύνη αὐτοῦ and the δίκαιος καὶ δικαιοῦν statement in the original pre-Pauline formulation. It is probable, however, that δίκαιος καὶ δικαιοῦν . . . was intended as a further explication of δικαιο-σύνη αὐτοῦ. Thus the pre-Pauline formula does not intend to suggest any sort of opposition or even separability between an attribute and an act of God. Granted that God is δίκαιος. But, as in the Jewish literature, whatever or whoever God is, He is only in relation to his creation and his people.[103] If a man can confess that God is righteous, that means, by definition, that God has manifested his righteousness. And that, according to the pre-Pauline formulation, God does by making righteous. According to this interpretation there is no material differ-ence between δικαιοσύνη αὐτοῦ and (αὐτος) δίκαιος καὶ δικαιοῦν . . . . "Righteousness of God" means that God is righteous

---

[103]In the OT and other Jewish writings (with the partial exception of Philo) one does not find speculation about God's "being" or his "nature." God is revealed and known as creator of the world, as deliverer of Israel, as Lord of the covenant, lawgiver, mighty warrior, merciful Father, vindicator, judge, etc. But all these designations imply God's _relationship_ to his world, his people, his enemies. It is _through these rela-tionships_ that He is known as God.

and that He makes righteous before Him τὸν ἐκ πίστεως 'Ιησοῦ[104]
How, then, is ὁ ἐκ πίστεως 'Ιησοῦ to be translated?
Again there seem to be two possibilities.  1) If διὰ πίστεως in
Rom. 3:25 does indeed refer to Jesus' faith, ὁ ἐκ πίστεως
'Ιησοῦ could be taken to mean:  "the one of Jesus' faith," that
is, the man who shares the faith of Jesus.  The fact that in the
phrase πίστις 'Ιησοῦ (which appears only here in the NT) the
formula employs the name "Jesus" rather than the title "Christ"
could be understood as support for this interpretation:  the
name "Jesus" points directly to the historical figure, Jesus
of Nazareth, and πίστις 'Ιησοῦ reflects the memory of this man's
own life stance, even in the face of death.  2) The reference
of the phrase is to "the man of Jesus-faith."  The "man of
Jesus-faith" would be not the man of faith-in-general but he
who has that faith of which Jesus is the source, the faith
which the crucified one "brought" or which "came" with him.

The central affirmation of the pre-Pauline formulation
in Rom. 3:25-26 can be paraphrased in this way:  God has
"regarded" Christ crucified as a means of expiation in order to
manifest his righteousness by making righteous the man who has
that faith whose source is Jesus (or:  the man who shares
Jesus' faith).  This act of justification is understood in terms
of forgiveness of sins.  (This is not stated explicitly but is
implied by the past situation over against which the divine act
was deemed appropriate, i.e., ἡ πάρεσις τῶν προγεγονότων
ἁμαρτημάτων. 'Ιλαστήριον also points to forgiveness of sins.)
According to an earlier suggestion regarding πάρεσις and ἀνοχή
the divine act being described is motivated by the plight of
the Gentiles.  It is therefore the Gentile of Jesus-faith (or
the Gentile who shares Jesus' own faith) whom God makes

---

[104]If the pre-Pauline formulation at Rom. 3:25-26 comes
out of hellenized Christianity and tells what God has done for
the Gentiles, the view of Käsemann ("Zum Verständnis . . . ,"
152-53) and Stuhlmacher (op. cit., p. 89), i.e., that here
δικαιοσύνη αὐτοῦ means God's "covenant loyalty," is thrown
open to question. Following Käsemann, Stuhlmacher (p. 90)
argues that v. 26 shows that Paul understood God's righteousness to be "die Treue des Schöpfers zu seiner Schöpfung." But
according to the interpretation offered in this study, this
idea would have been already expressed in the pre-Pauline
formulation since the δίκαιος καὶ δικαιοῦν phrase is a part of
the quotation!

righteous, thereby demonstrating His righteousness.[105]

E.  Conclusion

In the fragment of a pre-Pauline formulation preserved in Rom. 3:25-26 the death of Jesus is interpreted from the perspective of the Gentiles who now have been blessed with acceptance into the community of God's chosen ones, who can confess that through the death of the Lord of the church God was dealing with them to effect their salvation by removing the defilement of sin.  This is not to say, by any means, that the formulation must have been created by Gentile Christians or that it came from an exclusively Gentile congregation (even if there happened to be such, which at this early stage is quite unlikely). Rather, it came from a congregation which recognized that prior to the founding of churches consisting of Jews and Gentiles, Gentiles had been "outsiders" to the purpose of God as embodied in the people of Israel.  But now a new situation prevailed: uncircumcized Gentiles were an integral part of the salvation community, the church of Christ, which looked for his epiphany as the exalted one.  The one God, they affirmed, now accounted them righteous, they who did not define the God-man relationship by the Torah of Moses but by Jesus the Lord.  They claimed the πίστις that "came" with him (or:  they adopted his stance of faith) and thus they were accounted righteous by and before the one God, who is and makes righteous.

For these early Christians the death of Jesus was a "given," a concrete datum which from the beginning carried at least the potential for embarrassment, especially when viewed

---

[105]There are several exegetical problems relating to Rom. 3:24-26 which this chapter has touched upon very lightly or not at all.  If the πρὸς τὴν ἔνδειξιν phrase is a Pauline addition, for example, why does Paul repeat ἔνδειξις τῆς δικαιοσύνης αὐτοῦ?  Is there any significance in the fact that he substitutes πρός for εἰς and adds the article before ἔνδειξις?  What is the full import of the rather enigmatic addition ἐν τῷ νῦν καιρῷ?  Another question whose implications have not been worked out is this:  If (as I have argued) both the phrases διὰ πίστεως and ὁ ἐκ πίστεως 'Ιησοῦ belonged to the pre-Pauline formulation, is not the repetition of πίστις rather strange in the brief compass of a single confessional formula? An additional question which I have not attempted to answer is:  What is the Sitz im Leben of this formula--baptism, eucharist, or neither?

against the OT-Jewish idea of death as divine retribution for sin. Thus the death of Jesus was an apt subject for interpretation within the broad context of apologetic necessity. In the fragment at Rom. 3:25-26, we find preserved an early Christian affirmation that God, too, has "interpreted" the event of Jesus' death. That is, He has "regarded" it in a certain way, has responded to it so as to work salvation out of man's evil. Christ crucified He has set forth as a means of expiation of sins.

Where is one to look for the background and origin of this idea? This question provides the stimulus for the remainder of the present study.

Excursus:   Four Models of Event Interpretation

This thesis is an investigation of the background and
origin of a particular concept:  Jesus' death as saving event.
The historian who undertakes a project such as this is confronted by a two-fold situation:  on the one hand, an event; on
the other, an interpretation of that event which eventually
solidifies into dogma.  His task in this situation is to suggest
what elements in the thought spectrum of first century Christians were responsible for this particular interpretation of
this particular event.  He must attempt to describe the dynamics
of the interpretive process.

In the effort to facilitate that task I intend to
operate, especially in Chapter VI, on the basis of four models
of event interpretation.  The models I suggest result from a
conscious attempt to reflect upon the conceptions with which
historians work vis-a-vis the genesis and development of interpretations, particularly interpretations of events.  One
assumption on my part is that the historian should consistently
try to make a distinction between the general cultural-concept-
ual framework in which a given event interpretation is possible
and a more restricted circle of ideas which make that interpretation natural and persuasive or necessary or perhaps even
inevitable.  Thus popular terms such as "background," "source,"
"origin," and "influence" can be assigned distinct meanings.

For my investigation of the concept of Jesus' death as
saving event I propose the following four models of event
interpretation.  The first three, at least, should not be
considered mutually exclusive.

1.  The participants in an event are its initial interpreters.  Whatever the background or origin of the explanation
they offer, the subsequent history of interpretation presupposes
it as the normative point of reference.  (According to this
model, Jesus himself interpreted his death as a saving event;
his disciples remembered and proclaimed his words.)

2.  The interpreters of an event formulate an essentially novel concept from the most common and available elements of
the cultural heritage ("background").  (According to this model,
the concept of Jesus' death as saving event was a more or less
natural outgrowth of familiar OT ideas and current practices:
sacrifice, substitution, satisfaction for blood guilt, ransom,

etc.; it was developed and became a popular item of belief already in earliest Palestinian Christianity.)

3. As a means of explicating the significance or meaning of an event (or as an attempt to discover meaning), historical or conceptual parallels ("sources") are sought deliberately and self-consciously, that is, by a process of conscious reflection (although such reflection is itself culturally determined). The purpose of the interpreters is to clarify by analogy or to demonstrate continuity with the traditions from which a community or a people draws its life. (According to this model, the concept of Jesus' death as saving event was a result of the conscious search for the meaning of the crucifixion in scripture. The by-products of this endeavor would be the collection of Testamonia, the construction of typologies, and the citation of biblical proof-texts.)

4. Prior to a conscious attempt to discover the significance of an event or to formulate its meaning verbally (or perhaps also as a result of conscious reflection), the similarity of that event to events already interpreted appears so striking that the already-formulated interpretation functions as the lens through which the present event is viewed. In this case the existing event interpretation is not simply raw material that can be drawn upon in a search for antecedents and parallels. Rather it is, of itself, an impetus for, even a cause of, the interpretation of the present event. This impetus, the already-formulated event interpretation, might be designated the "creative source" of the interpretation of the present event. "Background" could designate whatever constellation of concepts and historical memories is responsible for the situation in which such an impetus could produce the interpretation of a present event. The "origin" of this interpretation can be thought of as that point--chronological or conceptual--of interaction between background and creative source, event and interpreter. (According to this model, the concept of Jesus' death as saving event had as its creative source a current tradition of effective and beneficial human death.)

CHAPTER II

TRADITIONS OF THE MACCABEAN MARTYRS FROM DANIEL
TO II MACCABEES AND JOSEPHUS

In conjunction with Rom. 3:25 it was observed that the
closest available parallel to ἱλαστήριον is διὰ . . . τοῦ
ἱλαστηρίου θανάτου αὐτῶν at IV Maccabees 17:22. The first step
toward understanding the meaning of this phrase in the context
of IV Maccabees as a whole is to compare the interpretation of
the martyrs' deaths in that writing with previous traditions
of steadfast Jews who had been put to death by command of
Antiochus Epiphanes. The five writings in which those traditions need to be examined are Daniel, Assumption of Moses, I
Maccabees, Josephus' Antiquities and II Maccabees. By comparing
the meaning of the death of the righteous Jews killed by
Antiochus in these five works with the interpretation offered
by IV Maccabees it should be possible, in a later chapter, to
indicate what features in that treatise are traditional and
which represent a development of or a departure from earlier
tradition.

I. The Death of the Righteous Ones in Daniel

        Critical scholars are almost unanimously agreed that
the book of Daniel, although incorporating much older traditional lore, was written in the early years of the Maccabean
struggle, that is, ca. B.C. 165.[1]  This writing, therefore,
may contain our earliest references to the persecution of
Antiochus Epiphanes and to the fate of those Jews faithful to
their God and his Law.

_____

        [1]R. H. Charles, A Critical and Exegetical Commentary on
the Book of Daniel (Oxford, 1929), p. lxx and following.
Charles observes that the author of Daniel refers to the desecration of the altar (168 B.C.; cf. 11:31) and the early
Maccabean victories (11:34); but that the prediction of the death
of Antiochus is in conflict with the actual facts and is therefore a genuine prediction ante eventum.  Moreover, for the
author, the rededication of the sanctuary in Dec. 165 is still
in the future (p. lxxv). Cf. O. Plöger, Das Buch Daniel
(Gütersloh, 1965), p. 27.

The most crucial passage for this study is Dan. 11:
32-35.  The main points for discussion are:  who is being
described, what is the purpose of those who suffer martyrdom
and what is the "effect" of their death?

Verse 32:  "He shall seduce with flattery those who
violate the covenant; but the people who know their God shall
stand firm and take action" (RSV).  "He" is Antiochus; his
desecration of the Temple the author has just described (v. 31).
"Those who violate the covenant" are the Hellenizers; "the
people who know their God," the traditionalists, those Jews
opposed to the hellenizing reforms of Jason and his party.
"Shall stand firm":  by contrast to the Hellenizers and their
sympathizers, the traditionalists are not affected by the
pressures brought to bear by Antiochus.  The absolute use of
the verb עשה ("act, do") leaves the author's meaning somewhat
in doubt.  As in other instances where the same verb is used
absolutely (Dan. 8:12, 24; 9:19; 11:28, 30; cf. II Chron. 31:
21, Jer. 14:7, Ez. 20:9) one must rely on the accompanying
verb(s) or the context to indicate the intention of the author.

Verse 33a:  "Those among the people who are wise shall
teach many (make many understand: יבינו )."  Other occurrences
of the verb בין (Qal and Hiphil) and the noun בינה suggest
that those who make many understand are not teachers or sages
in the general sense.  To be sure verb and noun are used
several times in Daniel in the more or less general sense of
"understand" or "give heed, regard" (8:5; ?10:11 and 10:12;
11:33, 37).[2]  In many other passages, however, verb and noun
have the near-technical meaning of understanding, interpreting
or explaining to others the visions of the end time.  (The
Hiphil verb can be used transitively or intransitively; thus at
times it is unclear whether the author means "understand" or
"explain, teach.")  In 1:17 it is said that one of God's gifts
to the four youths at the court of Nebuchednezzar was השכל
(LXX and Theod.: φρόνησιν).  Daniel, however, is singled out:
he "gave instruction" or "had understanding" (Hiphil הבין;

---

[2]Cf. also 1:4, 20.  The direct object gives the verb
(participle) in 8:23 a more specific sense but also creates
its own puzzle, for the actual subject is Antiochus Epiphanes
and the object is "riddles, enigmas"!  In 9:2 the verb is used
with reference to Daniel's calculation of the number of years
to the end.

LXX: τῷ Δ. ἔδωκε σύνεσιν . . .; Theod.: συνῆκεν . . .) in all dreams and visions. When in 8:15 Daniel says, "When I had seen the vision I sought understanding (בינה )," the noun clearly denotes the interpretation or explanation of his vision--which according to v. 16, was forthcoming. A voice orders Gabriel: "Cause this man to understand (הבן ; LXX and Theod.: συνέτισον) the vision." Gabriel then came to Daniel and said: "Understand (הבן --which could also mean "cause others to understand," as in v. 16) that this vision is about the end time" (8:17). At 8:27 Daniel admits: "I was appalled (or astounded) by the vision and I did not understand (אין מבין )." His response to the words of the divine meesenger at 12:8 is: "I heard but I did not understand (אבין )."

As a clue to the meaning of 11:33a the words of Gabriel to Daniel at 9:22 are especially interesting: "Now I have come להשכילך בינה " --that is, to teach you understanding, to instruct you in the interpretation of the vision. Gabriel continues (9:23): "Pay attention (Qal: בין ) to the interpretation and understand (or explain: הבן ) the vision." Finally, in 12:10 the messenger says to Daniel: "None of the wicked ones will understand (יבינו ) but those who are wise will understand (המשכלים יבינו )." The verb is used absolutely here; no direct object or prepositional phrase tells what will be understood. But vv. 8 and 9 leave no doubt whatever that what the wise will understand are the visions of the end time in the book of Daniel!

In light of these texts it would appear likely that the clause "those among the people who are wise shall teach" has the more specific meaning: those among the people who are endowed with visionary powers will instruct their fellows as to the meaning of the persecution of Antiochus within the plan of God and in view of the approaching end. This line of interpretation is supported by a suggestion made recently by Otto Plöger:

Wird insgesamt mit diesen letzten Versen [Dan. 11:33-35] der Schwebezustand angedeutet, der unmittelbar nach dem Religionsverbot begreiflich ist, als sich der aktive Widerstand der Makkabäer noch nicht voll und ganz auswirken konnte, die asidäische Gruppe zwar in ihrer Gesetzestreue verharrte und das Martyrium zu erdulden bereit war, sich aber zur Teilnahme am aktiven Widerstand noch nicht entschliessen konnte, dann wird mit den Weisen vielleicht an eine extrem eschatologische Richtung innerhalb der

asidäischen Gruppe gedacht sein, der sich der Verfasser
selbst zuzurechnet . . . .[3]

Thus if the designation "Hasidim" can be used in a very broad
sense to mean those traditionalist Jews who opposed the
programs and purposes of the Hellenizers, one can say that
"the wise" among the people (i.e., among the Hasidic group)
refers to a sub-group with a decidedly eschatological orientation who encourage their fellows with the assurance that soon,
at the time appointed (11:35b), God will give Antiochus his due
and the faithful will be delivered (11:45-12:3).

Who, then, are the "many" whom the wise will instruct?
It is difficult to say with certainty. "Many" may be intended
in a very general sense; but perhaps it is practically equivalent to the Hasidim (cf. I Mac. 1:62: πολλοὶ ἐν Ισραηλ).

Verse 33b: "And they shall fall by sword and by flame,
by captivity and by plunder for a certain time." Like most of
vv. 32-35, this statement is a vaticinium ex eventu. Who are
"they" who fall? The "many" of the preceding clause or "the
wise" alone? It is impossible to say with assurance. All one
can say is that from the perspective of the author of Daniel,
the ranks of the faithful had been thinned by the attempts of
Antiochus to enforce his decree (cf. Theod.: ἀσθενήσουσιν ἐν
ῥομφαίᾳ κτλ.).

Verse 34a: "And when they fall they shall be given a
little help." This statement is probably a reference to the
aggressive resistance of the Maccabees (and, perhaps, to non-
quietistic Hasidim; cf. I Mac. 2:42). To the author of Daniel,
according to this interpretation, ". . . the greatest victories
won by the arm of man are only 'a little help'. He looks for
deliverance not from this source but from the Lord."[4] If indeed
the author of Daniel was writing after some early successes of
Mattathias and Judas but before the rededication of the Temple
and the more substantial victories of the following years, he
need not take this "little help" too seriously; he still
believes that Antiochus will be crushed by no human effort (8:25).

Verse 11:34b:

MT: ונלוו עליהם רבים בחלקלקות

LXX: καὶ ἐπισυναχθήσονται ἐπ' αὐτοὺς πολλοὶ ἐπὶ
πόλεως καὶ πολλοὶ ὡς ἐν κληροδοσίᾳ.

---

[3]Plöger, op. cit., p. 165.

[4]Charles, Daniel, p. 309. Charles observes that in I
Enoch 90:6-12 the Maccabees are included among the Hasidim.

Theod.: καὶ προστεθήσονται πρὸς αὐτοὺς πολλοὶ ἐν ὀλισθρήμασιν.

Charles thinks that the MT is corrupt and suggests that the LXX has preserved the original reading since it ". . . supplies the right thought, and it explains how the corruption in the MT arose"--a statement that Charles supports in detail (p. 311). According to his reconstruction (which is adopted here), the text originally read: "There shall join them many in the city and many in their several homesteads."

Verse 11:35a. According to the MT 11:35a reads: ומן המשכילים יכשלו --"some of the wise shall fall." Theod., Peshitta and Vulgate follow the MT, but LXX reads διανοηθήσονται, a reading which clearly presupposes ישכילו (so Charles, p. 311). Which verb is original, which secondary-- שכל or כשל ? An alteration in either direction would be understandable as a copyist's error, but more probable is the change from שכל to כשל . Accordingly, as Charles suggests, ישכילו should be considered original. Two considerations support this contention: 1) The occurrence of כשל in the two immediately preceding verses could easily have triggered an unconscious switch from שכל to כשל in v. 35; the MT of v. 35 simply reproduces the language (word play?) of v. 33: משכילי עם . . . נכשלו. 2) Dan. 12:10, like 11:35, uses the language of purification and refining; there is also mention of the wise, but nothing is said about their falling. Nor is purification connected with persecution. One may conclude, therefore, that as it stood originally 11:35 did not repeat the "fall" of vv. 33 and 34. Rather the idea expressed was: "some of the wise shall give attention" (so שכל at Dan. 9:13)[5] or "shall give insight, teach" (so at Dan. 9:22) or simply "shall act wisely." The thought thus begun continues in three (or two) infinitival expressions (35b).

Verse 11:35b. Charles considers the reading of the MT very late: ". . . to refine among them ( בהם ) and to purify and to make white." In a complex argument drawing upon the readings of MT, LXX and Theod. at 11:35 and 12:10, he concludes that the original Hebrew reading was לצרוף אותם ולהחברר --"to

_____

[5]Note, however, that 9:13 may belong to a traditional prayer incorporated into the book of Daniel sometime before 145 B.C. Cf. Charles, Daniel, p. 221.

refine and make themselves pure." With the exception of
Charles' view that 11:35b originally contained only two verbs
("to refine and to purify")--a view here adopted as probable--
his reconstruction must be considered arbitrary and, therefore,
unconvincing. Unlike his explanation for the emendation of
34b, Charles cannot explain exactly how the "corrupt" reading
of our MT might have taken place. If Charles' emended text is
equivalent to the original, it is difficult to explain why the
simple אותם would have been changed to the more difficult
בהם or why the Hithpael (cf. MT Dan. 12:10) of ברר would have
been altered to the Piel. On the other hand the ἑαυτούς-αὑτούς
disparity between LXX and Theod. (LXX: εἰς τὸ καθαρίσαι
ἑαυτούς/Theod.: τοῦ πυρῶσαι αὐτούς) as well as their passive
and middle infinitives (LXX: εἰς τὸ ἐκλεγῆναι/Theod.: τοῦ
ἐκλέξασθαι) are understandable as different interpretations of
the puzzling בהם. Therefore, with the possible exception
of וללבן , one is justified in retaining the reading of the MT
at 35b.

Verse 35 would therefore read: "some of the wise shall
give attention (or act wisely, or teach) in order to refine
among them and to purify (and to make white) until the end
time . . . ." But to whom does "them" refer? There are three
possibilities: 1) "themselves" in a narrow sense, i.e., "some
of the wise will purify themselves"; but this restricted implication is not likely (cf. 12:10: "many") although it is
supported by the LXX (ἑαυτούς); 2) "themselves" in a broader
sense, i.e.,the Hasidic group in general; 3) more specifically,
the "many" who join them (v. 34) and who, being newcomers, need
to be properly instructed in things eschatological. In my
view, the last of these options is the most adequate, particularly in light of v. 33a. In either of the two latter options,
however, "to refine and to purify (and make white)" has reference not to cultic acts but to the instruction of the faithful
of Israel in order that they might understand the final woes,
be encouraged to stand faithful to the Law and therefore be
prepared for the end (cf. 11:33, 12:3).

According to the emended MT text adopted in the preceding pages (especially ישכילו for יכשלו in v. 35a) Dan. 11:32-
35 makes no mention of any "effect" of the death of the faithful. In v. 33 it is acknowledged that some of those who stand
fast will die. And in v. 35 it is said that some of the wise

ones will serve the wider group of the pious so as to purify
them (through instruction: causing them to understand) in
preparation for the .end. These two ideas appear side by side
but they are not connected with each other in any causal way.
Some of the wise will instruct and prepare, refine and purify,
and some of them (or, more broadly: some of the pious) will
suffer and be killed. That is all that the author of Daniel
intended to say at 11:33, 35 about the meaning of the righteous
ones' suffering and death.

The unemended MT ("shall fall, to refine among them and
to purify . . ."), on the other hand, could possibly be understood to imply that the death of "the wise among the people"
has a purifying effect upon the community. Even if this line
of interpretation is followed, however, nothing in the text
indicates vicarious purification from sin. The interpretation
of Bevan is more convincing: the death of some of the teachers
is a means of testing the other members of the group.[6]

Theodotion's translation is similar to the (unemended)
MT at Dan. 11:35, based as it is on a faulty MS which read
ישל instead of ישל : "Some of the wise will fall (ἀσθενήσουσιν) to refine them (τοῦ πυρῶσαι αὐτούς) and to purify themselves (τοῦ ἐκλέξασθαι)." Here the puzzling Hebrew בהם appears
to be rendered twice: once by αὐτούς, once by the middle voice.
Thus the death of the wise appears to have a double effect: by
example it refines and strengthens the faithful, and in God's
eyes it purifies those who are steadfast unto death.

The LXX reading gives no occasion to see in Dan. 11:35 a
reflection of any sort of vicarious suffering concept: "Some
of the wise ones shall be wise (have understanding) in order
to purify themselves and to be made pure . . . ."

At several points other than 11:30-35 the author of
Daniel mentions the decree of Antiochus, the desolation of the
Temple, etc. (8:11-13, 23-24; 9:26-27; cf. 12:1b). Likewise he
alludes several times to the suffering and death of those Jews
who held fast to the Law (7:21, 25; 8:24, 25); but these additional texts contribute nothing substantial to what one learns
from Dan. 11 about the death of the righteous ones.[7] In their

---

[6]A. A. Bevan, A Short Commentary on the Book of Daniel
(Cambridge, 1892), p. 195. Compare Charles (p. 311) on the
meaning of the MT: ". . . their martyrdom would have as its
effect the disciplining and purifying of the faithful wherever
found."

[7]Dan. 12:10 reads (RSV): "Many shall purify themselves,
and make themselves white, and be refined; but the wicked shall
do wickedly; and none of the wicked shall understand; but those
who are wise shall understand." Although some of the same
terms found in 11:33-35 recur here, this verse need not be
examined separately, especially since it does not even allude

contexts, however, they do provide definite confirmation of the impression given by Dan. 11:35, that is, that in God's plan for the world the present sufferings of the righteous are but a part of the "time of trouble" (12:1) which precedes divine intervention and the establishment of the everlasting kingdom of the saints of God (7:27). When that moment comes those faithful ones who have died will awake to everlasting life (12:2; cf. v. 3).

## II. The Death of the Righteous Ones in Assumption of Moses

A. The Original Work

In order to understand the meaning of the death of the righteous ones in the Assumption of Moses it is helpful to recognize at once that the order and content of this work as it now stands are very likely not equivalent to the original.

Chapter eight is, in Charles' words, a "faithful description" of the Antiochian persecution.[8] Just as clearly, a preceding chapter refers to Jewish history subsequent to the persecution of Antiochus: chapter six alludes to the Hasmonean dynasty (6:1) and describes the reign of Herod the Great (6:2-7). Very likely, the group described in chapter seven is the Sadducees of the period 15-70 A.D.[9] In any case, this group

---

to the death or persecution of the faithful ones. The statement at 12:10 is much more general than that at 11:35, appearing as it does as a summary-type affirmation right at the end of the book. It is not said by what means many shall purify themselves, etc.; but these words must certainly be read in light of 12:1-3. And if one can legitimately detect a chiastic pattern in the four statements of v.10 (many-wicked/wicked-wise) that verse directly associates "shall understand" (i.e., understand the place of these end-time events in God's plan) and "shall purify themselves."

[8] R. H. Charles, The Assumption of Moses (London, 1897), p. 30. I follow customary usage in referring to this work as the Assumption of Moses; however, as Charles observes (pp. xlv-l), the more legitimate designation of the extant work is the "Testament of Moses."

[9] Ibid., pp. 25-28. Charles points out numerous parallels with anti-Sadducean polemic in the Psalms of Solomon. He notes, however, that other scholars have identified this group as the Pharisees or as Roman procurators.

flourished subsequent to the reign of Herod and was probably contemporary with the author of chapters six and seven. At the same time, the Assumption of Moses in its present form makes no mention of the Antiochian persecution at that point in the work where such an allusion is certainly to be expected, i.e., after chapter five. The present text, then, has been either accidentally dislocated or intentionally revised.

Charles argues that the historical gap between chapters five and six was originally filled by what we know as chapters eight and nine; the transposition of this original text was the work of the "final editor."[10] I agree completely that there is an unnatural gap between chapters five and six and that chapter eight originally followed immediately upon chapter five, but I find Charles' solution unsatisfactory at two points. 1) He does not (and does not try to) account for the motivation that might have moved the "final editor" to transpose the text into its present form. 2) By suggesting that only chapters eight and nine have been transposed, he fails to recognize that originally chapters nine and ten belonged together. Any acceptable theory regarding the date and composition of the Assumption of Moses must take account of these two considerations in addition to the dislocation of the text that Charles acknowledges. Such a theory I wish to suggest in the form of progressive theses.[11]

1. Chapter ten was intended by the (original) author of the Assumption to follow chapter nine.[12] Taxo's words as well as chapter ten are concerned with God's vengeance upon the persecutors of His people. More specifically, 10:2-3, 7, 10 can only be understood as a counterpart to Taxo's final words (9:7).[13]

---

[10] Ibid., pp. 29-30.

[11] This proposal is indebted to the discussions of Jacob Licht, "Taxo, or the Apocalyptic Doctrine of Vengeance," JJS 12(1961), 95-103; and George Nickelsburg, Resurrection, Immortality, and Eternal Life in Intertestamental Judaism (unpublished Th.D. Dissertation, Harvard University, 1967), pp. 52-53.

[12] But the original text of chapter ten may not have been equivalent to the present text. Charles (pp. 39-44) notes significant divergences between vv. 1-2 and vv. 3-10, which suggest that the present chapter derives from two different authors. That possibility does not substantially affect the theory being set forth here.

[13] Licht, op. cit., 97.

68

2. Chapter nine was intended by the (original) author
to follow chapter eight. The reference to a "second visitation"
and "a punishment far exceeding the first" (9:2; cf. v. 3)
alludes to the "second visitation and wrath, such as has not
befallen them from the beginning until that time" (8:1). Furthermore, no closer historical parallel can be given for Taxo
and the cave than various accounts of faithful Jews hiding in
caves or being killed in a cave because they refused to resist
on the Sabbath--this during the Antiochian persecution (cf. I
Mac. 1:53, 2:29-38; II Mac. 6:11; Josephus, Ant. 12.272-75).

3. Chapters eight through ten (the Antiochian persecution through God's intervention) originally followed immediately
upon chapter five.

4. On formal grounds 10:11 through 12:13 also constitute a unity; that is, this section exhibits no gap where
chapters eight through ten could have belonged originally.

5. Chapters six and seven clearly seem to be an in-
trusion into an otherwise coherent work. Historically speaking,
there is nowhere in Assumption of Moses that these chapters
make sense. If placed after 10:10 they destroy the hymn's
essential point; if placed after chapter twelve they deprive
the work of its second literary and fictional "bracket" (cf.
chapter one). I conclude that chapters six and seven did not
originally belong to the "Testament of Moses"; the "original
edition" consisted of chapters one through five, eight through
ten, and probably (in some form) chapters eleven and following.
An unknown redactor added six and seven at a later period. How,
then, is one to understand the circumstances surrounding the
original composition and the later revision of the Assumption
of Moses?

6. Chapter ten looks forward to the imminent intervention of God or his appointed representative. The original
"Testament of Moses," therefore, was probably written after
the outbreak of Antiochus' persecution but before Judas and
his followers had achieved substantial success; the Temple has
not yet been restored (165 B.C.). The writing is thus very
nearly contemporary with, perhaps slightly earlier than, the
book of Daniel.[14]

[14]Ibid., 102-103; Nickelsburg, op. cit., p. 53, n. 121.

7. When history had continued apace and the prediction of heavenly intervention (chapter ten) had not yet come to pass, some unknown redactor, who apparently harbored intense eschatological hopes himself, updated the "Testament of Moses" by adding to it allusions to the Hasmoneans, Herod and his sons and (probably) the Sadducees. According to his revised edition, it is the iniquity of his own day--the iniquity of the Sadducees --which will bring that final time of distress that will precede divine intervention and Israel's salvation. In other words, the description of the Antiochian persecution in chapters eight and nine is excized from Jewish history and is transformed into a prediction of eschatological woes. Taxo is no longer a contemporary, but a figure of the end time. Thus the redactor can conclude the body of the revised work with an eschatological hymn--just as the original author had done![15]

B.  The Death of the Righteous Ones in Assumption of Moses

Chapters eight through ten--composed, with the probable exception of parts of chapter ten, in the depths of the Antiochian persecution--should be taken as a unit when one asks how the author of the Assumption of Moses understands the death of the righteous.

Chapter eight describes the fate of the righteous in general terms. Antiochus crucifies those who confess their circumcision (8:1). Those who circumcize (or: those who deny their circumcision) he tortures and imprisons (8:2; cf. Josephus, Ant. 12.251; Dan. 11:33: "by captivity"). Jewish women are given to the gods of the Gentiles (8:3; cf. II Mac. 6:4) and their sons are operated on to "uncircumcize" them. Others are punished by tortures, fire and sword (8:4; cf. Dan. 11:33). They are also forced to carry in public processions the idols of the Gentiles (8:4; cf. II Mac. 6:7) and to blaspheme God and the Law in other ways (8:5).

---

[15]If the differences between 10:1-2 and 3-10 are taken seriously, it would be reasonable to assume that one part of the present hymn belongs to the original author, the other to the redactor. If this is indeed the case, one would suppose that the original hymn was surely longer than two verses. In any case, the angel appointed chief, who will avenge Israel (10:2), is strikingly reminiscent of Daniel (e.g., 10:21, 12:1). On the other hand AMoses 10:9 reminds one of Dan. 7

In chapter nine the spotlight turns onto one individual figure. "In that day" a man from the tribe of Levi, Taxo, exhorts his seven sons: "Let us fast for the space of three days and on the fourth let us go into a cave which is in the field, and let us die rather than transgress the commands of the Lord of lords, the God of our fathers. For if we do this and die, our blood will be avenged before the Lord" (9:6-7, trans. R. H. Charles). The following (composite?) chapter then describes the divine intervention anticipated. According to 10:2 the angel appointed chief will avenge Israel of her enemies (cf. 10:3: God's wrath will burn on account of his sons). In other words, the reader is to understand that the blood of Taxo and his sons will indeed be avenged before the Lord. Thus, from the perspective of his eschatological schema, the author of the Assumption of Moses appears to understand the death of the righteous Taxo and his sons as the decisive event which will provoke divine vengeance against those enemies of Israel who now oppress her. Since God cannot allow innocent blood to go unavenged, their death is the crucial act which triggers the events of the end time.[16]

### III. The Suffering and Death of the Faithful in I Maccabees

According to I Maccabees, two years after he had plundered the Temple treasures upon returning from Egypt (1:20-24) Antiochus Epiphanes sent the captain of the Mysians[17]

---

and 12:3--a situation which warns against a simplistic solution regarding the composition and redaction of chapter ten. That is to say, in 10:3-10 the redactor is very likely combining the original hymn with his own eschatology.

[16]Cf. Licht, op. cit., 97. Licht (98) emphasizes the significance of Taxo's fasting and going into the cave: these acts insure true innocence and purity from sin; death will be wholly undeserved and so a certain means of provoking divine vengeance. But Licht may over-emphasize the place of penitence and purity here. In OT instances in which unjust death or undeserved suffering triggers God's vengeance (e.g., II Chron. 24:22-24; Ps. 9:12; 79:10) there is the implication that the murdered one was innocent of any act worthy of death, but no emphasis on penitence or purity from all sin.

[17]The text reads ἄρχοντα φορολογίας, but this reading is probably a mistranslation of the Hebrew original. Cf. Solomon Zeitlin in The First Book of Maccabees (New York 1950), p. 33.

(Apollonius, according to II Mac. 5:24) to Judah. He burned and plundered Jerusalem, pulling down its walls and houses. "And he took captive the women and children . . ." (1:32; cf. Josephus, Ant. 12.251). The forces of Antiochus also erected a citadel in Jerusalem and manned it with pagan soldiers (1:33-34; cf. Ant. 12.252). "And they shed innocent blood round about the sanctuary; and they defiled the sanctuary. And the inhabitants of Jerusalem fled because of them (δι' αὐτούς), and it became a dwelling place for foreigners" (1:37-38a).

The account in I Maccabees goes on to describe the decrees of Antiochus (1:41-42, 44-51) and the willing obedience given to the king's command by "many from Israel" (1:43)--that is, "everyone who abandoned the Law" (1:52). Then one is told about the "abomination of desolation," other pagan sacrifices, and the confiscation and destruction of books of the Law (1:54-56). Whenever a book of the covenant was found in the possession of someone who insisted on living according to the Law (εἴ τις συνευδόκει τῷ νόμῳ), that person was killed in accord with the king's command (1:57). "And according to the decree they killed the women who had circumcised their sons; and they hung (ἐκρέμασαν) infants from their necks and (they hanged) their families and those who had circumcised them. But many in Israel stood firm (ἐκραταιώθησαν) and they determined among themselves (or: they were strengthened/fortified within themselves or among themselves: ὠχυρώθησαν ἐν αὐτοῖς) not to eat unclean food. They even welcomed death in order not to be defiled by food and (thereby) profane the holy covenant. And die they did" (1:60-63; cf. Ant. 12.253-255).

In chapter two occurs the account of those who were killed because they refused to fight on the Sabbath. "Then [i.e., after the incident at Modein and the flight of Mattathias and his sons: 2:15-28] many who were seeking righteousness and judgment went down to the wilderness to settle there . . ." (2:29). The king's officers, finding out about this move, sent troops who attacked the Jews on a Sabbath. Preferring death to a breach of the Law, these Jews refused to resist or even to defend themselves. They died with the words: "Let us all die in our innocence; heaven and earth bear witness to us that you destroy us wrongly" (2:37). The pericope ends: "They arose in battle against them on the Sabbath and they

72

died--they and their wives and their children and their cattle, as many as a thousand people" (2:38).[18]

Mattathias and his followers decided that a strict policy of non-resistance on the Sabbath would soon result in the extermination of all faithful Jews and consequently they determined to fight whenever necessary, even on the Sabbath. They were then joined by "a company of Hasidim, strong and mighty men of Israel, each of whom offered himself freely for the Law (πᾶς ὁ ἐκουσιαζόμενος τῷ νόμῳ)" (2:42).[19]

In his last words to his sons, Mattathias exhorts them: ζηλώσατε τῷ νόμῳ καὶ δότε τὰς ψυχὰς ὑμῶν ὑπὲρ διαθήκης πατέρων ἡμῶν . . . καὶ δέξασθε δόξαν μεγάλην καὶ ὄνομα αἰώνιον (2:50-51; cf. 2:64). His final words include this advice: "Add to yourselves all those who keep the Law, and avenge your people. Render recompense to the Gentiles and give attention to the commandments of the Law" (2:67-68; cf. Ant. 12.279-84).

One further passage can suffice for this look at I Maccabees. In the author's song of praise for Judas, the following statement appears: "He went among the cities of Judah and he destroyed the ungodly out of it, and he turned away wrath from Israel" (3:8; cf. 1:64: "very great wrath came upon Israel").

By way of systematization or analysis of the passages mentioned above, attention is called to the following observations:

1. Compared with Daniel and Assumption of Moses I Maccabees is obviously written from a different chronological perspective and with an entirely different purpose. Daniel and AMoses were written during the years of early Maccabean successes. I Maccabees could not have been written before the death of Simon (cf. chapter 16). If the purpose of Daniel

---

[18]Cf. Ant. 12.272-75. In Josephus' version the king's troops burned the Jews in their caves so that they died from suffocation. He adds that "many" escaped and joined Mattathias.

[19]This passage appears to be somewhat at odds with Dan. 11. I Mac. 2:42 has the Hasidim joining the Maccabees at a very early date (i.e., before the death of Mattathias). Dan. 11:34, however, suggests a Hasidic attitude towards the Maccabees that falls far short of an enthusiastic embrace of their program--and this at a time which must have been a year or two after the death of Mattathias.

(and AMoses) was to encourage and fortify a persecuted people, the purpose of I Maccabees, by contrast, was to praise the Hasmoneans by recounting their exploits, their courage and their piety.

2. This being the case, it is not surprising that the intense mood of eschatological anticipation that pervades Daniel and AMoses leaves not a trace in I Maccabees. Whereas the author of Daniel expects Antiochus to be broken by no human instrumentality (Dan. 8:25) and anticipates the day that Michael will arise to deliver the faithful of Israel (12:1; cf. 10:21), I Maccabees ascribes the Jewish victories against the Seleucids to God's providence operating through the zealous Maccabean warriors (cf. several further passages not mentioned above, e.g., 3:18-24, 46-54; 4:8-15, 24-25, 30-34; 5:60-63).

3. Thus, the accounts of the death of faithful Jews plays a different role in I Maccabees than in Daniel and AMoses. In AMoses the death of Taxo and his sons triggers divine intervention. In Daniel the death of "some of the wise," as well as Antiochus' acts against the Jews and the desecration of the Temple, are aspects of the "time of trouble" which precedes the end. In I Maccabees these events are features of the historical background against which the author depicts the rise of the Maccabees.

4. In I Maccabees it is Judas and his brothers who avenge their people and punish the Gentiles (2:27-68). Similarly, by destroying impiety in Judah, it is Judas who averts wrath from Israel (3:8). Yet in light of previous statements (2:43-48) it is obvious that even in our author's eyes Judas did not accomplish everything alone. But the statement at 3:8 occurs in a song of praise to Judas and for literary reasons he alone must be the subject of the prowess described. Judas is not only the heroic and inspiring leader of his people; as the foremost among them, he stands also as a symbol of their success.

5. Implicit in the Danielic account is the underlying idea that loyal Jews were willing to die in order to uphold the Law and demonstrate their faithfulness to the God of their fathers. Taxo is willing to die rather than transgress the commands of the Lord (AMoses 9:6). But I Maccabees gives even more explicit expression to the reasons for which the people faithful to the Law were willing to die. Many chose

74

death "in order not to be defiled by (unclean) food, in order
not to profane the holy covenant (1:63)." Two closely related
motifs are detectable here: the desire to remain personally
undefiled before God and the desire to remain true to the
unique covenant between God and Israel.[20] According to 2:42,
the Hasidim offered themselves freely (that is, they were
willing to fight and die) "for the Law" (τῷ νόμῳ). And Judas
and his brothers are exhorted by their father to be zealous τῷ
νόμῳ and to devote their lives ὑπὲρ διαθήκης πατέρων ἡμῶν
(2:50).[21]

6. What effect does the death of the righteous ones
have in I Maccabees? It appears to have no direct effect at
all. There is, for example, no statement about the dying
righteous equivalent to what is said about the garrisoned
troops of Antiochus: δι᾽ αὐτούς the inhabitants of Jerusalem
fled (1:38). Two passages in chapter two suggest a very indirect effect, that is, the rise of the Maccabees. The death
of young men and infants in Israel is one aspect of the shock-
ing plight which created the determination of Mattathias and
his sons to resist actively the program of Antiochus (cf. 2:9
in its context). Further, the massacre of those Jews who refused to fight on the Sabbath persuaded Mattathias and his
followers that it would be necessary to fight even on that holy
day (2:29-41).[22]

7. In sharp contrast to Daniel, I Maccabees does not
mention a personal reward of life beyond the grave for the
righteous ones who die for the Law. Mattathias can exhort his
sons to devote their lives to the defense of the covenant "and

---

[20] Cf. Josephus, Ant. 12.274: The Jews who perished on
the Sabbath did not resist "on account of the day"; they did
not want to violate the honor of the Sabbath. The motivation
of those faithful unto death is emphasized even more in II and
IV Maccabees.

[21] Cf. Ant. 12.281-82: Mattathias exhorts his sons to
be prepared to die ὑπὲρ τῶν νόμων. Nor are they to shrink
from losing their lives ὑπὲρ αὐτῶν (=τῶν μεγίστων: the greatest of deeds).

[22] In the dying words of Mattathias, Josephus includes
the statement (Ant. 12.281) that when God sees the Maccabees
prepared to die for the sake of the laws, "He will not overlook
you, but admiring your virtue (ἀρετῆς) He will give them (i.e.,
the laws?) back to you again and your freedom . . . He will
restore."

you will receive great glory and an eternal name" (2:51; cf.
v. 64);[23] but there is no suggestion that they will be rewarded
by personal immortality if they fall.


## IV. Josephus on the Righteous Ones Who Suffered Under Antiochus

Because Josephus used I Maccabees as a source,[24] it is
not necessary to reproduce passages in the Antiquities which
parallel I Maccabees. Some of the pertinent similarities and
variations have already been noted in the previous section.

In one passage Josephus diverges rather considerably
from I Maccabees. Having written that many Jews, confronted
by the decree of Antiochus, acquiesced willingly or because of
fear, he continues: "But those most esteemed, men of noble
spirit, disregarded him, holding their ancestral customs
(πατρίων ἐθῶν) to be more important than the punishment with
which he threatened those who would not obey; for this reason
. . . they were put to death" (Ant. 12.255). In this and the
following sentence (12.256) Josephus enumerates the sufferings
endured by the righteous. The macabre detail of this single
sentence surpasses that in the account of I Maccabees and reflects a greater degree of fascination with pain and dying
than either Daniel, Assumption of Moses or I Maccabees. In
this respect Josephus is reminiscent of II and IV Maccabees.
According to his account, those who disregarded the royal
decree

--daily were tortured (αἰκιζόμενοι) and endured (ὑπομένοντες)
       bitter torments;
--they were whipped (μαστιγούμενοι);

---

[23]Cf. Ant. 12.282: "For although our bodies are mortal
and perishable, through the memorial of our deeds we receive a
position of immortality."

[24]Zeitlin, op. cit., p. 55. According to Ralph Marcus
in the Loeb edition of the Antiquities (vol. 7, p. 122),
Josephus paraphrases I Mac. 1:14-13:42 in Ant. 12.241 to
13.214.

--their bodies were mutilated (λυμαινόμενοι);

--still alive and breathing, they were crucified (ἀνεσταυροῦντο);

--their wives and the sons whom they had illegally circumcized
   were strangled [ἀπῆγχον--the verb apparently has an
   indefinite "they," i.e., the king's officials, as
   subject];

--the strangled children were then suspended from the necks of
   their crucified parents.

Josephus concludes this section with a remark about the fate of
those Jews in whose possession a copy of the Law was found:
"those wretches perished miserably." But as for any meaning
to their deaths, he does not go beyond what is said or implied
in I Maccabees.

## V.  The Suffering and Death of the Martyrs in II Maccabees

II Maccabees, the Epitome of the five-volume history by
Jason of Cyrene, provides a more detailed historical background
for the revolt of the Jews against Antiochus Epiphanes and the
rise of the Hasmonean dynasty than does I Maccabees (II 3-5);
but here it is not necessary to discuss either the additional
details or the disparity between I and II Maccabees regarding
the sequence of events.[25] The following paragraphs are limited
to an analysis of the description and interpretation in II
Maccabees of the suffering and death of righteous, loyal Jews.

Several incidents found in II Maccabees closely parallel
I Maccabees and (or) Josephus. At 5:12-14, Antiochus, having
returned from Egypt and marched on Jerusalem, "ordered his
soldiers to cut down unsparingly those they met and to kill
even those who had gone into their houses. The result was the
destruction of young and old, the annihilation of youths,
women and children, a slaughter of virgins and infants." In
three days eighty thousand had been killed and an equal number
sold into slavery (cf. I Mac. 1:20-24 where these atrocities

---

[25]It is assumed here that no literary relationship
between I Mac. and II Mac. (or Jason) can be demonstrated.

are not mentioned; but see Ant. 12.247). Subsequently he
ordered Apollonius to kill all in Jerusalem who were in the
prime of life and to sell others into slavery (5:24)--a command
which Apollonius dutifully carried out by treachery, so that
many were slain (5:25-26). Two women, charged with circumciz-
ing their children, were paraded around the city as public
spectacles, their infants hanging from their breasts; they were
then hurled from the wall headfirst (6:10).[26] Other Jews who
had fled to neighboring caves to observe the Sabbath secretly
were all burned together when they refused to resist on that
most sacred day (6:11, cf. Ant. 12.274).

These two incidents are introduced as examples of the
plight of loyal Jews in the face of the Seleucid campaign of
forced hellenization. Following them, and after an intervening
note of explanation (6:12-17), the author presents two rather
detailed martyrdoms: the separate but related stories of
Eleazar and of seven brothers and their mother.

In comparison with Daniel, I Maccabees or Josephus, the
most striking aspect of these two stories is perhaps the very
fact that they are included at all. Such descriptions of the
Antiochian persecution in terms of particular, individual
persons has its only antecedent parallel in the Assumption of
Moses.[27]

The means by which Eleazar and the seven brothers were
tortured and executed are described in much more vivid and
lengthy detail than in Daniel, Assumption of Moses, I Maccabees

_____

[26] The similarities and differences between this account
and that in I Mac. and Josephus are intriguing. Features
common to all three are: 1) women 2) who had circumcized their
children against the king's order 3) are apprehended and killed;
4) in some sense the infants "hang." It is at this point that
the most interesting point of divergence occurs. I Mac. 1:61:
they hanged (ἐκρέμασαν) the infants by their necks; Ant. 12.
256: they hung (ἀπαρτῶντες) the children from the necks of
their crucified parents; II Mac. 6:10: the officials paraded
the women around, hanging (κρεμάσαντες) their infants from
their breasts. The mothers are killed by different means in
all three instances.

[27] In the first story the old priest who resists unto
death is given a name and his reputation and personal characteristics are described (cf. 6:18, 23). Note also that while
I Mac. and Josephus mention "the women" who circumcized their
children and were put to death, II Mac. has, more specifically,
"two women."

or even Josephus. Eleazar, refusing to eat swine's flesh, went to the instrument of torture (6:20, 28) and was beaten and whipped to death (6:30: ταῖς πληγαῖς and μαστιγούμενος). The seven brothers were tortured by whips and cords (μάστιξιν καὶ νευραῖς: 7:1). The king ordered that one brother have his tongue cut out, his head scalped and his hands and feet cut off (γλωσσοτομεῖν καὶ περισκυθίσαντας ἀκρωτηριάζειν: 7:4); while he was still breathing he was brought to the fire and fried in a red-hot pan (τηγανίζειν: 7:5; cf. v. 3). The second had his scalp torn off and was threatened with dismemberment (7:7). The third brother apparently had his tongue and hands cut off (7:10) before he died; the king's officials abused and tortured the fourth brother in the same way (7:13). The fifth, too, they tortured (7:15). The author simply states that the last two brothers and their mother died without yielding; their tortures are not described, although of the youngest it is said that the king treated him even worse than the others (7:39).

Other new features in the stories of II Maccabees might be called "novelistic." The issue of apostasy is related in terms of a personal contest of protagonists and adversaries. One can note, for example, references to the king's anger (7:3, 24, 39) and the defiant, jeering attitude of the brothers and their mother (7:9, 16-17, 19, 27a, 31, 34-36). The rudiments of a "plot" (the king's repeated attempts, the martyrs' unyielding resistance) are accompanied by dialogue between protagonists and adversaries. The king's officials suggest a ruse by which Eleazar can meet the requirements of his religion and yet save his life, but to no avail (6:21-23). Antiochus himself tries to dissuade the youngest son with promises of wealth and position—also to no avail (7:24-25). More significant than this indirect or direct (7:7-8) dialogue are the "speeches" of the dying martyrs in which they express their defiance, their motivation and their hope.[28]

These "speeches" are one of the vehicles which bear the theologizing of II Maccabees about the reason for the suffering

---

[28]See 6:24-28, 30; 7:2, 6, 9, 11, 14, 16-17, 18-19, 22-23, 27-29, 30-38. In the accounts previously considered, the closest one gets to these "martyr speeches" are the words of the righteous who perish on the Sabbath (I Mac. 2:37) and the words of the dying Mattathias (I Mac. 2:67-68; Ant. 12.279-84).

of the righteous ones. This is a very significant step beyond the accounts in earlier Jewish works. In I Maccabees and Josephus the suffering of the righteous is but an entirely plausible result of the clash between the faithfulness of traditionalist Jews and the hellenizing program of Antiochus and his allies in the Jerusalem priesthood. The author of II Maccabees also presents these "historical" reasons, but he goes further. The first hint of his theologizing proclivities occurs at 4:16-17. Having described the hellenizing reforms of Jason and their enthusiastic support by the Jerusalem priests, the author continues: "On account of these things a grievous crisis overcame them. The very people whose modes of life they envied and wished to imitate in every way became their enemies and punished them. For to act impiously against the divine laws is no light matter . . . ." This passage suggests, without exactly stating, that the persecution of Antiochus was due to the divine intolerance of apostasy. This view is expressed directly in 5:17: "Antiochus did not realize that because of the sins of those inhabiting the city the Lord had been provoked to anger for a little while; thus His overlooking the Place" (i.e., the Temple) (cf. also v. 18). In 5:20 the Temple is said to have been "forsaken due to the wrath of the Almighty." The sixth brother informs the king: "It is our fault that we are suffering these things since we sinned against our own God . . ." (7:18). And his younger brother likewise asserts that "we are suffering on account of our own sins" (7:32).[29] By these statements the author appears to be suggesting the non-historical

_____

[29] In the context of II Mac. the "we" of these last two statements can only refer to the nation as a whole. Only various facets of the sin of apostasy and collusion have been described. No personal sin of any of the martyrs is ever intimated. Thus the martyrs are suffering because of the sin of some of their fellow Jews. That they nevertheless speak in terms of "we" points to the important element of representation. In II Mac. this "representation" can be read from two perspectives: it points up the reality of group solidarity (the sin of some Jews, thus God's wrath, thus persecution even for the faithful and righteous) and it serves to illustrate an historical phenomenon by concrete, "representative" examples of steadfastness under pressure.

"cause" behind the historical events of persecution: God responds to the nation's apostasy by withdrawing his protecting arm from his people. Thus, human sin and divine wrath are the "theological reasons" for the martyrs' suffering and death.

Nor does the author of II Maccabees stop here. God also has a purpose in the suffering of his people. In his introduction to the stories of Eleazar and the seven brothers the Epitomist consoles his readers with the statement that the dire events he is recounting were "not to destroy but to discipline (πρὸς παιδείαν) our nation." Immediate punishment, which does not allow sin to accumulate, he sees as a manifestation of divine mercy. Thus he can say that although God disciplines his people with misfortune He does not abandon them (6:12-17).[29a] And the seventh brother affirms that God has become angry for a little while in order to reprove and discipline (χάριν ἐπιπλήξεως καὶ παιδείας: 7:33). Again it should be observed that the earlier Jewish works previously considered attempt no such theological explanations; II Maccabees has taken a significant step beyond them.

The same assertion can be made when one considers the "effects" of the martyrs' deaths in II Maccabees. Ready to die, Eleazar speaks these words: "By departing life courageously . . . I shall have left a noble example (ὑπόδειγμα) to the youth of how to die readily and nobly for the sake of (our) revered and holy laws" (6:28). To this, the author adds in the third person: "In this way he died, leaving his own death as an example of nobility and as a memorial of virtue not only to the youth but also to most (πλείστοις) of the nation" (6:31).

According to II Maccabees, then, the death of Eleazar, especially his bearing in the face of death, was for his fellow Jews a paradigm of virtue to be emulated. As others are moved and motivated by his example of faithfulness unto death, one might say, Eleazar's death has continuing "effects."

The martyrs' steadfastness unto death also gains for them the personal reward of life beyond death. The second brother says to the king: "Because we died for the sake of his laws, the king of the universe will raise us up to an eternal resurrection life" (7:9). The third brother holds out his hands (to be cut off) with the words, ". . . from Him I

---

[29a]For a translation and discussion of this text cf. supra, p. 31.

hope to get these back again" (7:11). Says the fourth: "It is
better (αἱρετόν), as we are killed by men, to entertain hopes
(given, implanted?) by God that we will again be raised up by
Him; but for you there will be no resurrection to life" (7:14).
The mother encouraged her sons thus: God ". . . will give you
life again in mercy, since now you disregard yourselves on
account of his laws" (7:23; cf. vv. 28-29, where the hope of
resurrection is grounded in the belief that God created heaven
and earth οὐκ ἐξ ὄντων). Finally, the seventh brother affirms
that his brothers, having endured pain for a little while, have
drunk of everlasting life under God's covenant (7:36).[30]
Because the martyrs suffer for the sake of God's laws, God will
raise them up for life eternal. Thus their steadfastness unto
death has the "effect" of life everlasting--not a natural con-
sequence of physical death but a unique creative act by which
God rewards his righteous servants.

II Maccabees develops in greater detail a feature previously noted in I Maccabees and Josephus: the explicit
statement of the motivation for the martyrs' willingness to die.
Eleazar's motivations are varied: he does not want to set a
precedent which will lead the young astray (6:24-25); he wants
to show himself worthy of his old age by dying courageously
(6:27); he wants to leave a noble example of how to die on
behalf of the sacred laws (6:28); if he escapes the punishment
of Antiochus he knows that he cannot escape the hand of God
(6:26). As he dies he says: "I suffer these things because of
my reverence (for Him)" (6:30). The second brother expects
God to raise up him and his brothers "since we die for (ὑπέρ)
his laws" (7:9). Likewise, the third brother is willing to
suffer "because of (διὰ τούς) his laws" (7:11); and the mother
echoes his affirmation (7:23). The youngest brother asserts
his willingness to give up body and soul περὶ τῶν πατρίων
νόμων (7:37; cf. 7:30).

If the disastrous situation of persecution is understood
by II Maccabees in terms of man's sin and God's wrath, its

---

[30]Reading πεπώκασιν according to Hort's conjecture,
rather than πεπτώκασιν of the MSS. Hort's suggestion is adopted by J. Moffatt (AP, I, p. 142) and by F. M. Abel (Les livres
des Maccabées [Paris, 1949], p. 380), who finds no satisfactory
way to translate the text as it stands.

reversal is described in terms of mercy and reconciliation.
This is clearest at 7:33: "Even if, for reproof and discipline,
the living Lord has been angry (ἐπώργισται) with us for a little
while, He will again be reconciled (καταλλαγήσεται) with his
servants" (cf. also 5:20). The seventh brother concludes his
"speech" with this indirect plea of intercession: "I call
upon God to become merciful to the nation right away and with
afflictions and scourgings to make you [Antiochus] confess that
He alone is God and to check, in me and my brothers, the wrath
of the Almighty which has justly been laid upon the entire
people" (7:37-38).

This important passage introduces a larger question than
the theology of reconciliation and mercy in II Maccabees. That
question is: Does II Maccabees present a concept of vicarious
expiatory suffering and death? H.-W. Surkau represents the
positive response to this question; his supporting arguments
will therefore be considered here in some detail.

Surkau finds it illuminating that the particular text
quoted at II Mac. 7:6 is from Deut. 32: "And He will have
compassion on His servants" (32:36b LXX). The real significance
of this quotation is to be discovered from other parts of the
Song of Moses, i.e., 32:35 (". . . near is the day of their
destruction . . .") and 32:43 (". . . for He avenges the blood
of his servants, and takes vengeance on his adversaries, and
makes expiation for the land of his people"--RSV, following
MT). According to Surkau,

> Wenn unser Martyrium dieser Vers zitiert, dann sieht
> es in dem Sterben der Märtyrer, . . . den Beweggrund
> für Gott, einzugreifen. Das Blut der Märtyrer ist es,
> das hier die Sühne schafft und Gott auf den Plan ruft.
> Wir stehen dicht vor dem Gedanken des Sühneleidens.[31]

Do we really? The following considerations speak against
Surkau's position. 1) The fact that the author knows that
Deut. 32 consists of the "Song of Moses" does not mean that he
has in mind, or intends for his readers to recall, any other
particular verses in that Song. By using the phrase κατὰ

---

[31]Hans-Werner Surkau, Märtyrien in jüdischer und
frühchristlicher Zeit (Göttingen, 1938), p. 59.

πρόσωπον ἀντιμαρτυρούσης (7:6) with reference to Israel's enemy he disregards the fact that in Deut. the Song of Moses bears testimony against Israel herself. At most, then, one might assume that the author intends the quotation to bring with it recollection of its immediate context, i.e., perhaps v. 35 (vengeance upon the enemy). It is even more likely, however, that he knows, and intends his readers to remember, that the Song of Moses includes the motifs of the vindication of Israel and God's vengeance against her enemies. In any case, nothing in the text points to Deut. 32:43 in particular.

2) It is questionable whether II Maccabees views the death of the martyrs as an "inducement" for God to act. The implication of Deut. 32:35-36 is that the plight of God's servants is a sign of the impending destruction of Israel's enemies. But the causal notion suggested by "Beweggrund" is absent in Deut. 32 and in II Maccabees. Furthermore, even if one could accept Surkau's premise, the statement quoted above contains a non sequitur: if the author did understand the death of the martyrs to be an inducement for God to act it does not follow that "it is the blood of the martyrs which effects expiation" (of sins); it does not follow that there is re-flected here "the concept of expiatory suffering" (by which Surkau means vicarious expiatory suffering). Nothing a priori renders this connection impossible. The point is simply that II Maccabees does not take this step.

3) Even if one could be persuaded to agree with Surkau that the author intended the reader to recall Deut. 32:43 specifically, Surkau's interpretation still does not follow. He apparently quotes/translates v. 43 from the MT. At one point, however (i.e., "er . . . reinigt durch Sühne das Land seines Volkes") he seems to incorporate both MT (כפר: "He makes expiation:) and LXX (ἐκκαθαριεῖ: "He will purify"). It would be more appropriate for Surkau to follow the LXX alone since both Jason and the Epitomist wrote in Greek. At this point the observation is pertinent that only at Deut. 32:43 in the LXX does ἐκκαθαρίζειν translate כפר; (καθαρί-ζειν translates כפר only at Ex. 29:37, 30:10). Thus it is, at best, questionable whether the LXX translators had in mind the idea of expiation of sins at Deut. 32:43. Thus I object strongly to the implications of Surkau's contention that "In

84

Dt. 32,43 ist es das Blut der Feinde Israels, das die Entsündigung bringt; denn dort handelt es sich um die Sünde der Feinde
des Volkes . . . ."[32] LXX Deut. 32:43 says nothing about "Sünde"
or "Entsündigung." The Lord "purifies the land"--not from sins
but from Israel's enemies! Furthermore, since the quotation
itself (II Mac. 7:6 of Deut. 32:36) speaks only of vindication
and not of expiation, one must ask what evidence there is that
the author of II Maccabees had in mind the purification of the
land through expiation (i.e., Deut. 32:43 according to Surkau's
translation). II Maccabees never mentions the purification of
the land or its inhabitants by God or by anyone or anything
else.[33] Besides, Surkau himself has to admit that in Deut. 32:
43 it is the blood of Israel's enemies which purifies the land.
What, then, is the evidence for the statement that "the blood
of the martyrs effects expiation"? Deut. 32 offers none.

A much more plausible interpretation of II Maccabees at
this point assumes a degree of correspondence between the words
of the mother and brothers at 7:6 and their words in the following verses. In their subsequent "speeches" two motifs are emphasized: the expectation of resurrection (7:9, 10, 14, 23,
28-29, 36) and of reconciliation between God and Israel (especially 7:33), and the prediction that God will exact vengeance
upon Antiochus (7:17, 19, 31, 35, 36, 37). Read in this light,
7:6 echoes the same motifs. 'Ο κύριος . . . ἐφ' ἡμῖν παρακα-
λεῖται (plus the quotation from Deut. 32) alludes to the hope
of resurrection; with this hope the martyrs encourage each
other to die nobly (7:5). Again, κατὰ πρόσωπον ἀντιμαρτυρούσης
(ᾠδῆς), as an allusion to the theme of vengeance in the Song of
Moses (Deut. 32:35 is especially pertinent), looks forward to

---

[32]Ibid., note 6.

[33]The verb καθαρίζειν is used of the Maccabees' purification of the Temple (2:18; 10:3, 7; 14:36; cf. καθαρασμός at
2:16, 19; 10:5 and at 1:18, 36). The words εκκαθαρίζειν (LXX
Deut. 32:43), ἱλάσκεσθαι, ἱλάζειν, ἐξιλάσκειν do not occur in
II Mac., although ἐξιλασμός (expiation) is used with reference
to a special sacrifice intended by Judas to deliver the dead
from their sins and thereby qualify them for resurrection (cf.
12:43-45 in context). 'Αγνίζειν and καθαγιάζειν are used of
the ceremonial cleansing of persons (12:38), the consecration
of sacrifices (1:26, 33), or the sanctification of the Temple
(2:8; 15:18). At 1:25 ἁγιάζειν has God as subject: ". . .
chose our fathers and consecrated them." This text, then,
would be a half-way exception to the statement preceding this
note.

the torment and death of Antiochus. In a sense this promise of scripture (i.e., Deut. 32:36) is the basis for the brothers' warnings to Antiochus: Do not misinterpret our suffering; we will be raised, God will be reconciled to Israel, and you will get your due.

The suggestion offered here for an adequate interpretation of II Mac. 7:6 can be furthered by an examination of 7:37-38, Surkau's principal textual support for the thesis that II Maccabees reflects a concept of vicarious expiatory suffering. Surkau notes Grimm's paraphrase of 7:38a: "let me and my brothers be the last instances of God's punishment," but asks: Why are these the last instances of punishment? He answers:

> Hinter diesem Vers scheint mir der Gedanke des stellvertretenden Leidens bereits unabweisbar zu stehen. Der Zorn Gottes, der über das ganze Volk ergeht, macht an den Märtyrern halt, bleibt bei ihnen stehen und ergeht nicht weiter über das Volk; denn er ist durch das Sterben der Märtyrer gestillt. Diese Aussage ist noch in keiner Weise irgendwie klar dogmatisch oder systematisch formuliert, jedoch ist daran nicht zu zweifeln, dass hier der Gedanke des stellvertretenden sühnenden Leidens vorliegt.[34]

Furthermore, the phrase οἱ ἡμέτεροι ἀδελφοί (7:36) signifies to Surkau that the martyr not only speaks for the people but is also suffering for them!

The validity of this interpretation depends upon an affirmative answer to this crucial question: In the context of II Maccabees, does 7:37-38 contain any features which cannot be sufficiently explained by appealing to belief in the efficacy of the righteous man's intercessory prayer?[35]

One way to determine the theological import of the (indirect) intercessory prayer at 7:37-38 is to compare the requests made with the events recounted in the following chapters. The pleas are three in number: 1) to become merciful to the nation right away; 2) to make Antiochus confess, with afflictions and scourgings (or plagues), that He alone is God; 3) to check the wrath of the Almighty "ἐν me and my brothers."

---

[34]Ibid., p. 59.

[35]See Abraham's request at Gen. 18:23ff., 20:17; Moses' prayers at Ex. 32:11-14, 31-33 (but note also God's response!); Assumption of Moses 11:14, 17; 12:6. See also the prayers of the prophets: Amos 7:2-3, 5-6; cf. Jer. 7:16, 11:14, 14:11 and II Mac. 15:14. Further: I En. 13:4-6; with this contrast

Does God respond positively to these pleas? About the second there is no doubt at all: "The Lord, the God of Israel struck him with an incurable and invisible wound." Antiochus suffered pains in his bowels and sharp internal torments (9:5). He fell out of his speeding chariot and was badly injured (9:7). Worms swarmed from within his body; still living, his decaying flesh fell from him (9:9). His pains intensifying due to the divine scourging (9:11), Antiochus finally says: "It is right to submit to God and to realize that mortal man is not God's equal" (9:12). It can hardly be doubted that the author of II Maccabees wrote 7:37-38 and the account of Antiochus' demise and repentance in light of each other.

The divine response to the first and third pleas of the seventh brother is not quite so clear-cut. Nevertheless the author provides sufficient indications of the view he holds. As for linguistic parallels to 7:37-38, the most important text is 8:5: "When Maccabeus had assembled his forces the heathen could not withstand him since the Lord's anger had turned into mercy." The victories of Judas and his followers are due to God's "change of heart" from anger to mercy. But this verse does not answer one puzzling question: Why does God's anger turn to mercy? A second pertinent text, 2:22, supplies no clue either. There the Epitomist asserts that the Maccabees regained the Temple, liberated the city and reinstituted the laws "since the Lord, with all clemency (or fairness), became merciful to them." But why? A notice at 8:2-4 is as close as the author comes to an explicit answer. There it is said that Judas and his followers called upon the Lord ". . . to show pity (οἰκτεῖραι) to the Temple, desecrated by impious men, and to have mercy (ἐλεῆσαι) on the ruined city, about to be leveled to the ground; to give heed to the spilled blood crying out to Him and to remember the lawless murder of sinless infants and the blasphemies committed against his name; and to show his hatred of

---

II Enoch 53:1 and note the similarity with Ex. 32:32-33. Surkau himself (p. 59) recognizes that this element of intercession is a decisive one in II Mac.--although for him it is an additional element in the circle of ideas which includes vicarious expiatory suffering. He also maintains that "Das Gebet der Märtyrer hat vor Gott besondere Kraft: durch seinen um Gottes Willen erlittenen Tod hat er ein besonderes Gebetsrecht . . . ." This assertion goes beyond the evidence of the text, for there is nothing in II Mac. to suggest that the prayer of the martyr has any greater efficacy than that of any righteous man whose life is totally dedicated to God.

evil." Since the assertion of God's "change of heart" occurs in the following verse, one is justified in proposing a direct connection between the prayer of the Maccabees and God's turning from anger to mercy.[36] Therefore, the amazing victories of the Maccabees can be understood as due to God's merciful response to their prayers.[37] At the same time, although in less direct fashion, the successes of Judas are the divine reply to the prayer of the seventh brother at 7:37-38. The author of II Maccabees understands God's mercy to have been manifested in the reversal of a situation disastrous to His people; but as a matter of historical fact he knows that this reversal was accomplished by the Maccabees--albeit with a divine ally. The author operates with the theological categories of sin, estrangement and reconciliation, divine wrath and mercy; on the other hand, he is an historian and a sympathetic biographer of Judas Maccabeus.

The words of the seventh brother at 7:37-38, then, are to be interpreted in light of the author's view that the death of Antiochus and the successes of the Maccabees (which give evidence that God's anger is checked and his mercy again operative) are the divine counterpart, the "answer," to the martyr's dying plea.

But one clause of that plea remains to be interpreted: to check (let end) the anger of the Almighty ἐν ἐμοι δὲ καὶ τοῖς ἀδελφοῖς μου. The import of the whole prayer depends to a great extent on the meaning of this last phrase and especially on the preposition ἐν. The central question is: Does ἐν

---

[36] Cf. I Mac. 3:8, where Judas is said to have destroyed the impious out of Judah and ἀπέστρεψεν ὀργὴν ἀπὸ Ισραηλ. In I Mac. the death of Jewish youth is one aspect of the dire situation which arouses Mattathias and his sons (I Mac. 2:6-14 and the following pericope). In II Mac. 8:2-5 the blood of the murdered is one element of the situation to which the Maccabees implore God to give heed, which God "remembers" and because of which he acts through his chosen instruments, Judas and his company.

[37] Cf. the many passages in which Judas and his men pray for God's help or where victory is attributed directly to God or to his aid, e.g., 8:18ff.; 10:1, 7, 16, 26, 28, 38; 11:13: "the Hebrews were invincible since the mighty God fought with them." Note especially 11:9 (ἐλεήμονος θεός) and 11:10 (ἐλεήσαντος αὐτοὺς τοῦ κυρίου).

have here a connotation of means, of instrumentality? That it does is essential to Surkau's thesis that in II Maccabees the martyrs' deaths are vicarious and expiatory.

Eduard Lohse expresses most clearly this interpretation of 7:38a: ". . . die Märtyrer treten mit ihrem Leben stellvertretend für Israel ein und wenden durch ihren Tod den Zorn Gottes von seinem Volke ab."[38] Two considerations speak against this view. In the first place, it is God to whom the brother cries to check (or let end) the wrath of the Almighty. But the idea of God using an external instrument (ἐν ἐμοί . . .) to stay his own wrath is incongruous. More likely, ἐν is intended by the author to mark a fixed point: let the anger of the Almighty end at this point, i.e., with the death of me and my brothers.

In the second place, several aspects of the prayer of the Maccabees at 8:2-4 are incompatible with a conviction that through their death the martyrs avert the wrath of God (Lohse, Surkau). To be sure, God is implored to listen to the spilled blood crying out to Him; but, after all, the martyrs were nine of many whose blood had been shed under Antiochus (5:24-26; 6:9, 10, 11; cf. also 7:42). The stories of Eleazar and the seven brothers are only the most dramatic and impressive examples of a steadfastness exhibited by numerous others. Furthermore, God is requested to remember various other acts on the enemy's part which demand vengeance: desecration of the Temple, destruction of the holy city, the murder of infants, the blasphemies against his name. He is beseeched to show his hatred of evil by requiting those who represent and perpetrate that evil. Thus is God called upon to show mercy on his people and to take vengeance upon the enemy by acting for the sake of his name, his Temple, his city. There is no suggestion in this prayer that God's wrath has been averted through the death of Eleazar and the seven brothers. To suggest that the author of II Maccabees intended for the reader to infer that, is to pass beyond the evidence of the text into the happy realm of conjecture where all things are possible.[39]

---

[38]Lohse, op. cit., pp. 67-68.

[39]If one surmises that the prayer of the seventh brother and the story which provides its context originally circulated separately (i.e., independently of the broader historical context of the rise of the Hasmonean dynasty), then the

Viewed from this perspective, the significance of the seventh brother's prayer at 7:37-38 is not substantially different from that of the "prayer of the righteous" in I Enoch 47:1-2. There the ministering angels appeal to God on behalf of the blood of the righteous which has been shed, that the prayer of the righteous may not be in vain before God and "that they may not have to suffer for ever."[40] But in I Enoch 47 there is certainly no vicarious suffering or expiatory death.

For the Epitomist the meaning of the martyrs' suffering and death is discovered in the idea of God's gracious discipline, visited upon his people before their sins have reached their height (6:12-17).[41] In death they are illustrations of the barbarity of Antiochus (cf. 7:42); they are also models of steadfastness, to be cherished and imitated by all Jews (cf. 6:31). But--and the point must be stressed--II Maccabees does not suggest a direct cause-effect relationship between the death of the martyrs and the deliverance and purification of Israel. That work God effects through the righteous warriors, the Maccabees.

Yet, if II Maccabees does not make the connection between the martyrs' deaths and Israel's deliverance, Jason or the Epitomist appears to have prepared the way for it to be made by another. He has developed the martyr "speech" and the martyr's dying appeal to God for mercy and revenge. He has presented the persecution of Antiochus in terms of nine individual persons; thus he has made nine individuals into representatives of all steadfast Jews who suffered torture and death under Antiochus. The motivation for this feature of

---

argument that ἐν (ב?) was originally intended to have an instrumental sense is more compelling.

[40]The deterministic note of v. 4 ("because the number of the righteous had been offered") still does not endow the death of the righteous with expiatory power effective for others; besides, such an implication is absent from II Maccabees.

[41]The disparity between the understanding of God's mercy in chapters 8 and following (i.e., mercy is demonstrated by the cessation of persecution, victories of Judas, etc.) and in 6:12-17 is apparent. This disparity indicates that the view of chapters 8ff. is that of Jason of Cyrene since 6:12-17 is probably the work of the Epitomist.

representation in II Maccabees is rhetorical and literary.[42]
Nevertheless in its particular context in the course of II
Maccabees, this element of representation is extremely suggestive. For while on the one hand the martyrs represent numerous
other loyal and suffering Jews, on the other their story
clearly marks the crucial turning point from disaster to deliverance, from sin and divine wrath to mercy and reconciliation.
Thus is the stage set for the development of an even more
profound interpretation of martyrdom--an interpretation that
would emphasize the effectiveness of the death of the righteous.
Before turning to an examination of the writing which is evidence of that development, the present study will consider
ideas about suffering and death in the OT and Jewish writings
(Chapter III) and in Greek and Hellenistic literature (Chapter
IV).

---

[42]That is, for a "pathetic" historian the moving story
of nine individuals was a much more useful vehicle for recounting the dire straits of the Jews under Antiochus than would
have been a more generalized description set on a broader
scale.

CHAPTER III

SUFFERING AND DEATH IN THE OLD TESTAMENT

AND OTHER JEWISH WRITINGS

I. Suffering in the Old Testament and Other Jewish Writings

The presupposition underlying every attempt in the OT
and in extra-biblical Jewish literature to deal with the
problem of suffering is that God himself is ultimately the
cause of all suffering. Even when other powers are involved
they work only at God's behest (e.g., Judges 9:23; I Sam. 18:
10, 19:9; I Kings 22:21f.; Job 1-2:10).[1]

One of the most pervasive solutions to the problem of
suffering--which most other solutions either deliberately
rejected or to some extent incorporated--was the view that
misfortune was divine punishment by means of which God judged
the sin and guilt of all mankind (Gen. 6-8), pagan cities and
lands (Gen. 19, Ex. 7-12), wayward Israel (Ex. 32; Num 11, 14)
or individuals. But even when it is an individual who is
punished, he does not bear his suffering in isolation. Rather,
he is a member of the community and a link in the chain of
generations; therefore the effects of the sin for which he is
punished can also be felt by other members of the group and by
his descendants (cf. Gen. 20:7; Josh. 7; II Sam. 21, 24, 9-20).[2]

This retributive view of suffering was adapted and
furthered by the eighth century prophets and by the author of
Deuteronomy at the end of the seventh century. The fall of

---

[1] J. J. Stamm, Das Leiden des Unschuldigen in Babylon und
Israel (Zürich, 1946), p. 33. Only from such infrequent evidence as the ban against sorcerers, wizards, and soothsayers
(Ex. 22:18; Deut. 18:9-11, 14) does one learn that occasionally
other powers--magic, curses, spirits--were thought to be the
causes of suffering or misfortune. It is difficult to say
whether such powers exercized their influence independently of
Yahweh. In any case, to use Stamm's phrase, these other powers
appear "nur am Rand" in OT thought.

[2] Ibid., p. 34.

Israel and then Judah gave new impetus to this manner of understanding misfortune. The view of Deuteronomy was adopted in the Deuteronomic history ca. 550 B.C. The same principle of sin and retribution controls a later historical work, that of the Chronicler (probably composed in the fourth century B.C.), i.e., Chronicles, Ezra, Nehemiah. This principle colors the Chronicler's view to such a degree that he finds it necessary to explain every historical misfortune by some underlying sin (cf. e.g., II Chron. 35:20ff. and compare II Kings 23:29). Applied specifically to the individual, the doctrine of retribution also emerges frequently in the Wisdom literature of Israel.[3]

In the pre-exilic period the suffering of the prophet of Yahweh was a significant exception to the retributive understanding of suffering. The prophet himself certainly did not consider his suffering to be God's punishment for sins. Rather, suffering was the prophet's "occupational hazard," to be endured in the line of duty. Jeremiah, for example, suffers empathetically with his people (Jer. 4:19-22; 8:18-23; 13:17-19); yet he must also endure their enmity (11:19, 21; 20:1-2, 20; 36:26; 37:15; 38:6). Furthermore, he knows the anguish of conflict between his own inclination and the message he must proclaim.

Certain aspects of the prophet's suffering were sometimes required by God specifically as signs to the whole people. Hosea's marriage to a prostitute was a sign of alarm and warning, for that marriage was just as unnatural as God's continuing loyalty to an unfaithful people (Hos. 1:2, 14:1f.). Hosea accepts this special form of suffering, hoping by this "sign" to turn his people to repentance and thus gain their salvation. And when Jeremiah "sits alone" and foregoes the blessing of marriage and children, that mode of life points to Yahweh's impending judgment against His people (cf. Jer. 15:17, 16:1-13).[4]

---

[3]Ibid., pp. 36-39.

[4]Ibid., pp. 61-62, 66. Compare the suffering of the righteous ones in Is. 24-27 (a post-exilic apocalypse). Here, as an eschatological sign, the intensity of suffering is thought to indicate the proximity of divine intervention. (Cf. H. W. Robinson, Suffering Human and Divine [New York, 1939], p. 46.) This principle becomes standard in later Jewish apocalypses, wherein the nearness of the end is indicated by the nature and intensity of the eschatological woes (e.g.,

The post-exilic work of the Chronicler was the high
water mark for the retributive view of suffering and misfortune.
It was also in the post-exilic period, however, that this
"solution" came to be questioned with increasing intensity.
The central problem now became not suffering in general nor
even the suffering of the individual but the suffering of the
righteous or innocent man. Two factors were primarily responsible for the growing disenchantment with the "official" answer
to the problem of suffering. In the first place, it was becom-
ing ever more apparent that the retributive view simply was not
compatible with the facts of life. Accompanying that realization was a growing individualism which, at least in the area
of jurisprudence, is already reflected in the Deuteronomic
history (cf. II Kings 14:5f., Deut. 24:16). The new recognition
of the worth of the individual is expressed forcefully in
Jeremiah, Ezekiel, many post-exilic Psalms and in the Wisdom
literature. As the individual, viewed less in connection with
the community, became more and more a creature of worth in and
of himself, the question of the suffering of the innocent and
the prosperity of the godless became correspondingly more
pressing. No longer was there sufficient consolation in the
hope that future reward would be experienced by the community,
no matter what happened to individuals. And a distinct belief
in resurrection was not yet available as a source of comfort
for the individual righteous ones who asked questions about
their misfortune. Thus was it felt that just retribution and
reward had to be demonstrated in the brief span of an individual life. If God was indeed just, an explanation must be
found for the suffering of the righteous and for the good
fortune of the godless.[5]

---

Dan. 11:33-35, 12:1; AMoses 8-10; II Bar. 25:2-4, 70:1-71:1,
81:1-82:2; cf. Mark 13).

[5]W. Wichmann, Die Leidenstheologie (Stuttgart, 1930),
p. 2; Stamm, op. cit., p. 41. Stamm (p. 40) notes that only
two pre-exilic texts reflect the theological question of
the suffering of the righteous man: II Sam. 24:17 and Jer.
12:1-6 (and 31:29f. if this text is genuinely pre-exilic).

This dilemma was resolved in various ways by different authors. Some abandoned completely the previously dominant explanation;[6] others retained the basic concept of retribution but adapted it to conform to the reality of life.

The concept of retribution was frequently "adjusted" by means of the claim that the righteous who suffer unjustly will receive compensation in the future--either by reward in this earthly life (Ps. 37; Sir. 11:21), by the reputation of one's descendants (Sir. 11:28 LXX; the opposite: Wisd. 3:16f., 4:3-6), or by an immortal name (Sir. 44:8-15, 41:11-13; Wisd. 4:1, 19; 8:13b; Ps. Sol. 13:10f.).[7] Finally, of course, the belief in resurrection or immortality offered the most adequate opportunity for the righteous individual's future reward (e.g., Dan. 12:2; I En. 22:9-13, 103:3-4; TBenj. 10:8; Wisd. 3:4, 5:15-16, 15:3; II Mac. 7:9, 14, 23, 36; IV Mac. passim). Even so, belief in an afterlife did not completely eliminate attempts to find solutions to the problem of suffering "von innen her."[8] But whether compensation was expected in this life or in the hereafter, suffering gained meaning because it insured a reward in the future.

By far the most influential and widespread solution to the problem of the suffering of the righteous was the "disciplinary" view. That is, suffering was understood not as retribution but as the disciplinary act of a good and gracious God. Yahweh chastises his chosen ones not out of anger but out of love. This fundamental conception took three distinguishable forms in Jewish literature.[9] At least two of them, the first and third, presuppose that no man, not even the most righteous, is totally without sin. To use Wichmann's phrase, that "naive optimism" had been lost (p. 9).

---

[6]The author of Job views the suffering of the righteous as ultimately mysterious. God's wisdom and power are beyond human ken; so too is the divine purpose in the suffering of the innocent. Cf. H. Wheeler Robinson, The Cross in the Old Testament (London, 1955), pp. 42-47.

[7]Wichmann, op. cit., p. 3.

[8]Ibid.

[9]I am here following W. Wichmann, Die Leidenstheologie, pp. 5-15.

At times suffering was viewed as divine discipline in the narrow, literal sense.[10] This view is reflected in Amos, Hosea, and Jeremiah (e.g., Jer. 2:19, 30; 3:3; 5:3; 30:11, 14; 31:18), but it is found most often in the Wisdom literature. Proverbs 3:11-12 can be taken as an example: "My son, do not despise the Lord's discipline or be weary of his reproof, for the Lord reproves him whom he loves, as a father the son in whom he delights" (RSV).[11]

A second form of the disciplinary view of suffering (often combined with the first) is that God tests a man through misfortune; by testing and probing He discovers what is in a man's heart and how faithful he is to the commandments.[12] The prologue to the book of Job expresses this view forcefully through narrative and dialogue.[13]

Finally, suffering was sometimes understood as having an expiatory or purificatory function: a man's suffering was thought to remove the sin for which he would otherwise have to be punished more drastically in the future. Such expiatory suffering has very positive meaning because through it God gives one the opportunity for a new beginning. The beginnings of this view are to be found in the image of smelting and re-fining in the OT (Is. 1:25, Jer. 6:27-30; Ps. 66:10; Is. 48:10; Zech. 13:9); but the developed idea is first expressed dis-tinctly in Ps. Sol. (10:1f., 13:9, 18:4-6) and in II Maccabees (6:12-17). I quote from only one of these texts, Ps. Sol. 13:9: "The Lord spares his pious ones and blots out their errors by his chastening."

The disciplinary view of suffering is, in one sense, a complete reversal of the retributive view, although God is recognized as the cause of suffering in each case. In the retributive view, suffering is a mark of divine punishment, vengeance, rejection. In the disciplinary view suffering can

---

[10] The terms used most often are יסר (Piel)/παιδεύειν or יכה (Hiphil)/ἐλέγχειν, and related forms.

[11] Cf. also Job 5:17f. (Eliphaz), 33:19-28 and 36:8-12 (Elihu); Ps. Sol. 10:1, 16:11; Wisd. 12:2; Sir. 23:2f. For a study of "suffering as divine discipline" see the book by that name by J. A. Sanders (Rochester, 1955).

[12] The terms usually used are בחן /δοκιμάζειν and נסה (Piel)/πειράζειν.

[13] Cf. also Deut. 8:2, 16; Judges 3:4; Ps. Sol. 16:14; Judith 8:27; Wisd. 3:5, 11:9; Sir. 2:1.

be understood as a sign of acceptance and loving concern on God's part; it is precisely the righteous man that He disciplines and tests and to whom He gives opportunity for expiation through suffering. Conversely, God does not seek to bring the godless into the paths of righteousness through disciplinary action because He has already given them up to their sin; eventually the full measure of punishment will reward them.[14]

The theology of disciplinary suffering--Leidenstheologie, in Wichmann's terms--was destined to have a significant impact on Jewish thought, especially in its otherworldly, future form (i.e., in the present age the righteous suffer to expiate the few sins which they must have committed; so purified, they can expect a glorious reward in the next world for their good deeds). It is prominent in an apocalyptic writing composed after the beginning of the Christian era, II Baruch (cf. 13:1-12; 78:3, 5-6), as well as among the Tannaim and Amoraim.[15] Wichmann suggests (p. 15) that Leidenstheologie became so widespread because it answered two profound needs: the problem of suffering and the question of an effective means of expiation. Wichmann also makes this further observation (p. 14), which is not without significance for the present study:

> Es kann und wird nun nicht zufällig sein, dass die Leidenstheologie in der Generation ihre grösste Bedeutung bekommt, die die Zerstörung des Tempels in Jerusalem und damit das Ende der priesterlichen Sühnehandlungen erlebt hat.

## II. The Death of Individuals in the Old Testament

My intent in this section is not to examine the understanding of or attitude toward death in general but to observe how the deaths of individual persons are described and what, if any, significance or effects are attributed to those deaths.

Frequently in the OT the only significance that the death of an individual has is that it rids the community of the defilement of one who transgresses some law or taboo. For

---

[14]Wichmann, op. cit., pp. 9-10.

[15]Cf. Wichmann, op. cit., pp. 32-42, 51-80 and Appendix; Sanders, op. cit., pp. 105-17.

the offender himself, however, the punishment of death is wholly
negative. Examples can be taken almost at random. At Ex. 19:
12-13 whoever touches the mountain shall be put to death;
(compare II Sam. 6:7 = I Chron. 13:10, where an angry Yahweh
smites Uzzah because he touched the ark). At Ex. 21:12-17
death is prescribed for anyone who murders a free man or who
strikes or curses either of his parents (cf. Lev. 20:9; 24:17,
21; Num. 35:16-21). Other transgressions worthy of death are
sorcery, sodomy, idolatry (Ex. 22:18-20; cf. Lev. 20:15-16),
profaning the Sabbath (Ex. 31:14-15; cf. Num. 15:32-36),
sacrificing children to Molech (Lev. 20:2), adultery (Lev. 20:
10), incest (Lev. 20:11-12), homosexual acts (Lev. 20:13) and
blasphemy (Lev. 24:16). Deut. 24:7 gives a clear insight regarding the purpose of the death penalty: "If a man is found
stealing one of his brethren . . . and if he treats him as a
slave or sells him, then that thief shall die; so you shall
purge the evil from the midst of you" (RSV). By thus executing
the offender the community protects itself against the wrath
of Yahweh and restores its sacral order.[16]

As for specific instances of precipitous death, Jewish
authors seem little inclined to see any meaning or significance
in the act of dying. The Chronicler does interpret Saul's
death as God's punishment for his unfaithfulness, that is,
because Saul had sought counsel from the witch of Endor (against
the Lord's command) rather than from God (I Chron. 10:13-14).[17]
And the death of the rebels against Moses, Dathan and Abiram,
and their families is understood as a warning against the
"murmuring" congregation (Num. 16:25-35 with 26:64-65). But
usually the precipitous deaths of kings and princes, priests,
national heroes and ordinary men are noted without comment as
to "meaning."

In many texts a person is slain to exact vengeance or
punishment. Yet, even in those instances where the victims'
office or character might provide an opportunity to discover

---

[16]Cf. G. von Rad, Old Testament Theology I (New York,
1962), p. 264.

[17]Compare I Sam. 31, where there is no trace of such an
interpretation. A similar interpretive advance is obvious
when one compares II Chron. 35:20-24 with II Kings 23:29-30.

some positive meaning in their death, one finds no attempts at
such an interpretation.[18] The only "effects" mentioned in most
cases are grief (e.g., II Sam. 1:11-12, 3:31-34, 19:1-4), flight
or dismay (e.g., I Sam. 31:7, II Sam. 4:1), or revenge (Judges
9:53-56, II Sam. 4:11-12 and passim).

In comparison with Greek and Hellenistic literature (cf.
infra, Chapter IV, section on glorious death) one of the most
striking aspects of OT references to unnatural death is that no
meaning is sought for Israelite warriors who fall in battle.
Whatever the explanation,[19] there are, to my knowledge, no
passages in the OT which declare or suggest that the warrior
of Israel fights and dies for Yahweh, the land of Israel, the
Law, the king, or his own family; nor does he die in order to
attain a glorious name.[20] Rather he fights and dies because
that is Yahweh's will and because He promises to give the enemy
into Israel's hand.[21] The skill and daring of the Israelite
man of war is overshadowed by the conviction that for their
sake Yahweh fights on behalf of his people and to Him victory
is due (Josh. 10:42, 23:3, passim). Thus, even when thousands
of Israelite soldiers are said to have fallen (e.g. I Sam. 4:
10), one detects no inclination to find positive meaning or
significance in their death. For the Hebrew, the heroic conception of patriotic self-sacrifice is not familiar. In
Israel the closest equivalent to the Greek or Roman soldier who
gives himself for the fatherland is the prophet of Yahweh who

---

[18]E.g., Judges 16: the folk-hero Samson forfeits his
own life when he brings the temple of Dagon down upon the
Philistines, but no "meaning" (except revenge--cf. v. 28!) is
sought in his death. I Sam. 22:18 tells about the death of
the priests of Nob at Saul's command; but in spite of their
priestly office and the injustice of Saul's act, no significance is assigned their death.

[19]The tradition of Holy War? The idea that the victory
is Yahweh's alone? The absence of a vigorous individualism?
The covenant relationship which prevents the development of
patriotism in a Graeco-Roman sense?

[20]However, the "mighty man" of Israel did, of course,
gain fame among his peers by his exploits; cf. e.g., I Sam.
18:7, 30; II Sam. 23:8-39. And one does find at Judges 7:18
and 20 the battle shouts "for the Lord and for Gideon" and "a
sword for the Lord and for Gideon," "for" rendering ל and the
Greek dative (LXX).

[21]Among numerous texts cf., e.g., Josh. 8:1, 7; 10:8,
32; 11:6; Judges 7:14, 15.

endures suffering and sometimes death (cf. I Kings 18:13, 19: 10; Jer. 15:15) in faithfulness to his mission.   In Jewish literature the first appearance of the idea that the warrior fights _for_ Yahweh or the Law seems to be in I Maccabees (cf. 2:50-64).[22]

Five instances of precipitous death in the OT, described with unusual detail, deserve more than a cursory glance in the present context because of their connection with some sin or taboo.   They are:   the death of Achan (Josh. 7), the killing of the chiefs of the people (Num. 25:1-5), Phineas' slaughter of the Israelite and a Midianite woman (Num. 25:6-13), the sacrifice of Jephtha's daughter (Judges 11), and the hanging of Saul's sons by the Gibeonites (II Sam. 21:1-9).   The central question to be put to these texts remains:   What is the purpose and effect of these deaths?

In Josh. 7 God's anger is aroused against Israel because Achan saved and hid some of the booty from Jericho although the Israelites had been commanded to destroy everything totally except the precious items which were to be brought to the Lord (Josh. 6:17-19).   This deed is understood as a transgression of the covenant (7:11) which leads directly to military defeat (7:4-5, 12-13).   To rectify this situation the culprit is searched out and discovered; then Achan himself, his family and all his possessions are stoned and burned (7:24-25).   Only then does Yahweh turn from his burning anger.   The effects of the death of Achan and his household, then, are two:   the sin having been removed, God's anger is averted from Israel. Achan's death is therefore not presented first and foremost as punishment meted out to him but as the divinely ordered measure essential to the community's recovery of wholeness

---

[22]At Qumran the view of the warrior's role does not appear to be fundamentally different from that in the OT.   In the War Scroll one finds a detailed account of the preparation for and the purpose and execution of the final battle of the Sons of Light against the Sons of Darkness.   Here the purpose of warfare is simply to defeat the enemies of God (IQM 1.1, 9.5-6 etc.).   Mention is made of Israel's valor (11.7), and on the day of battle the priest is expected to exhort the congregation to be courageous and valiant (10.3-4, 15.7-8).   But the only reasons given for undertaking this courageous venture are that the great battle is an aspect of God's predestined plan (1.10, 13.14) and that the victory is to be won by His power is certain (cf. 6.3, 5-6; 10.1, 4; 11.4-5; 14.5; 16.1; 18.13; 12.10-12; 19.2-4).   With his angels God fights for Israel and for the glory of His name (11.8, 14; 18.8).

within the covenantal relationship. His death--which in its
context is not only deserved but also unavoidable--effects both
expiation and propitiation, but the latter depends directly
upon the former. Yahweh's anger will not subside until the
sinful situation is reversed.

The two incidents recounted in Num. 25 can be considered
together. Because some of the Israelites began to worship
Baal of Peor, Yahweh's anger was kindled against Israel. In
accord with the Lord's command, Moses instructed the judges of
Israel to kill every man who had become a worshipper of Baal.
This was to be done so that the fierce anger of Yahweh might
turn away from Israel (25:4). (The text proceeds to the
Phineas episode without stating that the command of Yahweh was
actually carried out.)

In the second incident, Phineas, grandson of Aaron, ran
a spear through an Israelite man and a Midianite woman who were
seen together at the tent of meeting. This act, the reader is
told, stayed the plague which was afflicting Israel. The plague
was stayed because God's wrath was averted by the zealous act
of Phineas (25:8, 10-11). Thus, again Yahweh is propitiated
because a rankling transgression had been removed from the
congregation. By his act of zeal Phineas "made expiation for
(יכפר על / ἐξιλάσατο περί) the sons of Israel" (25:13). In
both incidents of Num. 25, transgressors against the commandments of Yahweh are slain in order to rid the community of sin
and thereby to avert the anger of the Lord of the covenant.

In II Sam. 21 the implication is clear that the famine
afflicting Israel is due to blood guilt on the house of Saul
because he had broken the oath to spare the Gibeonites and had
slain them instead (vv. 1-2). David asks the survivors how he
can expiate the wrong that has been done (21:3).[23] In accordance with their response he delivers into their hands seven
sons of Saul, whom the Gibeonites hanged on a mountain before
the Lord (21:5-6, 8-9). After the Israelites had properly
disposed of their remains, the pericope concludes, Yahweh

---

[23]The text reads: במה אכפר / ἐν τίνι ἐξιλάσωμαι (in
neither case does the verb have an object). The idea seems to
be that of the expiation or removal of a wrong; the element of
blood guilt tends to inject a connotation of compensation.
"Propitiate" is hardly the sense of the verb here. The fundamental aim of David's question is not the appeasement of the
Gibeonites but the cessation of the famine, and that necessitates "making expiation" (i.e., for a wrong done). Incidentally,

granted entreaties for the land (21:14)--apparently by bringing
the famine to an end.

In this text there is no mention of Yahweh's anger,
although the implication is present that the famine is due to
His displeasure. The three elements involved are Saul's transgression of an oath to non-Israelites, the resultant blood
guilt upon Saul's house, and the necessity of removing that
blood guilt by the compensatory death of members of Saul's
family who were in no sense personally responsible for their
father's transgression but are vulnerable because of the customs
of blood guilt and vengeance. In a word, the death of Saul's
sons--themselves innocent of any wrongdoing--expiates the stain
of blood guilt from his descendants and removes the hardship of
famine from the people whom Saul had ruled and represented.
This text differs from Josh. 7 and Num. 25 in that those who
are killed are not, and do not include, the transgressor.
Nevertheless, this text is still a great conceptual distance
from the idea of "vicarious expiation" or of self-sacrifice
for the welfare of others. Rather, the conceptual framework
is that of group (family) corporateness, blood guilt and
vengeance.[24]

The final text for consideration at this point is the
well-known story of Jephtha's daughter (Judges 11). In accord
with a rather mindless vow made to Yahweh, Jephtha offered up
his daughter as a burnt offering (11:30-31, 34, 39). Behind
this story apparently lies the pagan practice--known and sometimes indulged in by Israel--of human sacrifice; and of this
practice the OT, of course, has nothing positive to say.[25] It

---

here one finds a good example of an act of the king (Saul)
affecting the entire people (i.e., the famine).

[24]Furthermore, on the historical level it is likely that
with David's consent the Gibeonites were indulging in a
Canaanite fertility rite at the expense of Saul's sons. For
parallels with a Ras Shamra text and the suggestion of this
thesis, cf. R. de Vaux, Studies in Old Testament Sacrifice
(Cardiff, 1964), pp. 61-62.

[25]Deut. 12:30f., 18:10; II Kings 16:3, 21:6, 23:10; Jer.
7:31, 32-35; Micah 6:6f. Cf. W. Eichrodt, Theology of the Old
Testament I (London, 1961), pp. 149-52. A more extensive
study of human sacrifice in Israel can be found in R. de Vaux,
op. cit., pp. 52-90; on Jeptha's daughter: pp. 65-66.

102

is strictly forbidden as an unthinkable sin against Yahweh.[26]
Jephtha's daughter is willing to be sacrificed, but her acquies-
cence does not mean that she dies for the good of anyone.  She
dies simply because she must:  a vow made to Yahweh cannot be
broken.[27]


III.  Vicarious Expiatory Suffering and Death in the Old
Testament[28]


A.  Introduction

Many OT scholars espouse the view that the concept of
vicarious expiatory suffering is clearly and unambiguously set
forth in only one OT text, Isaiah 53.[29]  This text above all

---

[26]Deut. 12:31; 18:10; Lev. 18:21, 20:2-5.  At I Kings
13:2 the "sacrifice" of human beings is foretold by a "man of
God."  He declares that Josiah will slay upon the altar at
Bethel those non-Levitical priests who had collaborated with
Jereboam and officiated at the "high places" in the Northern
Kingdom.  But this predicted event, of course, is without a
modicum of positive meaning.  It will be a punishment deserved
by apostates, and the "man of God" revels in such an ironic
retribution.

[27]In spite of the haggadic expansion of the story in
Pseudo-Philo 39-40, its point remains fundamentally unchanged.
Pseudo-Philo emphasizes the willingness of Seila to die,
heightens the pathos of the situation, and adds this declaration
by God:  ". . . et erit mors eius preciosa ante conspectum meum
omni tempore."  But there is no suggestion that Saila died "for"
anyone or that her death had any expiatory significance.

[28]By "vicarious expiatory suffering" I mean the suffering of one person which effects expiation for the transgression
of another.  "Expiatory suffering," however, without reference
to the vicarious dimension, means only that by suffering a
person expiates his own sins.  Similarly, "vicarious suffering"
does not necessarily include the element of expiation, since
vicariousness could be envisioned as substitution in a more
immediate, literal sense; for example, "vicarious punishment"
would mean simply that one person bears the punishment which
was due another.

[29]E.g., Robinson, Suffering, pp. 43-44; cf. Lohse, op.
cit., p. 97.

others must therefore be given careful consideration.

Ex. 32:30-32 is not included in this examination because the interpretation that Moses expresses his willingness to die in place of or even on behalf of the people of Israel is incorrect. To be sure, Moses tells the people that he will try to effect forgiveness of their sins before the Lord, but the means to this end is his prayer of intercession, not a willingness on his part to offer himself on their behalf. The alternatives expressed by v. 32 are not: forgive their sin (without any sacrificial act) or accept my life as an expiatory offering for their sin. Rather, the alternative is: forgive these people and let us live or if you will not forgive these people, destroy me with them. By his request to be blotted out of the book of life if the people are not forgiven, Moses expresses his desire to stand with them and to share their fate.[30] The only other interpretation that seems possible is that in v. 32 Moses, the intercessor for his people, is bargaining with God, almost daring Him to destroy His servant (cf. Num. 11:15). In a sense Moses confronts Yahweh in a showdown and forces the divine hand--almost. God's response is: the sinners, not you, will I destroy; but not right now (cf. vv. 33-34)! In any case, v. 33 is sufficient rebuttal to the notion that the concept of vicarious expiatory suffering is held by the author(s) of Exodus.

Likewise, I do not think it possible to sustain the argument that the idea of vicarious expiatory death is echoed in Zech. 12:10-13:1, as has been suggested by Stamm[31] or by J. Scharbert.[32] The idea is not there and the text can be quite adequately explained without any recourse to it.[33]

B. Transference and Substitution in the Old Testament

By way of introduction to the following discussion of Isaiah 53, I wish to raise a two-fold question: Leaving aside this text, what role do the ideas of transference and substitution play in the writings of the OT?

---

[30] Cf. J. J. Stamm, Erlösen und Vergeben im Alten Testament (Bern, 1940), p. 60, who also cites Gressmann.

[31] Stamm, Leiden, pp. 74-75.

[32] Scharbert, "Stellvertretendes Sühneleiden in den Ebed-Jahwe-Liedern und in altorientalischen Ritualtexten," BZ 2 (1958), 212.

[33] Cf. Paul D. Hanson, Studies in the Origins of Jewish Apocalyptic (unpublished Ph.D. thesis, Harvard University, 1969), pp. 322-33.

In contrast to the ideas of magic and transference preva-
lent in Babylonian religion, one finds in an OT cultic setting
only two occasions on which defilement is transferred from man
to animal. In order to purify any leper who has been cured,
one of two living birds is killed; the other, having been dipped
in the blood of the first, is released to fly away (Lev. 14:2b-
7). One gets the definite impression that the rite of purification in this instance includes the element of transference. The
second occasion is the Day of Atonement. According to Lev. 16:
15-22 (cf. 6-10), after the goat of the sin offering has been
slain and Aaron has performed the proper rites with its blood
for purification of the holy place, the tent of meeting and the
altar, he shall lay his hands on the head of the live goat and
confess over him all the transgressions and sins of the people
of Israel. Then the goat is to be sent away into the wilder-
ness--to Azazel, adds v. 10. "And the goat shall bear (or carry
or take away: נשא / λήμψεται) all their impurities upon him to
a land apart" (v. 22). The sins of the whole community are thus
transferred to a single living thing.

As for the second part of my question, R. B. Townshend
has expressed the view that "the whole Jewish theory of
national religion was based on redemption by substitution."[34]
That is an over-statement. The texts in which Townshend sees
this principle at work in the substitution of one person for
another--Ex. 32:32 (Moses' intercession); II Sam. 24:17 (David's
plea for his people); Judges 11 (Jephtha's daughter)--must be
disallowed. And his understanding of a sacrifice as the substitution of an animal death for that of a man is by no means
shared by all scholars. W. Eichrodt and R. de Vaux, for
example, represent quite a different view. Eichrodt writes:
"The substitutionary value of the victim is restricted to the
quite general principle that, if man were to omit the prescribed form of expiation, he would _irrevocably_ fall under the
just and annihilating wrath of God . . . ."[35] He gives four
summarizing statements of the principal arguments against a
substitutionary interpretation of the sacrificial animal's
death, of which I mention three: the victim is in fact considered holy, whereas if it were thought to be laden with sin
and guilt it would be unclean; if the sacrifice were a _satis-
factio vicaria_ it could not be replaced by a meal offering

---

[34]Townshend in AP, II, p. 663.
[35]Eichrodt, _op. cit._, I, p. 165.

(cf. Lev. 5:11ff.); in P none of the sins expiated by the sacrifice are transgressions worthy of death. R. de Vaux writes:
". . . the victim does not become 'sin'; it is pleasing to God,
who in consideration for this offering removes the sin."[36]

It should be noted that there are unusual situations in
which the substitutionary function of the slain is essential
to the episode recounted.[37] But these are better understood
as ad hoc events rather than reflections of a generally operative conception of substitution. Further, in Gen. 22, for
example, the animal's death does not effect expiation. God
commanded Abraham to offer Isaac not in order to expiate his
sins but to manifest his devotion and obedience.

Nevertheless, there are two OT texts in which the substitution of a less valuable for a more valuable animal and
(apparently) of an animal for a human being is an integral
aspect of Israel's cultic life. Ex. 13:13 and 34:20 (with
minor differences in wording) state: "And every firstborn of
an ass you shall redeem ( תפדה ) with a sheep; but if you do not
redeem (it) you shall break its neck. And every firstborn of
man among your sons you shall redeem."[38] The text does not
state how the firstborn of man is to be redeemed, but one can
infer that the practice was to substitute an animal which was
offered to God in place of the human child upon whom God held
a rightful claim.

---

[36]R. de Vaux, op. cit., p. 94. In n. 5 de Vaux cites
literature wherein the same position is argued. Cf. also
Stamm, Leiden, p. 69; Robinson, Suffering, p. 44. I might
note that whereas Eichrodt (op. cit., I, pp. 165-66) is certain
that the laying of hands on the sacrificial victim does not
reflect a substitutionary concept, von Rad (op. cit., I, p.
256) leaves the question open.

[37]E.g., the sacrifice of Isaac in Gen. 22; possibly the
redemption of Jonathan in I Sam. 14:45.

[38]The translations of these two verses in the LXX are
intriguing. Ex. 13:13: "Every firstborn of an ass you shall
exchange (ἀλλάξεις) for a sheep; but if you do not exchange
you shall redeem (λυτρώσῃ) it." Ex. 34:20 has: ". . . you
shall pay a price (τιμὴν δώσεις--A adds αὐτοῦ)." Apparently,
for the translators of the LXX the meaning of ערף (to break
an animal's neck) was uncertain (cf. Deut. 21:4, 6, where it
is rendered by νευροκοπεῖν--to hamstring). Note the distinction in Ex. 13:13 LXX between to "exchange" or "substitute"
and to "redeem"; in Ex. 34:20 LXX, between "redeem" and "pay
the price (for it)."

Three additional texts require brief consideration. In Deut. 21:1-9, directions are given about how to purge the guilt of innocent blood from the community when a man is found slain in the open country and no one knows who murdered him. In that situation, the elders of the city nearest the site of the murder shall take a heifer and break her neck; washing their hands over the heifer, they shall declare their innocence and pray that the defilement of blood guilt be removed from Israel. Since blood guilt is expiated by the death of the offender when his identity is known, it would appear that in Deuteronomy 21 the slain heifer is understood as a "stand in" for the unknown transgressor. Thus the animal is a substitute for the murderer, but in a different way than if he had been discovered and the death of the heifer had nevertheless served to expiate the blood guilt which rested upon him.

Some scholars have argued that the substitution of one human life for another is suggested by the story in I Sam. 14: 24-46. Jonathan, having unwittingly broken an oath imposed upon the people by Saul (i.e., not to eat before evening), must now die for his "transgression." But the people would not allow this to happen: "The people redeemed (יפדו) Jonathan and he was not put to death" (v. 45). The text does not say how the people redeemed Jonathan, however. Stamm, following Ewald and Wellhausen, thinks it probable that one of the people was sacrificed in Jonathan's place.[39] But, although this possibility cannot be dismissed on the level of historical event, there is nothing in the text to suggest that the author of Samuel understood the episode in this way. Nothing suggests a transaction different in kind from that provided for at Ex. 13:13 and 34:20, that is, the substitution of an animal (or possibly money) for a human life.[40] In any case, the act of substitution in I Sam. 14 is not related to the expiation of sin against the covenant but to recognition of the power of oath and curse (cf. Judges 11).

---

[39] Stamm, Erlösen, p. 13; cf. Lohse, op. cit., p. 95.

[40] Significantly, the LXX translators do not even consider an animal (or money) substitute necessary. They render: "And the people prayed for (περί) Jonathan on that day, and he did not die." Redemption has given way to intercession!

The idea that persons <u>can</u> substitute for other persons
in the sight of Yahweh is most clearly attested in Num. 3:11:
God says to Moses that He has taken the Levites in place of the
firstborn of the Israelites.

In addition to those texts where the substitution of a
living thing for a human life is involved, there are others
where provisions are made for a <u>money</u> substitute for a human
life. At Ex. 21:29-30 the owner of an ox which gores a person
to death shall be put to death himself unless he pays the
ransom laid upon him as the redemption for his life. At Ex.
30:12 Yahweh tells Moses that "each shall give a ransom (כפר )
for himself to the Lord when you number them, that there be no
plague among them when you number them" (RSV). The money so
given is called כסף הכפרים and its purpose is לכפר for the
people (v. 16).

This brief preliminary inquiry has shown that the ideas
of transference and substitution are indeed present in the OT,
but that in connection with rites of purification and expiation
they are not as pervasive and fundamental as scholars (e.g.,
Townshend) often imply. With this point clarified, the present
study turns to Isaiah 53.

C. Isaiah 53: The Prophet's Intent

The meaning of the suffering of the servant in Is. 53
has long been debated and, no doubt, will continue to be for
generations to come. Instead of trying to resolve an extremely
complex problem here, I will be content to suggest three possible responses (among many!) to a more specific question:
Does Second Isaiah operate, in chapter 53, with a concept of
vicarious expiatory suffering?

1) The customary response given to this question by
scholars is an affirmative one. Furthermore "vicarious" is
usually tacitly assumed to be synonymous with "substitutional."
A statement by J. Lindblom represents this view: "Through his
suffering the servant makes expiation for a multitude of men,
taking their punishment upon himself. By means of all this a
sublime plan of Yahweh will be fulfilled, the salvation of
many."[41]

---

[41]J. Lindblom, The Servant Songs in Deutero-Isaiah

2) This widely-held view has recently been challenged by
Harry M. Orlinsky.[42] His arguments against the traditional
view of "vicarious suffering" in Isaiah 53 fall roughly into
three categories:  (a) It is difficult to believe that Second
Isaiah could say that the servant is suffering in the place of
other nations (b) or in Israel's place; (c) the idea of vicarious suffering is simply not present here; the point lies
elsewhere.  I quote several statements from Orlinsky which
develop the above points.

(a) It is evident at once that neither Babylonia nor any
    other gentile nation can be involved here [re: vv.4-6,
    which O. calls the crucial passage in the chapter]:  they
    had experienced no sickness and no pain, and, as is clear
    from the preceding section, they were guilty of no trans-
    gression or iniquity, and they were not going to be healed;
    quite the contrary:  the prophet held out for them nothing
    but shame and ignoble defeat.  There is only one party who
    had transgressed and sinned, who had, consequently, ex-
    perienced sickness and pain, and who would soon be healed
    of its wounds--and that was the people Israel, now in
    exile [pp. 53-54].

(b) All scholars are in agreement, and rightly so, that the
    covenant lay at the heart of biblical thought. . . .
    This altogether legal contract, then, assured both the
    obedient and the rebellious, both the guiltless and the
    wicked, their proper due.  Nothing could be farther from
    this basic concept of quid pro quo, or from the spirit
    and letter of biblical law, or from the teachings of
    the prophets, than that the just and faithful should
    suffer vicariously for the unjust and faithless . . .
    [pp. 54-55].[43]

---

(Lund, 1951), pp. 47-48.  Cf. also H. W. Wolff, Jesaia 53 im
Urchristentum (Berlin, 1950), pp. 27-28, passim; O. Cullmann,
The Christology of the New Testament (Philadelphia, 1959),
pp. 55-56.

[42]First in his 1964 Goldenson lecture:  "The So-Called
'Suffering Servant' in Isaiah 53," in Interpreting the Prophetic Tradition (Cincinnati, 1969), pp. 227-73, and then in
an expanded, more technical version of that address:  "The So-
Called 'Servant of the Lord' and 'Suffering Servant' in Second
Isaiah" in Studies on the Second Part of the Book of Isaiah,
with N. H. Snaith (Leiden, 1967).  Here I refer to the later
work.

[43]Orlinsky has on his side the fact that when Second
Isaiah does use substitution or exchange language, it is other
nations which are given in exchange for Israel-- תחת is used
three times in 43:3-4 to express this idea!  This term is not
used in Is. 53 except in the expression תחת אשר ("because":
v. 12).

How could our author be talking of vicariousness, that is, how could he be asserting that sinful Israel would be spared punishment, when Israel had already experienced that punishment--in the form of destruction at home and two generations of captivity abroad . . . [p. 58]?

As for point (c), Orlinsky sees the servant as the prophet of God who, like his prophetic forebears, experienced intense suffering as a result of his unpopular mission.

Like all spokesmen and prophets of God, from first to last, this person too suffered on account of and along with the people at large, the latter directly because of their transgressions and the former, though not guilty of transgression, because of his unpopular mission. And when the people were made whole again, when their wounds were healed, it was only because the prophet had come and suffered to bring them God's message of rebuke and repentance [p. 57].

To Orlinsky, then, such statements as "he shall bear their iniquities" mean only that God's innocent and faithful servant had to suffer the chastisement which fell upon a wicked people.[44]

In my view Orlinsky's strongest point is made in the second quotation under (b) above, i.e., that no prophet writing during the exile could have intended to say that Israel escaped punishment because her punishment had been borne by the servant. On the other hand, with regard to the quotation under (c), one may properly ask whether the assertion that "with his stripes we are healed" is merely a hyperbolic, poetic expression of the belief that the chastisement which brought healing to us also fell upon him who did not deserve it. Does not v. 5, above all, claim that in some way the servant's suffering was beneficial for others? Orlinsky is unable to deal with such a question because he defines "vicarious" exclusively in terms of substitution (cf. p. 51)--a definition which he adopts without question because that is the definition central to the interpretation that he wishes to refute.

3) It is possible to understand the suffering of the servant in Isaiah 53 quite differently, that is, in terms of a second connotation of "vicarious": performed or suffered by one person with results accruing to the benefit or advantage of another." Morna D. Hooker, for example, can speak of "Israel as the Servant of Yahweh, whose sufferings are powerful to

---

[44]Cf. L. Waterman, "The Martyred Servant Motif of Is. 53," JBL 56(1937), 28-30.

convert the nations . . . ."[45] More specifically she writes:
". . . the change will be so profound that other nations will
be forced to admit that their attitude to her [Israel = the
servant] must have been wrong: so her very suffering will be
transformed into a means of bringing other nations to worship
her God."[46]

One might ask, however, whether the text of Isaiah 53
allows such a direct joining together of the idea of Israel's
mission as "a light to the nations" and the affirmation that
"with his stripes we are healed." Miss Hooker's interpretation
seems to require that the "we" of verses 4-6 be taken as a
reference to peoples other than Israel. But must not "our
griefs" and "our sorrows," on the one hand, and "our transgressions" and "our iniquities," on the other, refer to Yahweh's
punishment (devastation and exile) for Israel's sin?

Perhaps all that one can say with relative certainty--
especially in light of Orlinsky's comments--is that the servant's suffering somehow eventuates in the healing and making
whole of the people of God.[47] Whether the prophet intended to
speak of "vicarious expiatory suffering," however, is very
much open to question.

One additional observation seems appropriate at this
point. If one decides that Isaiah 53 does indeed present the
idea of vicarious expiatory suffering, he should take quite
seriously the possible implications of the fact that Second

---

[45]M. D. Hooker, Jesus and the Servant (London, 1959),
p. 61.

[46]Ibid., p. 48.

[47]This healing and being made whole is a necessary
aspect of Yahweh's restoration of Israel to her own land. In
the new exodus event the glory of Yahweh will be revealed and
"all flesh shall see it together" (Iṣ. 40:5). Israel will be
a "light to the nations" in that the nations will recognize
the power and covenant loyalty of Yahweh and will turn and
become worshippers of Israel's God. This interpretation takes
into full account a feature of Second Isaiah's thought that is
frequently overlooked, i.e., his thoroughgoing nationalism
(cf., e.g., 49:22-26). On this point see Orlinsky, op. cit.,
pp. 97-117 and N. H. Snaith, "The Servant of the Lord in
Deutero-Isaiah" in H. H. Rowley (ed.), Studies in Old Testament Prophecy (Edinburgh, 1950), pp. 191-200; also: Snaith,
"Isaiah 40-66. A Study of the Teaching of the Second Isaiah
and Its Consequences" in Studies on the Second Part of the
Book of Isaiah, pp. 154-65.

Isaiah wrote during the exile in Babylonia. The question which this fact brings with it is: Has Second Isaiah been influenced in any way by Babylonian concepts and practices?[48] This question cannot be explored here; it can be said, however, that an affirmative answer would help to explain why Isaiah 53 is the only passage in the OT where a concept of vicarious expiatory suffering or death might be found.

D. Isaiah 53 and Post-Exilic Jewish Literature

The chief purpose of the preceding pages has been to indicate that the question of the presence and meaning of a concept of vicarious expiatory suffering in Isaiah 53 should probably be considered an open one. In the final analysis, however, what Second Isaiah intended to say is a secondary question for the present study. Of primary concern is another query: How did Jewish writers from the sixth century B.C. until the first century A.D. understand Isaiah 53? Specifically, is there textual evidence that, subsequent to Second Isaiah, chapter 53 was understood in terms of vicarious expiatory suffering? For the most part the way in which Isaiah 53 was "understood" in ancient Judaism is reflected not in commentary and exegesis but by allusions, by the borrowing of terminology or structure, or by echoes of particular ideas.

1. Zech. 12:9-10. Miss Hooker thinks it doubtful that these verses contain a reminiscence of Isaiah 53.[49] And although Wolff insists that in these verses one finds the "same message" as Isaiah 53 (i.e., "der Opfer- und Sühnetod eines Unschuldigen"), he can detect no stylistic or terminological evidence of influence from that chapter.[50] In this admission

---

[48]J. M. P. Smith and W. Irwin (The Prophets and Their Times [Chicago, [2]1941], pp. 234-37) are among the scholars who answer this question affirmatively; more specifically, they suggest that Second Isaiah was probably influenced by the Babylonian New Year's ritual. For others who adopt this view in some form cf. Scharbert, op. cit., 201-202. Scharbert himself rejects this position on the grounds that the central concepts of Is. 53 (vicarious expiatory suffering and the guilt of the "we") have no counterpart in the Babylonian ritual.

[49]Hooker, op. cit., p. 53.

[50]Wolff, op. cit., p. 40.

112

Wolff is unquestionably correct; his assertion of conceptual parallelism, however, is at best open to question.

2. Daniel 11:33-35, 12:3. Several scholars have seen in these verses an instance of direct influence by Isaiah 53 (especially 52:13 and 53:11).[51] There are terminological parallels which are probably not coincidental.[52] But, as I have noted in Chapter II, the suffering of the wise in Daniel is not the means whereby they turn many to righteousness. The conception of vicarious suffering effective for others is absent from the book of Daniel. This writing, then, can offer no evidence that Isaiah 53 was understood in such terms.[53]

3. The Septuagint. Although in LXX Isaiah 43, 49, 52: 1-12, and 54 the servant is understood collectively, Isaiah 53 LXX describes the death of a single man.[54] In describing the fate of that man, the LXX text diverges rather significantly from the MT at several points. Those deviations and their significance as clues to the translators' understanding of the servant's suffering and death must now be evaluated.

---

[51]E.g., R. H. Charles, Commentary on Daniel, p. 331; H. L. Ginsberg, "The Oldest Interpretation of the Suffering Servant," VT 3(1953), 400-404; Wolff, op. cit., pp. 38-39; Nickelsburg, op. cit., pp. 44-48.

[52]Is. 52:13: ישכיל; Dan. 12:3: המשכילים. Is. 53:11: יצדיק; Dan. 12:3: מצדיקי.

[53]Cf. Wolff, op. cit., p. 39.

[54]Karl Friedrich Euler, Die Verkündigung vom Leidenden Gottesknecht aus Jes 53 in der griechischen Bibel (Stuttgart, 1934), p. 125. From his investigation Euler concludes that in Aquila the figure of Is. 53 is apparently described as a sacrificing priest who is ignored and ostracized because of his appearance; but then his detractors recognize him as a priest of God (pp. 31-32). Symmachus sees in the suffering man the characteristics of a prophet whose suffering and martyr death have expiatory power; cf. vv. 4, 11, 12, but especially εἰς θυσίαν in v. 7 (pp. 35-36). Euler thinks that Theodotion depicts the suffering one as a Job-figure: a man who has to bear bodily suffering but throughout his ordeal nevertheless maintains his piety. Exalted (or resurrected) by God, he can now absolve those who repent of their wrongdoing toward him (pp. 39, 41). Of these three Greek translations, one should note that only Theodotion--assuming a (pre) Theodotionic translation earlier than the person by that name--has any real claim to reflect a Jewish reading of Is. 53 prior to 100 A.D.

Verse 4. For הלינו (our sickness) LXX has τὰς ἁμαρτίας
ἡμῶν (with the MT compare Vulgate and Peshitta); but an important deviation from this LXX reading is found in Matt. 8:17 (cf.
Ignatius to Polycarp 1:3), and the textual tradition at this
point exhibits further variations (Euler, p. 59). Having ana-
lyzed the evidence, Euler concludes (p. 62): "Mt 8, 17 bietet
den ursprünglicheren LXX-Text, dagegen der heutige LXX-Text ist
erst in christlicher Zeit entstanden und hat den Text von Mt 8,
17 verdrängt." If one follows Euler, then, this verse must be
eliminated as evidence for the LXX translators' understanding
of the servant's suffering. If one adopts the present LXX text
as original, however, LXX Is. 53:4 says not only that the
servant "suffers on our behalf" (περὶ ἡμῶν ὀδυνᾶται) but also
that he "bears our sins" (τὰς ἁμαρτίας ἡμῶν φέρει).

Verse 6. For MT's "the Lord caused to fall upon him
(הפגיע בו ) the iniquity of us all," LXX has: καὶ κύριος
παρέδωκεν αὐτὸν ταῖς ἁμαρτίαις ἡμῶν. The intent of the shift
in meaning from הפגיע בו (plus direct object) to παρέδωκεν
αὐτόν (plus dative) is difficult to interpret. The Greek can
be translated "the Lord delivered him up for our sins." But
the dative is subject to a different interpretation: "the
Lord delivered him up to our sins"--i.e., to their evil acts
against him. It is possible to see in this verse a reflection
of vicarious expiation, but if the translators were operating
with that concept in mind, if they understood Isaiah 53 in that
way, it is surprising that the idea is not expressed here more
forcefully, for example by ὑπέρ or περί (cf. I Clement 16:7!).[55]

Verse 10. The first clause reads: καὶ κύριος βούλεται
καθαρίσαι αὐτὸν τῆς πληγῆς. This represents a significant
divergence from the Hebrew ( ויהוה חפץ דכאו החלי ). Euler

---

[55]In verse 7, for MT לטבח LXX has ἐπὶ σφαγήν. Whereas
טבח in the OT usually refers to the slaughter of an animal
for food or the killing of men in battle, σφαγ- in Greek authors
typically has reference to the immolation of a sacrificial
victim. But nothing can be drawn from this general state of
affairs in connection with Is. 53:7 because the LXX translators
did not make such a distinction. טבח terms are frequently
translated by σφαγή (and related words). Thus while ἐπὶ
σφαγήν may indicate that the LXX translators were thinking of
the servant in terms of a sacrificial victim (so Euler, p. 119),
there is no way to demonstrate this. Vv. 11 and 12 do not
constitute proof since in the OT the sacrificial animal is
never said to "carry away" sin.

114

takes this as corroboration of his view that the servant expiates sins by taking them upon himself (vv. 8, 11, 12), for "hatte er sich bei der ταπείνωσις mit Sünden verunreinigt, so wird er nun von dem versöhnten Gott gereinigt" (p. 120). Since v. 10 says that God purified the servant, he must have been laden with the sins of others, especially in light of v. 9b. But Euler's argument cannot be considered conclusive. In the first place, according to the text the Lord does not wish to purify the servant of sins (which had been transferred to him) but τῆς πληγῆς, that is, from his sickness; compare τοῦ πόνου in the last clause of the verse. In the second place, one should note that this strange expression (the infinitive phrase) very likely has another, less "theological" explanation. The shift from דכאו to καθαρίσαι αὐτόν is probably due to the connotation of דכא in Aramaic, where it is equivalent to the Hebrew זכה : to be clear or pure. "It is no uncommon occurrence for LXX to interpret a Hebrew word in accordance with the signification borne by a word externally resembling it in the Aramaic dialect spoken at the time when the translation was made."[56]

Although the next clause is difficult in Hebrew (אם תשים נפשו אשם ), the LXX is both clear and clearly different from the MT--however the Hebrew might be rendered or the text emended: ἐὰν δῶτε περὶ ἁμαρτίας, (ἡ ψυχὴ ὑμῶν . . .). "You" refers to those people responsible for the death of the servant, "sin," that deed for which they stand guilty. If they would see their off-spring they must make an offering to expiate their sin.[57] Whereas the MT can be understood to say that the servant becomes a sin offering, in LXX v. 10 the servant is not said to affect the sin and guilt of the wicked in any way. Quite the contrary: those who killed him must make expiation for themselves! Thus the movement of the translation in v. 10 appears to be _away from_ a concept of vicarious expiation.

---

[56] S. R. Driver and A. Neubauer, _The Fifty-Third Chapter of Isaiah According to the Jewish Interpreters_ (New York, 1969; first published: 1877), p. 3, n. on v. 10. Driver and Neubauer give ten examples of this phenomenon.

[57] Euler, op. cit., p. 27. In Euler's view this verse determines the special connotation of ἁμαρτία and ἀνομία throughout the entire passage: ". . . sie bezeichnen geradezu die Schuld am Tode des παῖς (vs 6)."

The deviations of the LXX from the MT which have been noted here do not compel the conclusion that the translators worked under the influence of a conception of vicarious expiatory suffering. With the possible exception of v. 4 there is no instance in Isaiah 53 of an expression which can be understood as the translators' intensification of an idea of vicarious suffering.[58] If such an idea had been operative it is difficult to explain why, at several points where a vicarious interpretation would have been appropriate, the movement seems to be away from such an interpretation.[59] Nevertheless, the uncertainty regarding the original LXX reading in v. 4 prevents a final and conclusive judgment about the translators' conception of the meaning of the servant's death.

4. II Maccabees. H. W. Wolff finds several terminological parallels between Isaiah 53 and II and IV Maccabees. The alleged parallels with IV Maccabees will be considered later. Here I note only the two in II Maccabees to which Wolff points. Παιδεία is found at II 7:33 and LXX Is. 53:5; but a word used so frequently in the LXX, often to translate מוסר, is no proof of anything. Wolff compares the prayers and entreaties of the martyr for his people (II 7:37f.) with Is. 53:12. But the Bible read by the author of II Maccabees was probably a Greek version. Neither the LXX nor the other Greek versions, however, contain terms of intercession or supplication in Is. 53:12; and terms of "bearing" or "taking away" the sin of others are not used in II Maccabees 6 or 7. In fact, as I have already argued, vicarious expiatory suffering is a conception not to be found in II Maccabees at all. This writing, then, cannot serve as evidence that Is. 53 was understood in such terms.

5. Wisdom of Solomon. H. W. Wolff has written:

Here we find . . . for the first time such clear reminiscences of Is. 53 that not only can one speak of the borrowing of individual motifs; one must speak as well

---

[58] Verse 4 would be an exception only if one disagrees with Euler and argues that the present LXX reading ("he bears our sins") is original.

[59] Note especially "you" (ἐὰν δῶτε) at v. 10 and the dative (v. 6) instead of ὑπέρ or περί (cf. also ἀπό in v. 8 and διά in vv. 5 and 12).

116

of an actual interpretation of the servant. For here
in 5:1ff. the author apparently has followed the ancient
prophecy verse for verse.[60]

In this chapter and in chapter 2 numerous parallels with Isaiah
53 can be cited.[61] As for themes or concepts, that which most
prominently reflects Deutero-Isaiah is the affliction of the
righteous by the wicked and God's subsequent vindication of the
suffering righteous. This being the case, it is all the more
remarkable that the idea of vicarious suffering is completely
absent from the Wisdom of Solomon.[62]

6. I Enoch. Several scholars have detected conceptual
and terminological parallels between Second Isaiah and I Enoch
which point to the influence of the former upon the latter.
Strack-Billerbeck, followed by J. Jeremias, among others,[63]
maintain that the designation "the righteous one" in the parables of Enoch (38:2; 47:1, 4; 53:6) is taken from Is. 53:11 and
that the attitude of the kings of the earth toward the Son of
Man/Elect One (46:4, 62:5f.) is described according to Is. 52:
13-15. Nickelsburg[64] notes several similarities between Is.
52-53, Wisdom and I Enoch 62-63 and concludes (p. 146):
"Wisdom and Enoch represent a common interpretation and
reworking of Isaiah 52-53." Even when this Deutero-Isaianic
influence is accepted as probable, however, one must not overlook one additional--and rather important--fact: although the
righteous are said to have been persecuted (En. 46:8 and ch.
47) and will be vindicated (ch. 50), the Son of Man in the
Parables does not suffer. "If some of the attributes of the
Son of Man have in fact been taken from the Servant, therefore,

---

[60]Wolff, op. cit., p. 45.

[61]Cf. 2:19 and 53:7, 2:20 and 53:8; λογίζεσθαι at 5:4
and 53:3; ἄτιμος at 5:4 and ἠτιμάσθη at 53:3; ἐπλανήθημεν at
5:6 and 53:6; ὁδός at 5:6, 7 and 53:6. Ibid., p. 46.

[62]Ibid., p. 47; Hooker, op. cit., p. 54.

[63]Strack-Billerbeck, I, p. 481; J. Jeremias, "Erlöser
und Erlösung im Spätjudentum und Urchristentum," in Deutsche
Theologie II. Der Erlösungsgedanke (Göttingen, 1929), pp. 109-
10. Cf. also W. Manson, Jesus the Messiah (Philadelphia, 1946)
pp. 145, 235-36; W. D. Davies, Paul and Rabbinic Judaism
(London, 1955), pp. 279-80.

[64]Nickelsburg, op. cit., pp. 141-46.

the absence in Enoch of the idea of suffering, which is the
most distinctive feature of the Servant, is the more remarkable."[65]

7. Qumran. The Isaiah scroll IQIs[a] exhibits numerous
minor variations from the MT and a few more important ones, but
none which, for present purposes, affects the text significantly.
The only possible exception to this statement is the reading
משחתי (for MT משחת) in 52:14. William H. Brownlee has argued
that the Qumran sectaries, taking advantage of the ambiguity of
the original reading, altered it to mean "I anointed . . . ."[66]
Accordingly, Isaiah 53 was apparently understood by the sect as
a description of the suffering messiah. Although the added
final yod in the Qumran reading is problematic, Brownlee's
solution creates more problems than it solves.[67] Even if
Brownlee's interpretation be accepted, however, it does not
constitute evidence that bears on the question of whether the
sectaries saw in Isaiah 53 the idea of vicarious suffering.

One must also ask whether other Qumran documents appear
to reflect an understanding of Isaiah 53 in terms of vicarious
suffering. Although echoes of the language in Second Isaiah
are found in the scrolls, it is extremely questionable whether
certain passages in IQS contain allusions to the servant of
Second Isaiah, as Brownlee would have us believe.[68] Nickelsburg thinks that at IQH 4.8 the author uses the language of
Isaiah 53 (despised, not esteemed).[69] But there is no reference in IQS, IQH or any other Qumran writing to the idea that
the suffering of the servant in Second Isaiah brings salvation
to others.[70]

8. I Baruch. The song of lamentation and comfort at
4:5-5:9 has been influenced by the language and ideas of Second

---

[65]Hooker, op. cit., p. 54; cf. Wolff, op. cit., p. 43.

[66]Brownlee, "The Servant of the Lord in the Qumran
Scrolls," BASOR 132(1953), 10-12.

[67]Cf. Joseph Reider, "On MŠHTY in the Qumran Scrolls,"
BASOR 134(1954), 27, 28. Brownlee, in replies on the same
pages, does not successfully refute Reider's criticism.

[68]Brownlee, op. cit., 135(1954), 33-38. Brownlee's
propensity for overinterpretation is apparent in his designation of IQS 8.5-10 and 4.15-23 as "two important Servant
sections" (33)!

[69]Nickelsburg, op. cit., p. 175.

[70]Whether the concept of vicarious expiatory suffering
is to be found in any form in the Qumran scrolls is a question
which will be dealt with in the following section.

118

Isaiah.[71] But neither in these verses nor elsewhere in Baruch does the author show any acquaintance with a conception of vicarious suffering.

9. **IV Ezra.** Allusions to Isaiah 53 in IV Ezra are questionable.[72] Of course, "my servant (or son) the anointed one" does die (7:29), but: 1) so do all other men; 2) he is not put to death by men; 3) prior to his death he does not in any way suffer--7:28 implies the contrary.[73] Most importantly, the death of this figure has no saving or expiatory function whatsoever.[74] Even if the language of IV Ezra 4 and 9:38-10:28 echo passages in Deutero-Isaiah,[75] such echoes are insignificant beside the recognition that IV Ezra's response to the problem of Israel's suffering does not include the idea of vicarious suffering.[76] Consequently IV Ezra is useless as evidence that Isaiah 53 was understood in terms of vicarious expiatory suffering.

10. **II Baruch.** II Baruch, too, wrestles with the problem of sin and suffering, but he is more easily satisfied-- satisfied with a more traditional solution than was IV Ezra. He declares that the righteous who suffer in this world will, in the next, be given a crown with great glory (15:7-8). II Baruch's problem of sin is solved: because of one's present suffering, God pardons sins completely while one lives upon

---

[71]O. C. Whitehouse in AP, I, pp. 591-95, various notes.

[72]Against Jeremias, "Erlöser," 110-11. Even if one should read "my servant the anointed" at 7:29, that designation by no means points necessarily to Second Isaiah, as Jeremias insists it does. Nor is it likely that 13:33 contains an echo of Is. 53, as Wolff (op. cit., p. 44) suggests.

[73]Jeremias' opinion needs no comment: ". . . angesichts der Bezugnahme auf den Gottesknecht des Deuterojesaja [ist] ein Heilswert des Todes des Erlösers nicht ausgeschlossen" ("Erlöser," 110).

[74]Cf. Wolff, op. cit., pp. 44-45, who cites Volz and Bultmann.

[75]Hooker, op. cit., p. 59.

[76]Cf. 4:26; 6:18f., 27f.; 7:16: the end will bring appropriate reward and retribution. But this answer has problems: what about those who die before the end (5:41)? Answer: the resurrection will enable them to share the eternal reward (5:42, cf. 7:32). But the seer finds this solution ultimately unsatisfactory since all men are sinners, due to Adam's sin (cf. 7:119-126). If the seer can find little comfort in the knowledge that "few shall be saved" (8:3 with

earth. Thus does suffering actually become a positive asset in view of the future life![77]

Since I Baruch, IV Ezra, and II Baruch attempt to deal with the same problem as does Second Isaiah--that is, Israel's sin and suffering--one might expect to find significant use of the servant figure. Furthermore, if the authors of these writings understood Isaiah 53 in terms of vicarious suffering, one might expect some trace of that concept in their work, either because they accepted it and found it useful or because they disagreed and rejected it. In neither case is the expectation fulfilled. These three writings give no evidence that Isaiah 53 was understood as a statement about the great worth of vicarious suffering. One might go even further and suggest that they are negative evidence; that is, they seem to indicate that Isaiah 53 was not so understood--at least not in the first centuries B.C. and A.D. in the circles from which I Baruch, IV Ezra and II Baruch came.[78]

11. Targum of Jonathan.[79] To what degree the Targum reflects midrashic tendencies in vogue prior to, say, 100 A.D. is an open question. The Targum on Isaiah 53 may reflect an anti-Christian interpretation of the prophet's words,[80] but one cannot say with certainty that it represents the rejection of and polemic against an opposing conception. Jeremias' view is founded on the presupposition that the Suffering Servant idea of Isaiah 53 was much more influential in the early church than

---

vv. 4ff.), he must finally be satisfied with the assurance that God's ways are inscrutable to man (e.g., 4:1-11).

[77]Cf. W. Wichmann, op. cit., pp. 32-40, 48. For the relationship between IV Ezra and II Baruch: pp. 43-50. Wichmann argues that II Baruch was written as a polemic against IV Ezra, whose revolutionary attitudes the author found intolerable. Other scholars argue for a literary relationship in the opposite direction.

[78]Cf. Hooker, op. cit., pp. 58-59.

[79]For pertinent literature cf. Cullmann, op. cit., p. 58.

[80]So, following Dalman, J. Jeremias, "Zum Problem der Deutung von Jesaja 53 im palästinischen Spätjudentum," in Aux Sources de la Tradition Chrétienne (Neuchatel, 1950), pp. 114-15, 118-19.

Miss Hooker has shown it to have actually been. The targumic
interpreter seems rather to have been interested in the positive
messianic use of the text.[81] In any case, in the Targum Isaiah
53 is consciously a description of "my servant the messiah"
(52:13). But the more remarkable feature is that the servant
messiah does not suffer! All suffering in the passage is interpreted either as punishment to befall the Gentiles (53:3, 7, 11)
or as God's purifying chastisement of his people (53:10). The
messiah does not "bear" the sins of the people. Rather he
prays for their sins and they are forgiven for his sake (53:4,
cf. v. 6); by his instruction and by devotion to his words the
sins of the people are forgiven (53:5). There is present the
idea of transference of sin, but it is the Gentiles who have
transferred to them the sins which Israel has committed (53:8)!
Totally absent, then, is any hint of an idea that the servant
(messiah) suffers vicariously and thereby expiates the sins of
his people.

From the foregoing one can only conclude that Jewish
writings subsequent to Second Isaiah provide no evidence that
Isaiah 53 was understood as the picture of a figure whose suffering expiates the sins of his fellows. The authors of the
works considered may have wondered what the prophet meant by
some of his statements, but--judging from echoes and illusions,
borrowing of ideas and terminology, and translations into Greek
and Aramaic--they did not think that he intended to say that
the servant's suffering effected expiation of sins. Rather
they seem to have understood Isaiah 53 as a prototypical biblical example of the persecution of the righteous man and his
vindication by God. At least in several cases (Daniel, Wisdom,
I Enoch) the tradition of the suffering and vindication of the
righteous man appears to have developed, in part, from Isaiah
53.[82]

---

[81]Cullmann, op. cit., p. 60.

[82]Cf. Nickelsburg, op. cit., pp. 44-48, 121-25, 141-46.
On pp. 162-63 Nickelsburg writes: "At some time between the
writing of Second Isaiah and the time of Antiochus, civil persecution of (the religious leaders of) the Jews led to the interpretation of Isaiah 52-53 as a scene of the post-mortem
exaltation of the persecuted ones and the (impending) judgment
of their persecutors. This interpretation was crystallized in
a tradition that preserved the basic structure of the servant
poem and conflated with it materials from Isaiah 13 and 14,

IV.  Vicarious Expiatory Suffering and Death in Judaism Prior
to A.D. 70

A.  Introduction

The investigation of the preceding section has yielded
two results significant for the present study:  1) With the
possible exception of Isaiah 53, the OT fails to exhibit a
conception of vicarious expiatory suffering; 2) even if such
a concept underlies and is expressed by Isaiah 53, one must
recognize that evidence for such an understanding of this
chapter in Jewish writings from the sixth century B.C. to ca.
100 A.D. is not forthcoming.  The vicarious suffering of Isaiah
53 would even appear to be an anomaly in the entire spectrum
of Jewish thought prior to Jamnia.

Such an impression would be controverted at once by
numerous scholars who claim that the idea that a righteous man
can suffer or die vicariously for the sins of others was a
widespread theologumenon in Judaism prior to the destruction
of the Temple.  This claim has, in fact, become at least as
widespread among modern scholars as the supposed first century
theologumenon is thought to have been.  It is necessary, therefore, to include in this chapter a careful examination of the
texts to which scholars frequently point as evidence for the
pre-70 A.D. concept of vicarious expiatory suffering and death.

B.  Rabbinic Sources--and Josephus

Eduard Schweizer has written as a self-evident fact:
"The idea that the suffering and death of the righteous . . .
atone vicariously for the sins of others is so widespread that
we will only mention where to find the evidence."[83]  The most

---

using them to describe the judgment/punishment of the persecutors.  This conflate tradition . . . emerged as a new entity
unto itself which then pursues its own form history.  Elements
within this form develop without reference back to its Isaianic
roots and often in a direction that moves away from these
roots."

[83]Schweizer, Lordship and Discipleship (London, 1960),
p. 26.

important primary sources to which he points as evidence are: II Maccabees 7:37f., IV Maccabees 1:11, 6:28, 17:20ff.; the texts cited in Strack-Billerbeck II, pp. 278-82 and in G. F. Moore, Judaism, I, pp. 546ff.

I have already taken the position (Chapter II) that the idea of vicarious expiatory suffering is not present in II Maccabees. Thus I must hold that Schweizer's first proof text does not support his contention. Such an idea is found in IV Maccabees although within a particular context which is frequently not taken into account.[84] That this concept is found in IV Maccabees does not necessarily mean that it was familiar throughout all branches of first century Judaism.

Both Strack-Billerbeck and Moore cite the IV Maccabees passages plus numerous rabbinic texts. Regarding the latter, it is striking that a great majority of the rabbis who are quoted lived in the third and fourth centuries. Even the few significant exceptions[85] do not antedate 135 A.D. Thus the crucial observation to be made regarding every one of the texts cited by Moore and Strack-Billerbeck is this: the traditions which they reflect regarding expiatory death have no certain claim to a first century date!

This situation does not appear to bother many students of first century Judaism who confidently cite one rabbinic text after another to support the contention that the idea of vicarious expiatory death was a natural and normal item of belief among first century Jews. Their confidence appears to rest upon an unspoken presupposition regarding the origin and continuity of rabbinic tradition, that is, that due to an intrinsic stability, the theology reflected in the Targums and in rabbinic writings represents essentially the uninterrupted continuation of pre-70 and pre-Christian Pharisaic theology-- further developed, of course, but unaltered in its essentials. A corollary assumption follows easily: Any important post-70 doctrine must have been present, at least in its rudiments, in pre-70 Pharisaic Judaism.

---

[84]Cf. infra, Chapter V.

[85]pSanh 11, 30c, 28: R. Jochanan (died 279) said in the name of R. Simon ben Zakkai (ca. 150) . . .; Mekilta Ex. 12:1 (2a): R. Jonathan (ca. 140) said . . . .

Such assumptions as these have not been without their detractors recently. With specific reference to B. Gerhardsson's Memory and Manuscript, Morton Smith[86] refers to a study by G. 'Allon which shows that such revolutionaries as Akiba were by no means utterly conservative or "bound to tradition," for A.D. 65-140 were years of revolution in Palestine and of consequent religious readjustment. Smith notes that most of the relatively few halakoth preserved from the last days of the Second Temple are anonymous and he sees this as proof that a radical change did take place after A.D. 70.

J. Neusner, discussing some implications of E. R. Goodenough's basic hypothesis, suggests that ". . . the impact of the catastrophic events of 70 and 132-35 C.E. is reflected in new concern for personal, as well as cosmic, salvation . . . ."[87] Neusner is thinking specifically of such manifestations as merkabah mysticism and the adoption of pagan symbols, but his observation may well have relevance to the development of the concept of vicarious expiatory death.

Commenting on the work of J. Jeremias and E. Lohse, John Downing expresses the opinion that these scholars fail to take into account the influence which the events of A.D. 70 and 132-35 exerted on Jewish (especially rabbinic) thinking about the meaning of suffering. Thus his scepticism regarding ". . . the value of producing catenae of third-century rabbinic statements about the substitutionary power of suffering. For there is no statement to this effect in rabbinic sources which can be dated before the Bar Cocheba rising."[88]

The position that the doctrine of vicarious expiatory suffering and death among the rabbis is a post-70 development has at least one explicit rabbinic statement in its favor. It is associated with the name of R. Hoshaya (ca. 225).

> Moses said to God: 'Will not the time come when Israel shall have neither Tabernacle nor Temple [i.e., as a pledge, to prevent destruction]? What will happen with

---

[86] M. Smith, "A Comparison of Early Christian and Early Rabbinic Tradition," JBL 82(1963), 169-76.

[87] J. Neusner, "Jewish Use of Pagan Symbols after 70 C.E.," Journal of Religion 43(1963), 293.

[88] J. Downing, "Jesus and Martyrdom," JTS 14(1963), 280. Downing (279) observes that his view is supported by Büchler's investigation in Studies in Sin and Atonement.

them then?' The divine reply was: 'I will then take one of their righteous men and retain him as a pledge on their behalf, in order that I may pardon all their sins.' Thus too it says, And He hath slain all that were pleasant to the eye (Lam. II, 4).[89]

Here it is clearly because of the destruction of the Temple that it is necessary for God to "take"--apparently by death--a righteous man to expiate Israel's sins.

In light of the preceding it would appear that scholars who create a first century doctrine of vicarious atoning death out of traditions which are first attested in the second century are proceeding on risky methodological assumptions. They do, however, have one card yet to be played. Strack-Billerbeck (II, p. 275) write: "Wie geläufig diese Vorstellung vom stellvertretenden Leiden gewesen ist, beweist der alte Ausruf pietätvoller Liebe u. Verehrung: Ich will eine Sühne sein für den u. den אֲנִי כַפָּרָה!" The initial text to which Strack-Billerbeck refer (p. 280) is Sifre Num. 161 on 35:34 (62b). In this passage the phrase is used by a man involved in an episode which evidently occurred before the destruction of the Temple.[90]

With regard to this text several observations are in order. 1) The origin of the pertinent phrase is uncertain and its precise reference is unclear. In the parallel texts, for example, there is some disparity between the first and third persons--thus a question about whether the subject (i.e., the "expiation") is the slain priest or his surviving father. 2) The expression does not appear in texts which can be dated prior to A.D. 70. In the rabbinic writings the earliest rabbi with whom it is associated is R. Ishmael. 3) The form כפרה is not found in the OT or in those Qumran texts covered by Kuhn's concordance.[91] 4) The only evidence that the phrase

---

[89]Ex. Rabbah 35 to 26:15 (95a), trans. S. M. Lehrman in H. Freedman and Maurice Simon (eds.), Midrash Rabbah. Vol. 3: Exodus (London: Soncino Press, 1939), p. 432.

[90]Parallels given by Strack-Billerbeck are TJoma 1,12 (181); TSchebu 1,4 (446); pJoma 39d, 13; Joma 23a. Other texts, are (Str.-B. III, on Rom. 9:3:) Sanh. 2,1 and Neg. 2,1 (R. Ishmael, died ca. 135), the only two pertinent Mishnaic texts; Sifra Lev. 13:2 (235a); Qid. 31b Bar.; Sukka 20a; Jeb. 70a Bar.

[91]Karl Georg Kuhn, Konkordanz zu den Qumrantexten (Göttingen, 1960).

itself is early (i.e., pre-70) is the fact that it occurs in an
episode whose setting is the Jerusalem Temple. The crucial
question then becomes: Is the report of the father's words
historically accurate; or does the story as one finds it in
Sifre Num. and parallel texts, even if based on an historical
incident, include the embellishments of subsequent tradition--
among them the phrase אני כפרה ? The likelihood, or at least
the possibility, of the second alternative again calls into
question the methodological soundness of the attempt to argue
from the Sifre Num. text (and parallels) to the existence of a
doctrine of vicarious atoning death in pre-70 Judaism.

Although he holds that "Der Gedanke einer stellvertretenden Sühne liegt hier nicht vor" (i.e., in the Sifre Num.
text and par.), Eduard Lohse asserts that Paul (Rom. 9:3) and
Josephus (War 5.419) are testimony to the great antiquity of
this "Jewish formula."[92] This view is untenable. The relevant
sentence in Josephus reads: ἀποκτείνατε αὐτούς, λάβετε μισθὸν τῆς
ἑαυτῶν σωτηρίας τὸ ἐμὸν αἷμα · κἀγὼ θνήσκειν ἕτοιμος, εἰ μετ'
ἐμὲ σωφρονεῖν μέλλετε. This statement comes toward the end of
a long and impassioned speech in which Josephus himself pleads
with the citizens of Jerusalem to abandon their futile struggle
against the Romans. Immediately preceding the quotation he
voices his awareness that his fellow Jews might think that his
advice to capitulate is given "because of them"--that is,
because of his concern for his family's safety. Whatever the
meaning of his words, then, the purpose of Josephus' expression
of his willingness to die and have his family killed is to
demonstrate that his advice is not motivated by selfish personal reasons. The μισθὸν . . . αἷμα statement, however, is
probably not a Greek rephrase of אני כפרה . It certainly has
nothing to do with sin and expiation; "salvation" here simply
means the avoidance of total destruction by the Roman army.
Just how Josephus thinks that his death might effect the deliverance of his people is not clear. In attempting to interpret his words allowance must surely be made for his desire for
dramatic effect. Nevertheless his language ("my blood as the
price for your salvation") does seem to express the underlying
idea that the death of one individual can have beneficial
effects for others. It will be seen in the present study that

[92]Lohse, op. cit., p. 101.

126

in first century Judaism one finds clear expression of this idea in only one other writing: IV Maccabees. Regarding Rom. 9:3 (ηὐχόμην γὰρ ἀνάθεμα εἶναι αὐτὸς ἐγὼ ἀπὸ τοῦ Χριστοῦ ὑπὲρ τῶν ἀδελφῶν μου . . .), the assertion that "behind this statement stands the Jewish concept of vicarious expiatory suffering" (so Lohse) cannot be demonstrated. More likely, Paul's words are an expression of intense loyalty and concern, entirely understandable without reference to this concept.[93]

C. Testament of Benjamin 3:8

With one exception, Eduard Lohse offers no additional texts of significance as evidence that vicarious expiatory suffering was a familiar theologumenon in first century Judaism. The exception is one of the few pertinent texts for which Lohse explicitly claims a pre-Christian date: Testament of Benjamin 3:8.[94]

The textual problem is complicated.[95] Lohse notes the Christian interpolations in the Greek and Slavonic MSS

---

[93]Even if Lohse (and Strack-Billerbeck, whom he follows) is right, I would argue that one should posit that behind Paul's statement stands not a widespread theologumenon but a particular idea at home in rather limited circles of first century Judaism. Cf. infra, Chapter V.

[94]Lohse, op. cit., pp. 85-87.

[95]For a critical text based on the Greek MSS, with variants in the Armenian and Slavonic versions, cf. R. H. Charles, The Greek Versions of the Testaments of the Twelve Patriarchs (Oxford, 1908). I reproduce here the pertinent verse, minus critical apparatus, from Charles' text:

| c, β, s¹ | A |
|---|---|
| 8. Πληρωθήσεται περὶ σοῦ προφητεία οὐράνιος [περὶ τοῦ ἀμνοῦ τοῦ θεοῦ καὶ σωτῆρος τοῦ κόσμου], ὅτι ἄμωμος ὑπὸ ἀνόμων παραδοθήσεται καὶ ὁ ἀναμάρτητος ὑπὲρ ἀσεβῶν ἀποθανεῖται [ἐν αἵματι διαθήκης ἐπὶ σωτηρίᾳ ἐθνῶν καὶ τοῦ Ἰσραὴλ καὶ καταλύσει Βελίαρ καὶ τοὺς ὑπηρέτας αὐτοῦ]. | 8. Πληρωθήσεται ἐπὶ σὲ ἡ προφητεία οὐράνιος ἢ λέγει ὅτι ὁ ἄμωμος ὑπὲρ ἀνόμων μιανθήσεται καὶ ὁ ἀναμάρτητος ὑπὲρ ἀσεβῶν ἀποθανεῖται. |

(bracketed in Charles' text) but sees no reason for considering
the Armenian version of v. 8 a Christian addition:

Denn es finden sich zwar christliche Interpolationen
an verschiedenen Stellen der Testamente--aber immer
dort, wo schon vorher ein Anknüpfungspunkt vorhanden
war, um christliche Gedanken einzuschieben. Es muss
also an unserer Stelle bereits vor der christlichen
Überarbeitung eine Leidensaussage gestanden haben,
wie sie uns die armenische Version bietet. Sonst
wäre es unerklärlich, warum die Christen ohne jede
Veranlassung gerade in ein Wort über den Stamm Joseph
eine Deutung auf Jesu Leiden eingefügt haben sollten,
da Jesus mit dem Stamm Joseph nichts zu tun hatte,
sondern aus dem Geschlecht Davids kam.[96]

Lohse rejects as "hardly correct" the view of J. Jeremias
that one can see in this text traces of an early tradition about
a suffering Messiah ben Joseph--a tradition which can be documented no earlier than the second century A.D. and even then
includes nothing about the expiatory effect of his death.[97]
His scepticism is fully supported by TJoseph 19:11: a messianic
figure will arise from Judah and Levi! What does Lohse do
with TBenj. 3:8 then? "Wohl aber ist es gut denkbar, dass man
Joseph . . . als einen Gerechten angesehen hat, der stellvertretend für andere sühnt."[98] But this is no solution at all to
the problems raised by the text. Not only is it incompatible
with the future verb ("will be fulfilled," but Joseph had
already suffered at the hands of his brothers); it also presupposes the concept of vicarious expiation for which TBenj.
is, outside IV Maccabees, Lohse's only certainly pre-Christian
evidence! And yet one must agree with Lohse, for the reasons
he gives, that it is impossible to explain the whole of v. 8
as a Christian interpolation. What, then, is the alternative
to his non-solution?

---

[96]Lohse, op. cit., p. 86. For a study of Christian
interpolations throughout the Testaments see J. Jervell, "Ein
Interpolator interpretiert. Zu der christlichen Bearbeitung
der Testamente der Zwölf Patriarchen" in Studien zu den Testamenten der Zwölf Patriarchen (Berlin, 1969), pp. 30-61.

[97]Cf. also M. Rese, "Überprüfung einiger Thesen von
Joachim Jeremias zum Thema des Gottesknechtes im Judentum,"
ZTK 60(1963), 25-28.

[98]Lohse, op. cit., pp. 86-87.

The basic fact that any adequate "solution" must take into account is that as it stands in the Armenian version TBenj. 3:8 simply does not make sense, either as a statement about Joseph himself or as a prediction about a descendant of Joseph. For reasons already noted it is extremely improbable that this is a reference to a Messiah ben Joseph. On the other hand, nowhere does one find evidence of a tradition which includes the idea that Joseph died for anyone. The brief statement about Joseph's death at TJos. 20:4-5 certainly gives no hint of such an idea, nor does any statement in TBenj. In fact, TBenj. 3:4 in the Greek and Slavonic MSS implies quite the contrary. It is difficult to reconcile peaceful death at a ripe old age with the notion of a vicarious death "for" others.

The fact that in v. 8 the Armenian version has no immediately self-evident Christian interpolations does not automatically demonstrate that every word and phrase in the Armenian version is a preferred reading over the Greek MS tradition. Charles himself considers παραδοθήσεται of MS c and the recension β (plus S[1]) preferable to μιανθήσεται of A; he also prefers the reading ὑπὸ ἀνόμων of c to ὑπὲρ ἀνόμων of β, S, and A. Now if this reading is taken as the original, we have an obvious difference of meaning between the two clauses of the ὅτι statement: a blameless one will be delivered up by lawless men; the sinless one will die for ungodly men. According to TJos. and TBenj. the first statement is completely understandable as a "prophecy" of Joseph's fate at the hands of his brothers. The second statement is not understandable; nor would it be if one reads ὑπέρ (instead of ὑπὸ) ἀνόμων.

I suggest, then, that the phrase ὁ ἀναμάρτητος ὑπὲρ ἀσεβῶν ἀποθανεῖται, found in all extant MSS, is a Christian interpolation which had occurred already in an archetypal copy from which the entire MS tradition known to us is descended.[99] The trigger for this interpolation would have been the preceding phrase, which recalled the Christian interpretation of Jesus' death as a fulfillment of prophecy and thus set up an

---

[99] For a parallel phenomenon (i.e., a Christian alteration which was present in an archetypal copy and has entered all MS families) cf. "virgin" at TJos. 19:8 and Charles' note thereon; also J. Jeremias, "Das Lamm, das aus der Jungfrau hervorging," ZNW 57(1966), 219: "Ergebnis: Test. Jos. 19,8 ist christlich . . . ."

ad hoc Joseph-Jesus typology which was elaborated with a corresponding phrase.[100] Supporting this hypothesis is the fact that,
in the Greek MS tradition, ἄμωμος is anarthrous and therefore
indefinite whereas ὁ ἀναμάρτητος (the reading of c, preferred
by Charles over β, where the article is omitted) is definite.
The definite noun--the, i.e., a particular, sinless one--can
reasonably be viewed as a reference to Jesus. The strongest
support for the proposed hypothesis, however, is the difficulty
of understanding "the sinless one will die for ungodly men" as
a "prophecy" about Joseph. This statement does not at all fit
into the context of the Greek or Armenian versions. On the
other hand the first part of the ὅτι clause, while it may seem
inappropriate and intrusive at this point, is not totally
incongruous in the context of Joseph's request for Jacob to
pray that God would not reckon his brothers' evil against him
as sin (3:6-7) and of Benjamin's exhortation to imitate Joseph's
mercy and compassion (chapter 4).

I see only one major problem with the proposal that, in
its original form, TBenj. 3:8 included only a single clause
after ὅτι. That is the future verb πληρωθήσεται. For if "you"
refers to Joseph himself, the prophecy must already have been
fulfilled in Joseph's past experience and that fact was being
expressed in the present by Jacob. To this dilemma two solutions are possible. 1) Πληρωθήσεται is the rendering by a dis-
interested (i.e., non-Christian!) translator of the Semitic
imperfect. Compare Eccl. 1:8 and 6:7 where in the LXX πληρωθήσεται (with a different sense, however) translates MT תמלא,
although from the context it is clear that a future event is
not involved. 2) More likely, the future tense is due to a
Christian redactor who wanted to suggest that the heavenly
prophecy about a righteous man being delivered up by (or for)
lawless men would be fulfilled in the death of Christ. Quite
possibly this redactional hand is also responsible for the
addition of the second part of the ὅτι clause in all extant
MSS of TBenj.

Admittedly my hypothesis cannot be proved conclusively.
My intention in presenting it here has been to suggest that a

---

[100]It is misleading for Lohse to say that there is "no
motive" in the text for the interpolations of the Greek MSS

sufficient number of questions can be raised against Lohse's confident assumption (i.e., that the Armenian version preserves the original text at 3:8) to render unacceptable the assertion that TBenj. 3:8 is unassailable evidence of a first century doctrine of vicarious expiatory death.

## D. Qumran

A. Dupont-Sommer has asserted, without reservations of any kind, that ". . . it is impossible to overlook the fact that the doctrine of atonement for the sins of others was fundamental to the sect . . . ."[101] This statement is imprecise, for it is not clear whether "atonement for the sins of others" differs from the function of the Jerusalem priesthood. Accompanying statements are open to further questions, for Dupont-Sommer thinks that the Righteous Teacher naturally shared this "doctrine" and therefore understood his own sufferings in terms of vicarious expiation for the sins of others!

I do not wish to undertake an inquiry into the self-understanding of the Righteous Teacher. Rather, in the following paragraphs I will look briefly at those texts which Dupont-Sommer considers evidence for "the doctrine of atonement for the sins of others": IQS 8.6, 10; 9.4; Saying of Moses 3.11, 4.3. Again the central question will be: Do these texts reflect any conception of vicarious expiatory suffering?

IQS 8.5-7:

The council of the community will be established in truth
for (ʔ) an eternal planting:
a house of holiness for (ʔ) Israel
and a company of great holiness for (ʔ) Aaron,
witnesses of truth
    for (ʔ) judgment

---

unless the original text was equivalent to the Armenian version at v. 8. The phrase προφητεία οὐράνιος and the initial clause of the ὅτι statement (whether one reads ὑπό or ὑπέρ are quite sufficient inducements for a Christian interpolator to expand the ὅτι clause in an explicitly Christian direction.

[101]Dupont-Sommer, The Essene Writings from Qumran (Cleveland, 1961), p. 366, n. 1.

and the chosen of (divine) favor
to make expiation for the land ( לכפר בעד הארץ )
and to bring upon the wicked their recompense.

IQS 8.10:

They will be the ones who are acceptable ( היו לרצון )
to make expiation for the land ( לכפר בעד הארץ )
and to decree the judgment of wickedness.

In both texts the word רצון occurs. Often in the OT this term
has to do with being favored or found acceptable to God. This
idea is completely compatible with the present context. The
community is chosen, elected by God, and is therefore acceptable
before Him as those who shall make expiation for the land (or
earth).

In both texts the expiation idea is immediately connected
with and paralleled by a statement about the community's
responsibility to judge or punish evil. Whether this and the
expiatory function are constant responsibilities or are to be
exercised only at the very end of the age is not clear from the
texts.

The term ארץ is also ambiguous. It could mean the
whole earth as man's dwelling place, distinct from heaven (cf.
IQM 10.8, 12; 12.5; IQH 1.13, 3.32, 8.23, 13.9, 16.3). One
could compare Jubilees 6:2, where it is said that Noah "made
expiation for the earth" and "for all the guilt of the earth"
(cf. Gen. 8:20-22 where this idea is missing). Noah is not
making expiation for the sins of others, since all life was
destroyed by the flood except the men and animals on the ark.
He is, rather, purifying the earth itself which had been defiled
by the sins of men. On the other hand, ארץ could mean "land"
in these two texts (cf. CD 5.20, 21; also IQM 10.7, 9; 12.12 =
19.4; IQH 4.8, 8.4; CD 1.8, 3.10). The close connection between making expiation for the land and requiting the wicked
may point to the sort of idea represented best of all by Deut.
32:39-43, where God, by taking vengeance on his adversaries,
"makes expiation for his land, his people" (MT v. 43). If the
mere probability were not sufficient, we know from the Sayings
of Moses and from the large number of Deuteronomy MSS found at
Qumran that this biblical book was of special importance to
the sect; furthermore, IQM, especially such passages as 12.10-
12, can be considered an apocalytic expansion of the latter
part of the Song of Moses. I might call specific attention to

132

IQM 7.2 where those who purify the land are mentioned side by
side with those who strip the dead, plunder, watch the weapons,
etc.  If these parallels are sufficient to point to eschatological warfare as the context of the two texts in IQS 8, making
expiation for the land of Israel would be accomplished by the
sons of light precisely by punishing (that is, destroying) the
wicked.  In that case one must insist that no idea of vicarious
expiation is even faintly perceptible here.

If, however, the eschatological note is not predominant
in IQS 8.6, 10, the expiatory function must be a continuous and
generalized one.  But in that case it is difficult to perceive
a distinction between Qumran and the Jerusalem sacrificial
system so fundamental as to allow the novel idea of vicarious
expiatory suffering.

IQS 9.4.  The ordinances established for the ordering
of the community (9.3) are intended, in part, "to make expiation for the guilt of transgression and sinful infidelity and
for acceptance for the land ( לרצון לארץ ) . . . ."  Whose
guilt is not specified, but lines 4-5 point to members of the
sect.  The interesting assertion is made there that "the
offering of the lips in accordance with the Law shall be as an
agreeable odor of righteousness, and perfection of way shall
be as the voluntary gift of a delectable oblation" (Dupont-
Sommer's translation).  But how this "spiritual sacrifice"
makes the land acceptable before God is not clear.  Nevertheless, I cannot detect here a doctrine of atonement for the sins
of others.  Quite the contrary, each man can and should make
his own sacrifice to God:  the offering of a life totally dedicated to a striving for perfection before Him.

Sayings of Moses (= Qumran Cave I, No. 22) 3.11-4.3.
At 3.11 the clause "on the tenth day of the month they shall
make expiation" is followed by a lacuna.  At 4.1 a phrase that
can be reconstructed as "for the children of Israel and for
the earth (or land)" is preceded by a lacuna which Dupont-
Sommer thinks was occupied by the words "they shall make
expiation."[102]  At 4.3 the letters ופר להם[ ] appear.  In
this passage, then, it appears that Moses is giving instructions for the proper rituals on the Day of Atonement.

---

[102]Ibid., p. 309, n. 4.

133

Apparently expiation is to be made for the people of Israel and for the earth (or land). Whether ארץ refers to the land of Israel or to the earth, the action involved belongs to the sphere of ritual; those responsible for this ritual action are the Aaronic priests. Since the priests make expiation for the people of Israel, in some sense a "doctrine" of atonement for the sins of others is, of course, implied here. But how this differs fundamentally from the OT, as Dupont-Sommer implies, is not clear.

One further text remains for discussion. William H. Brownlee translates IQS 8.3-4 thus: "to expiate iniquity[103] through doing the right and through the anguish of the refining furnace"; this he takes to be a reference to the suffering of the community's leaders and an allusion to the servant's atoning work in Isaiah 53.[104] According to his interpretation the suffering of the leaders serves as a means of expiating the sins of other members of the community. Even on the face of it, this interpretation is improbable in light of the code of IQS 6.24-7.25 and 8.20-9.2. Ultimately Brownlee's interpretation rests fully on his translation of ב as "through" (by means of). Is this translation preferable? The text reads:

לרצת עון בעושי משפט וצרת מצרף

The ב phrase here seems to parallel the preceding ב phrase, where the preposition must have an instrumental sense ("with a firm intent and a broken spirit") and might appear to justify Brownlee's translation. One must observe, however, that "intent" and "spirit" are impersonal nouns whereas עושי should be taken as a personal participle: "those who do or practice." But after "justice" comes "and distress of the crucible (or testing)." Is this phrase dependent on the participle?--so Dupont-Sommer (p. 90), who translates "those who practice . . . and undergo . . . ." Or does it depend on the ב ?--so Brownlee: "through practicing . . . and (through) anguish . . . ." Assuming the

---

[103]To distinguish from כפר I would translate לרצת : "to make satisfaction for iniquity"; cf. Lev. 26:41, 43.

[104]Brownlee, The Meaning of the Qumran Scrolls for the Bible (New York, 1964), p. 207.

134

necessity of choosing between these two alternatives, Dupont-
Sommer's translation/interpretation is to be preferred. However,
a different solution altogether has been proposed by John Strugnell. Strugnell finds another option possible "if one may postulate the existence at Qumrân of a noun $^c$wš . . . ." Taking
this noun to mean "trouble" one could then translate: "to
expiate iniquity in the troubles of the Judgment and the affliction of the Testing."[105] At any rate, the very ambiguity of
IQS 8.3-4 renders this text questionable as evidence that the
idea of vicarious expiatory suffering was at home at Qumran.

From this brief look at Qumran texts cited by Dupont-
Sommer and Brownlee I conclude that none of them clearly enun-
ciates a principle of expiation of sin through vicarious suffering. Only one text (IQS 8.3-4) even allows debate at this point
and that text is, at best, ambiguous.

If the texts considered fail to yield positive evidence
for the concept of vicarious suffering at Qumran, others constitute what amounts to negative evidence, that is, evidence
that such a concept was not held at Qumran. The Thanksgiving
Psalms are filled with descriptions of the suffering that befell
their author.[106] And yet there is no hint that he understood
his misfortune as vicarious suffering which could effect expiation of his fellows' sins. The motif of suffering and vindication runs throughout the Hymns, but the concept of vicarious
suffering is absent. The most that can be said about the
"meaning" of his suffering is that it is interpreted as the
birth pangs of the community (cf. IQH 3.7-18). The absence of
a vicarious suffering concept is particularly interesting
alongside the importance which the prophecies of Second Isaiah
obviously had for the author of the Hymns.[107] Nor do other

---

[105]John Strugnell, "Notes on IQS 1,17-18; 8,3-4 and IQM
17, 8-9," CBQ 29(1967), 581-82. Strugnell makes the significant observation that if one detects some expiatory force in
(the suffering of) the "distress of testing," that is an interpretation "for which no clear Qumrân parallel . . . can yet be
adduced" (581).

[106]IQH 2.14-17, 23-29, 31-34; 4.8-10; 5.16-17, 22-39;
6.23-24; 8.26-35; 9.4-6, 23-25.

[107]Cf. Is. 50:4 and IQH 8.36; Is. 61:1-2 and IQH 18.14-
15; Is. 49:1 and IQH 9:29-31.

Qumran writings understand the persecution of the sect or the
Righteous Teacher in terms of suffering for the sins of others.



E.  Conclusion

On the basis of the foregoing consideration of texts
frequently cited as evidence that the concept of vicarious
expiatory suffering and death was a familiar and widespread
theologumenon in pre-70 Judaism, I conclude that the texts do
not in fact support that claim.  The concept, apparently, was
not a familiar one among first century Jews.  In fact, it can
be documented with certainty in only one pre-70 Jewish writing,
and that is IV Maccabees.

CHAPTER IV

SUFFERING AND DEATH IN GREEK AND
HELLENISTIC LITERATURE

The various sections of this chapter will strike the
reader as rather disparate--as indeed they are; for here I
intend to make neither a thorough nor a systematic investigation
of the meaning of suffering and death among the Greeks. Nor
has originality been my aim. My purpose in this chapter is
much more modest, namely, to present briefly 1) some of the
more frequently encountered views regarding the "meaning" of
suffering and death, and 2) several influential traditions or
noteworthy dramatic portrayals of suffering or death willingly
accepted because of higher principles or on behalf of other
people. The subject matter of the different sections of the
chapter was thought to be particularly appropriate and significant for the present study because of its similarity to or
(usually!) its contrast with the Jewish ideas and traditions
discussed in Chapter III or because of its potential relevance
for the subsequent analysis of IV Maccabees (Chapter V).

I. Suffering as Education

One of the most widespread views regarding the meaning
of suffering in the Greek world was that it is a discipline by
which the gods intend to educate and improve the sufferer or
to bring him to σωφρονεῖν. This understanding is succinctly
expressed by Aeschylus.[1] In the Agamemnon the Chorus proclaims

---

[1]For a discussion of the παθεῖν-μαθεῖν theme in Greek
literature (and for many additional texts) cf. H. Dörrie, Leid

138

that πάθει μάθος is a reality ordained by Zeus himself (177-78).
Later the Chorus declares: Δίκα δὲ τοῖς μὲν παθοῦσιν μαθεῖν /
ἐπιρρέπει (Ag. 250-51). In another play Aeschylus writes: ξυμ-
φέρει / σωφρονεῖν ὑπὸ στένει (Eum.520-21). In the Oedipus at
Colonus (7f.) Sophocles can have the blind Oepidus say:
στέργειν γὰρ αἱ πάθαι με . . . διδάσκει.

Challenging a view sometimes found in the poets (Homer
and Aeschylus are quoted) that the gods are responsible for
evil as well as good in human affairs, Plato asserts that men
should rather declare that "what God did was just and good, and
those who were chastised profited" (οἱ δὲ ὠνίναντο κολαζόμενοι:
Rep. 380B). The poet may be allowed to say that "evil men were
miserable because they needed chastisement and by being punished
they were benefited by God" (διδόντες δὲ δίκην ὠφελοῦντο ὑπὸ
τοῦ θεοῦ: ibid.); but to call God a cause of evil to anyone is
a lie.

The educative value of suffering is also expressed by
Herodotus. He includes these words in a brief speech by
Croesus (1.207): τὰ δὲ μοι παθήματα ἐόντα ἀχάριτα μαθήματα
γέγονε.

Sometimes when suffering is understood as punishment
for evil or foolish deeds, the sufferer's pain serves as a
"learning experience" for others who observe his suffering and
benefit by their determination to avoid his missteps. For
example, when Prometheus cautions him against angering Zeus,
Oceanus replies: "Your misfortune, Prometheus, is (my) teacher"
(Prometheus Bound 393). The same idea is implicit in the
words of the Chorus at 526-53.[2]


II.  Ὁ πόνος ἀγαθόν


According to Diogenes Laertius, Antisthenes (ca. 446-
366 B.C.), the actual founder of Cynicism, "by means of the

---

und Erfahrung (Mainz, 1956). Dörrie notes the role that the
play on words had in the origin and widespread popularity of
this idea. It is in Aeschylus, he writes, that one sees a
"Wort- und Klangverbindung" become a genuine "Gedanken-Verbind-
ung" (p. 324).

[2]Cf. also Plato, Symposium 222B; Gorgias 525B; Plutarch,
De stoic. repug. 1040C.

great Heracles and Cyrus demonstrated that hardship is good" (ὅτι ὁ πόνος ἀγαθὸν συνέστησε: Diogenes Laertius 6.2).[3] The view attributed here to Antisthenes can be taken as a representative--even if somewhat overstated--expression of the positive evaluation of suffering which courses throughout Cynic-Stoic ethical tradition from Antisthenes to Dio Chrysostum. H. Höistad writes:

> According to Cynic views there is no suffering from which a positive value may not be extracted, in other words which may not become an ἀγαθόν . . . . suffering is a δόξα against which one fights by submitting to it, by declaring it paradoxically to be a good. Πόνος, πενία, ἀδοξία etc., which in the eyes of the world are evil, all have the epithet ἀγαθόν in Cynic propaganda.[4]

Already, judging from his Ajax and Odysseus[5], Antisthenes sees combined in the royal figure of Odysseus the features of suffering (especially self-abasement) and philanthropia.[6]

In the Cynic-Stoic tradition hardships appear to be considered a necessary dimension of the wise man's mission, his quest for virtue. Dio Chrysostom tells a story about Diogenes at the Isthmian games. Asked if he came to see the contest, Diogenes answered that instead he came to participate. Asked who his opponents were, he replied: τοὺς πόνους (Or. 8.13). His rather extended response also includes these statements: "The noble man considers hardships his greatest antagonists and with them he desires to do battle always, day and night, . . . for the sake of happiness and virtue throughout all his life . . . ." Such a man must contend eagerly with hunger and cold; he must endure thirst and the pain of

---

[3]This is a corollary of the preceding statement, i.e., that Antisthenes emulated Socrates' disregard of feeling: τὸ ἀπαθὲς ζηλώσας. On the relationship of Antisthenes to Diogenes of Sinope and the beginnings of Cynicism, cf. Ragnar Höistad, Cynic Hero and Cynic King (Uppsala, 1948), pp. 5-21.

[4]Ibid., p. 61.

[5]Published in F. Blass (ed.), Antiphontis Orationes et Fragmenta (Leipzig, 1871), pp. 166-74.

[6]Höistad, op. cit., pp. 97-99. Cf., e.g., Odysseus 9: εἴτε δοῦλος εἴτε πτωχὸς καὶ μαστιγίας ὢν μέλλοιμι τοὺς πολεμίους κακόν τι δράσειν . . . . Od. 8: καὶ ἔγωγε καὶ σὲ καὶ τοὺς ἄλλους ἅπαντας σώζω.

being beaten, cut or burned without exhibiting any weakness;
nor can he fear exile or dishonor (Or. 8.15-16). Thus the pain
of enduring hardships would appear to be an important feature
of the Cynic program of "double training" (ἡ διττὴ ἄσκησις--i.e.,
of body and soul) for the attainment of ἀρετή.[7]

Among those influenced by Stoic thought, too, suffering
was sometimes thought of as a γυμνάσιον.[8] Seneca, for example,
tells Lucilius that God allots good men toil, hardships and
suffering for their own good; such experiences give a man the
opportunity to test himself, achieve greater strength of character, and thus become a noble example for others (De Prov. 2.6-7,
3.4). Actually it is those whom He loves that God hardens and
makes strong by training in adversity.[9]

Physical suffering or abuse by the crowd can also be
viewed as one mark of the true king. This identification is
made by Dio Chrysostom (Or. 9.9) with respect to Diogenes. Like
Odysseus (!) "he was really like a king and master although he
wore the clothing of a beggar"; thus his "servants," made foolish by ignorance, did not recognize his true identity. Just as
the ideal king is δοῦλος and διδάσκαλος, a solitary, poor and
suffering figure,[10] so the suffering σοφός, although a δοῦλος,
is the true king. Here one finds an important example of the
radical Cynic reversal of normal social values.

One may generalize about the significance of suffering
in the Cynic tradition: to a hostile world it helps to identify
the wise and noble man in pursuit of virtue. It also reassures
the Cynic himself that he is what he claims to be. In this
sense οἱ πόνοι constitute an essential ingredient of Cynic
ethics. Not only is suffering viewed positively; it is considered a necessity--so that if the world should relent, the Cynic
would not hesitate to inflict hardship on himself.

---

[7]Cf. Diogenes Laertius, 6.70-71.

[8]Cf. James Adam, "Ancient Greek Views of Suffering and
Evil" in The Vitality of Platonism and Other Essays (Cambridge,
1911), p. 203. (This essay pointed me to some of the texts
quoted in section I above.)

[9]De Prov. 4.7; that struggling against hardships makes
men strong Seneca stresses at length in 4.11-16. See also
Epictetus 1.24.1.

[10]Cf. Höistad, op. cit., chapt. 3, especially pp. 174ff.,
218, 221.

I append here an additional note regarding the significance of suffering--the suffering of one particular man:  the
Cynic Diogenes.  At one point Epictetus describes him as a man
so gentle and kind that ὑπὲρ τοῦ κοινοῦ τῶν ἀνθρώπων τοσούτους
πόνους καὶ ταλαιπωρίας τοῦ σώματος ἄσμενος ἀναδέχεσθαι (3.24.
64).  Here Diogenes' hardships are salutary in the sense that
they are willingly endured as the unavoidable concommitants of
his mission as teacher and social critic.

## III.  Traditions of the Steadfast Philosopher

From several ancient sources we have evidence of traditions about the steadfastness of the philosophers Zeno of Elea
(fifth century B.C.) and Anaxarchus (fourth century B.C.) in
the face of torture and death.  According to Diogenes Laertius
(9.26-27) Zeno plotted to overthrow Nearchus the tyrant but was
arrested.  Diogenes notes that, according to different traditions, Zeno managed to bite off either the tyrant's ear or his
nose; then he was either stabbed or beaten to death.  Diogenes
reports Zeno's last words to the bystanders:  "I am amazed at
your cowardice (and that) you serve the tyrant lest you suffer
these things which I am now enduring" (εἰ τούτων ἕνεκεν ὧν νῦν
ἐγὼ ὑπομένω).  He later gives a similar tradition about Anaxarchus (9.58-59).

Similar stories about Zeno and Anaxarchus are known to
Philo of Alexandria.  In Quod omnis prob. lib. sit 106 he
writes:  "Although tormented by savage tyrants . . . by means
of ingeniously contrived tortures, they disregarded the terrors
with great disdain, offering their bodies as if they were foreign objects or belonged to their enemies."  More specifically,
Philo relates that Zeno, when stretched on the wheel, bit off
his own tongue and spit it at his torturer (ibid., 109).
Plutarch is familiar with the same tradition and explains
further why Zeno bit off his tongue:  "Zeno the philosopher
bit off his tongue and spat it at the tyrant in order that his
body might not be forced by tortures to let slip something that
should not be spoken (τι τῶν ἀπορρήτων)."[11]

---

[11]Plutarch, De garr. 505D; cf. Adv. Col. 1126E.

Philo quotes Anaxarchus as having said: πτίσσε τὸν
'Αναξάρχου ἀσκόν · 'Ανάξαρχον γὰρ οὐκ ἂν δύναιο.[12] And Philo
himself ventures the opinion that the glory and reputation of
Zeno and Anaxarchus is founded upon virtues freely willed,
whereas the glory of the heroes, offspring of gods and men, is
due to their parentage.

Philo is also one of the ancient authors who transmits
a version of the exchange between Alexander the Great and the
Indian gymnosophist Calanus. When, persuasion having failed,
Alexander tried to force Calanus to accompany him, the Indian
wrote him a letter which included these words: "There is
neither king nor ruler who will force us to do what we do not
deliberately choose."[13]

Far more significant in the Greek-Hellenistic world
than the stories about Zeno, Anaxarchus and Calanus, however,
is the pervasive and influential tradition of the death of
Socrates. Werner Jaeger has written:

> Socrates is one of the imperishable figures who have
> become symbolic. The real man . . . shed most of his
> personality as he entered history and became for all
> eternity a 'representative man'. It was not really
> his life or his doctrine (so far as he had any doc-
> trine) which raised him to such eminence, so much as
> the death he suffered for the conviction on which his
> life was founded.[14]

He can even be considered, as Jaeger asserts a few pages later,
"the central point in the making of the Greek soul."[15] Thus
the primary "effect" of Socrates' death was its continuing
influence as an example to emulate and as a source of strength
and inspiration. That this indeed was the case can be demonstrated from Plato, Seneca and Epictetus.

In the Apology Plato several times has Socrates express
his determination to obey the god, his refusal to turn aside

---

[12] "Pound Anaxarchus' skin (body); Anaxarchus you cannot
pound": Quod omnis prob. lib. sit 109. Cf. Diogenes Laertius
9.59.

[13] Ibid., 96. Compare the words of Zeno, quoted in the
same work at 97, regarding the impossibility of forcing a
virtuous man to do anything against his will.

[14] W. Jaeger, Paideia: The Ideals of Greek Culture, II
(New York, 1943), p. 13.

[15] Ibid., p. 27.

from philosophy, and his serenity in the face of death. To a
hypothetical detractor Socrates replies: "You do not speak well,
mister, if you think that a man of any worth whatever must
calculate the risk of living or dying and not look to this alone
when he acts: whether he acts justly or unjustly and whether
his works are those of a good or an evil man" (28B). When a
person has been stationed, as Socrates has, where he considers
it best for him to be, "there, it seems to me, he must remain
and accept the risk, taking nothing into consideration, neither
death nor anything else, in preference to disgrace" (28D). To
those who would vote for his acquittal or condemnation (and in
response to the possibility of release upon the condition that
he no longer pursue philosophy) Socrates declares: "Men of
Athens . . . I shall obey the god rather than you and so long
as I can breathe I shall not cease examining (φιλοσοφῶν) and
exhorting you . . ." (29D). One further quotation from the
Apology must suffice: ". . . whether you acquit me or not, I
will not do otherwise, not even if I have to die a thousand
times" (30B; cf. 37E-38A).

As do the martyrs in IV Maccabees, Socrates approaches
death serenely (Apology 40ff., Phaedo 63ff.) and he predicts
severe retribution upon those who condemn him: younger and
even more critical men will reprove and annoy the citizens of
Athens (Apology 39C-D). He also expresses the firm belief
that οὐκ ἔστιν ἀνδρὶ ἀγαθῷ κακὸν οὐδὲν οὔτε ζῶντι οὔτε τελευ-
τήσαντι (41D).

These last two assertions are echoed in a single statement attributed to Socrates by Seneca: "Leap upon me, make
your assault; I shall conquer you by enduring (ferendo vos
vincam). Whatever attacks that which is firm and insurmount-
able employs its power to its own harm" (De vita beata 27.3).
Something of Seneca's great regard for Socrates is evident in
his words at 27.1: Ecce Socrates ex illo carcere, quem
intrando purgavit omnique honestiorem curia reddidit . . . .

In even more admiring tones Epictetus praises a recal-
citrant Socrates: τοῦτ᾽ ἔστιν ἄνθρωπος ταῖς ἀληθείαις συγγε-
νὴς τῶν θεῶν (1.9.25). Socrates is admired because he does
not save himself dishonorably. "He saves himself by dying,
not by flight" (ἀποθνῄσκων σῴζεται, οὐ φεύγων: 4.1.165). He
did wish to save something, οὐ τὸ σαρκίδιον, ἀλλὰ τὸν πιστόν,
τὸν αἰδήμονα (4.1.161).

In light of Socrates' example Epictetus asks rhetorically: "If we are useful while we live, would we not be much more useful to men by dying when we should and as we should?" (4.1. 168). He continues: "Now that Socrates is dead the memory of him is no less useful--or even more useful--to men than what he did or said while still living" (4.1.169). That Socrates' conduct in the face of death is indeed a cherished example to be emulated is clear from this injunction: "Pay attention to these things, . . . look at these examples if you wish to be free" (4.1.70).


IV. Glorious Death Among the Greeks

In Greek literature one finds the widespread sentiment that the noble warrior who dies in battle has been granted the most glorious of deaths. According to Plutarch (Mor. 192C), for example, the Theban general Epaminondas (d. 362 B.C.) used to say: τὸν ἐν πολέμῳ θάνατον εἶναι κάλλιστον. Lysias asserts that those who have died in battle have chosen the noblest death of all (Epitaphios 79). In the funeral oration ascribed to him by Thucydides, Pericles expresses the view that "they are fortunate who draw for their lot a death as glorious as that which these now have" (Thucydides 2.44.1).

This view of glorious death was apparently not merely a source of comfort for those who survived the fallen but a motivating force for the warrior himself. One reason for his readiness to die was the glory he knew death would bring.[16] His would be long-lived fame and honor. Lysias (ca. 459-ca. 380 B.C.) avows that "those who have fallen in battle are worthy of being honored with the same honors as the immortals" (Epitaphios 80). They are even to be envied (81): "I deem them blessed (or, I congratulate them: μακαρίζω) for their death and I envy them" (cf. also 69). Similarly Plato can write: "Of those who die on foreign campaigns, whoever

---

[16]See Isocrates, Panegyricus 83.

should die gloriously--shall we not in the first place say that he belongs to the golden race?" (Rep. 468E). Apparently the honor paid them is due to men's realization that they willingly chose noble death rather than dishonorable life.[17]

A frequent component in the glorious death complex is the rather natural claim that the fallen warrior has given his life for the deliverance or safety of city or fatherland. Isocrates can declare: "Responsible for our great good fortune and worthy of our highest praise, I think, are those men who bore the brunt of battle with their bodies, for Hellas (τοῖς σώμασιν ὑπέρ τῆς ʿΕλλάδος)."[18] Plato writes that "they exchange their death for the deliverance of the living."[19] Later he describes the noble dead as those ὅσοι ὑπέρ τῆς πόλεως τετελευτήκασι (Men. 246A). In the Troades (386-87) Euripides has Cassandra say: "The Trojans in the first place died for their fatherland (ὑπέρ πάτρας ἔθνῃσκον)--the noblest glory of all!"

The antiquity of these ideas is manifest from the fact that they are already at home in the Greek world by the time of Homer. The blind poet, for example, has Hector encourage his men with the words: "Not in unseemly manner do we die fighting for our country" (Iliad 15.496-97: οὐ οἱ ἀεικὲς ἀμυνομένῳ περί πάτρης / τεθνάμεν). In one of the extant fragments of his works, the elegiac poet Tyrtaeus (seventh century B.C.) writes: . . . θυμῷι γῆς περί τῆσδε μαχώμεθα καὶ περί παίδων / θνήισκωμεν ψυχέων μηκέτι φειδόμενοι (". . . let us fight with courage for our land and let us die for our children, no longer sparing our lives").[20]

Noble death on behalf of the fatherland not only brings glory for those who fall in battle. Death with valor also serves as an example to be imitated by those who survive the

---

[17]See Demosthenes, Epitaphios 26 and 37.

[18]Isocrates, Panegyricus 75; cf. 77: καλῶς ὑπέρ τῆς πόλεως ἀποθνήσκειν.

[19]Menexenus 237A. Whether the Menexenus is a genuine Platonic work is a question immaterial for my present purpose.

[20]Fragment 6.13-14 (Diehl). See the whole of Fr. 6-7, especially 6.1-2. Compare the following lines of Callinus, also a seventh century poet: τιμῆέν τε γάρ ἐστι καὶ ἀγλαὸν ἀνδρὶ μάχεσθαι / γῆς πέρι καὶ παίδων κουριδίης τ᾿ἀλόχου / δυσμενέσιν (Bergk II.1.6-8). See also Thucydides 2.43.2. For other pertinent texts illustrating the motif of glorious death for

146

fallen heroes. The survivors should resolve to meet the enemy just as courageously as did those who have already given their lives.[21] Mnasalcas (ca. 250 B.C.), describing "these men who delivered their country" in one of his epigrams, concludes with this injunction: "Let a citizen look at them and dare to die for his fatherland (θνάσκειν τλάτω ὑπὲρ πατρίδος)."[22]

## V. Sufferers With a Cause: Prometheus and Antigone

R. Höistad has written that in Euripides' play Mad Heracles ". . . the theme philanthropia through suffering is clearly delineated" and that "Through his πόνοι Heracles becomes a εὐεργέτης . . . ."[23] Unless Höistad's position is misrepresented by the juxtaposition of these two statements, he has, in my opinion, misstated the case. Why? Because the πόνοι by means of which Heracles becomes the benefactor of mankind are described in Mad Heracles in terms of exertion and heroic feats accomplished rather than in terms of pain and suffering endured.[24]

The suffering of Heracles is a vivid and memorable aspect of the play, but not in connection with the Twelve Labors. Rather, the only real suffering emphasized is the anguish Heracles experiences when his madness subsides and he comes to realize that he has murdered wife and children. And this suffering is hardly beneficial for anyone! If it has any positive meaning at all that is only because from his experience of act and anguish Heracles has learned the value of σωφροσύνη and friendship.[25]

---

one's country see the sepulchral epigrams in Anthologia Graeca 7.225-58, especially 226, 231, 245, 250-55, 258; also 442, 512, 541. Further cf. M. Evaristus, The Consolations of Death in Ancient Greek Literature (see bibliography), pp. 63-75.

[21]Thucydides 2.43.1.

[22]Anthologia Graeca 7.242.

[23]R. Höistad, op. cit., p. 27 and p. 26

[24]Cf. 17-21, 225-26, 296-700, 851-53.

[25]W. C. Greene, Moira (Cambridge, 1944), p. 186. In

Thus, if one insists that "suffering" denotes more than hard work and physical exertion, that it refers rather to the experience of pain and anguish, then he can justifiably disagree with Höistad's view that the theme of philanthropia through suffering is present in the Mad Heracles of Euripides. The theme that Höistad detects here is more obvious in a drama by one of Euripides' two great precursors, the Prometheus Bound by Aeschylus.

The words of Kratos in the opening lines of the Prometheus Bound announce the protagonist's offense and the punishment decreed for him by Zeus. A Titan, son of Uranus and Themis (Earth), Prometheus had stolen fire, the source of all crafts (παντέχνον πῦρ), and had given it to mortals; this is his initial overt ἁμαρτία (9). Therefore he is to be chained indefinitely to a high-jutting crag in the Scythian wasteland. In this way he must make satisfaction (δοῦναι δίκην) to the gods so that he might learn to acquiesce in the sovereignty of Zeus and to cease his habit of philanthropia (φιλανθρώπου . . . τρόπου: 11; the phrase is repeated at 28). The two themes here introduced, philanthropia and suffering, along with the motifs of the ruthlessness of Zeus and the "fatal flaw" and recalcitrance of Prometheus, are of fundamental importance for the structure and development of the drama.

To say merely that Prometheus benefits mankind is to describe a less heroic figure than Aeschylus himself presents, for Prometheus is, in a quite literal sense, the savior of mankind. Successful in his attempt upon his father's throne, Zeus at once assigned the various gods their privileges and

---

general, similar conclusions can be drawn with regard to other authors who make use of the Heracles myth. For example, in both Sophocles' Trachiniae and Seneca's Hercules Oetaeus--both of which, in plot, differ greatly from Euripides--Heracles suffers excruciating torment from the poisoned robe innocently sent him by Deianeira (Tr. 765-71, 785-806, 1046-1111; HO 796ff. 823ff., 1218ff.); but the effect of this suffering and subsequent death is anything but beneficial. In both plays Deianeira kills herself. In Hercules Oetaeus Seneca has her announce the major "effect" of her husband's death: the evils which Heracles subdued--tyrants, monster, wild beasts, cruel gods--will again gain prominence and afflict mankind (874-79; cf. 1143ff.).

powers (230-32). But of mankind he took no account; in fact he wanted to destroy the whole race and create a new one (233-35). "No one resisted these plans except me," declares Prometheus, "but I dared. I rescued mortals so that they might not go to Hades, utterly destroyed" (236-38). Although it is not stated in this particular passage, other lines throughout the play leave no doubt that Prometheus' "loosing" of the race involved the several benefits that he granted mankind. In the first place, he prevented men from foreseeing their death by implanting blind hopes in them (250, 252)--a deed which the Chorus pronounces μεγ' ὠφέλημα. In addition, Prometheus explains, he gave men fire, "from which they shall learn many arts" (254, 256; at 110-111 fire is διδάσκαλος τέχνης πάσης). Those arts are enumerated elsewhere: building with bricks, woodworking, astronomy, arithmetic, writing, animal husbandry, shipbuilding (450-68); the healing arts, divination, minerology (478-503). All these, men could learn because Prometheus had given them understanding (443f.). In a word, as he himself declares, πᾶσαι τέχναι βροτοῖσιν ἐκ Προμηθέως (506).

And this is precisely why he was punished: because he bestowed upon mortals greater honors than was proper (30: τιμὰς πέρα δίκης, and cf. 107-108, 82-84, 945-46). He suffers, in other words, "because of too much love for mankind" (διὰ τὴν λίαν φιλότητα βροτῶν: 123)--love the more incomprehensible because Prometheus could expect no help from mankind in return (cf. 545-551). His suffering is dwelt upon by the playwright. Such words as πάσχειν, πόνος, πῆμα, αἰκεία, and μόχθος occur again and again.[26] Significantly, the play ends with the words (addressed to Themis): ἐσορᾷς μ' ὡς ἔκδικα πάσχω.

A third structural motif in Prometheus Bound is the protagonist's steadfast refusal to capitulate. Relatively early in the play (259-62, 309-31) the observer is given the impression that Zeus would consent to release Prometheus if the Titan would simply "repent" and submit wholly to the chief god's will. But throughout the play Prometheus obstinately

---

[26] E.g., 66, 93, 99, 103, 118, 159, 169, 179, 181, 240, 258, 269, 284, 300, 308, 316, 318, 328, 341, 413, 471-72, 512, 614, 754, 1026. The sufferings of Prometheus are described in some detail at 20-27, 31-34, 64-65; Hermes predicts still worse tortures--including having his body rent and his liver devoured repeatedly by a ravenous eagle--unless Prometheus relents: 1014-25.

refuses although he is threatened with still worse tortures.
This adamant willfulness the other <u>dramatis personae</u> characterize as ὕβρις or as an unwillingness σωφρονεῖν--a fatal flaw
indeed[27] and illustrated above all by Prometheus' refusal to
make known the secret by which Zeus might prevent his own future
overthrow.[28] This refusal, however, is prompted not by some
desire to benefit mankind yet further but by mere personal
motivation, namely the desire for vindication and revenge
against an arbitrary, unjust god. Therefore one must look
elsewhere for the inner connection between suffering and philanthropia that can point to the "meaning" of suffering in the
Prometheus Bound.

Most obvious (and least significant) is the idea that
Prometheus' suffering is educative for others although he himself will not learn σωφρονεῖν from that experience. It
impresses upon lesser divinities the necessity of submission
to the will of Zeus (393; cf. 526-53). Of considerably greater
significance is the observation that Prometheus <u>realized</u> the
personal risks involved in his daring deeds on behalf of mankind. In his own words: ἑκὼν ἑκὼν ἥμαρτον, οὐκ ἀρνήσομαι · /
θνητοῖς ἀρήγων αὐτὸς ηὑρόμην πόνους (268-69).[29] Even so, he
adds, he did not expect to receive punishment so horrible as he
now experiences (270-72). The meaning of Prometheus' suffering,
then, must be seen in terms of his willingness to suffer punishment as a result of his effort to save mankind. However,
one does not find here an idea of "effective suffering" because,
except for its educative value, the suffering of Prometheus has
no subsequent effects beneficial for mankind or for the lesser
deities. That, at least, is the definite impression that one
gets from the Prometheus Bound.

---

[27]Esp. 82-83, 983; cf. 313-23, 964-65, 999-1000;
further: 970, 1009-13, 1037-39, 1078.

[28]Cf. 168-79; also 522-25, 752-66, 944-52, 984, 1001-
1006.

[29]Cf. ἐτόλμησα at 237. The danger of such insubordina-
tion is implied already by emphasis on the fact that none of
the other deities dared to resist Zeus's plan to destroy mankind: 233-36.

It is possible to get a rather different impression if one looks at the suffering and recalcitrance of Prometheus from the wider perspective of the other dramas written by Aeschylus, including the two other plays of the Prometheus trilogy. Unfortunately, the Prometheus Unbound and Prometheus the Firebearer do not survive. However, references to these works in ancient literature plus the picture of Zeus in extant plays such as the Agamemnon allow the suggestion that, within the framework of Aeschylean theology, the unrepentant suffering and steadfastness of Prometheus was a factor in the transformation of Zeus into a more understanding, moral and gracious deity.

> We shall find in the Agamemnon that, as contrasted with all the previous rulers of Heaven, Zeus has a new and extraordinary faculty: the power to think and to learn by suffering. Before Zeus the world was governed by beings who were like blind forces of nature. But with Zeus came something new: what the Greeks called Ξύνεσις or Understanding.30

Whence this new and beneficent faculty? It is probable that at least one element in the evolution of Zeus into a more intelligent and moral deity was the suffering of Prometheus. ". . . Prometheus, caught between the power of Zeus and his pity for man, made his choice, but by his suffering helped to close the gap between Zeus and man, between power and right." [31]

No matter how legitimate this more profound interpretation of the significance of Prometheus' suffering, for spectators of the enacted drama or for readers of the published play, the most enduring impression left by the Prometheus Bound was very likely the vivid picture of a noble hero who suffers terribly because he now refuses to capitulate to the ruthless tyrant god. [32] One might venture to suggest that for those gripped by this picture, the suffering of Prometheus has meaning primarily because of what it represents and celebrates: philanthropia and endurance.

---

[30] G. Murray, Aeschylus: The Creator of Tragedy (Oxford, 1940), p. 101; cf. further pp. 99-110.

[31] Greene, op. cit., p. 125; cf. further pp. 117-25 and the bibliographical references in the notes.

[32] The unjust ruthlessness of Zeus is particularly emphasized by the sufferings imposed upon the innocent Io; cf. especially 640-86 and Greene, op. cit., p. 111.

The Antigone of Sophocles presents another heroic figure who refuses to capitulate to a tyrant's will. From the wider perspective the underlying conflict in the Antigone is between the ancient principle of religious duty and the claims of the polis and its ruler.[33] As for the plot, Antigone, the daughter of the dead Oedipus, desires to bury her brother, Polynices, killed in his attempt to wrest the throne of Thebes from his brother. But Creon, now king of the city, forbids proper burial because Polynices had plotted against city and kinsmen. A resolute Antigone persists, is caught in the act, and is condemned to a rocky cavern where Creon expects her to die of starvation (cf. 773-80). In fact, her end comes quickly, for Antigone hangs herself and her lover, Creon's son, kills himself as well.

Antigone does not merely die. From the beginning she anticipates her death and approaches it with unflinching resolve (26-38, 72, 96-97, 447-48, 555). But what is her motivation and how does she understand the significance of her death? Antigone believes that to comply with Creon's decree would be to betray her brother (45-46) and to dishonor the ordinances of the gods (77; cf. 519). Creon's law does not annul the unwritten and unalterable laws of the gods (ἄγραπτα κἀσφαλῆ θεῶν νόμιμα) which exist eternally (453-57);[34] and these laws Antigone dares not abrogate lest she suffer punishment from the gods (458-59). Thus her willingness to die protects her from the divine wrath which would otherwise fall upon her. And yet, avoidance of divine wrath is by no means the impulse which drives Antigone; that is really but an afterthought. Her primary motivation is much less egocentric: in a word she suffers in defense of religion. In a plea directed to the gods of Thebes she cries: "Behold . . . what fate I suffer from such men because I honored piety" (οἷα πρὸς οἵων ἀνδρῶν πάσχω, / τὴν εὐσεβίαν σεβίσασα: 942-43).

On the most superficial level Antigone's death has quite definite "effects." It is, first of all, the immediate cause of Haemon's suicide which, in turn, leads Creon's wife to kill herself--two deeds which plunge Creon into the depths of

---

[33]Ibid., p. 144.

[34]The precisely opposite view, i.e., that the laws of the state or its ruler are absolute and tolerate no appeal to

anguish and self-deprecation. Antigone views her own death
from other perspectives. Anticipated as a release from misery,
death she counts as gain (463-64). And while she must forego
the joys of marriage and motherhood (809-14, 916-18), the
Chorus reminds her that she departs life not only renowned and
commended (817-18; cf. 688-95) but αὐτόνομος, before debilitated
by disease or sword (819-22). Antigone herself appears to
find great consolation in the fact that she dies a noble death
(cf. καλῶς θανεῖν at 97) and by the deed which prompted it she
will achieve most glorious fame (502-503).

But Sophocles introduces yet another element which bears
upon the significance of Antigone's death. In one of the most
puzzling passages in the play he has her say to her sister,
Ismene: "You live, but I have already died so as to benefit
the dead" (σὺ μὲν ζῆς, ἡ δ'ἐμὴ ψυχὴ πάλαι / τέθνηκεν, ὥστε τοῖς
θανοῦσιν ὠφελεῖν: 559-60). Πάλαι τέθνηκεν can only mean that
Antigone has already made the decision that brings her condemnation, and she knows her death is irrevocably assured. Τοῖς
θανοῦσιν ὠφελεῖν must reflect the ancient belief that the living are responsible for the welfare of the dead; of special
importance in this regard is the performance of the proper
burial rites.[35] Antigone's decision to defy Creon and thereby
court a certain death can therefore be interpreted as an act
for others--even though these "others" no longer dwell among
the living.

To summarize: the central significance of Antigone's
death lies in the reasons for which she is willing to die: to
win glorious fame, to speak with her life on behalf of religion
and to benefit the dead. In this sense, she dies on behalf of
other persons and for the sake of principles more profound by
far than her own immediate self-interest. Her death has repercussions beyond the fact of physical demise. W. C. Greene can
assert that "The suffering of Antigone assists in the vindication of the moral order . . . ."[36] If that is so, it is only

higher principles, is represented vigorously by Creon: 163-
210, 666-80. To Creon, Antigone's steadfastness is nothing
less than ὕβρις (482)--a view with which, in different words,
her sister concurs (68).

[35]Cf. E. Rohde, Psyche (New York, 1925), pp. 162-66.

[36]Greene, op. cit., p. 141. The suffering of Antigone,
viewed in the wider picture of human and divine events, Greene
compares with that of Philoctetes, Ajax and Oedipus.

because she is willing to uphold religion with her life.
Antigone does not want to die. But she prefers death to the
renunciation of her firmest conviction. Certainly in this
sense she is a true martyr--perhaps the first in Greek literature.


## VI.  Deliberate Self-Sacrifice for the Good of Others in the Plays of Euripides

Although Iphigenia at Aulis is not one of Euripides'
better plays according to the canons of Greek tragedy (Greene
calls it "a loosely constructed melodrama" and contrasts it
sharply with the powerful Bacchae),[37] the picture of the noble
maiden who sacrifices herself for the welfare of countrymen and
fatherland is one which cannot be omitted from the present
survey.

Assembled to sail against Troy, the Greek fleet is
weather-bound at Aulis because no favorable wind blows. The
seer Calchas advises that only by sacrificing Agamemon's eldest
daughter, Iphigenia, to Artemis would the fleet be able to set
sail and capture Troy. Much of the play's structure depends on
Agamemnon's vacillating response to this advice (he refuses,
changes his mind and sends for his daughter, then again relents
--but this time too late) and on Iphigenia's own response to
the prospect of her precipitous death.

In the broad context of the suitors' binding oaths (55-
67), Paris' abduction of Helen (71-83), and the oracle communi-
cated by Calchas (87-93), the death of Iphigenia seems fated.
On the other hand, her sacrifice is self-willed. When first
informed of her father's intent, of course, Iphigenia is
hesitant and despairing (1211-52), but then she resolves to
give herself bravely and gloriously (cf. 1374ff.). Why this
reversal of attitude? Euripides seems to provide four motivations:  to resist would be futile anyway because the army

---

[37]Ibid., p. 210.

clamors for her to be sacrificed (cf. 1346, 1348); by sacrificing herself she can insure the safety of Achilles (1371-73);
besides, the gods will it (1395-96, 1408-1409); and by this act
she believes she will insure not only victory for the Greeks
but the future welfare of Hellas (e.g., 1378ff.).

To recognize these various motivations is already to
perceive the "effects" of Iphigenia's self-sacrifice.[38] One
is her personal reward. Her memorial among men will be the
destruction of Troy (1398-99; cf. 1504). But already she lives
among the gods.[39]

---

[38]A few words are necessary here about the "happy ending"
of the play as it stands, that is, the fact that Iphigenia
(according to bystanders) was not actually slain; rather, she
having miraculously disappeared, a deer was seen slain upon the
altar. It is quite likely that this ending is not the work of
Euripides. The play seems to have been completed by someone
else and later to have received even further interpolations
(cf. Greene, op. cit., pp. 208-209 and n. 158. On the present
ending cf. Kjellberg, "Iphigeneia," Pauly-Wissowa, Real-
Encyclopädie [Stuttgart, 1916], IX, 2614). Certainly this play
would constitute less of a contradiction to the plot of the
Iphigenia Among the Taurians if it originally ended with, say,
the words of the Chorus at 1510-31. Such an ending--Iphigenia
is on her way to the altar--would leave open the possibility
of the miraculous rescue of Iphigenia and her transportation
by Artemis to the land of the Taurians, which is presupposed by
Taurians. Furthermore, the human figure of Iphigenia in
Taurians is hardly intelligible when set against her apotheosis
in the long ending of Aulis. On the other hand, according to
the story in the Cypria, one of the poems of the Epic Cycle
(which Euripides may be following to some degree), Iphigenia
was snatched away by Artemis and a deer was substituted in her
place (cf. H. J. Rose, "Iphigenia," The Oxford Classical Dictionary [Oxford, 1949], pp. 457-58).

But whether the work of Euripides or someone else, the
"happy ending" is a device which avoids actual human sacrifice
while insuring the point that Iphigenia's self-sacrifice was
acceptable to Artemis and therefore would indeed have the
effects anticipated. The reader cannot afford to overlook the
warning cue provided by Clytaemnestra's words at 1616-18.
Furthermore, one should note that even in the context of the
long ending Iphigenia still gives herself; her parents are
bereft for a very good reason: their daughter is no longer a
part of the human scene.

[39]Cf. ζῶν δ'ἐν θεοῖσι at 1614; ἔχει γὰρ ὄντως ἐν θεοῖς
ὁμιλίαν at 1622; and 1608. These assertions, of course, may
not be from the hand of Euripides. But they were most likely
a part of the play by the first century A.D.

The other major effect of Iphigenia's sacrifice that is anticipated by her, Calchas and the Chorus (cf. 1524-31), is the reversal of an external situation (previously weatherbound, the fleet now will sail) and the "historical" event of victory over Troy. The relationship between her deed and these expected results is to be seen above all in Iphigenia's own words, all of which must be understood from a two-fold perspective. On the one hand the sacrifice of Iphigenia can only be taken as a propitiatory offering to Artemis. Angry for whatever unstated reason, the goddess will be placated only by the death of Agamemnon's eldest daughter. Only then will favorable winds be granted the ships of Hellas. On the other hand, Iphigenia views her impending self-sacrifice as equivalent to the death of the soldier who dies for (ὑπέρ) Hellas (1387ff.). In this sense, she does no more than any noble Greek warrior would consider an honorable duty. With these two points in mind I would call attention to several significant examples of the language used to describe the self-sacrifice of Iphigenia and its (anticipated) effect.

Just before approaching the altar, Iphigenia tries to console her mother with these words: "All these [cf. 1379-82] by dying shall I deliver (κατθανοῦσα ῥύσομαι) and, since I have set Hellas free (ἠλευθέρωσα), mine shall be a happy fame" (1383-84). "It was for the good of all Greeks that you bore me, not for yours alone" (1386). To Achilles, who tries to dissuade her, she protests: "Let me save (σῶσαι) Hellas, if we might" (1420). And just before the procession to the altar she cries: "I come with the intention (or hope) of giving to the Greeks deliverance victorious" (ὡς σωτήριαν / ˝Ελλησι δώσουσ᾽ ἔρχομαι νικηφόρον: 1472-73). Thus does she hope to become the benefactor (εὐεργέτις) of Greece (1446).

For the reader of IV Maccabees and the student of the New Testament, three further passages from Iphigenia at Aulis appear particularly striking. In the long speech to her mother Iphigenia declares: δίδωμι σῶμα τοὐμὸν ˊΕλλάδι (1397; cf. 1395). This intention she repeats, in the long ending, in these words to her father: "My body I give to be sacrificed for my country's sake and for all Hellas-land" (τοὐμὸν δὲ σῶμα τῆς ἐμῆς ὑπὲρ πάτρας / καὶ τῆς ἁπάσης ˊΕλλάδος γαίας ὕπερ /

156

θῦσαι δίδωμι: 1553-55).[39a] Finally, in that last long speech
Iphigenia says (1484-86): "So by my bloodshed and my sacrifice,
if need be, shall I cancel what the goddess decreed" (ὡς ἐμοῖ-
σιν, εἰ χρεών / αἵμασι θύμασί τε / θέσφατ' ἐξαλείψω); that
is, by her death Iphigenia would fulfill the conditions for
Greek success which Artemis made known in the oracle of Calchas.

It is significant, I think, that neither in the brief
references of Pindar and Sophocles to the sacrifice of Iphigenia
(Pyth. 11.22-23; Electra 270-74) nor in Aeschylus' depiction of
that grim deed (Ag. 205-49)[40] is there the slightest hint of
willing submission on the victim's part. Indeed, Aeschylus
mentions her entreaties and appeals to her father (228) and
the piteous glance shot from her eyes to each of those who would
slay her (240-41). This is not the courageous maiden that one
finds in Euripides, willing, even eager, to give her life for
the good of her homeland. Rather, it is a moving, pity-
inspiring account of a human sacrifice necessary to appease
an angry goddess. Euripides, apparently, has refined the
story of the sacrifice of Iphigenia that is reflected in
Aeschylus and Sophocles. He has moralized it by transforming
Iphigenia's death into a voluntary offering freely willed.
She is no longer a passive and pitiful victim but a noble
benefactor who views her death as opportunity and blessing.
In a sense she accepts and internalizes necessity and thereby
rises above it through the sheer power of her free will.

It is worthwhile to compare the heroine of Iphigenia at
Aulis with other Euripidean figures, particularly Polyxena,
Macaria, Menoeceus and Alcestis. In the plays in which they
appear one can argue that Euripides engages in the same process
that is reflected in Aulis: the moralization of human sacrifice. To be sure, that is less evident in the Hecuba than,
say, the Heraclidae; for in the Hecuba the sacrifice of Polyxena is demanded by the Achean host in order to honor the ghost

_____

[39a]Cf. Euripides, Electra 1025-26 (Clytaemnestra on her
husband's deed): (κεἰ) . . . τ'ἐκσώσων τέκνα / ἔκτεινε πολλῶν
μίαν ὕπερ . . . .

[40]Aeschylus does not describe the actual sacrifice; in
fact, he does not actually assert that Iphigenia was slain.
It is difficult, however, to understand 249 to mean anything
else: τέχναι δὲ Κάλχαντος οὐκ ἄκραντοι.

of Achilles (90-95, 107ff., 188-90). But her death does not
benefit her countrymen, as does Iphigenia's. The only positive
significance of her death is that it is an escape from the
miseries of defeat and disgrace (cf. 214-15). The most noteworthy aspect of Polyxena's death, however--and this is a point
that Euripides emphasizes--is that she dies of her own free
will. She asks that the youths holding her for the death blow
be commanded to release her, because, she says, ἑκοῦσα θνῄσκω
(548). She wishes to die free (ἐλευθέρα) in order that she not
be called a slave among the dead (550-52).

The sacrifice of Macaria in the **Heraclidae** is more similar to that of Iphigenia. Like Polyxena, Macaria wants to die
freely (ἐλευθέρως θάνω: 559; cf. 547-51). But unlike Polyxena,
she dies believing that her death would have beneficial effects.
The plot is this: fleeing from the persecution of Eurystheus,
king of Argos, Iolaus and his charges, the children of the dead
Heracles, take sanctuary in the temple of Zeus at Marathon.
Demophon, king of Athens (to which Marathon belongs) defends
the cause of Iolaus and the children and refuses to surrender
them to Eurystheus. Having assembled the Athenian troops to do
battle with the king of Argos, Demophon reports that seers and
oracles agree that victory depends upon the sacrifice to Kore
of a nobleman's virgin daughter (398-409). In spite of his
good will and desire to help, Demophon refuses to slay his own
daughter or any other Athenian child (410-12). The only alternative seems to be that Iolaus and the children of Heracles
leave their precious sanctuary (492-97). At this point Macaria,
daughter of Heracles, learns of the situation and suggests that
she be sacrificed (500ff.). Realizing that such a sacrifice is
necessary for their deliverance (σωθῆναι: 498), she cries:
"Lead me where this body now must die . . . and conquer your
enemies; this life is ready, willing and not constrained. And
I promise to die on behalf of (ὑπέρ) my siblings and myself"
(528-32). When Iolaus tries to persuade her to consent to the
casting of lots among her and her sisters, Macaria insists that
she not die by lot, χάρις γὰρ οὐ πρόσεστι (548). Rather, she
volunteers eagerly (προθύμῳ): τὴν ἐμὴν ψυχὴν ἐγὼ / δίδωμ'
ἑκοῦσα τοῖσδ', ἀναγκασθεῖσα δ'οὔ (550-51). An admiring Iolaus
relents, for, as he says to Macaria, ἀδελφοὺς δ'ὠφελεῖς θανοῦσα
σούς (557). Thus she can call herself their savior (σώτειρα:
558). Moreover, as suggested already by the very plot of
the play, the motif of substitution is explicitly voiced:

Macaria gives up the possibility of marriage "by dying in their place" (ἀντὶ τῶνδε κατθανουμένη: 580).

Even more similar than the deed of Macaria to the sacrifice of Iphigenia is that of Menoeceus in the Phoenician Women. Thebes is threatened by the armed attempt of Polynices to gain his rightful year of rule--an attempt which his brother Eteocles resists with his own army. According to Tiresias the seer, Thebes will be utterly destroyed unless Creon (a descendant of Cadmus: 940ff.) slays his son Menoeceus ὑπὲρ πάτρας (193). This deed will placate Ares and thereby gain the god as an ally for Thebes (930-36). Tiresias explains the anticipated effects of Menoeceus' death in these words: θανὼν πατρῷαν γαῖαν ἐκσώσειεν ἂν (948). For Creon the choice is simply stated: ἢ γὰρ παῖδα σῶσον ἢ πόλιν (952). He refuses to slaughter his child (962ff.); but Menoeceus, having deceived his father, determines to do the deed himself in order not to betray the city of his birth by flight (996): "I will go and save the city and give my life to die for the land" (εἶμι καὶ σώσω πόλιν / ψυχήν τε δώσω τῆσδ᾽ ὑπερθανεῖν χθονός: 997-98). And again he says: σφάξας ἐμαυτόν . . . ἐλευθερώσω γαῖαν (1010, 1012; cf. 1013-14: θανάτου δῶρον οὐκ αἰσχρὸν πόλει / δώσων). Furthermore, Menoeceus views his self-sacrifice as but an example of what every man owes his country (1015-18).

There is one further Euripidean portrait, consideration of which is appropriate here: Alcestis, in the play of the same name. Unlike most of the other figures previously discussed, Alcestis is willing to give herself not for the sake of her fatherland but in the place of her husband. Apollo, banished from Olympus for a time and by Zeus made servant to a mortal, Admetus, succeeds in obtaining from the Fates the promise that Admetus shall escape imminent death if a substitute consent to replace him. But no one, including his father and mother, would die in the place of Admetus--with one exception: his wife Alcestis (cf. 8-21). Although the play ends happily because Heracles overpowers Death and leads Alcestis back from Hades, the following expressions of the purpose and "effect" of Alcestis' death are nonetheless pertinent to this study. A handmaid wonders: "How could anyone give greater honor to her husband than by desiring to die for him (ὑπερθανεῖν)?" (154-55). Alcestis speaks of "this man in whose stead I die" (οὗ θνῄσκω πέρι: 178); and she emphasizes that she acts without constraint (θνῄσκω, παρόν μοι μὴ θανεῖν ὑπέρ σέθεν: 284). Admetus gratefully acknowledges her noble act: "You do save me by giving all you love in place of my own life" (σὺ δ'ἀντιδοῦσα τῆς ἐμῆς τὰ φίλτατα / ψυχῆς ἔσωσας: 340-41). And again he declares that "she alone has died in my stead" (τέθνηκεν ἀντ' ἐμοῦ μόνη: 434; cf. also 524, 383). Thus, in the most direct fashion imaginable, Alcestis is presented as a voluntary substitute figure. In the most immediate and literal sense, her free act of self-giving is an instance of vicarious, substitutionary death.[41]

These dramatic presentations by Euripides of lives given for others or for the fatherland have their particular background and context in the historical currents of the poet's own time. During the trying years of the Peloponnesian Wars Euripides adapted ancient sagas to powerful dramas of patriotic self-sacrifice. Alcestis is but a more intensely personal example of what one student of Euripides has called his "Verherrlichung der freiwilligen Hingabe des Lebens."[42] The fervent devotion which he felt for fatherland and countrymen urged him to fashion his unforgettable scenes of men and women freely

---

[41]An intriguing piece of evidence for the impact of the Alcestis story (known from Euripides' play) is found in the Anthologia Graeca 7.691. A woman named Callicratia speaks her epitaph: "I am a new Alcestis, and I died for (ὑπέρ) my good husband Zeno . . . ."

[42]J. Schmitt, Freiwilliger Opfertod bei Euripides (Giessen, 1921), p. 2. For the motif of patriotic self-sacrifice in two lost plays, the Erechtheus and the Phrixus (of which we have only fragmentary quotations in other works of ancient literature), cf. pp. 63-72. For the influence on later generations of the Euripidean dramas of the self-sacrifice of Macaria, Menoceus, Polyxena, the daughter of Praxithea and Phrixus, cf. pp. 84-103. On Iphigenia's self-sacrifice in Greek and Latin literature after Euripides cf. Kjellberg, op. cit., 2615-18. The rather considerable posthumous influence of Euripides in the ancient world has been discussed by W. Schmid and O. Stählin, Geschichte der griechischen Literatur, III (Munich, 1940), pp. 823-33. Among their observations not altogether irrelevant for the present study (particularly Chapter V) are the following: the early Stoa did not hesitate to borrow from the wisdom of Euripides; the Cynic diatribe quotes no poet except Homer more frequently; Plutarch (de Alex. fort. 5) speaks of the diffusion of the tragedies of Euripides (and Sophocles) in the Orient (although perhaps in somewhat exaggerated fashion); in the third century B.C. Euripides was already a model for Roman tragedy; educated Romans of the first centuries B.C. and A.D. were familiar with his verse; decorative vase painting shows a pronounced preference for Euripidean scenes; Clement of Alexandria quotes Euripides frequently.

160

giving themselves as sacrificial offerings ὑπὲρ πάτρας. That
devotion is nowhere more succinctly expressed than in these
words from a fragment of the lost Erechtheus, probably spoken
by Praxithea: φιλῶ τέκν᾽ ἀλλὰ πατρίδ᾽ ἐμὴν μᾶλλον φιλῶ.[43] A
similar statement might well summarize the conviction of the
other Euripidean figures to whom attention was called in the
preceding pages: "I love life, but I love my country more."

The motif of effective self-sacrifice for the benefit of
others is, of course, not without parallels in Latin literature.[44] In Book Eight of his History Livy preserves the legend
of the self-sacrifice of Decius. The Roman Senate having
agreed upon war with the Latins (ca. 340 B.C.), two consuls,
Titus Manlius and Publius Decius, marched into battle with
their armies. During the night before the battle, the consuls
had identical visions: a majestic figure declared that the
commander of one side and the army of the other must be offered
up to the gods. Thus, if a Roman commander should "devote"
himself, the enemy would fall and his side would be victorious.
Upon comparing visions in the morning, the two consuls agreed
that on whichever flank the Roman army began to yield, the one
of them in charge "should devote himself on behalf of the Roman
people and Quirites" (se consul devoveret pro populo Romano
Quiritibusque: 8.6.13).

When the line on the left began to give way before the
Latins, Decius called for the Roman pontiff accompanying the
army. After the appropriate rites he sent word to his fellow
consul that he had devoted himself "for the army" (pro exercitu:
8.9.9). Then he girded himself, mounted his horse and charged
into the ranks of the enemy, appearing "as though sent from
heaven as a means of appeasing all anger of the gods" (sicut
caelo missus piaculum omnis deorum irae) that he might turn
destruction away from his own side and bring it upon his enemies
(8.9.10). Wherever he rode, men cowered, and when he fell the
Latin troops fled from the field (8.9.12). Of Decius it is
said: "he had turned all the threats and menaces of the
supernal and infernal gods upon himself alone" (8.10.7).

---

[43]Quoted from Schmitt, op. cit., p. 66.

[44]Nor is it without parallels in Greek literature outside the dramas of the tragic poets. For example, Lycurgus,
the Athenian statesman (ca. 390- ca. 325 B.C.), in his oration
against Leocrates (Leoc. 84-87), preserves the legend of Codrus,
an early king of Athens who by his self-imposed death delivered
the city from certain defeat at the hands of Peloponnesian
invaders. For Lycurgus, Codrus (in contrast to Leocrates) is
a foremost example of ἄνδρες γενναῖοι οἱ τότε βασιλεύοντες,
ὥστε προῃροῦντο ἀποθνήσκειν ὑπὲρ τῆς τῶν ἀρχομένων σωτηρίας
. . . (86). He further describes such earlier rulers as men
οἱ γε προῃροῦντο . . . ἀποθνήσκειν ὑπὲρ αὐτῆς [i.e., τῆς πατρί-
δος] καὶ τὴν ἰδίαν ψυχὴν ἀντὶ τῆς κοινῆς σωτηρίας ἀντικαταλλάτ-
τεσθαι (88).

A second story involves Curtius. When a huge chasm
opened in the midst of the Roman forum, soothsayers advised
the Romans to sacrifice what they prized most highly if they
wanted the Republic to endure. Thereupon, having devoted himself, Curtius rode into the chasm fully armed, and it closed
over him (Livy 7.6.1-5). According to Pliny's account (HN 15.
78) ". . . when the foundations of the Empire were collapsing
in portent of disaster, Curtius had filled up the gulf with
the greatest of treasures, I mean virtue and piety and a glorious death" (trans. H. Rackham in the LCL edition).

Postscript:  A Brief Comparison

Perhaps the most vivid impression left by a comparative
look at the views outlined in Chapters III and IV is that a
positive understanding of the causes and effects of suffering
or death is more characteristic of the Greeks than the Hebrews.
To be sure, the Hebrew often acknowledged the disciplinary value
of suffering; and the prophet of Yahweh accepted suffering as a
necessary aspect of his calling.  But rare would have been the
Hebrew, prophet or no, who (for example) could have agreed with
the Cynic that hardship is a good thing.

At one point the Greek and Hebrew attitudes toward suffering are quite similar.  The Hebrew view of suffering as
divine discipline reminds one forcefully of the Greek motif
παθεῖν-μαθεῖν.  This similarity, however, is outweighed by
several readily apparent differences of attitude and emphasis.

Typically, Hebrew-Jewish "answers" to the problem of
suffering and death involve the assumption that the sufferer is
a sinful man.  For example (to consider the two most influential
views) suffering was thought to be divine punishment for sin,
or it was thought to expiate a person's sins (so that they would
not "pile up" and interfere with his future reward).  (Exceptions include the suffering of the prophet, Isaiah 53 in particular, and the idea that suffering is God's testing of a man's
heart.  The author of Job forcefully rejects the notion that
suffering implies sin.)  Thus, even the "positive" attitude
that suffering insures future reward involves the presupposition that the sufferer is guilty of some sin, large or small.
By contrast, except in connection with the παθεῖν-μαθεῖν motif
or in the special sense of the poets' "tragic flaw," among the
Greeks suffering and death are not usually understood as the
effect of sin or wrongdoing.

In Jewish literature, even when suffering or death is
thought to have a positive function (i.e., by educating one or
by expiating one's sins), that experience tends to be viewed
only in relationship to the individual immediately concerned.
(Exceptions include the suffering of the prophet as a sign to
the people; Achan, the hanged chiefs, etc.; possibly Isaiah 53;

Josephus' assertion at <u>War</u> 5.419.) In Greek literature, however, in addition to the idea that the individual involved will obtain a personal reward (e.g., glorious fame), one frequently finds expressed the idea that the suffering or death of one person--often in defense of principles unrelated to his own immediate self-interest--effects benefits for others. This observation leads to another, namely, that whereas the notion of patriotic self-sacrifice is deeply imbued in the Greek mind, it is an understanding of death foreign to the OT and non-hellenized Jewish literature.

CHAPTER V

THE DEATH OF THE MARTYRS IN IV MACCABEES

In Chapter II it was seen that in five Jewish writers,
from Daniel to Josephus, the deaths of the righteous Jews who
died at the hands of Antiochus are not interpreted in terms of
vicarious expiation. On the other hand, it has also been noted
previously that IV Maccabees uses the language of ransom, purification and expiation with reference to the martyrs' deaths.
From the perspective provided by the two preceding chapters, it
is now possible to attempt an answer to the question posed by
this "new" element in IV Maccabees, i.e., what are the sources
of the author's statements about the meaning and effect of the
martyrs' deaths?


I.  The Death of the Martyrs and Its Effects

The historical situation which provides the setting for
the martyr story of IV Maccabees is described in terms of
Jason's hellenizing program (4:19-20). Implicit, of course, is
the fact that Jason had accomplices, but this point is never
stated. Jason is the subject of the sentences preceding this
statement (4:21): "Because of these things the divine justice
became angry and made Antiochus himself their enemy." IV Maccabees includes no assertions equivalent to II Maccabees 5:17-
18 and 7:32 about the sins or guilt of the people. The noun
ἁμάρτημα is not used at all; ἁμαρτία appears twice. Once it
occurs in the phrase "the nation's sin" (17:21). What the
nation's sin was is indicated by 5:19, where Eleazar explains
to Antiochus that eating forbidden food is not an insignificant
sin. Clearly the nation's sin is apostasy, the most conspicu-
ous example of which is the eating of swine's flesh. Yet it

is only in terms of Jason and his program that this sin is
described explicitly.

This is the historical scene into which the author sets
the story of Eleazar, the seven brothers and their mother--a
story which he apparently does not create ex nihilo but which,
already existing in some form, he reworks freely in accord with
his own purpose and theology.[1]

According to his own statement, however, the author of
IV Maccabees does not intend to narrate history but to discuss
the subject εἰ αὐτοδέσποτός ἐστιν τῶν παθῶν ὁ εὐσεβὴς λογισμός
(1:1). It is not unnatural, given this stated purpose, that he
lays special stress on the motif of the martyrs' remarkable
endurance under torture, for this steadfastness proves as no
other evidence could that the passions of man can be subjected
to godly reason (cf. 13:1, e.g.). The feature of the martyrs'
endurance, of course, is not lacking in II Maccabees; the point
that the martyrs stood firm is essential to the story in any

---

[1]The question of possible literary dependence on II
Maccabees is complex and does not enjoy the honor of scholarly
consensus. J. Freudenthal (Die Flavius Josephus beigelegte
Schrift Ueber die Herrschaft der Vernunft (IV Makkabäerbuch)
[Breslau, 1869], pp. 72ff.) argues that IV Maccabees, like II
Maccabees, is dependent upon the historical work of Jason of
Cyrene but is independent of II Maccabees itself; Freudenthal
thinks that at many places--e.g., the prayer of Eleazar!--IV
Maccabees gives a much fuller version of Jason's text than
does II Maccabees. Deissmann (in Kautzsch, II, p. 156, n. e)
accepts Freudenthal's thesis that Jason served as a common
source. Surkau, however, rejects Freudenthal's conclusions
regarding literary relationship (op. cit., pp. 25-29). He
points to significant variations in parallel texts (e.g., II
7:24ff. and IV 12:1) which "bei schriftlicher Grundlage nicht
verständlich wären" (p. 28). Surkau suggests, instead, that
the martyrdoms in II and IV Maccabees presuppose a common tradition "die, älter als diese Texte, selbst nicht der grossen
Literatur angehört, sondern unliterarisch ist" (p. 29). Both
authors used this tradition rather freely in writing their own
pieces, but not so freely as to erase all traces of the common
Vorlage.

M. Hadas, in The Third and Fourth Books of Maccabees
(New York, 1953), considers a literary relationship between II
and IV Maccabees obvious. "Closer examination makes it equally
certain that the fuller and more ornate account in IV Maccabees
is an elaboration of that in II Maccabees, and indeed that the
author of IV Maccabees used no other source for the substance
of his story" (p. 92). ". . . all divergences can be adequately explained by the different purpose of the author of IV
Maccabees and the different historical circumstances in which
he wrote" (p. 93).

version. But by comparison, the overriding emphasis in IV Maccabees on the martyrs' endurance is apparent. Thus, the author expends an inordinate amount of literary energy on lingering and detailed descriptions of the tortures which Antiochus concocted. These descriptions set the stage against which he presents his central thesis: if men could endure such tortures as these for the sake of their beliefs, surely godly reason is indeed master of all human emotions and passions.

The emphasis on ὑπομονή and ὑπομένειν is indicated above all by the sheer frequency with which these and equivalent terms appear. The martyrs were admired by everyone for their courage and endurance (1:11)--even by Antiochus and his council (17:17). The mother exhorts her sons to endure any pain for God's sake (16:19), just as Daniel and the three youths did (16:21); (cf. also v. 20 where οὐκ ἔπτηξεν is used with regard to Isaac). The mother is eulogized for her own courage and endurance (15:30, 32; cf. 12:7). Eleazar, likewise, is praised for fortifying his people's faithfulness to the law through his endurance (plural!) unto death (7:9).[2]

From the perspective of this thesis the most significant aspect of the martyrs' endurance unto death is the author's assertions concerning the effects of that endurance. In the verse just referred to (7:9) Eleazar's endurance has effects as an example for his people to emulate: σύ, πάτερ, τὴν εὐνομίαν ἡμῶν διὰ τῶν ὑπομονῶν εἰς δόξαν ἐκύρωσας . . . . In less explicit language, the example motif is echoed at 5:33-36, 6:18-21, and 16:16.

The martyrs' endurance unto death also assures for them the personal reward of immortality. This "effect" is affirmed or alluded to numerous times, but perhaps most clearly at 17:18: δι'ἥν [i.e., αὐτῶν τὴν ὑπομονήν--v. 17] καὶ τῷ θείῳ νῦν παρεστήκασιν θρόνῳ καὶ τὸν μακάριον βιοῦσιν αἰῶνα. See also 17:12 (τὸ νῖκος ἀφθαρσία . . . .) and 18:23 (ψυχὰς ἁγνὰς καὶ ἀθανάτους ἀπειληφότες παρὰ τοῦ θεοῦ).[3]

_____

[2]See also 7:22; 9:8, 30; 17:7, 10, 23 (twice). The noun or verb is often accompanied by διά with acc. of εὐσέβεια, νόμος, θεός, ἀρετή, πίστις. Other terms, equivalent in meaning to ὑπομονή/ὑπομένειν are found at 6:30 (ἀνθιστάναι); 9:28 (καρτερεῖν); 13:5 (οὐκ ἐπιστρέφειν); 13:10 ("μὴ δειλανδρήσωμεν"); 14:4 (οὐκ ὀκνεῖν); 16:14 (καρτερία); 16:23 (ἀνθίστασθαι τοῖς πόνοις).

[3]Additional texts: 9:8, 13:17; cf. 7:19, 9:22, 10:15,

More startling by far--especially in comparison with previous examples of writings dealing with the Maccabean martyr tradition--is a third kind of claim made by the author of IV Maccabees: the martyrs' endurance unto death had objective benefit for the nation, i.e., it was effective in breaking the power of Antiochus over Israel and causing him to leave. This claim is most clearly expressed early in the work, in the author's introductory remarks: "Because they were admired for their courage and endurance not only by all men but even by their torturers, they served as causes of the destruction of the tyranny against the nation, conquering the tyrant by endurance so that through them the fatherland was purified" (1:11).[4] The precise way in which they were, or served as, causes of the destruction of tyranny is not specified here, but the point is emphasized that they were victorious over the tyrant by means of endurance.

The same point is made in 9:30: "Don't you think, most cruel of tyrants, that you are being tormented more than I am? --because you are watching the arrogant plans of your tyranny overcome by our endurance for the sake of piety."[5] Here ὑπομονή is clearly the means by which Antiochus' intention is thwarted.

A fitting memorial to the martyrs, says the author, would include these words: "They avenged the nation by looking to God and by enduring the tortures until death" (17:10).[6] If the participles here can be interpreted as having causal or

---

14:5-6, 15:3, 16:25, 17:5, 18:3. The motifs of example and future life have already been observed in II Maccabees, where the martyrs anticipate the resurrection of their bodies. At II Mac. 6:26-28, 31, the example motif is articulated with greater force than in IV Mac. but in conjunction with Eleazar's death alone.

[4]θαυμασθέντες γὰρ οὐ μόνον ὑπὸ πάντων ἀνθρώπων ἐπὶ τῇ ἀνδρείᾳ καὶ ὑπομονῇ, ἀλλὰ καὶ ὑπὸ τῶν αἰκισαμένων, αἴτιοι κατέστησαν τοῦ καταλυθῆναι τὴν κατὰ τοῦ ἔθνους τυραννίδα νικήσαντες τὸν τύραννον τῇ ὑπομονῇ ὥστε καθαρισθῆναι δι᾽ αὐτῶν τὴν πατρίδα.

[5]οὐ δοκεῖς, πάντων ὠμότατε τύραννε, πλέον ἐμοῦ σε βασανίζεσθαι ὁρῶν σου νικώμενον τὸν τῆς τυραννίδος ὑπερήφανον λογισμὸν ὑπὸ τῆς διὰ τὴν εὐσέβειαν ἡμῶν ὑπομονῆς;

[6]οἳ καὶ ἐξεδίκησαν τὸ γένος εἰς θεὸν ἀφορῶντες καὶ μέχρι θανάτου τὰς βασάνους ὑπομείναντες.

modal force, we have essentially the same causal connection between the endurance of the martyrs and the departure of Antiochus that is expressed at 1:11.

According to these passages the deaths of the martyrs-- more specifically: their endurance unto death--had quite objective results: Antiochus departed from the country and peace was restored. The claim is made that the martyrs' deaths are effective. The martyrs die efficaciously; the nation benefits from their deaths.

The uniqueness of this claim becomes apparent in light of three considerations: a) The assertion that the deaths of the martyrs were directly responsible for the departure of Antiochus and the restoration of peace is not supported by the historical record as we have it from I and II Maccabees and Josephus. b) Such a claim was apparently not an element in the stories of Eleazar and the seven brothers prior to their reworking at the hands of our author. It is not found in II Maccabees. 2) This assertion is in no way necessary to the author's central (stated!) thesis. He needs only to show that the martyrs did endure amidst tortures unto death, thus that godly reason is master of human passions; he has no cause to show that these deaths were in any way "effective."

In additional passages which express the significance of the martyrs' deaths the word ὑπομονή does not appear. However, the emphasis throughout IV Maccabees on endurance as the outstanding feature of their deaths leaves little doubt that also in these other passages the ὑπομονή motif, although unexpressed, is not absent; in other words, it is not death qua death that is effective but the martyrs' steadfastness, their endurance, to the point of death itself. This point is clearest in 11:24-25, where the sixth son speaks to Antiochus from the torture wheel: "We six youths have destroyed your tyranny. For is not your impotence to affect our resolve and to force us to eat polluted food your downfall?" And at 17:2 the author eulogizes the mother: "O mother who with (your) seven sons did make impotent the tyrant's power and did thwart his evil designs . . ."; (her steadfastness is described in the next verse).

In 17:20-22 the author says the martyrs are honored by the fact that

> because of them the enemies did not prevail over our nation, and the tyrant was punished, and the fatherland was purified; as if they had become [or: since they had become, as it were] a ransom for the nation's sin. And through the blood of these pious ones and (through) their expiatory death Divine Providence delivered Israel, which

170

previously had been afflicted.[7]

Another relevant passage is 18:4-5:

Thanks to them the nation came to be at peace; and having restored the right observance of the Law in our fatherland, they overcame their enemies. And the tyrant Antiochus was punished upon earth and is being punished now that he is dead. For when he failed completely in forcing the citizens of Jerusalem to adopt foreign ways and depart from the customs of their fathers, then he left Jerusalem and fought against the Persians.[8]

Here two key ideas are εἰρήνευσεν τὸ ἔθνος and τὴν εὐνομίαν . . . ἀνανεωσάμενοι. This is exactly the same terminology used to describe the situation in Israel prior to Jason's Hellenizing reform: βαθεῖαν εἰρήνην διὰ τὴν εὐνομίαν οἱ πατέρες ἡμῶν εἶχον (3:20). Furthermore, the situation for which Jason is responsible is described in terms of παρανομία (4:19; cf. 5:13, 9:3)-- a term which is used very infrequently in the LXX. The author of IV Maccabees, then, appears to be expressing the belief that the deaths of the martyrs were collectively effective in restoring the "pre-sin" situation!

In all of these passages, in fact, the author apparently intends to suggest a direct causal connection between the martyrs' endurance unto death and the collapse of Antiochus' power over Israel. The very novelty of his claim raises intriguing questions of how and why it originated. The attempt to answer such questions is greatly facilitated by certain clues within the writing itself. One such clue consists of a certain tension between the author's overt claim and the implications of several other statements.

A cursory reading of one verse of the last passage discussed (18:4) gives the impression that the author is once again affirming that the endurance of nine Jewish martyrs convinced Antiochus to leave the country. But a more careful analysis of vv. 3-5 yields a different impression.

_____

[7]δι' αὐτοὺς τὸ ἔθνος ἡμῶν τοὺς πολεμίους μὴ ἐπικρατῆσαι καὶ τὸν τύραννον τιμωρηθῆναι καὶ τὴν πατρίδα καθαρισθῆναι, ὥσπερ ἀντίψυχον γεγονότας τῆς τοῦ ἔθνους ἁμαρτίας. καὶ διὰ τοῦ αἵματος τῶν εὐσεβῶν ἐκείνων καὶ τοῦ ἱλαστηρίου θανάτου αὐτῶν [here I deviate from Rahlf's text, omitting τοῦ with A; see supra, Chapter I, n. 87] ἡ θεία πρόνοια τὸν Ισραηλ προκακωθέντα διέσωσεν.

[8]καὶ δι' αὐτοὺς εἰρήνευσεν τὸ ἔθνος, καὶ τὴν εὐνομίαν τὴν ἐπὶ τῆς πατρίδος ἀνανεωσάμενοι ἐκπεπόρθηκαν τοὺς πολεμίους
. . . .

The problem is introduced by 18:4: "Thanks to them
[i.e., ἐκεῖνοι of v. 3] the nation came to be at peace; and
having restored the right observance of the law in our fatherland, they overcame their enemies." From a strict grammatical
standpoint, the participle and verb in the latter clause have
no antecedent; being plural, they need a plural antecedent, but
the only noun subject of the sentence is τὸ ἔθνος. From the
historical perspective "the nation" (under the Maccabees!)
would indeed be a more appropriate subject for "restored the
law" and "overcame their enemies," especially since ἐκπορθεῖν
has definite connotations of plundering and pillaging--actions
difficult indeed to attribute to our nine martyrs! This interpretation is also possible on grammatical grounds, for τὸ ἔθνος
does not connote an indivisible object but a host of individuals,
a company of people living together and thus constituting "a
people." I suggest, then, that the "they" implicit in ἀνανεωσάμενοι and ἐκπεπόρθηκαν represents an historical reminiscence
of those faithful Jews who took up arms against the Seleucids,
restored the law and pillaged their enemies (cf. 17:23). More
specifically, one can suppose that underlying this statement at
18:4 is the memory of Judas' cleansing of the Temple and his
victories against the generals of Antiochus. Furthermore, in
the phrase δι'αὐτούς there may be a faint echo of the connection
already noted in II Maccabees between the death of the martyrs
(especially the seventh brother; cf. his dying prayer) and the
subsequent successes of the Maccabees. The important point is
that while the author of IV Maccabees appears to echo certain
facts from Israel's past, he seems to be uninterested in their
actual historical significance. Thus, he does not explicitly
mention the Maccabees and their contributions but concentrates
almost exclusively upon the nine martyrs.

That the author is indeed aware of the deeds of the
Maccabees as reported in Jason of Cyrene or II Maccabees is
implied also by 18:5. The assertion that Antiochus was punished upon earth is followed matter-of-factly by the statement:
"for . . . he left Jerusalem and marched against the Persians."
Nothing further is said about Antiochus, but that there is some
connection between Antiochus' punishment and his marching off
to Persia is an unavoidable inference. Such an implication on
the author's part is most easily understandable if one assumes
that he was familiar with the death of Antiochus as it appears
in II Maccabees 9:1-29.

Another factor is the author's explanation in 18:5 of
why Antiochus left Jerusalem: "When he failed completely to
force the people of Jerusalem to adopt foreign ways and abandon
the customs of their fathers . . . ." In the context of IV
Maccabees, the significance of the plural τοὺς Ιεροσολυμίτας
can hardly be overemphasized. In the first place, by implication it contradicts other assertions by the author (e.g., at
9:30, 11:24-25, 17:2, 17:10) which suggest that Eleazar, the
seven brothers and the mother singlehandedly convinced Antiochus
by their endurance that his attempts were futile. In the second
place "the people of Jerusalem" indicates the author's full
awareness that the nine martyrs of his story were not the only
Jews who stood fast when confronted by persecution.[9] Here the
author is repeating, in intensified form, a notice already
given in 4:24-26. There it is said that Antiochus was completely unsuccessful in destroying the nation's observance of
the Law through the decrees enforced by his subordinates. All
his threats and punishments were totally disregarded; therefore
he himself, through tortures, pressured each individual in the
nation to deny Judaism by tasting unclean food. The remainder
of IV Maccabees shows that even this personal effort was useless too.

Two other brief notices which parallel the plural "inhabitants of Jerusalem" at 18:5 appear at the beginning of the
martyrdom proper. At 5:2 it is said that Antiochus ordered his

---

[9] I should mention the opinion of Hadas that the latter
part of v. 5 "does seem to be a gloss on v. 4" (op. cit., p.
238, n. 5). This appears likely only if Antioch is the setting
of the martyrdom--a view that Hadas defends. But if the scene
is Antioch, what about the term πατρίς at 18:4, 1:11 and 17:21?
It is not clear how the endurance of martyrs in Antioch could
have been instrumental in the purification of the "fatherland."
In Hadas' favor is the author's remark that Eleazar was known
to many in the king's circle because of his philosophy (reading with Venetus). On the other hand, in view of 4:22-26, I
find Hadas incomprehensible when he writes that if Antiochus
were actually present in person "no site other than Antioch is
possible" (p. 111). Perhaps it would be more reasonable to
postulate that this martyr tradition developed in Antioch,
where, by the fourth century, a "cult of the martyrs" was
associated with their (supposed) tomb in that city. The Anti-
ochene tradition, however, preserved the memory that the
martyrdoms occurred in Palestine. The author of IV Maccabees
is aware of this fact. On the possible relationship of IV
Maccabees and Antioch cf. infra, Chapter VI, Part IV (B. 2.).

bodyguards to bring up "each Hebrew in turn" (ἕνα ἕκαστον Εβ-
ραῖον). Those who refused to eat swine's flesh and meat
sacrificed to idols were executed (5:3). "And many having
been seized and carried off, the first one of the herd, a man
named Eleazar, . . . was brought before him" (5:4). The clear
implication of these scattered statements (4:24-26, 5:2-4,
18:5) is that many Jews were arrested and subjected to tortures
designed to force them to renounce Judaism, and many remained
faithful unto death. Nevertheless, just as clearly, IV Maccabees is a martyr story which centers on only nine individuals,
and, with the probable exception of 18:3-5, all the affirmations
about the import and meaning of martyrdom are confined to statements about these nine persons.

Taken as a whole, then, IV Maccabees seems to reflect a
certain tension between the individual martyrs whose suffering
is described in detail and the faithful people as a whole. This
situation can be accounted for to a considerable degree by the
author's purpose in telling the martyrs' story.

In the first place, the martyrs described here are a
typical example which serves as a paradigm--a paradigm on two
levels. According to the author's introduction, he intends
them as the most appropriate illustration of his central thesis
(1:7-9). But further, as suggested earlier, the author seems
also to present them as examples for his hearers to emulate.
The author-speaker affirms that "you, father [i.e. Eleazar],
by your endurance fortified our observance of the Law" (7:9).
At 8:16-26 the speaker recites various arguments and excuses
that the brothers might have used to rationalize compliance and
escape death. Rhetorical embellishment is hardly sufficient
explanation for the speaker's inclusion of these hypothetical
escape routes. More likely, the author intends to counter
some of the reservations he supposes his hearers might have
about standing fast unto death, or else he is combatting
definite erroneous ideas held by some Jews, to the effect that
compliance with paganism under extreme duress would be forgiven
by God (cf. especially 8:22, 25).

That one of the author's purposes is exhortation to
steadfastness is supported above all by his words at 18:1-2:
"O Israelites, children born of Abraham's seed, obey this Law
and practice piety in every way; for you know that godly
reason is master of the passions--not only over internal pains

but over external ones as well." Here the author clearly com-
bines his stated theme with what one suspects is his real
driving purpose, that is, to exhort his hearers to stand fast.
Even the syntax of the sentence (πείθεσθε--εὐσεβεῖτε--γινώσ-
κοντες) indicates which concern, exhortation or philosophical
discourse, is subservient to the other.

This hortatory concern is a complement to what might be
called the speaker's purpose of occasion. IV Maccabees was, in
all likelihood, composed for a particular occasion, namely a
commemoration of the Maccabean martyrs, perhaps at the traditional site of their tomb in Antioch.[10] The hypothesis of such
an occasion best explains the passages of unrestrained rhetorical display where the martyrs are eulogized with metaphors
sometimes set on a universal scale.[11] It is from this perspective of barely restrained encomium that one must consider the
author's statements regarding the effect of the martyrs' deaths

---

[10]That the occasion was a commemoration of the martyrs'
has been argued by A. Dupont-Sommer, Le Quatrième Livre des
Machabées (Paris, 1939), pp. 67-68, and Hadas, op. cit., pp.
104-109. Note especially τοὺς κατὰ τοῦτον τὸν καιρὸν . . .
ἀποθανόντας (1:10). Cf. also 3:19 (ἤδη δὲ καὶ ὁ καιρὸς ἡμᾶς
καλεῖ . . .).

[11]See especially 7:1-15, 14:2-8; chapt. 15, esp. vv.
29-32; cf. 17:11-16. Note some of the figures employed:
Eleazar pilots the ship of religion (piety) in the sea of
passions (7:1-3); he is described as the philosopher of life
divine (7:7) and is called a "great king over the passions"
(7:10). Of the brothers, note the play on the sacred number
seven (14:7-8). The mother is compared with Noah's ark, which
bore the world (κοσμοφοροῦσα) in the universal cataclysm (15:
31-32). At 15:17 the author bursts forth with this ecstatic
line: "O solitary woman who gave birth to perfect piety."
At 17:14 "the world and the life of men" were the spectators
at the "divine contest" between Antiochus and the martyrs. On
one occasion the mother is called μήτηρ ἔθνους (15:29). Similarly, Eleazar is called "father" (7:5, 9)--even as is Aaron
(7:11)--apparently because he defended the Law with his blood
and strengthened his people's faithfulness to their religion
(7:8-9). In their steadfastness, then, Eleazar and the mother,
by noble example, defended and preserved the religion of their
people. Thus they can be described as the "ancestors" of a
people who have passed through suffering to attain a deepened
loyalty to their God. Such a view must be seen in its historical perspective, that is, from the standpoint of the speaker-
author, decades after the fact, when the resistance of faithful
Jews in the Antiochian persecution could naturally enough be
understood as the beginning of the nation's "rebirth."

for the benefit of the nation. The eulogy context is particularly self-evident in the "editorial" assertions of the author-narrator (1:10-11, 17:2-5, 17:8-10, 17:17-24; cf. 18:3).
Although he apparently knows of the resistance of other loyal Jews and the successful uprising of the Maccabees, as the keynote speaker at a "memorial service" for those individual martyrs (around whom a quasi cult had developed?) his purpose is already limited by the occasion. He intends to praise those being remembered and honored. Thus he describes the Antiochian persecution from the restricted viewpoint of the nine individuals whose praises he sings. Likewise, the historical effects of anti-Seleucid resistance are expressed in terms of the resistance of nine indivuduals. Furthermore, since according to the tradition, they did not take up arms but resolutely died for their faith, the known historical results of resistance he describes as the effect of their endurance unto death. In other words, the narrative of a whole span of historical events is concentrated into the story of the nine martyrs. The importance (and the rewards!) of unswerving loyalty to God and to his Law is formulated in terms of the effect of the martyrs' deaths.

As an impressive medium for his eulogy, the speaker adopts the form of philosophical discourse--a fact which tells a great deal about the speaker and his anticipated hearers. Having praised the martyrs for whom the occasion demands veneration, the speaker draws the appropriate moral: As they conquered passion with pious reason, so let us.

My argument in the preceding pages has been that a) in IV Maccabees one can detect a certain tension between statements that the martyrs were solely responsible for breaking the hold of Antiochus upon Israel and remarks which indicate the author's awareness that other faithful Jews shared this honor; b) this tension can be illuminated by assuming actual memory of historical events on the one hand while, on the other, taking into account the author's double purpose of encomium and exhortation. The single purpose of this argument is to suggest the appropriate context for understanding his assertions about the meaning of the martyrs' deaths, namely, his purposes.

Intent on "congratulating" his heroes (cf. μακαρίζειν at
1:10) and moving his hearers, the author of IV Maccabees
heightens not only the marvelous aspects of their suffering but
also the impact of their death. In short, one must say that it
is from the perspective of his eulogizing and hortatory purposes
that the author affirms that the martyrs' deaths were effective
and beneficial for the nation. Do such affirmations constitute
a "doctrine of expiatory death," with which IV Maccabees is so
frequently credited? One may begin to answer this question by
noting that at 1:11 "they conquered the tyrant by endurance"
and "through them the land was purified (= God purified the land
through them)" refer to the same historical event. The second
statement simply repeats the first in religious-cultic terminology. Similarly, at 17:21a, "because of them . . . the
fatherland was purified" cannot be understood except as a reference to Antiochus' departure, which IV Maccabees insists is a
result of the martyrs' endurance (not their spilled blood).
Similarly, 17:22 intends to say nothing more than: "through
their death God delivered Israel" (i.e., from Antiochus).

Another very important text at this point is a passage
not mentioned heretofore in this chapter: the prayer of the
dying Eleazar at 6:28-29. This is the only statement in IV
Maccabees in which the beneficial effect of the martyrs' deaths
is expressed exclusively in what appear to be religious terms:
"Be merciful to your people--satisfied by our punishment for
them. Let my blood serve for their purification and accept my
life as a ransom for them."[12] This text is often cited as the
prime example of the author's doctrine of vicarious expiatory
death. According to this interpretation, the martyrs suffer
and die in the place of their fellow Jews so that they don't
have to; the martyrs take upon themselves the fury of God's
wrath, etc. That view does appear to be substantiated by
Eleazar's words, but reservations are justified on two grounds.

In the first place, the particular formulation of
Eleazar's prayer raises questions. It is significant that
Eleazar does not say "I am dying so that my blood . . ."; he
prays rather: "make my blood . . ." and "take my life (as)

---

[12]ἵλεως γενοῦ τῷ ἔθνει σου ἀρκεσθεὶς τῇ ἡμετέρᾳ ὑπὲρ
αὐτῶν δίκῃ. καθάρσιον αὐτῶν ποίησον τὸ ἐμὸν αἷμα καὶ ἀντίψυχον
αὐτῶν λαβὲ τὴν ἐμὴν ψυχήν.

. . . ." In other words, the effectiveness of his death is dependent upon the way in which God regards it and whether or not He accepts it for purification and ransom. This, of course, is exactly what God does every time that a priest makes an offering on behalf of his people. Now it can hardly be accidental that Eleazar's priesthood is greatly emphasized in IV Maccabees. He is described as coming from a priestly family (5:4; in II Maccabees he is "one of the foremost scribes"-- 6:18). He declares that he will never deny his "honorable priesthood" (5:35). At 7:6 the author praises him: "O priest worthy of (your) priesthood"; at 17:9 he is "an aged priest."

Most illuminating, however, is 7:11-12: "For just as our father Aaron, armed with the censer, ran through the multitude and overcame the fiery angel, so Eleazar, son of Aaron, did not forsake reason even though he was consumed by the fire." Here Eleazar's steadfastness in the flame is compared with Aaron's overcoming the angel who destroys by fire. The biblical account in Numbers 17 mentions no "fiery angel" (but cf. Wisdom 18:20-25!), but that chapter does contain a divine word which later tradition easily enough expanded into a consuming ἄγγελος: "The Lord said to Moses and Aaron, 'Go away from the midst of this congregation, and I shall utterly consume them all at once'" (Num. 17:9-10; cf. 16:35). The account in Numbers continues by relating how Aaron, in accord with Moses' advice, ran into the midst of the congregation with the censer "and made expiation ( יכפר /ἐξιλάσατο) for the people" (17:12). This act of expiation effected the cessation of the plague brought upon the people by God's wrath (v. 11). One need only recall how popular (and useful) allegory was among hellenized Jews to account for the idea that Eleazar, like his priestly ancestor, makes atonement for the people by overcoming the flames. Eleazar's prayer at 6:28-29 can be interpreted as but an explicit formulation, in different language, of the basic idea present at 7:11-12; and that is an idea likely dependent in some way upon an allegorization of the fire/atonement elements in the Aaron episode.

In the second place, insofar as IV Mac. 17:21-22 expresses God's response to Eleazar's plea,[13] even 6:28-29 cannot

---

[13]Compare ἵλεως γενοῦ with διέσωσεν, and καθάρσιον with καθαρισθῆναι and ἱλαστήριος. Also αἷμα and αἷμα, ἀντίψυχον and ἀντίψυχον (used only in these two passages in the entire LXX!).

be separated radically from the objective historical effect of the martyrs' endurance unto death (17:20). In other words, the specifically religious categories used to express the effect and meaning of the martyrs' deaths in 6:28-29 (and 17:21-22) do not constitute an independent affirmation. Rather, they supplement the central assertion that the deaths were effective and beneficial for the nation in that Antiochus departed. This situation appears to involve a very "theological" motive. Whether or not IV Maccabees be regarded as an encomium, it is nonetheless clear that in most of the passages commenting on the effect of the martyrs' deaths the martyrs themselves are definitely the agents of victory.[14] It is only when the author explicitly ascribes the nation's deliverance to God--as is only fitting for an aspiring philosopher to do (cf. 1:1-21)--that he employs specifically religious-cultic concepts and terminology, that is, in 6:28-29 (the plea for mercy etc. is addressed to God) and 17:21-22 (in v. 22 the active subject is ἡ θεία πρόνοια; the martyrs' deaths have become the means through which God accomplishes his purpose).[15] Apparently the author considers religious categories, and them alone, appropriate to affirmations about God. On the other hand, statements about God appear to be the only context in which he considers strictly religious categories necessary.

From the foregoing I conclude that, strictly speaking, IV Maccabees does not intend to present a "doctrine of expiatory death." The "removal" of the nation's sin is not described as the forgiveness of personal wrongs or as the assuaging of guilt --we hear nothing about the Hellenizers being "forgiven"--but as the reversal of an overt situation: the land was purified. The sin of apostasy is thought of as that which defiles the land--that is, defiles by the pollution of apostasy itself and also by Antiochus, who had been sent against Israel by God because He was angered by that sin. According to the author,

---

[14]Cf. 1:11: "they"; 9:30: "our endurance"; 11:24-25: "we six youths"; 17:2: "mother and seven sons"; 17:10: "they."

[15]In those passages where the terminology used is somewhat ambiguous or where it suggests a religious interpretation without stating it explicitly, the subject of the action is also ambiguous. Cf. 1:11: καθαρισθῆναι (passive!) δι᾽αὐτῶν. Similarly 17:21a: καθαρισθῆναι (δι᾽αὐτούς--v. 20); compare δι᾽ αὐτούς at 18:4.

the deaths of the martyrs were instrumental in removing that
defilement: the army of Antiochus on the one hand, the apostasy
of the Jews on the other. (This double sense is suggested by
εἰρηνεύειν and εὐνομία at 18:4.) Only in this sense can one
speak at all about ideas of expiatory death in IV Maccabees,
much less about a "doctrine." I find it more appropriate by far
to speak of "effective death" in IV Maccabees. The author
repeatedly asserts that the martyrs' endurance unto death had
objective, beneficial effect. The religious dimension of that
effect (or: that effect as a religious event) he can then describe with language from Israel's cultic-religious tradition.[16]

One further observation. The transition from "historical" to "religious" statement at 17:21-22 is introduced by
ὥσπερ: "they having become as it were (or: so to speak) a
ransom for the nation's sin." This ὥσπερ may be altogether
without significance. It may, however, provide an inadvertent
clue for evaluating more adequately the meaning of the martyrs'
deaths in IV Maccabees. Ὥσπερ points to the possibility that
ἀντίψυχον, αἷμα, and ἱλαστήριος θάνατος are intended more in a
metaphorical sense than as identification indicators.[17] That
is, the author may not be saying that the martyrs are sacrificial victims slain or ransoms paid. Rather: in light of the
extraordinary faith in which they offer their lives for the
sake of the Law, God accepts that supreme offering as He accepts
a perfect sacrifice; He regards it as an act of expiation. Perhaps it is in this sense, then, that their deaths become the
means through which God works to purify his people and his land.

---

[16]The foregoing paragraphs--especially the last one--
are intended in part as a reaction and corrective to the
tendency of scholars to treat "the doctrine of expiatory
death" in IV Mac. as a separable and self-contained entity for
the sources of which one should turn immediately to the OT.
Cf., e.g., H. Wenschkewitz, Die Spiritualisierung der Kultusbegriffe (Leipzig, 1932), pp. 20-21; Surkau, op. cit., pp. 60ff.
Also Lohse, op. cit., pp. 70-72; Townshend in AP, II, pp. 663-
64; Hadas, op. cit., pp. 121-22.

[17]Cf. Liddell and Scott at ὥσπερ II.: "to limit or
modify an assertion or apologize for a metaphor . . . ."
Ὥσπερ is used in three distinguishable ways in IV Mac.: to
mean "as (also)" with other examples or instances following
(2:6, 16; 7:19; 16:25); "as though" or "like" plus a simile or
some expression of comparison (6:5; 7:1, 5, 11; 8:29; 9:22;
14:5; 15:15; 16:13); simply "as" or "as if" (5:22; 6:16; 8:6;
9:5; 17:7).

These statements require some elaboration. Regarding
the possible metaphorical use of cultic terms E. Lohse has
observed that

> Weil die Juden in der Diaspora den Opferkult nicht
> selbst vollziehen konnten, ist im hellenistischen
> Judentum die Opferterminologie häufig im übertragenen
> Sinne verwendet worden, besonders in der Anwendung auf
> ethische Fragen.[18]

One should not conclude, however, that the metaphorical use of
cultic terms originated in Hellenized Diaspora Judaism. The
ultimate roots of this usage undoubtedly are to be sought in
the prophetic protest against cultic acts as substitutes for
righteousness. In Hosea 6:6 Yahweh declares: "I desire steadfast love and not sacrifice, the knowledge of God, rather than
burnt offerings" (RSV).[19] The element of polemic against the
sacrificial cult is present also in the Psalms (e.g. 40:6, 50:
12-13, 51:16--but cf. v. 19), but there one finds also the
expression of a recognition that prayer or praise can be as
acceptable in God's eyes as a rich sacrifice. At Ps. 50:14 one
is enjoined to offer God a "sacrifice of praise" (LXX 49:14:
θυσία αἰνέσεως); and at LXX 49:23 God says: θυσία αἰνέσεως
δοξάσει με . . . . In Ps. 141:2 the psalmist asks that his
prayer be counted by God as an evening sacrifice (cf. also 40:
6-8, 69:30-31). More significant is Ps. 51:17: "The sacrifice
acceptable to God is a broken spirit; a broken and a contrite
heart, O God thou wilt not despise" (RSV). Here it is not a
specific act which is understood as a substitute for cultic
sacrifice; rather, in a more generalized sense, cultic terminology describes the attitude of the man who stands before God.
Nevertheless his "contrite spirit" is still directly related
(apparently) to a sin for which sacrifice would be an appropriate response in light of God's anticipated forgiveness.

Greater distance from the realm of cultic sacrifice is
evident in Tobit 4:11, where alms-giving is called a "good
offering" (δῶρον ἀγαθόν) before God. Even more reminiscent of
Ps. 51:17 is a Qumran text, IQS 9.4-5: ". . . the offering
of the lips in accordance with the law shall be as an agreeable
odour of righteousness, and perfection of way shall be as the
voluntary gift of a delectable oblation" (trans. Dupont-Sommer).

---

[18]Lohse, op. cit., p. 71.

[19]See also I Sam. 15:27, Amos 5:21-24, Micah 6:6-8, Is.
1:10-17, Zech. 7:1-10.

As the earlier quotation from Lohse suggests, however, the metaphorical use of cultic terminology appears to have been most frequent in hellenized Judaism. In several passages in Aristeas, Wisdom of Solomon and Philo one finds cultic terms employed not simply to describe acts closely related to sacrifice (e.g., prayer, thanksgiving). The "distance" over which the conceptual transference has to be made becomes greater; cultic terms are used to describe attitudes and life stances (e.g., faith, a pious life, noble character) as well as specific acts completely unrelated to the cultic act of sacrifice. To illustrate this last point first, one reads in Aristeas 19 and 37 that the offering which Ptolemy makes to the supreme God is the setting free of 100,000 captives![20]

In Wisdom of Solomon 3:4-6 one finds sacrifice language used in a striking simile. The context here is a description of the fate of the righteous, having been condemned to a shameful death by evil men:  "For even if they are punished in the sight of men, their hope is satisfied by immortality; and although they were chastened a little, they shall receive great reward because God tested them and found them worthy of Himself. Like gold in the smelting furnace he proved them, and like a whole burnt offering he accepted them (ὡς ὁλοκάρπωμα θυσίας προσεδέξατο αὐτούς)."

In Philo allegorization of cultic institutions is the umbrella under which the metaphorical use of cultic terms can be understood. Yet there are passages where the movement is not directly from cult object/act to allegory; rather, at times, an independent act (for example) can be described with cultic metaphors. At det. pot. 21, for example, Philo says that God welcomes all genuine acts of worship. And what are they? The worship (plural!) of a person who offers truth as his single, unpretentious sacrifice (γνήσιοι δ'εἰσὶν αἱ ψυχῆς ψιλὴν καὶ μόνην θυσίαν φερούσης ἀλήθειαν . . .).[21] In the

---

[20]This metaphorical use of cultic language is accompanied in Aristeas by an anti-cultic polemic on the one hand (e.g., 234) and a rationalizing allegorization of cultic practice on the other (e.g., 169-70).

[21]This statement is made in a polemical context; here Philo is not engaged in an allegorizing interpretation of Israel's institutions.

course of interpreting Num. 28:2, Philo (de Cher. 85) writes
that "He who has learned these things . . . will offer to God
a superior sacrifice without blemish, faith, at feasts given
by no mortals" (ἄμωμον καὶ κάλλιστον ἱερεῖον οἴσει θεῷ πίστιν
ἐν οὐ θνητῶν ἑορταῖς).

A rhetorical question at vit. Mos. 2.108, while not
itself an item of allegorical explication, does fall within a
general context of allegorization:  "For true worship--what is
it except the piety of a life devoted to God?" (ἡ γὰρ ἀληθὴς
ἱερουργία τίς ἂν εἴη πλὴν ψυχῆς θεοφιλοῦς εὐσέβεια;)(cf. de
Somn. 2.74).  The same provision must be made regarding a
statement at spec. leg. 1.272:  "And indeed they need bring
nothing else, since by offering themselves they present the
best sacrifice:  a most perfect fulfillment of good and noble
character" (αὐτοὺς φέροντες πλήρωμα καλοκἀγαθίας τελειότατον
τὴν ἀρίστην ἀνάγουσι θυσίαν . . .).[22]

Such texts as these show that in Diaspora Judaism acts
of self-denial as well as attitudes of devotion to God could be
described in cultic terms.[23]  It is unlikely that this type of
metaphorical description can be entirely discounted as a
factor in IV Maccabees 6:28-29 and 17:21-22.[24]

---

[22]Some of these and other Philonic texts may be able to
provide some insight into the development from cult ritual to
the metaphorical use of cultic language. At vit. Mos. 2.106-
108 Philo emphasizes the intention of the worshipper as the
essential factor in sacrifice; without purity of heart one's
sacrifice does not effect forgiveness but serves merely as a
reminder of past sins. At spec. leg. 1.290 Philo holds that
God considers a sacrifice to consist not in the victims but in
the worshipper's intention and zeal based on virtue.  Thus,
from motive and character as the central and effectuating
elements of sacrifice or worship it seems to be only a small
step, for Philo, to the absolutizing of those elements so that
they constitute worship in such a way that the ritual acts in
which they can express themselves are not really essential in
the eyes of God.

[23]Cf. Corpus Hermeticum, Tractate 1 (Poimandres):
δέξαι λογικὰς θυσίας ἁγνὰς ἀπὸ ψυχῆς καὶ καρδίας πρὸς σέ
ἀνατεταμένης . . . .

[24]A note to prevent one possible misimpression:  I am
not suggesting that the "metaphorical" use of cultic language
has anything to do with the concept of effective death in IV
Mac.  Rather:  the step from "effective death" to "expiatory
death" may have occurred because there was available a tradition of the metaphorical use of cultic terms.  Obviously IV
Mac. 1:11, 6:28-29, 17:21-22 are saying a great deal more than,
say, Wisdom 3:4-6.  For one thing, the martyrs' deaths have
repercussions for the whole nation; that is not the case in
Wisdom.

## II.  The Sources and Origin of the Concept of Effective Death
in IV Maccabees

In the foregoing section I suggested that IV Maccabees
reflects a concept of "effective death" which several times
(1:11, 6:28-29, 17:21-22) is expressed (metaphorically?) in
categories found also in the Old Testament:  blood, purification,
expiation, ransom.  Of course, some of the words used in 6:28-29
and 17:21-22 (i.e., καθάρσιον, ἀντίψυχον, and ἱλαστήριος [to
describe anything except the lid of the ark]) are not used in
the Greek versions.[25]  Nevertheless, the ideas of purification
and expiation are frequently expressed in the LXX by words with
καθαρ- and ἱλασ- roots, and the components of ἀντίψυχον (i.e.,
ἀντί and ψυχή) make it an obvious synonym for λύτρον.  Moreover,
two of the words in these IV Maccabees texts (αἷμα, καθαρίζειν)
are commonplace cultic-religious terms in the LXX.[26]  Thus for
two of the exact words and for the ideas underlying most of the
remainder, there is no good reason to question the assertion
that the author draws upon the Old Testament.

The possible exception to this statement is the ἀρκεσθείς
phrase:  "(Be) satisfied by our punishment for them" (6:
28).  It is noteworthy that the verb ἀρκεῖν is never used
in this sense in the LXX to speak of God.[27]  Nor, so far
as I can determine, is punishment ever connected with the
idea of God's being satiated by it.  When God punishes his
people, his purpose is their repentance (cf. e.g., Lev. 26).
Evidence of repentance, not degree of suffering, is what
propitiates an angry Yahweh.  Even when it is said (e.g.,
Is. 40:2) that Israel has received double punishment for
all her sins, the prophet does not intimate that He has
been "satisfied."  Nor when He exacts vengeance upon his
enemies is there any hint of his being "filled" or "satisfied"
by their suffering (cf. e.g., Deut. 32).

---

[25]All three words are found in Greek texts; cf. Liddell
and Scott, s. v.  On ἱλαστήριος/ἱλαστήριον see Deissmann's
important article in ZNW 4(1903), 193-212.

[26]For καθαρίζειν with respect to Jerusalem, Judah or the
land, cf. Jer. 13:27; II Chron. 34:3, 5, 8; Ez. 39:12, 14, 16.

[27]In Is. 1:11 שבע (Qal) has God as subject, but the
reference is to unacceptable sacrifices.  In Jer. 46:10 "sword"
is the subject of the same verb:  "That day is the day of the
Lord God of hosts, a day of vengeance, to avenge himself on
his foes.  The sword shall devour and be sated, and drink its
fill of their blood" (RSV).

On the other hand, in the Greek world--although ἀρκεσθαι is not used in this sense among the Greeks either--arbitrary deities often wreck havoc or withhold their favor, not until men repent but until they (the gods) are "satisfied" by the death of a human being! In my opinion, then, the idea behind the ἀρκεσθείς phrase at IV Mac. 6:28 can be most adequately understood by assuming influence from the Greek world.

But if, as I have argued, this cultic-religious terminology is used to formulate differently a more fundamental concept, then a more important question than whether καθαρίζειν or ἀντίψυχον appear in the Old Testament is this: From where does the concept of effective human death derive? Whence the influences that issue in this interpretation of the martyrs' suffering and death? An answer to these questions can now be attempted on the basis of the surveys in chapters three and four and of the preceding analysis of IV Maccabees' presentation of the martyrs' deaths.

\*    \*    \*

In his discussion of the expiatory power of vicarious death and the concept of vicarious expiation, Eduard Lohse implies that the idea of vicarious expiatory death can be adequately accounted for by the Old Testament views of substitution (I Sam. 14:45) and intercession (Gen. 18:23ff., Ex. 32: 32); the prescriptions for the expiation of blood-guilt (Ex. 21:23, 32:30, II Sam. 21:1ff., etc.); the picture of the suffering servant of the Lord in Isaiah 53; and the conception of community solidarity. Of particular significance is the ancient idea that life is in the blood and that life surrendered effects expiation.[28]

With the possible exception of Isaiah 53 one can assume that all the texts and ideas mentioned were familiar to the author of IV Maccabees and that they contributed, in some way, to his interpretation of the martyrs' deaths. The key question nevertheless remains: Does the Old Testament provide a sufficient background for the concept of effective death as it is formulated in IV Maccabees?

The preceding survey of the tradition of the righteous ones killed by Antiochus (Chapter II) has indicated that prior to IV Maccabees no claim was made that the martyrs' deaths were

---

[28]Lohse, op. cit., pp. 94-104, 106-107.

effective either as expiation for the land and its people or in
any other way.  That fact, in itself, is significant--albeit not
finally conclusive--when set against Lohse's contention that the
concept of vicarious expiatory death is of Palestinian origin
(p. 71).  In Assumption of Moses, of course, the death of Taxo
and his sons is in some sense "effective" since it appears to
trigger God's wrathful intervention.  But this view of the
martyrs' deaths as an eschatological event is not echoed, however faintly, in IV Maccabees.

In the Old Testament and other Jewish literature Isaiah
53 is the only text which might be interpreted as expressing a
concept of vicarious expiatory suffering or death.  But, as has
been shown, evidence is lacking that Isaiah 53 was so understood
in the intervening centuries between Second Isaiah and IV Maccabees.  Nor is there real evidence, terminological or otherwise,
that the interpretation in IV Maccabees is dependent upon Isaiah
53 in any way, although Isaiah 43:2 is quoted (18:14).  Wolff's
supposed linguistic parallels are either actually non-existent
or too general to be of value as evidence.[29]

Some of the texts discussed in a previous chapter (for
example, the episodes of Achan, Phineas, the hanged chiefs, the
sons of Saul) may legitimately be considered important elements
in the Old Testament background with which the author of IV
Maccabees was familiar and upon which he drew.  In these
episodes there is a direct connection between human deaths and
expiation.  But one must avoid speaking of "parallels," for in
all these texts those who are slain are either passive victims
(involved only because of the concept of corporate solidarity:
Saul's sons, Achan's family) or they are guilty of some transgression worthy of death.  Neither statement is true about the
martyrs of IV Maccabees.  They are faithful, noble, pure--
innocent of the sin for which the nation is being punished.
But they are not passive victims; on the contrary, they are

---

[29]E.g., Is. 53:5: διὰ τὰς ἀνομίας ἡμῶν /IV Mac. 6:27:
διὰ τὸν νόμον.  Is. 53:5: παιδεία /IV Mac. 6:28: δίκη.  Is.
53:12: "für die Vielen"/IV Mac. 6:28: ὑπὲρ αὐτῶν.  Is. 53:7,
10: אשם/IV Mac. 17:21: ἀντίψυχον and 17:22: ἱλαστήριον.
Wolff, op. cit., pp. 47-48.  Even with his interpretation of
Is. 53, Wolff has to recognize that conceptual contrasts
between that chapter and IV Mac. are far more striking than
any parallels (pp. 48-49).

given every opportunity to renounce their religion and escape the tortures. In my opinion, then, there is a conceptual gap between these texts and IV Maccabees which the Old Testament alone does not fill. It is not enough to look for the source of vicarious expiatory death in the idea that blood makes expiation, for in the Old Testament it is the blood of <u>animals</u> which expiates human sins. Without convincing evidence, it is much too facile to assert that the ancient Jew could easily have "jumped" to the conclusion that <u>human</u> blood, especially innocent human blood, could make expiation for the sins of others.[30]

*      *      *

Without question the author of IV Maccabees was a loyal Jew who did not distinguish between ethical and cultic purity when characterizing the faithfulness that God expects of his people. Nevertheless, it is equally clear that this author moved in a Greek-Hellenistic thought world and that he was influenced by its language and its ideas. That his work plainly reflects his mastery of that language and his extensive adoption of many of those ideas can be demonstrated without difficulty.

The style and vocabulary of IV Maccabees indicate that this work is not written in "translation Greek." Its author was a master of the Greek language, with a firm control of its vocabulary and idioms.[31] He uses numerous terms which appear frequently in classical and Hellenistic texts but rarely in the LXX. We find, for example, φιλοσοφεῖν and φιλοσοφία (only here in the LXX); εὐσέβεια, ἀρετή, πρόνοια, πάθος, σωφροσύνη, φύσις, and καλοκἀγαθία; (cf. also ἡδονή, τύραννος and τυραννίς). Also

---

[30] In Num. 33:35 one reads: "blood pollutes the land, and no expiation can be made for the land, for the blood that is shed in it, except by the blood of him who shed it" (RSV). But this statement has nothing to do with the expiation by one man's blood of the sins of others. The point is that murder defiles the land itself and only the blood of the murderer (i.e. a <u>guilty</u> man, deserving of death) can remove that defilement. The claim of IV Mac. that the innocent blood of the martyrs purifies the land involves a very different set of presuppositions.

[31] Townshend, AP, II, p. 655. Cf. A. Dupont-Sommer, <u>Machabées</u>, pp. 57-66, on language and style.

of interest is ἡ θεία δίκη. Used practically as a divine appel-
lation,[32] this phrase calls to mind Δίκη, the Greek personifi-
cation of justice.[33]

The author of IV Maccabees is also clearly familiar with
various popular Platonic and Stoic ideas:[34] the necessity for
reason's control of the passions (the stated subject of the
work); four cardinal virtues (1:18, 2:23-24, 5:23; cf. 5:10);
the wise man as the true king (2:23, 14:2) and additional Stoic
concepts.[35] He also makes effective use of the ἀγών-motif, a
motif which has its background not in the Old Testament but in
Greek philosophy and which was especially popular in Cynic-
Stoic circles.[36] By certain formal features, too, IV Maccabees
reflects the pervasive influence of the Greek world. Whatever
the occasion or place for which it was written or delivered
orally, many scholars have observed that IV Maccabees exhibits
stylistic characteristics of the Cynic-Stoic diatribe.[37]

The creative influence of Greek ideas can be demonstrated in other ways which bear more directly upon IV Maccabees'
interpretation of the martyrs' deaths.

---

[32]Cf. 4:21, 8:22, 9:9, 18:22; 9:15: ἡ οὐράνιος δίκη.
8:14: ἣν σέβεσθε δίκην. 12:12: ἡ δίκη.

[33]Cf. Euripides, Heraclidae 941; Acts 28:4; Pausanius
5.18.2. Further: G. Schrenk, "δίκη κτλ.," TDNT, II, p. 181.

[34]See A. Dupont-Sommer, Machabées, pp. 33-56.

[35]The definition of wisdom at 1:16 is identical with
that of Cicero, Tusc. 4.26.57. Compare Philo, De congr. erud.
gratia 79; Cicero, De off. 2.2.5; Plutarch, Placit. philos.
1.2; Seneca, Epist. 89: so Dupont-Sommer, Machabées, pp. 34-
35. On some other Stoic terminology and ideas, at 3:11, 14:6,
15:4, see M. Hadas, op. cit., pp. 159, 215, 220. Freudenthal,
op. cit., p. 41, suggests the reason for the great influence of
Stoicism on writers like the author of IV Mac.: "Das stoische
System . . . fesselte auch die bibelgläubigen Juden durch die
straffe Richtung seiner Ethik . . . ."

[36]Cf. 6:9-11; 9:8, 23-24; 11:20; 12:14; 15:29; 16:14,
16; and especially 17:11-16. Further: Victor C. Pfitzner,
Paul and the Agon Motif (Leiden, 1967), pp. 57-65; on the
motif in Greek and Hellenistic philosophy: pp. 23-37.

[37]E. Norden, Die Antike Kunstprosa (Leipzig, 1898), I,
p. 417; C. C. Torrey, The Apocryphal Literature (New Haven,
1945), p. 103; U. Luck, Makkabäerbücher," RGG, IV, 622; Hadas,
op. cit., p. 101.

188

Whether or not the author actually has in mind the
figure of Socrates as presented specifically in Plato's
Gorgias,[38] it seems virtually certain that he does draw upon
the tradition of Socrates' death which is found in Plato,
Seneca and Epictetus.[39] Like Socrates, Eleazar is an old man
(5:5, 7) and a well-known philosopher (5:4, 7, 11, 22ff.).
Like Socrates, he experiences the attempts of others to dissuade him from death (5:6-13, 6:12-14) but he rejects their
appeal. His resolve remains unshaken (5:16-38, 6:16-23).
"Like Socrates too he disdains purchasing a necessarily brief
extension of life at the price of betraying the long career
that had preceded."[40]

A remarkable parallel between the Socrates tradition
and IV Maccabees has to do with the effect of endurance. At
IV Maccabees 9:30 the second brother tauntingly suggests that
Antiochus' arrogant plans are being overcome "by our endurance
for the sake of piety." And at 1:11 the author himself affirms
that the martyrs conquered the tyrant by endurance. These two
texts remind one forcefully of the similar declaration which
Seneca attributes to Socrates: "Leap upon me, make your
assault; I shall conquer you by enduring" (De vita beata 27.3).

In the preceding chapter I referred to numerous Greek
texts indicating a positive attitude toward suffering and
death in certain circumstances. Against that backdrop, an
observation by Johannes Leipoldt is apt. Commenting about
how strange II Maccabees 6:12-17 would have seemed to a Greek,
he writes:

> Der Grieche braucht den Tod des Blutzeugen kaum zu
> rechtfertigen; dieser Mann gilt von vornherein als
> ein Held, wie Leonidas. Aber der Jude muss erklären,
> warum der Fromme ein so schreckliches Ende nimmt.[41]

By thus betraying his need to explain the martyrs' deaths, the
Epitomist (or Jason) reflects his fundamental agreement with a

---

[38]Hadas, op. cit., pp. 101, 116-17.

[39]In my opinion this assertion can also be made of his
source. I cannot agree with Hadas (Hadas and Smith, Heroes
and Gods [New York, 1965], p. 92) that II Mac. "suggests
neither Platonism nor Socrates." Of course, IV Mac. intensi-
fies the parallels between Eleazar and Socrates, notably by
describing Eleazar as a philosopher (7:7; cf. also 5:7, 11,
22, 35; 7:9.

[40]Hadas and Smith, op. cit., p. 91; cf. pp. 90-92.

[41]J. Leipoldt, Der Tod bei Griechen und Juden (Leipzig,

predominant Jewish solution to the problem of the suffering
righteous.[42] At the same time--in spite of many indications
that he was a hellenized Jew--he reveals the extent to which his
interpretation of the martyrs' deaths is foreign to Greek thinking.

The situation is quite different in IV Maccabees. Here,
as in Greek literature, the author does not feel constrained to
give theological explanations about the trans-historical cause
of the martyrs' sufferings. To paraphrase Leipoldt, he feels no
compulsion to justify their deaths. They are heroes and heroes
do not need to be explained or justified. To my mind, this is
an extremely significant indication of the degree to which the
author of IV Maccabees is controlled by Greek views about the
precipitous death of noble men.

From the constellation of ideas among the Greeks which
centered around the high honor of glorious death, more specific
parallels with IV Maccabees can be enumerated.

In Greek literature the point is often emphasized that
those who die gloriously on the field of battle have given
their lives in defense of (or to protect the reputation of)
their country or city-state. Moreover, it is remembered by
those who survive that those who fell did not shirk this fate;
rather, they approached death willingly, sometimes even eagerly.[43] IV Maccabees, like II Maccabees, repeatedly stresses the
fact that the martyrs die in defense of or for the sake of their
religion.[44] Their willingness to endure torture and to die is
likewise a motif that underlies the whole work.[45] In effect,

---

1942), p. 72. (II Mac. 6:12-17 has been quoted in full earlier
in this thesis, p. 31.)

[42]Cf. Wichmann, op. cit., pp. 18-21.

[43]Cf. supra, Chapter IV.

[44]Διὰ τὴν εὐσέβειαν: (7:16), 9:7, 9:29, 30; 11:20, 15:
14, 16:17, 18:3; cf. 13:10. Ὑπὲρ τῆς εὐσεβείας: 6:22 (14:6),
15:32, 16:13; cf. 9:24. The following expressions are also
used: διὰ τὸν νόμον: 6:27, 30; cf. 6:21, 7:8, 9:15, 13:13,
15:32; διὰ τὸν θεόν: 16:19, 25; cf. vv. 20, 21; διὰ τὴν πρὸς
θεὸν πίστον: 15:24; ὑπὲρ (τῆς) ἀρετῆς: 1:8, 11:2; cf. 9:18,
7:22; ὑπὲρ τοῦ νόμου: 16:16.

[45]See especially 5:32; 6:23; 9:7, 18, 29; 10:4, 16, 19-
20; 11:16; 14:1, 5-6; 15:12. Of special significance is 11:12,
where the fifth son embraces suffering eagerly as an opportunity

the seventh brother and the mother commit suicide (12:19, 17:1)
--an act which certainly has more parallels in Greek than in
Jewish literature!

In the realm of Greek rhetoric and literature the most
highly developed means of honoring the brave dead, while encour-
aging those who survived them, was the funeral oration.[46]
Examples are extant from Thucydides (ascribed to Pericles),
Lysias, Gorgias, Xenophon, Plato, Isocrates, Hyperides and
Demosthenes.[47] Typically these orations ended with an exhortation to the living to submit to their destiny as heroically as
the fallen warriors had done.[48]

IV Maccabees, of course, is not a funeral oration, but
I consider completely plausible and convincing the argument that
it was an edifying address delivered on a day commemorating the
death of the martyrs.[49] At any rate, even when one takes into
account the formal characteristics of the diatribe, the previous
analysis of IV Maccabees has indicated the considerable role
played by encomium in the address/writing.[50] And there are

---

to demonstrate steadfastness to the Law. On the other hand, at
11:1-3 the same brother welcomes his torture in order to insure
even greater retribution upon Antiochus.

[46]For the custom and some indication of the number of
such orations cf. Isocrates, Panegyricus 74; Lysias, Epitaphios
1-2; Demosthenes, Epitaphios I.

[47]Evaristus, op. cit., p. 61.

[48]Sister Evaristus summarizes the typical pattern thus:
a eulogy on the dead, their country and ancestors; comfort from
the renown they had gained; the honor paid them by the state;
their reception in the lower world; the care to be given their
parents and families by the state; finally, an exhortation to
the survivors.

[49]Supra, p. 174, n. 10. If in Palestine (?) the Jews
built tombs for the prophets and decorated the monuments of the
righteous (Matt. 23:29), the veneration of the martyrs would be
even less surprising in regions beyond Palestine where Hellenistic influence--including the phenomena of hero cults and
shrines in honor of fallen warriors--was more intense. Writes
Hadas (Hadas, op. cit., pp. 105-106): "The widespread practice
of commemorating figures who had served their people well must
have been peculiarly attractive to leaders of Hellenized com-
munities who wished to strengthen national pride and cement
religious loyalties." ". . . it is as probable that a practice
so widespread, so edifying, and so servicable should be adapted
to Jewish use as it was for the philosophic ideas and rhetorical form of IV Maccabees to be adopted."

[50]Cf. Dupont-Sommer, Machabées, p. 67: "C'est essenti-
ellement un panégyrique . . . ."

numerous passages which can only be understood as unabashed
exhortation[51] or as more subtle encouragement to faithfulness.[52]

IV Maccabees has several other, more specific, elements
in common with extant examples of the Greek funeral oration:
the ἀγών-motif;[53] the motif of death preferred to dishonor;[54]
the idea of punishing or avenging the enemy.[55] With Lysias,
Epitaphios 70, "they paid back the fatherland for their nurture,"
one might compare IV Maccabees 16:18-19: "Remember that because of God you had a share in the world and enjoyed life; for
this reason you ought to endure every torment διὰ τὸν θεόν."
Finally it can simply be recalled here that several of the
texts cited in chapter four regarding the effects of glorious
death come from funeral orations.

Related to the custom of funeral orations is that of
inscribing appropriate epitaphs on the tombs of those who died
gloriously in battle. According to Herodotus (7.228) the inscription over the Spartans who fell at Thermopylae read:

ὦ ξεῖν' ἀγγέλλειν Λακεδαιμονίοις ὅτι τῇδε
κείμεθα τοῖς κείνων ῥήμασι πειθόμενοι. [56]

Another epitaph attributed to Simonides was inscribed on the
tomb of the Corinthians who fell at Salamis (480 B.C.):

ἀκμᾶς ἐστακυῖαν ἐπὶ ξυροῦ 'Ελλάδα πᾶσαν
ταῖς αὐτῶν ψυχαῖς κείμεθα ῥυσάμενοι. [57]

---

[51]Especially 18:1-2, but see also 7:9 (ἡ εὐνομία ἡμῶν)
and 8:16-26.

[52]E.g., 16:25 and the frequent mention of the martyrs'
reward.

[53]See the oration attributed to Pericles in Thucydides
2.42.1; also Demosthenes, Epitaphios 18.

[54]E.g., Demosthenes, Epitaphios 26; cf. Isocrates,
Panegyricus (which is not really a funeral oration) 95; compare
IV Mac. 6:20-21.

[55]Thucydides 2.42.4.

[56]"Stranger, go tell the Spartans that we lie here
obedient to their words." In the Anthologia Graeca (7.249)
this epitaph is attributed to Simonides. The epitaphs for the
whole Peloponnesian force and for Megistias the seer are
found at 7.248 and 677 and in the Herodotus passage cited. For
other epitaphs, cf. supra, p. 145, n. 20 and Demosthenes,
De corona 289.

[57]"(Here) we lie, by our lives having delivered all
Hellas when she stood on a razor's edge" (Anth. Gr. 7.250).
Cf. also 251 and 253 which, according to W. R. Paton (The

The probability that many (most?) of the epigrams found in Book 7 of the Anthologia Graeca are the products of mere poetical exercise and were not epitaphs actually engraved on tombstones or monuments is particularly illuminating with regard to IV Maccabees 17:9-10 because the epitaph suggested there appears to be a parallel example of rhetorical display by an author who utilizes the familiar epigram form.

I leave now the complex of ideas and customs related to the death of those who fall in battle, and turn to the tragic poets, where even more striking similarities with the language and ideas of IV Maccabees can be adduced.

That such similarities are indeed apparent is not totally surprising in light of the familiarity with the Greek tragedians among Hellenized Jews. In addition to IV Maccabees, Philo of Alexandria is the strongest evidence supporting this claim of familiarity. It is sufficient here to refer to one essay alone, "Every Good Man Is Free." Philo acknowledges the educative value of the poets in these words (98): "Witnesses to the liberty of virtuous men are poets and writers; nourished upon their wisdom (γνώμαις) from their cradles, Greeks and barbarians alike are accustomed to improve their character (βελτιοῦνται τὰ ἤθη)." Later he writes (143): "If it is worthwhile to heed the poets--and why should we not? For they are (our) educators for all of life (παιδευταὶ . . . τοῦ σύμπαντος βίου) . . . ." It would appear that Philo was expressing a genuine opinion because in this essay alone he quotes the tragic poets at least eight times.[58]

Philo is not merely quoting popular aphorisms from the poets. He quotes, rather, from first-hand, personal acquaintance with their works. That he attended the plays is demonstrated by his own words (141):

A short time ago, when some players were acting a
tragedy, and reciting those lines of Euripides,
The name of freedom is worth all the world;
If one has little, let him think that much,

Greek Anthology in the Loeb Classical Library), were probably on the tombs of the Spartan and Athenian dead, respectively.

[58]Once (152) he says he is quoting a tragic poet but does not name him. By name he quotes Ion (134), Aeschylus (143), and Euripides (99 and cf. 25; 116, 141). In 101-103 he quotes and summarizes extensively from an unnamed play; these quotations are not introduced by a direct identification of the poet, but following, as they do, so close upon 99, where Euripides is quoted, they can confidently be attributed to him.

I saw the whole audience so carried away by enthusiasm
that they stood upright to their full height, and . . . 
burst into shout after shout of applause, combining[59]
praise of the maxim with praise of the poet . . . .

An important inscription provides indisputable evidence
that Philo's experience of attending the plays was not unique
among Diaspora Jews. Brought to public attention by Adolf
Deissmann, this inscription comes from one of the rows of seats
in the theater at Miletus. As to its date Deissmann ventures
no more than that it is "doubtless of Imperial age." According
to his translation the inscription reads: Place of the Jews,
who are also called God-fearing.[60] Thus we have engraved testimony that Jews of this Asia Minor city were regular theater-
goers.[61]

The degree to which some Diaspora Jews were familiar
with the form and conventions of Greek tragedy is indicated by
the Exagoge of Ezekiel the Tragedian. This composition, which
unites biblical narrative and Greek tragic form, exhibits
several phraseological and conceptual parallels with the great
tragedians, especially Euripides.[62]

In IV Maccabees itself there are several parallels with
the tragic poets at points not directly related to the interpretation of the martyrs' deaths. Moses Hadas, for example, calls

---

[59]Trans. F. H. Colson in the LCL edition of Philo's
works.

[60]Τόπος Εἰουδεων τῶν καὶ ϑεοσεβίον. Deissmann, Light
from the Ancient East (New York, 1911), p. 446.

[61]Another inscription (CIG, III, No. 5361) states that
a stele, inscribed by the Jews of Berenice in Cyrenaica in
honor of a prominent official, was set εἰς τὸν ἐπισημότατον
τόπον τοῦ ἀμφιθεάτρου (1. 27). But this is not certain evidence
that the Jews of Berenice attended the theater. The citizen so
honored was apparently not a Jew himself (cf. 11. 15ff.) and
the Jews could honor him with an inscription in the theater
without going there themselves. However, this very method of
honoring a distinguished person indicates, at the very least, a
relaxed and tolerant attitude toward theater-going. Incidentally, I might point out at least two rather widespread Greek
terms which this inscription and IV Maccabees have in common:
ἀνὴρ καλὸς καὶ ἀγαθός (1. 10; cf. IV 4:1) and καλοκάγαθία (1.
20 and five or six times in IV Mac.); the latter expression is
not found elsewhere in the LXX, the former only in Tobit and
II Mac. 15:12.

[62]Cf. Jerry Robertson, "Ezekiel the Tragedian: Scholia."
Unpublished paper submitted for the graduate New Testament Seminar at Harvard Divinity School, May 8, 1970, pp. 27, 39, 40,
42-43.

attention to 12:8 (an unexpected prospect of reversal of the plot before the final catastrophe) and 15:26 (the figure of the two "ballots," death and deliverance). More important is the presentation of the brothers themselves as a chorus (8:4, 13:8, 14:8), which, for heightened effect, can be broken up into the voices of individual members (13:11-13).[63]

I am more concerned, of course, with those descriptive and conceptual parallels between the tragedians and IV Maccabees that involve more directly the meaning of the martyrs' suffering and death. The relevant dramas have already been discussed; I can therefore state the important comparisons briefly.

a) Aside from II Maccabees, I am aware of no closer parallel in Greek or Jewish literature (including the book of Job) to the description of the martyrs' suffering than that in the Prometheus Bound of Aeschylus.

b) The recalcitrance of the martyrs has significant parallels in the dramatic portrayals of Prometheus, Antigone, Iphigenia, Macaria, Menoceus. By those who seek to dissuade them, their resolve is deemed folly (compare especially IV 12:3).

c) Most significantly, the concept of effective death in IV Maccabees parallels that in the tragic poets, particularly as developed by Euripides. In the plays of Euripides discussed earlier, as in IV Maccabees, human deaths effect the reversal of an overt, "historical" situation. In both cases, that effect can be described in terms of salvation or deliverance: Iphigenia at Aulis 1383-84, 1420, 1472-73; Heraclidae 499; Phoenician Women 948, 952, 997-98; compare IV Maccabees 17:22. The language used also includes that of death "for" (ὑπέρ) others, usually the state, in Euripides; this is often accompanied by religious-sacrificial language, since the pertinent deaths are, in Euripides at least, actual sacrifices!

As for specifics, one can compare ἀρκεσθείς at IV 6:28 with the Euripidean necessity of sacrificing a person in order to placate a temperamental deity. With ὑπέρ αὐτῶν compare, for example, Iphigenia at Aulis 1553-55; Heraclidae 532; Alcestis 154-55. With ἀντίψυχον αὐτῶν (IV 6:29) compare

---

[63]See Hadas, op. cit., in notes on the pertinent verses.

Alcestis 340-41, 434; Heraclidae 580. Although the ἀντι-
language is not typical of the other plays, the underlying
concept can hardly be denied, for those who give themselves
and thus appease the deity grant their compatriots release from
the fate of defeat and death. Thus one life is given in the
place of other lives.[64]

*        *        *

To conclude this chapter I offer a theory concerning
the origin of the concept of effective death in IV Maccabees.
According to my theory several components feed into this
concept. They include:

a) The general Old Testament-Jewish background, including the ideas and practices of sacrifice, ransom, payment
of blood-guilt, intercession, expiation and purification.[65]

b) The inherited material, that is, the basic stories
of Eleazar and the seven brothers and their mother, including
the martyrological motif (death rather than apostasy), the
martyrs as representatives of a faithful people, the intercessory martyr prayer for mercy and revenge,[66] and the "meaning"
of the deaths in terms of example and afterlife. To these
elements of the martyr stories themselves I would add another,
available from Jason or II Maccabees, i.e., knowledge of the
exploits and successes of the Maccabees.

c) The occasion and purpose. On the occasion of a
commemoration of the martyrs' deaths the author of IV Maccabees
sought to honor them by panegyric. By emphasizing the remarkable effect of their deaths he also sought to inspire and

---

[64]There are important differences as well. In IV Maccabees 17:21 it is said that divine providence delivered Israel
through their blood; in Euripides it is said that the acts of
self-sacrifice save city or individuals. More importantly, the
elements of sin, punishment, and expiation or purification have
no obvious parallels in the Greek tragic dramas.

[65]I do not include Is. 53 and the suffering servant
here because I find in IV Mac. no evidence of dependence on or
direct influence from that text.

[66]The importance of intercessory prayer for the author
is indicated in two ways: he increases the number of such
appeals, direct or indirect (cf. II 7:37 and IV 6:28, 12:18,
9:24); he emphasizes the effect of such prayer in a separate
incident. Onias ηὔξατο περὶ αὐτοῦ [Apollonius]. καὶ ὁ μὲν
παραδόξως διασωθεὶς . . . (4:13-14). In the corresponding II
Mac. story of Heliodorus, Onias offers a sacrifice instead of
an intercessory prayer.

encourage his hearers to stand fast in the faith and to follow
their example.

Both II and IV Maccabees view the Antiochian persecution
as a result of the nation's sin (apostasy) and God's response.
Therefore the departure of Antiochus or the defeat of his
generals, and the cessation of punishment at the hands of the
Seleucids, implies the expiation of the nation's sin.  II
Maccabees presents this "event" in terms of the victories of
the Maccabees and their purifying of temple, city and land.
Because of the circumstances of occasion and purpose, however,
IV Maccabees telescopes this extended event and identifies it
as the effect of the martyrs' faithful suffering unto death:
it was through their death that God delivered Israel; because
of them the land was purified.  By making such a claim he
apparently feels that the example of the martyrs would be more
impressive and prone to imitation.

In my opinion, however, it would be entirely erroneous
to suggest that the concept of effective death in IV Maccabees
was a natural development from the creative mutual influence of
Old Testament background, inherited material and the circumstances of purpose and occasion.  For such a suggestion fails
to come to terms with two key questions:  Given these three
factors alone, how could the author of IV Maccabees be so bold
as to make such a unique claim about the effect of the martyrs'
deaths?  And how could he expect that claim to be convincing or
meaningful to his hearers?  I submit that he could do so
because of the particular thought world in which he and his
hearers were immersed.  Its ideas and attitudes they had,
perhaps unconsciously, adopted.  The author of IV Maccabees
adapts some of those ideas to a particularly Jewish understanding of the relationship between God and his people.  More
specifically, he draws upon the concept of effective death that
is most clearly expressed in the Greek funeral orations and in
the dramas of the tragic poets, especially Euripides.  The
idea of deliverance through the death of another or of others
he incorporates into his own theology.

Of the idea of human death as a propitiatory sacrifice
à la Iphigenia there is only one real echo in IV Maccabees:
ἀρκεσθείς at 6:28.  The deaths of the martyrs are not presented
as θυσίαι which God demands.  Rather they are understood as
acts of complete devotion, and so, like perfect sacrifices,

God can regard them as effective for purification, expiation, ransom. As suggested earlier, it seems almost certain that an allegorical (or at least metaphorical) impulse played some role in those formulations employing the ideas of purification, expiation, and perhaps ransom, but it is difficult to define that role precisely.

The foregoing chapters of this thesis have, I believe, established the following: a) The concept of effective or vicarious expiatory suffering/death is found only once (if at all) in the Old Testament and other Jewish literature, with the exception of IV Maccabees; if Second Isaiah intended Isaiah 53 to express such an idea, there is no evidence that this chapter was understood in that way by subsequent generations of Jews prior to Jesus. b) The concept of effective death is found frequently in Greek-Hellenistic literature. c) The interpretation of the deaths of the martyrs as effective, beneficial and "expiatory" occurred only in a writing significantly influenced throughout by Greek-Hellenistic ideas.

In view of these results and the analysis undertaken in the present chapter, I conclude that Greek-Hellenistic ideas-- above all the concept of effective, beneficial death for others --were an essential catalyst for the interpretation of the martyrs' deaths in IV Maccabees.

## III. The Date of IV Maccabees

The implications of the preceding analysis for the central question of this thesis depend to a large extent upon the date of IV Maccabees. Therefore some support is necessary for the assertion made earlier that this writing is "earlier than or contemporary with primitive Christianity" for this judgment is contested by some modern scholars. A. Dupont-Sommer is perhaps the most prominent proponent of a late dating for IV Maccabees. He thinks that since IV Maccabees was composed to celebrate the anniversary date of the Maccabean martyrs, one should not assign too early a date for its composition.

Il convient de laisser au culte des martyrs le temps de s'instituer et de se développer. D'autre part, le Pseudo-Josèphe a utilizé II Mac.; ce livre . . . est probablement du 1<sup>er</sup> siècle de notre ère, et un certain temps a dû s'écouler entre II Mac. et IV Mac.[67]

All three points made here can be contested. The extremely rapid development of Christianity in the Hellenistic world should warn against such a generalized opinion as Dupont-Sommer's first statement. In the second place, the date of II Maccabees is, at best, uncertain; one can say with assurance only that it was written between 161 B.C. and 70 A.D.[68] Finally, the "certain temps" that would have had to elapse between II Maccabees and IV Maccabees--even if our author did use II Maccabees as a source--could as well be very brief as very lengthy.

Further attempts to place the date of IV Maccabees more precisely are subject to the same charge: Dupont-Sommer elevates mere possibilities to the status of positive proof. For example, he notes that the author manifests no aversion to artistic depiction in relation to the veneration of the martyrs (17:7). He finds it hardly conceivable that such an attitude was held even by a Diaspora Jew in the first century, citing Josephus (Contra Apion 2.75) as evidence that at this time pictorial representation was not allowed. However, he observes, several synagogues, especially Dura-Europas, show that by the beginning of the third century, attitudes among at least some Jews had changed. Inexplicably, Dupont-Sommer continues a tortuous line of reasoning in this fashion: a Jewish pictorial art must have been current before this date (i.e., third century)--indeed, perhaps the cautious attitude of IV Maccabees was the starting point of a new orientation. Then, even more inexplicably: "Cette considération pourrait nous conduire jusqu'au début du 2<sup>e</sup> siècle"![69]

Several comments. In the first place, Josephus is responding to Apion's charge that the Jews do not erect statues of the emperors (2.73). Whatever his attitude toward painting, in this passage Josephus, referring to the second commandment, appears to be speaking only of plastic images, statues. Furthermore, the author of IV Maccabees does not say that pictures

---

[67]A. Dupont-Sommer, Machabées, p. 75.

[68]Cf. James Moffatt, AP, I, pp. 128-29.

[69]Machabées, p. 76.

of the martyrs had been painted or that anyone had even considered such a means of honoring them. His statement is purely
hypothetical: εἰ δὲ ἐξὸν ἡμῖν ἦν . . . ζωγραφῆσαι. In itself
this statement is ambiguous. Does ἐξόν mean "permissable" or
"possible"? Is the author saying" "If we Jews were allowed to
. . ." or "If an artist could actually capture this . . ."? In
either case, this one passage from Josephus the apologist is
hardly grounds upon which to base sweeping conclusions about
the attitudes of all Diaspora Jews in the first century. On
the other side one might observe that the cumulative weight of
Erwin R. Goodenough's Jewish Symbols in the Greco-Roman Period[70]
now casts grave doubt upon the veracity of Dupont-Sommer's
position  that all first century Jews were averse to pictorial
art.

The rhetoric of IV Maccabees, thinks Dupont-Sommer,
places the work in the "second Sophistic" period (cf. pp. 60-
66). This literary movement, he asserts, was already popular
under Nero and the Flavians, attaining its apogee under Hadrian,
Antonius and Marcus Aurelius. "We are thus brought to about
the end of the first century or the first half of the second
rather than to the beginning or even the middle of the first"
(p. 76). But are stylistic considerations reliable grounds
upon which to assign a date to a writing like IV Maccabees?
That they are is, at best, questionable.[71]

Dupont-Sommer thinks that a dating even more precise
than the last of the first or the beginning of the second
century can be attained. Assuming that the philosophy of IV
Maccabees must necessarily reflect "to a certain extent" the
philosophy of his time, he notes that after Domitian Hellenistic philosophy experienced a veritable renaissance (p. 76).
The philosophy of one of the men who represented that renaissance, Dio Chrysostom, bears, in Dupont-Sommer's view, a noteworthy resemblance to IV Maccabees. Quoting from a French
scholar (Croiset), who notes the influence of Stoicism, Platonism, Aristotelianism, Pythagoreanism and popular mythology

---

[70]New York, 1953-65, 12 vols.

[71]Cf. Hadas, op. cit., p. 98.

in Dio, he asks: "Cet éclectisme et ce syncrétisme, . . . n'est-ce pas l'image même de la philosophie du Pseudo-Josèphe?" (p. 77). One can only respond that such points of similarity, fancied or real, prove nothing. Could not much the same be said about Philo and Wisdom of Solomon? Nor can the coincidence that both the author of IV Maccabees and Dio were philosophers and rhetors be made to bear much weight.

One must conclude, therefore, that the period to which the career of Dio points Dupont-Sommer (the reign of Trajan or Hadrian) is not confirmed by relevant data. Consequently no firm grounds have been given for the suggestion that IV Maccabees was written at the beginning of Hadrian's reign, that is ca. 117 or 118 (p. 78; p. 81, n. 45). The similarities which IV Maccabees bears to the Epistle to the Hebrews and the letters of Ignatius (pp. 83-84) are no reason to alter this negative judgment. These similarities could as well have been mediated through some Hellenistic synagogue or church, and there is no a priori reason to exclude the possibility that Ignatius or Hebrews was familiar with IV Maccabees.

The late dating proposed by Dupont-Sommer--or at least the arguments with which he supports that dating--must therefore be rejected. In the final analysis, his primary evidence consists of rather general similarities between the style and philosophy of IV Maccabees and that current in the early second century.

If the evidence that Elias J. Bickerman presents for the dating of this writing appears to be less grand and impos- ing, it is nevertheless more convincing; for Bickerman bases his dating on three rather minor but very concrete bits of textual evidence. Dupont-Sommer's labored arguments he dis- misses, perhaps too facilely, with a single stroke: "Every unprejudiced reader of IV Macc. cannot but be impressed by the fact that the Temple and its service are regarded as existent in the book."[72] Similarly, a pre-Empire date cannot be

---

[72]Bickerman, "The Date of Fourth Maccabees" in Louis Ginzberg Jubilee Volume (New York, 1945), p. 108; compare Grimm, IV, p. 293 and Townshend in AP, II, p. 654.

adopted: ". . . Louis Robert [in Études Épigraphiques et Philologiques (1938), 234] has shown that the term θρησκεία ('religion') was never used in the Hellenistic age but became modish from Augustus onward."[73] Nor is the designation νομικός used for Jews learned in the Torah until the Roman period (cf. IV 5:4).[74]

The most important evidence, however, is found at IV Maccabees 4:2. There Apollonius is called strategos of "Syria, Phoenicia and Cilicia"; in II Maccabees 3:5 he is called strategos of "Coelesyria and Phoenicia." Bickerman sees this divergence as the modernization by IV Maccabees of a detail no longer understandable for the author's readers, and he takes it for granted that "Syria, Phoenicia and Cilicia" is the official nomenclature of an administrative province in the author's own time.[75] One inscription and three literary sources (including Gal. 1:21 and Acts 15:23) show that in the first century C.E. Syria and Cilicia were considered a joint province. But two passages in Tacitus allow an even more precise dating of the period during which Cilicia was united with Syria under the Empire: Annals 2.58 and 13.8. These texts show that in 18 C.E. Cilicia was not yet a part of the province of Syria and in 55 C.E. Cilicia was no longer a part of Syria. Thus the two constituted a joint province at some period between 18 and 55 C.E. Consequently, IV Maccabees must have been written sometime during this time span.[76]

In a footnote (p. 112, n. 27a) Bickerman expresses the opinion that "The absence of any allusion to the persecution of Caligula suggests the date before 38 C.E., that is in the twenties or thirties." On the contrary, M. Hadas[77] thinks that the reign of Caligula "is exactly suitable as providing a

---

[73]Bickerman, op. cit., p. 108. The term appears also in Wisdom 14:18, 27 (and in A at Sir. 22:5; B and S read θρασεῖα).

[74]Ibid., p. 107, n. 8.

[75]Ibid., pp. 108-109.

[76]Ibid., pp. 109-12.

[77]Hadas, op. cit., p. 96.

historical conjuncture which would evoke such a consideration of religious persecution as is contained in our book." By way of support Hadas mentions the decree of Caligula that his statue be erected in Jerusalem, the imperial order for Petronius to enforce the decree, the meeting of Petronius with Jewish leaders and his march to Judea (cf. Philo, Ad Gaium 185-90, 207, 222-24; Josephus, Ant. 18.262-72; 19.279). For purposes of the present thesis, the difference between Bickerman and Hadas at this point is not crucial. Either way, the composition date of IV Maccabees is fixed at a time antedating the period of Paul's literary activity by at least a decade.[78]

---

[78]J. Jeremias, Heiligengräber in Jesu Umwelt (Göttingen, 1958), p. 19, agrees with a date of "around 35 A.D."; cf. "Lösegeld," 227. Lohse, op. cit., p. 69, n. 2: a date in the first half of the first century is "rather certain." J. Obermann, "The Sepulchre of the Maccabean Martyrs," JBL 50(1931), 263: "about 35 A.D."

CHAPTER VI


THE BACKGROUND, SOURCE AND ORIGIN OF THE CONCEPT

OF JESUS' DEATH AS SAVING EVENT

Much earlier in the present study I suggested four
models of event interpretation which might be helpful in the
attempt to account for the origin of the concept of Jesus'
death as saving event. Now, on the basis of the intervening
chapters (two through five) and the analysis of Romans 3:24-26
in chapter one, that attempt can be made.

The hypothesis which I propose in Part Four below is
formulated in terms of the last model suggested previously.
However, because most NT scholars have accounted for the origin
of the concept of Jesus' saving death in terms of one or another
(or all three) of the other options, I have thought it necessary
to consider them in some detail. Although I examine them in
three distinct sections, they are not to be thought of as
mutually exclusive options.

## Part I:  Jesus Said So

According to the first option being considered, Jesus
himself interpreted his death as having saving significance
for others. His immediate disciples and then other early
Christians simply appealed to Jesus' own words in their understanding of the meaning of his death. In its most frequently
encountered form, this option assumes that Jesus patterned his
own ministry after the Suffering Servant of Deutero-Isaiah;
Isaiah 53, it is thought, must have made an especially deep
impression on Jesus and played an inordinate role in shaping
his self-understanding. As the Servant suffers and dies "for
many," so did Jesus conceive his own mission.[1]

---

[1]Cf. e.g., O. Cullmann, op. cit., pp. 65-69, esp. p. 68.
J. Jeremias, "Lösegeld," esp. pp. 225-27. V. Taylor, Jesus and

It should be admitted immediately that the possibility
that Jesus interpreted his own death as a salvation event can
hardly be disproved. Nor is such an attempt the historian's
concern. The question is, rather: What is the evidence for
this view? The textual evidence is scanty--even proponents of
this option must admit that.[2] The texts usually cited are the
eucharistic words of Jesus in the Synoptics and in I Cor. 11
and Mark 10:45. Nevertheless, this evidence is sufficient to
demonstrate the validity of option one if it can be shown that
the texts cited do include authentic Jesus words which reflect
the concept of vicarious expiatory suffering or death.


A.  The Eucharistic Texts


For present purposes, there are two questions to be put
to the eucharistic texts:  Does any one of these texts in its
present form report accurately what Jesus actually said?  If
none does, what can we assume that Jesus did say?[3]
A glance at the relevant texts (Mark 14:22-25, Matt.
26:26-29, Luke 22:15-20, I Cor. 11:23-26) in a synopsis indicates at once that the first question must be answered negatively.  The parallel texts are not parallel in their particulars.
And while it may be possible to trace a development of eucharistic tradition with some degree of success, the suggestion that
the earliest form of the tradition so discovered was equivalent
to the words actually spoken by Jesus would be a non sequitur.
The very recognition that the eucharistic tradition was subject
to a development within which changes were effected with relative freedom--cf. especially Luke 22:15-17 in comparison with
Matt. and Mark; also John 6:51-59--should make one aware of the
possibility that a development of the tradition likewise antedates even its earliest forms as recoverable from the different

His Sacrifice (London, 1937), pp. 39-48.  R. Otto, The Kingdom
of God and the Son of Man (London, 21943), pp. 250-52.  Wolff,
op. cit., pp. 55-71.  W. Manson, op. cit., pp. 154-58.

[2]Lohse, op. cit., p. 117.

[3]It will be noted that both of these questions make the
implicit assumption that there was such an occasion, the last
supper, on which Jesus did say something about the meaning of
the meal.  This assumption can be questioned, but here it is
adopted uncritically; without it, there is only one relevant
text:  Mark 10:45!

NT accounts. Thus, the necessary attempt to determine the oldest form and wording cannot yield a composite result which
could be described without further ado as the authentic Jesus
word. The eucharistic prayers of Didache 9:1-5 support such
scepticism; they make no mention of the bread as Jesus' body or
of the wine as Jesus' shed blood which institutes the new
covenant.

The answer to the second question posed above must be:
We do not know what Jesus said. Furthermore, we should probably
recognize that the attempt to recover Jesus' precise words is
futile because of the very nature of our sources and the fact
that the traditions they include are already the end results of
an historical development. Perhaps more enlightening ultimately
would be the attempt to understand correctly the nature and
import of Jesus' last meal with his disciples and any words
spoken on that occasion, although informed conjecture is the
main technique upon which such an endeavor would rely. The
phrase "informed conjecture" is used in view of the fact that
modern critical scholarship has arrived at a broad consensus
regarding the nature of Jesus' message and ministry. Agreeing
with many NT scholars that Jesus was an eschatological prophet
who proclaimed the inbreaking rule of God, one can ask: Which
elements of the preserved eucharistic traditions harmonize most
naturally with Jesus' mission as proclaimer of the Kingdom, and
which ones appear strange and intrusive? Two possible answers
seem to stand out above the rest.

1. The first claims that the words over bread and cup
were intended by Jesus as enacted parables, similar to those of
several OT prophets. The breaking of the bread was an action-
parable of the death that Jesus anticipated, that is, death by
stoning; the wine was intended to symbolize his shed blood.[4]

This interpretation is initially intriguing because
it promises some degree of compatibility between the eucharistic words and the eschatological message of Jesus--a feature
often missing in other theories of the Last Supper. That

---

[4]For those scholars holding some form of this view see
Norman A. Beck, "The Last Supper as an Efficacious Symbolic
Act," JBL 89(1970), 192-93.

promise, however, is threatened by several arguments which can be brought to bear against the symbolic act theory as a whole (a.-c. below) or as it applies separately to the bread word (d. below) and the cup word (e. through h.).

a. Those scholars who adopt the symbolic action interpretation of the Supper find antecedents for it in the symbolic acts of the OT prophets, pointing to such texts as Is. 8:3, 20:2f.; Jer. 19:10f., 27:1ff., 28:10-14; and Ez. 4 and 5; (cf. Acts 21:11). What is overlooked is that not a single one of these texts provides a really close parallel to the eucharistic words. In the OT the prophet's act always pointed to the future of Jerusalem or the people of Israel (or to another nation) but never to his own fate. The dramatized parable of the prophet is a word of Yahweh to His people; it is a sign and a warning and it calls for repentance. The words of Jesus are no parallel to this.[5]

b. When the OT prophets performed a symbolic act they intended to say thereby: "This will happen to Jerusalem (or the nation, etc.)." If one views the action and words over bread and cup as a parallel to these prophetic acts, he understands Jesus to be saying, in effect: "What happens to this bread and wine will happen to me." But the bread was broken and eaten and the wine was drunk. Surely Jesus did not anticipate actually having his body eaten and his blood drunk. For a second reason, then, it is doubtful whether one can legitimately speak of a genuine parallel to the symbolic acts of the OT prophets.

c. J. Jeremias considers the eucharistic words to be parallel with parabolic actions which Jesus had performed during his ministry.[6] But again, these acts are never signs of his own personal fate. Furthermore, although according to the synoptic accounts Jesus sometimes accompanied such an act with a (verbal) parable or an explanatory word, the succinct and enigmatic words over bread and cup bear them little resemblance.

---

[5] Only the cup word could possibly be--and then only if it is concerned with the covenant of the new Israel; but that would be a word of salvation, not of judgment and repentance.

[6] J. Jeremias, The Parables of Jesus (New York, 1963), pp. 227-29.

d. Scholars who endorse the symbolic action theory tend to argue that Jesus anticipated death by stoning and pointed to that fate by the breaking of the bread. Just how appropriate the breaking of bread would have been as a symbol of stoning, however, is questionable. After all, when a person is stoned his body remains intact. Would the breaking bread = stoning analogy have been apparent to Jesus' disciples?

e. A similar objection can be raised against the cup word: death by stoning is a singularly unbloody death. That fact suggests the inappropriateness of any reference to his blood by Jesus, especially any statement about its being "poured out."

f. The accounts of the Supper mention no action with the wine to correspond with the breaking of the bread. With regard to the wine, then, one finds at most a static symbol, not a symbolic action.

There are additional reasons for doubting that the cup word of Mark 14:24 par.--in any form and however interpreted --derives from Jesus himself.[7]

g. In several relatively early but non-canonical Christian writings bread appears to be the only eucharistic element.[8]

h. The short text (D) of Luke omits completely the word over the cup.

In view of these last two factors it seems likely that, at most, an eschatological vow of abstinence (Mark 14:25, Luke 22:18; cf. I Cor. 11:26) was the only word originally associated with the cup and that Mark 14:24 par. represent a later stage of tradition in which a cup word was made parallel to the bread word.[9]

---

[7]Some scholars insist that a word which suggests that the wine was Jesus' blood is difficult to imagine on the lips of a Galilean or Palestinian Jew. Cf., e.g., C. G. Montefiore, The Synoptic Gospels (London, [2]1927), I, p. 332; J. Klausner, Jesus of Nazareth (New York, 1925), p. 329. Whether the wine/ blood metaphor used in the OT (e.g., Gen. 49:11, Deut. 32:14; Zech. 9:15 LXX) provides sufficient grounds for denying this objection is a question which needs further discussion.

[8]H. Lietzmann, Mass and Lord's Supper (Leiden, 1958: Fasc. 4), pp. 195-203. Lietzmann also shows that, in some circles, when the eucharist did include an element to be drunk, that element was not wine but water!

[9]C. H. C. McGregor, Eucharistic Origins (London,

This probability is supported by the problems which beset the position that either of the basic cup-word traditions (i.e., Mark and Paul) represents an authentic Jesus word.

The phrases "my blood of the covenant" and "poured out for many" (Mark 14:24), almost certainly, do not derive from Jesus.[10] That is apparent above all from a comparison with I Cor. 11:25, which represents an earlier tradition at this point.[11] To support his contention that the Markan cup word is authentic, J. Jeremias vigorously defends the position that the Greek "my blood of the covenant" is a translation from Hebrew (or Aramaic).[12] In so doing, he reverses not only the opinion he previously held (cf. p. 194) but his usual methodology as well. At other points in his analysis of the eucharistic texts (e.g., pp. 174-82) he argues that when the word order of the Greek text corresponds to Semitic word order, that correspondence indicates a Semitic original. Now he contends that it is an error to assume that "the sequence of words in Greek must have been also that of the Semitic original" (p. 194). Not even Jeremias can be allowed to have it both ways. Why such a strain to make a point? I believe Jeremias exposes his motivation when he writes (ibid.): "In truth the Semitic requires another word order than the Greek . . ." (emphasis mine). Jeremias thus starts from the presupposition that the original language of "my blood of the covenant" was Semitic and then tries to account for the Greek order. It would be fairer to begin with the Greek text as it stands and ask whether this text reflects a Semitic origin. When Jeremias did exactly that in an earlier edition of Eucharistic Words, he concluded that "my blood of the covenant" can hardly in its present form be Palestinian."[13]

---

1928), pp. 64-68, 72-73; Otto, op. cit., pp. 273-74, 285-88; J. W. Hunkin, "The Origin of Eucharistic Doctrine" in The Evangelical Doctrine of Holy Communion (Cambridge, 1930), pp. 9-10; C. T. Craig, "From the Last Supper to the Lord's Supper," Religion in Life 9(1940), 166-68; Beck, op. cit., 195-96.

[10]M. Dibelius, From Tradition to Gospel (New York, 1965), pp. 206-207.

[11]A. Suhl, Die Funktion der Alttestamentlichen Zitate und Anspielungen im Markusevangelium (Gütersloh, 1965), pp. 110-14. Suhl stresses the development from the shared cup as an act symbolizing the consummation of the table fellowship (cf. the "new covenant") to the contents of the cup, which no longer involves an affirmation about the table fellowship. See also G. Bornkamm, "Lord's Supper and Church in Paul," in Early Christian Experience (New York, 1969), pp. 142-43.

[12]J. Jeremias, The Eucharistic Words of Jesus (New York, 1966), pp. 194-95.

[13]First ET ed., 1955, p. 133. Strangely, a "material difficulty" that Jeremias noted here drops out of the later edition, namely the fact that in "late Judaism" the phrase "blood of the covenant" was the recognized term for the blood of circumcision! If this is the meaning of the phrase among Palestinian Jews, that is additional evidence that "my blood of the covenant" in Mark 14:24 was first formulated in Greek-speaking Christianity.

On the other hand, even if it is earlier, the cup word of I Cor. 11:25 is not assuredly authentic either. The fact cannot be lightly dismissed that in the synoptic gospels Jesus never again mentions a covenant, new or otherwise. That the (new) covenant idea was so important in the self-understanding of the sectaries of Qumran[14] only underlines the probable significance of this silence. Furthermore, with the exception of Ex. 24:8 (where the covenant blood is thrown or sprinkled) the OT and other Jewish literature do not directly associate the covenant idea with accompanying rites which center in the shedding of blood (cf., as a special example, Jer. 31:31-34). These two facts suggest the improbability of Jesus' having affirmed that the cup at the last supper represented the new covenant which would be effectuated through his death. More likely, an early Christian rite is being accounted for etiologically.

Assuming (for the moment) that the bread word, in some form, is authentic, one must observe that Mark (and Matthew) and the short text of Luke omit the phrase ὑπὲρ ὑμῶν. Thus most of the scholars who adopt the symbolic action interpretation accept only "this is my body" as the original bread word. Even Jeremias acknowledges that the "presumably oldest text" read "this is my body/flesh."[15] But without "for you" the bread word does not point to a concept of vicarious expiatory death!

2. A second answer to the question of which elements of the eucharistic tradition harmonize well with Jesus' mission and message has been ably presented by J. Jeremias in The Eucharistic Words of Jesus. Jeremias holds that, following a vow of abstinence at the beginning of the meal, Jesus pronounced a word over the bread ("this is my body") and over the cup ("this is" plus a primitive phrase in Hebrew or Aramaic, of which we have two expressions: "my blood of the covenant/ the covenant in my blood" plus "which is poured out for many"--pp. 172-73). With these words Jesus probably intended to speak of himself as the paschal lamb. "He is the eschatological paschal lamb, representing the fulfillment of all that of which the Egyptian paschal lamb and all the subsequent sacrificial paschal lambs were the prototype" (p. 223). Thus Jesus describes his death as a saving death (p. 225). As the eschatological passover sacrifice, his vicarious death brings into operation the final deliverance, the new covenant of God (p. 226).

---

[14]Cf. e.g., CD 6.19, 8.21, 19.34, 20.12.

[15]Eucharistic Words, p. 168.

In addition to the objections that have already been
brought against those elements of the text which Jeremias considers original, I mention three others which, in my view,
disallow his interpretation.

a. If Jesus intended to describe himself as the
eschatological paschal lamb, it is inexplicable that his words
are associated with the bread rather than with the passover
lamb itself. It is also difficult to explain how a reference,
over the cup, to his _blood_ would fit into this context since
the blood of the passover lamb was not distributed and drunk!

b. In spite of Jeremias' attempt to prove from
rabbinic texts the connection between passover and covenant
(p. 225, n. 5), it remains questionable how appropriate a sol-
emn pronouncement by Jesus about "my blood of the covenant/new
covenant through my blood" would have been in the context of a
passover meal. After all, Jeremias can point to no text where
"blood of the covenant" is a designation for the blood of the
passover lamb or where the (or a) covenant is effected "through"
the blood of the passover lamb. Furthermore, as Jeremias
acknowledged in an earlier edition (ET 1955, p. 134), "blood
of the covenant" was apparently understood by Jews to mean the
blood of circumcision. More likely than Jeremias' view, then,
is the assumption that references to Passover and covenant
alike were later Christian contributions to the eucharistic
tradition, not authentic Jesus words.

c. In spite of his thorough and erudite defense
(pp. 15-84), Jeremias has not conclusively demonstrated his
most fundamental presupposition, namely, that the last supper
was a Passover meal. Without this supporting assumption
Jesus' alleged self-description as the eschatological paschal
lamb is deprived of its necessary context.[16]

There is no good reason to doubt that the last supper of Jesus with his disciples was "a meal eaten under the
shadow of the Passover season."[17] It is also clear that the
synoptic evangelists understood the Supper as a Passover meal.

---

[16]This in spite of Jeremias' assurances slightly to
the contrary (p. 88, last sentence), for just a few sentences
earlier he emphasizes that the words over bread and cup would
have been "in themselves puzzling" _if they had not been preceded by a (clarifying) Passover meditation!_

[17]Craig, _op. cit._, 165.

Nevertheless, the most that Jeremias can demonstrate is that
the last supper could have been a Passover meal; the sources
themselves, by their very nature, cannot yield positive proof
that what could have been actually did occur.[18] When all is
said and done,

> Formgeschichtliche Beobachtungen zeigen, dass die
> Schilderung von Jesu letztem Mahl erst sekundär mit
> dem "Einsetzungsbericht" verbunden wurde. Im Mahlbericht
> selbst spricht nichts für die Passasituation.[19]

The foregoing pages include a consideration of two
interpretations of the eucharistic texts which appear to offer
the greatest promise of compatibility with the eschatological
message and ministry of Jesus of Nazareth. It was seen, however, that substantial objections can be brought against both
of these interpretations. These objections indicate that to
rely on the eucharistic texts as evidence of Jesus' own understanding of the meaning of his death is to build upon uncertain
foundations. It is conceivable (but barely, in my view) that
these texts do accurately reflect Jesus' own interpretation of
his impending death, but there is no way to verify that assumption and several factors argue against adopting it as a methodological starting point.[20]

## B.  Mark 10:45

This verse probably represents an originally separate
logion which Mark (or Urmarkus?) has connected with the preceding verses because of a catchword, διάκονος (v. 43); (note

---

[18]See above all the trenchant remarks of G. Bornkamm,
"Lord's Supper and Church in Paul," pp. 132-33. Also: K. G.
Kuhn, "The Lord's Supper and the Communal Meal at Qumran" in
K. Stendahl (ed.), The Scrolls and the New Testament (New York,
1957), pp. 82-83.

[19]Thyen, op. cit., p. 163, n. 3.

[20]A third interpretation of the eucharistic texts is
based on the view that "this is my body (for you)" and "this
cup is the new covenant through my blood" (or "this is my blood
of the covenant") sound strange within the context of Jesus'
ministry and proclamation. That these words actually reflect
a stage at which the Lord's Supper tradition had come under the
influence of (non-eschatological) ideas in the Hellenistic
world is a theory supported by the results of the present
study.

212

διακονηθῆναι and διακονῆσαι in v. 45).[21] Thus, the present
context is of little help regarding the question of authenticity.
Mark 10:45 must be examined as a self-contained unit.

If this verse is considered the result of combining two
originally separate logia, comparison with Luke 22:27 would
suggest that 45b ("his life a ransom for many") is an interpretive expansion of a more original saying (i.e., 45a: "not to
be served but to serve"). On the other hand, if 45a and 45b
are not understood as two originally separate logia, the view
that Mark 10:45 expresses Jesus' own self-understanding rests
heavily on the authenticity of this verse as one of the Son of
Man sayings.[22] One need only note the impressive arguments that
can be marshalled in support of the view that all Synoptic Son
of Man sayings are creations of the post-Easter Christian community[23] to conclude that Mark 10:45, on methodological grounds
alone, is unacceptable evidence for Jesus' understanding of the
significance of his death.[24]

I conclude that both the eucharistic texts and Mark
10:45 are inadequate foundations upon which to rest the argument that the concept of Jesus' death as saving event originated
with Jesus himself.

---

[21]Thyen, op. cit., p. 155. Thyen finds the καί γάρ
jolting and argues that 45a stands in considerable tension with
43-44 in that suddenly the figure of the Son of Man is connected
with instructions for right relations in the community. He
notes Matthew's smoother ὥσπερ (20:28).

[22]Ferdinand Hahn, The Titles of Jesus in Christology
(Cleveland, 1969), pp. 36, 56, and Thyen, op. cit., p. 156,
represent, respectively, the affirmative and negative positions
on the question of whether Mark 10:45 is the result of joining
two originally separate logia.

[23]See especially Ph. Vielhauer, "Gottesreich und
Menschensohn," in Festschrift für Günther Dehn (Neukirchen,
1957), pp. 51-79; "Jesus und der Menschensohn," ZTK 60(1963),
133-77, esp. 170. Also: H. Conzelmann, "Jesus Christus," RGG,
III, 630-31; H. Koester, "One Jesus and Four Primitive Gospels,"
HTR 61(1968), 214-19.

[24]Jeremias' suggestion ("Lösegeld," p. 227) that the
opposition διακονηθῆναι/διακονῆσαι perhaps allows us to perceive the "inner struggle" of Jesus, who "stood before two
ways," must be totally rejected.

Part II:  Primitive Palestinian Christianity Said So

A second option claims that the doctrine of Jesus' expiatory death (even if it originated with Jesus himself) became a popular article of belief in earliest Aramaic-speaking Christianity.  This could be expected because this concept was such a natural outgrowth of familiar OT ideas and current Jewish practices.  That this was the case is demonstrated by the fact, so the argument goes, that several NT texts which express the idea of Jesus' expiatory death betray their Aramaic origins. The texts to be considered here are Mark 10:45, Mark 14:22-25, and I Cor. 15:3-5.

### A. Mark 10:45

Jeremias holds that the Semitic origin of this verse is especially clear from 45b.  Even if 45b is a Christian expansion of 45a, he thinks that he has proved that the ransom-word could not have originated outside Palestine.[25]  From a phrase by phrase comparison of Mark 10:45 with I Tim. 2:6 he concludes that "die semitisierende Markus-Fassung im ersten Timotheus-Brief grazisiert ist . . . ."  But to recognize the Semitic coloring of 45b is not necessarily to agree that this verse therefore reflects an Aramaic _Urtext_ more accurately than does a grecianized counterpart, I Tim. 2:6; for there is no way to verify the opinion that these two texts are merely translation variants of one original Aramaic saying.[26]  Quite as defensible as Jeremias' Aramaic _Urtext_ is the claim that "Alle Semitismen des Spruches Mk. 10,45 sind nichts als vielfach zu belegende Septuagintismen."[27]  To be sure, "the Son of Man" is a literal rendering of _bar nascha_, but that does not necessarily mean that anything except this designation goes back to Aramaic speaking Christianity.  In fact, if the post-Easter application of the Son of Man title to Jesus is taken seriously and if the contrast implied by "not to be served but to serve"

---

[25]_Ibid._, pp. 225-27.

[26]Cf. Thyen, _op. cit._, p. 158.

[27]_Ibid._, p. 159.

214

is recognized, it is legitimate to interpret Mark 10:45 as a
criticism of and an alternative to an accepted view of the Son
of Man and the early (Palestinian!) Christology dependent upon
it.[28]

Jeremias asserts that (δοῦναι) τὴν ψυχὴν αὐτοῦ is a
Semitism meaning "to give his life freely" whereas δοῦναι
ἑαυτόν (I Tim. 2:6) is the more natural Greek translation. The
texts to which Jeremias appeals as evidence for this Semitic
expression are those cited by A. Schlatter (Der Evangelist
Matthäus, p. 602). But all five of these texts are rabbinic
and late--a situation which, by contrast, makes five pre-
Christian Jewish texts quite interesting. In I Maccabees 2:50
Mattathias exhorts his sons: ζηλώσατε τῷ νόμῳ καὶ δότε τὰς
ψυχὰς ὑμῶν ὑπὲρ διαθήκης πατέρων ἡμῶν. Here, as the context
(especially vv. 64, 67-68) makes clear, "give your lives" does
not mean "go die for the Law" (contrast IV Maccabees!) but
"devote your full energies"; this injunction may include the
idea of being willing to die, but it points primarily to living
and fighting. At I Maccabees 6:44 ἔδωκεν ἑαυτὸν τοῦ σῶσαι τὸν
λαὸν αὐτοῦ certainly means "he died," but note that this Greek
translation of a Hebrew original has ἑαυτόν rather than τὴν
ψυχὴν αὐτοῦ. On the other hand, one should note that in a work
thoroughly Hellenistic in style and vocabulary, III Maccabees,
the expression διδόναι ἑαυτούς does not mean "give their lives"
but "give themselves up" (i.e., capitulate: 2:31) or "give
themselves (to revelry)" (5:17). But when the author of this
work wishes to say of the three youths that they gave their
lives to the flames, he writes: τὴν ψυχήν . . . δεδωκότας (6:
6)! Thus the neat distinctions that Jeremias makes between "to
give his life" and "to give himself" are questionable; so is
his implication that the one phrase reflects a more direct relationship to a Semitic original than the other.

When one turns to several Greek texts Jeremias' thesis
becomes even more untenable. In the Heraclidae of Euripides,
Macaria insists (550-51): τὴν ἐμὴν ψυχὴν ἐγὼ / δίδωμ' ἑκοῦσα
τοῖσδ' . . . . Earlier she had asked to be led to where she
would be sacrificed, ἥδε γὰρ ψυχὴ πάρα (530). Antigone (559)

---

[28]Cf. C. K. Barrett, "The Background of Mark 10:45,"
in New Testament Essays. Studies in Memory of Thomas Walter
Manson (Manchester, 1959), p. 8; Thyen, op. cit., pp. 156-58.

215

says to her sister: οὐ μὲν ζῇς, ἡ δ'ἐμὴν ψυχὴ πάλαι/ τέθνηκεν. The exact phrase δοῦναι ψυχήν appears again in the <u>Phoenician Women</u> of Euripides (998).<sup>29</sup>

Jeremias argues that πολλοί as an inclusive designation is a Semitism; its meaning is correctly rendered by πάντες (as in I Tim. 2:6).<sup>30</sup> One can agree that when πολλοί does have the meaning "all, everyone" it is very likely a Semitism.<sup>31</sup> But to acknowledge that is not to agree with Jeremias that Mark 10:45 reflects an Aramaic original. In the first place Jeremias fails in his attempt to show that this verse is dependent on Isaiah 53;<sup>32</sup> thus the claim that πολλοί translates רבים (MT Is. 53:11, 12) is open to serious question. Further, רבים in Jewish texts does not always have an inclusive, universal sense.<sup>33</sup> It can be an <u>exclusive</u> designation for the community, as at Qumran, so that "for us" would be an appropriate way to render its sense.<sup>34</sup> Thus in Mark 10:45 πολλοί could very well mean just what it seems to mean, i.e., "many (not just a few)": not every person alive but those who are disciples of Jesus. In that case πάντες in I Tim. 2:6 would not be simply a more acceptable Greek translation of רבים ; it would reflect a real <u>theological</u> divergence from the tradition known to Mark.<sup>35</sup>

---

<sup>29</sup>In other texts the expression "give one's <u>body</u>" is preferred to "give oneself"--e.g., Euripides, <u>Iphigenia at Aulis</u> 1397, 1553; Thucydides 2.43.2; Demosthenes, <u>Epitaphios</u> 18, cf. 23.

<sup>30</sup>Jeremias, "Lösegeld," p. 226; cf. <u>Eucharistic Words</u>, pp. 179-82.

<sup>31</sup>But see, e.g., Thucydides 2.40.4, where Pericles contrasts the Athenians with τοῖς πολλοῖς--i.e., everyone else.

<sup>32</sup>Cf. Barrett, <u>op. cit.</u>; Thyen, <u>op. cit.</u>, pp. 159-60.

<sup>33</sup>Dan. 11:33, 34; 12:3, 10; possibly 12:2, 4; often at Qumran, e.g., IQS 6.1, 7, 8.

<sup>34</sup>Thyen, <u>op. cit.</u>, p. 160. Cf. Titus 2:14.

<sup>35</sup>Note I Tim. 2:1: "for all men"; 2:4: "who desires to save all men"; also 4:10; II Tim. 2:24; Titus 2:11. This point assumes that the author of the Pastorals is dependent on tradition more generally than in I Tim. 2:6 alone.

Jeremias refers to Rom. 5:15, 19 as prime examples of οἱ πολλοί meaning, in effect, "all men." It seems to me that these instances actually undermine considerably his contention that "for many" at Mark 10:45 points to an Aramaic original. For Paul is not translating from Hebrew or Aramaic. Either his use of this term can be ascribed to the particular categories in which his thought is moving[36] or to the influence of the LXX.

Jeremias lays special stress on the "fact" that the religious λύτρον concept was at home in Jesus' thought world. He finds especially noteworthy the closely parallel statements of IV Maccabees about the deaths of the martyrs; he sees these parallels as the more important because IV Maccabees is to be dated between 30 and 50 A.D. But I have already demonstrated the degree to which IV Maccabees is dominated by Greek ideas. The claim that the ideas embraced in this hellenized writing belonged also to the thought world of Aramaic-speaking Palestinian Jews or Christians is an empty one, for the concept of suffering or death as a λύτρον for others cannot be documented in non-hellenized, pre-Christian Jewish texts.

Perhaps the most questionable aspect of Jeremias' argument is also the most fundamental one, namely his methodological presupposition. As Thyen has correctly observed, Jeremias sets the question of the authenticity of Mark 10:45 not at the end but at the beginning of his discussion. Thus, he does not investigate a text (i.e., what it says and how it was transmitted) so much as he inquires about a "speaker" and his self-understanding. The text, therefore, is naturally viewed as a translation from the Aramaic, and the sense of the Greek can be illuminated only by a retroversion into Aramaic. Furthermore, Jeremias makes Isaiah 53 his point of departure, assuming that this OT text is the source of Jesus' self-understanding.[37] His methodological predisposition enables Jeremias to pass all too easily over certain difficulties caused by his interpretation of the text, e.g., the near-technical term ἦλθεν[38] or the disparity between πολλοί as

---

[36]Namely those related to Adam-Anthropos speculation. Cf. E. Brandenburger, Adam und Christus (Neukirchen, 1962), p. 235, n. 1 and pp. 68-153.

[37]Thyen, op. cit., p. 157.

[38]Ibid., p. 157. n. 4.

inclusive-universal and early traditions reflecting a mission to Jews alone (Mt. 10:5-6, 23; 15:24).

I agree with Suhl that "eine an Semitismen reiche Sprache allein nicht für den Erweis eines hohen Alters einer Überlieferung ausreicht, wenn nicht zwingende sachliche Gründe hinzukommen . . . ."[39] The strong possibility that the Semitic coloring of Mark 10:45 is due to Septuagintal influence and the further possibility that the saying is a reaction to an early Palestinian Christology (cf. above) render this Markan text unacceptable evidence for the thesis that primitive Aramaic-speaking Christianity interpreted Jesus' death as a "ransom" for others.

B. Mark 14:22-25

The view that the "words of institution" in our present eucharistic texts represent variations of a common Aramaic tradition depends primarily upon the alleged Semitisms and Palestinian idioms in Mark 14:22-25.[40]

According to Jeremias, the verb εὐλογεῖν, when used to mean "bless" or "say a grace," is a Semitism--certainly when used absolutely, as in Mark 14:22. This point can be granted. Again, the expression "break bread" is strange to classical Greek and appears but twice in the LXX (Jer. 16:7, Lam. 4:4). In rabbinic writings, however, it appears to be a technical term for the breaking of bread before meals (Words, p. 176). These three facts tend to support the argument that the expression is Semitic in origin and was used in early Aramaic-speaking Christianity; but Acts 27:35 shows how apparently natural this usage was for a Greek-speaking Christian.

Much less compelling is the argument that the word order at several points in Mark 14:22-24 is indicative of a Semitic Urtext. According to Jeremias, "the position of the personal pronoun in Mark [i.e., τὸ σῶμά μου and τὸ αἷμά μου] corresponds to the Semitic suffix . . ." (p. 178). True. But

_____

[39]Suhl, op. cit., p. 119.

[40]Jeremias, Eucharistic Words, pp. 186-89 and 173-84. Since v. 25 involves Jesus' eschatological vow of abstinence (which is compatible with his eschatological message but has nothing to do with the meaning of his death), I am concerned here only with those alleged Semitisms in vv. 22-24.

this fact is not equivalent to a demonstration that the position
of the pronoun points to a Semitic original. (Nor does the
position of μου in I Cor. 11:24, "possible only in Greek," mean
conversely that any other word order is non-Greek.) Similarly,
Jeremias' assertion that the Greek phrase τὸ εκχυννόμενον
ὑπὲρ πολλῶν "corresponds to Semitic word order" (p. 182) does
not constitute proof that it derives from a Semitic original.

Additional arguments which Jeremias develops in support
of his thesis are unconvincing. Little weight can be given,
for example, to the six-fold καί in Mark 14:22-24 (which Jeremias takes as a "Semitic usage"). Given the fact that asyndeton
is highly characteristic of Aramaic,[41] it seems likely that the
καί style in the eucharistic text is Mark's own, especially
since this style is a feature of Markan editorial sentences as
well as of inherited material.[42] On linguistic grounds, therefore, it is by no means necessary to ascribe the six καί's of
Mark 14:22-24 to Aramaic-speaking Palestinian Christianity.
The difference between Mark and Matthew at this point is a
typical difference of style.[43]

If, as Jeremias asserts (p. 175), the participle λαβών
refers to a distinct, observable action (i.e., raising the
bread slightly from the table), it is meaningless to insist
that "having taken bread and blessed" is at the same time a
typically Semitic idiom ("took and did"). Although "took and
did" may be typically Semitic, Jeremias actually seems to undermine his case by acknowledging this idiom in Acts 9:25, 16:3,
and 27:35. In these instances Luke is hardly dependent on
Semitic sources. This situation suggests that an expression
Semitic in origin has become the property of Greek-speaking

---

[41]M. Black, An Aramaic Approach to the Gospels and Acts
(Oxford, [2]1954), p. 38.

[42]Cf. F. Blass and A. Debrunner, A Greek Grammar of the
New Testament and Other Early Christian Literature (Chicago,
1961), par. 458. Blass-Debrunner note that Aristotle distin-
guishes two types of Greek style, periodic and continuous. The
latter type
    is characteristic of plain and unsophisticated language in
    all periods, and thus of the earliest Greek prose as well
    as of the narrative sections of the NT on the whole. The
    latter conform at this point to Semitic style. . . . This
    produces a monotonous style which has left its imprint on
    the narrative of Mark . . . .

[43]This view is supported by the observation that three
instances of καί in Mark's text occur in expressions (i.e., he
gave, he gave, they drank) which probably represent a later
stage of tradition than the Pauline account. (The Pauline
tradition includes no direct reference to the congregational
actions of taking, eating, drinking.)

Jews and Christians,[44] probably due to the influence of the
LXX.[45]

A similar response is appropriate to Jeremias' argument
that "to give" (meaning to distribute or hand out) without the
accusative object is a Semitic idiom (p. 177). Even if this
expression is Semitic in origin, that fact cannot constitute
evidence that an Aramaic (or Hebrew) Vorlage underlies its
occurrence in Mark 14:22. The expression would have been
familiar from the LXX to Greek-speaking Jews and Christians.[46]
Likewise, one can agree that to "take a cup and give thanks"
is certainly a Jewish practice, but a few parallels from rabbinic texts do not convincingly demonstrate that the expression is
a Semitism pointing to an Aramaic source.[47] Nor can the pair
of terms "body/flesh-blood" really be called a Semitism since
this pair is found in Philo and in the LXX (a point acknowledged
by Jeremias himself: Words, p. 222).

The argument that the terms ἐκχυννόμενος and ὑπέρ are
derived from Isaiah 53 (MT!) can be quickly dismissed.[48] Nor
is there good reason to suppose that this present participle
must be dependent on an Aramaic (atemporal) participle. Rather,
possessing a timeless/theological (rather than a future/histor-
ical) sense, it is to be accounted for by liturgical considerations. That is why the participle is not future--as it would
be if the interest of those who transmitted these words had
been historical.

For Jeremias, any instance of coincidence with a

Semitic expression is considered a Semitism which points to

an Aramaic (or Hebrew) original. But most of Jeremias' Semi-

tisms can be more satisfactorily designated Septuagintisms:

expressions or stylistic peculiarities familiar to Greek-

speaking Christians from their scriptures. Only the objectless

---

[44]Cf. Wisdom 13:13 (ξύλον . . . λαβὼν ἔγλυψεν); II Mac.
10:30, 15:46. In addition to the Acts texts cf. I Clement
43:2: καὶ λαβὼν αὐτὰς ἔδησεν καὶ ἐσφράγισεν . . . . (This
sentence does not occur in LXX Num. 17.)

[45]LXX Gen. 2:15, 3:6, 8:9, 9:23, 16:3, 17:23, 18:8,
21:14, 21:27; I Kings 8:14, 30:11, etc.

[46]Cf. LXX Gen. 3:6, 18:7, 20:14, 21:14, 21:27, 24:41,
38:18; Judges 14:9, 21:22; I Kings 9:8, 25:27, etc. Whether
the expression occurs in Philo cannot be ascertained readily
because διδόναι is not included in Leisegang's index; but see
Joseph and Asenath 4.3: καὶ ἐξήνεγκαν πάντα τὰ ἀγαθά, ὅσα
ἐνήνοχαν . . . καὶ ἔδωκαν τῇ θυγατρὶ αὐτῶν (Gk. MS D and
Slavonic MS; the pertinent phrase is omitted in Gk. MS B). Cf.
also Wisdom 8:21, II Mac. 15:33, I Cor. 3:5.

[47]The claim that εὐχαριστεῖν without object is a
Semitism depends on the prior assumption that this word represents a translation from a Semitic language. If the phrase at
Mark 14:23 was originally formulated in Greek and means "give
thanks," however, an object is neither necessary nor appropriate.

[48]Cf. Thyen, op. cit., p. 162. On πολλοί as a
"Semitism" cf. above, pp. 215-216.

εὐλογήσας and ἔκλασεν clearly point to a tradition originally
formulated in Aramaic. One can conclude that the communal
meal in early Aramaic-speaking Christianity involved at least
the saying of a blessing and the "breaking of bread"; this
conclusion is entirely consonant with Acts 2:42. One cannot
prove from Mark 14:22-24, however, that Aramaic-speaking Christians celebrated a Eucharist which involved words over bread
and cup that reflected the concept of Jesus' death as saving
event.

## C. I Corinthians 15:3-5

In The Eucharistic Words of Jesus J. Jeremias asserts
at one point (p. 96) that I Cor. 15:3b-5 was "originally drawn
up in a Semitic language." Later (p. 102) he is more cautious:
"There are, if not strict proofs, at any rate signs that the
core of the kerygma is a translation of a Semitic original."

Jeremias' argument will not hold.[49] Several of his
"signs" are attributable to Septuagintal influence or to the
confessional-liturgical nature of this tradition. The reference to Isaiah 53 is irrelevant because it is improbable that
"according to the scriptures" alludes to that text.[50] The
contention that ὤφθη with the logical subject in the dative is

---

[49]For refutation and disagreement see H. Conzelmann,
"On the Analysis of the Confessional Formula in I Corinthians
15:3-5," Interpretation 20(1966), 18-20; W. Kramer, Christ,
Lord, Son of God (Naperville, 1966), pp. 34-37; Thyen, op.cit.,
pp. 153-54. That "Christ" (without article) argues against an
Aramaic original: Ph. Vielhauer, "Ein Weg zur neutestamentlichen Christologie?" EvTh 25(1965), 56-61. Jeremias' reply
to Vielhauer and Conzelmann: "Artikelloses Χριστός. Zur
Ursprache von I Cor 15 3b-5," ZNW 57(1966), 211-15, which in
turn is rejected forcefully by E. Güttgemanns, "Χριστός in 1.
Kor. 15,3b--Titel oder Eigenname?" EvTh 28(1968), 533-54.
Jeremias is supported by B. Klappert, "Zur Frage des semitischen oder griechischen Urtextes von I Kor. XV. 3-5," NTS 13
(1966-67), 168-73 (others in agreement: 168, n. 2). In my
view Klappert's argument is singularly unsuccessful. It centers on the contention that "for our sins" is a rendering of
Is. 53:5aβ Targum. In light of the meaning of Is. 53 in the
Targum, I find this argument rather incredible.

[50]Even if the phrase does point to Is. 53, the relationship with the Greek text (περί) would be stronger than with the
MT (מן). Cf. Conzelmann, "Analysis," 19.

a Semitism pointing to an Aramaic Urtext is puzzling in light
of the identical expression in Acts 9:17, 13:31, 26:16; Heb.
9:28; and I Tim. 3:16.[51]

One can agree with Jeremias this far: that the kernel
of the kerygmatic formulation at I Cor. 15:3-5 had its origin
in Aramaic-speaking Palestinian Christianity. But that "kernel"
was limited to a statement about the resurrection of Jesus.[52]
I Cor. 15:3, therefore, cannot serve as convincing evidence
that Jesus' death was interpreted as saving event in Aramaic-
speaking Christianity.


Part III: The Scriptures Said So


According to the third option suggested earlier in the
Excursus on models, the concept of Jesus' death as saving event
was the result of a conscious attempt to find in scripture a
meaningful explanation of the crucifixion. In view of the
extensive use of scriptural quotations in early Christianity
and the important purposes served by them,[53] this option has a
certain inherent probability. Of course, every pertinent OT
quotation or allusion does not automatically imply a movement
from crucifixion to OT to interpretation of Jesus' death. As
with other items of belief, the movement might have been from
interpretation to the OT text as warrant and proof. Often it
is impossible to make clear distinctions between the two types
of movement; it is not always clear whether believers searched
the scriptures to discover clarifying insights or to bolster
and legitimate beliefs which had already been formulated. In
most cases the movement was probably two-directional, either in
alternating or simultaneous fashion. Thus it should be recognized right at the beginning of this discussion that the mere

---

[51]See also Mark 9:4, Lk. 1:11, 24:34; Acts 2:3; 7:2,
26, 30, 35; I Cor. 15:8; the verb absolutely: Rev. 11:19, 12:1.

[52]Cf. the quotation to that effect from W. Kramer,
infra, p. 232.

[53]Cf. K. Stendahl, The School of St. Matthew and Its
Use of the Old Testament (Philadelphia, 1968); E. Ellis, Paul's
Use of the Old Testament (Edinburgh, 1957); A. Suhl, op. cit.;
B. Lindars, New Testament Apologetic (Philadelphia, 1961).

appearance of an OT quotation or allusion does not necessarily point to the OT as the source of a particular concept nor to its origin in the searching of scripture.  In each separate case one must decide whether an OT reference is a clue to the source of an idea or an indication of a secondary attempt to support that idea from scripture.

In the form most frequently encountered among scholars, this option is equivalent to the view that Jesus' death as saving event was interpreted as the fulfillment of Isaiah 53. The point of departure for this interpretation is often the assumption that κατὰ τὰς γραφάς at I Cor. 15:3 must refer to Isaiah 53.[54]  In my opinion this is little more than specula- tion.  By now Qumran, if nothing else, should have taught NT scholars the danger of understanding first century views of scriptural proof in terms of modern canons of what is appropri- ate and convincing.  There is as little reason to see "scrip- tures" at I Cor. 15:3 as a reference to one OT text as there is to do the same for Matt. 26:54 (note the expansion in v. 56!) or Mark 12:24 or Luke 24:32, 45 (cf. vv. 27 and 44!) or Rom. 1:2 or Rom 15:4.  Most importantly, κατὰ τὰς γραφάς at I Cor. 15:3 cannot be interpreted apart from a consideration of the identical phrase at 15:4.  In v. 4, however, "he was raised on the third day" is hardly drawn from a single OT text.  Indeed, it is uncertain to what text(s) this statement does allude. The evidence that it alludes to any specific OT texts must be provided by other early NT passages where quotations from or clear allusions to such texts make exegetical dependence likely. Likewise, sound methodology requires that I Cor. 15:3 be taken as a reference to Isaiah 53 only if Isaiah 53 is quoted or alluded to in other early NT material as a proof text for the belief that Jesus died "for our sins."

## A.  Quotations From Isaiah 53 in the New Testament

Isaiah 53 (including 52:15) is cited and quoted six times in the NT.  At Rom. 15:21 Paul introduces a quotation from 52:15 with the formula "as it is written":  "They shall

---

[54]Cf., e.g., G. Wiencke, Paulus über Jesu Tod (Güters- loh, 1939), p. 80; Cullmann, op. cit., p. 76.

see what has not been told about him, and they who have not
heard shall understand." Paul appeals to this statement as
scriptural backing for his missionary practice of preaching the
gospel where it has not already been heard (v. 20). At Rom.
10:16 Paul quotes Is. 53:1a ("for Isaiah says") to show that
the prophet had foreseen that the gospel would not be accepted
by all men. The whole of Is. 53:1 is quoted at John 12:38.
But here the point is that "the word spoken by the prophet
Isaiah" has been fulfilled by the unbelief of the people, even
though Jesus had done so many signs among them. These three NT
passages, then, are concerned with the preaching of the gospel
and its reception; so far, there has been no mention of Jesus'
suffering and death or of expiation of sins.

In Matt. 8:17 the evangelist introduces a quotation
from Is. 53:4 with a variation of his standard formula: "thus
was fulfilled what was spoken by the prophet Isaiah (saying)."
The quotation reads: αὐτὸς τὰς ἀσθενείας ἡμῶν ἔλαβεν καὶ τὰς
νόσους ἐβάστασεν. The Greek is not that of our LXX or the
other Greek translations. Matt. 8:17 may, therefore, be a
direct translation from the Hebrew; the quotation may, however,
represent a more original LXX reading.[55] In any case, the most
significant aspect of the quotation in Matt. 8 is that the
context has nothing to do with Jesus' bearing the sins of
others. Rather the act of Jesus which fulfilled the prophet's
words was this: "He cast out the spirits with a word and he
healed all those who were sick." Nothing of suffering and
death or bearing of sin here! The significance of this text
has been forcefully stated by Morna D. Hooker:

> . . . far from proving that Jesus was thought of as One
> who suffered because of the sins of others, directly
> bearing their guilt, it will, unless other passages are
> found to be used with this meaning, point to exactly the
> opposite conclusion. For if the very quotations which
> would, used in certain contexts, make abundantly evident
> the identification of Jesus with the Servant who by his
> suffering expiates the sins of others are instead used
> only of his work in other spheres, then this is strong
> evidence that such an identification was never made,
> either by Jesus or by his earliest followers.[56]

---

[55]Euler, op. cit., p. 62.

[56]Hooker, op. cit., p. 83.

Only two quotations from Isaiah 53 have to do with Jesus' personal fate. In view of the passion narrative, the words spoken by Jesus at Luke 22:37 ("this scripture must be fulfilled in me: 'And he was reckoned with transgressors'"--Is. 53:12) are taken most naturally as a reference to Jesus' trial and crucifixion.

The story of the Ethiopian eunuch in Acts 8 contains the most extensive quotation from Isaiah 53. The passage the eunuch is reading, which serves as the basis of Philip's proclaiming to him the Jesus-gospel (8:35), is Is. 53:7-8 (LXX). These words are understood as a prophecy of Jesus' undeserved suffering and death. The crucial observation--as likewise in the case of the previous five quotations--is that nothing is intimated in Acts 8 about the meaning of Jesus' death, certainly not in terms of vicarious or expiatory suffering.

B.  Possible Echoes of Isaiah 53 in Other New Testament Texts

I turn now to those NT texts in which scholars frequently detect echoes of or allusions to Isaiah 53.

1.  Mark 10:45. That this verse is dependent on Is. 53:10-12 is held by J. Jeremias, among many others.[57] He compares δοῦναι τὴν ψυχήν with נפשו . . . תשׂים אם (53:10) and πολλοί with רבים (53:11, 12); διακονῆσαι points to the Servant of God, and λύτρον is a "free translation" of אשׁם (53:10). These alleged parallels, however, have been fully discounted by several scholars and I need not duplicate their arguments here.[58]

2.  Mark 14:24 par. The widespread use of the phrase "to pour out blood" in the OT (especially in connection with sacrificial rites), the frequent occurrence of "many" in the OT, and the fact that the phrase "poured out for many" has no parallel in Isaiah 53 make untenable the claim that the words of Mark 14:24 par. echo Isaiah 53:12 in particular.[59] One need

---

[57]Jeremias, "Lösegeld," p. 227. Others include Lohse, op. cit., pp. 119-20; Lindars, op. cit., pp. 78-79; Taylor, Jesus and His Sacrifice, p. 102.

[58]See above all C. K. Barrett, op. cit., pp. 1-18. Also Hooker, op. cit., pp. 74-79; Thyen, op. cit., pp. 159-60.

[59]As Jeremias (Eucharistic Words, pp. 226-27) and Lohse (op. cit., pp. 126, 129) claim.

only observe with Thyen that "für das Gottesknechtslied sind weder der Opfer- noch der Bundesgedanke konstitutiv." That ἐκχυννόμενον in Mark 14:24 is intended to recall הערה in Isaiah 53:12 is improbable, "denn vom Blutvergiessen ist Jes. 53,12 nicht die Rede, dagegen steht ἐκχεῖν αἷμα in der Septuaginta ständig für die Opferdarbringung."[60]

3. Romans 4:25. According to O. Cullmann[61] Rom. 4:25 is the only Pauline text in which Isaiah 53 is "directly quoted." True, the last clause of Isaiah 53:12 LXX reads καὶ διὰ τὰς ἀμαρτίας αὐτῶν παρεδόθη. However, Rom. 4:25 uses a different word for "transgressions" than does Isaiah 53:12 LXX: ὃς παρεδόθη διὰ τὰ παραπτώματα ἡμῶν. Thus it can be called a precise quotation only if it is considered a direct translation from the Hebrew. Translation directly from the Hebrew is a theoretical possibility if this verse is a pre-Pauline formulation,[62] but it is not very likely in view of the fact that only three times in the LXX (Is. 47:3; 53:6, 12!) does παραδιδόναι render פשע. If one observes the use of παραδιδόναι in the NT in connection with the person of Jesus, it is obvious that the term often refers simply to Jesus' betrayal and arrest.[63] Sometimes it is used to describe the fate that faithful disciples can expect (e.g., Matt. 10:17, 19, 21; 24:9). But even when παραδιδόναι appears to bear heavier theological import (e.g., Rom. 8:32, Gal. 2:20, Eph. 5:2, 25; cf. John 3:16), there is little to suggest Isaiah 53 in particular. Therefore, while Rom. 4:25 might reflect this text, that possibility cannot be demonstrated conclusively. And even if the wording of Rom. 4:25 does depend on Isaiah 53:12, it is far more likely that this "borrowing" reflects the attempt to couch an already-formulated idea in biblical phraseology than that Isaiah 53 was the initial source of that idea.

---

[60]Thyen, op. cit., p. 162. Cf. Hooker, op. cit., pp. 79-83. Miss Hooker concludes (pp. 82-83): "Any exegesis which sees a fundamental connection with Isa. 53 can only arise from reading Mark 14.24 in the light of an already accepted doctrine of Atonement."

[61]O. Cullmann, op. cit., p. 76.

[62]For those scholars who support its pre-Pauline character cf. Kramer, op. cit., p. 30, n. 48.

[63]Mt. 10:4, 17:22, 20:18; 26 passim; 27:?, 3, 4, 18; cf. parallel passages in Mark and Luke, similar ones in John.

4. John 1:29, 36. Jeremias thinks that the "highly singular" genitive combination ὁ ἀμνὸς τοῦ θεοῦ "can be explained only in the light of the Aramaic."

In Aramaic the word טַלְיָא has the twofold significance of a. lamb and b. boy or servant. Probably an Aramaic טַלְיָא דֵאלָהָא in the sense of עֶבֶד יְהֹוָה underlies the Greek ὁ ἀμνὸς τοῦ θεοῦ, the original reference thus being to Jesus as the servant of God.[64]

The improbability that we have here an early allusion to Isaiah 53 is apparent at each stage of the argument. In the first place, neither Jeremias nor Burney[65] nor C. J. Ball[66] has furnished any texts in which טַלְיָא is used for a special representative of God. In none of the texts they cite is this Aramaic term one of honor; it seems to denote strictly the unprivileged status of the child or slave. Thus the Greek phrase of John 1:29, 36 is not one whit more "singular" than the phrase in Aramaic would have been. Furthermore, the Hebrew cognate טְלֶה is never translated by ἀμνός in the LXX.[67]

In the second place, even if the Aramaic טַלְיָא and its double meaning (lamb/servant) does stand behind the Johannine ἀμνός, it does not follow that the servant/lamb of God points to Isaiah 53. Jeremias implies that the more appropriate translation of the supposed Aramaic phrase would have been ὁ παῖς τοῦ θεοῦ. And, after all, this precise designation appears in Isaiah 52:13! But one cannot afford to overlook the fact that παῖς, translating עֶבֶד, is frequently used to refer to Moses or David, or even Caleb, Isaiah or Eliakim, as "the servant of the Lord" or the equivalent "my servant" or "your servant."[68] There is no warrant, then, for an appeal to Isaiah

---

[64] J. Jeremias, "ἀμνός, ἀρήν, ἀρνίον," TDNT, I, p. 339.

[65] Burney, op. cit., pp. 107-108.

[66] C. J. Ball, "Had the Fourth Gospel an Aramaic Archetype?" ET 21(1909-10), 93.

[67] Cf. Hooker, op. cit., p. 104, who writes that this theory "rests on a supposition" and "lacks any supporting evidence."

[68] Moses: Josh. 1:7, 13; 9:24; 11:12, 15; 12:6; 13:8; 18:7; 22:2, 5; I Chron. 6:49(34); II Chron. 1:3; Neh. 1:7, 8; cf. Baruch 1:20, 2:28. David: II Chron. 6:15, 17; Is. 37:35; Caleb: Num. 14:24; Eliakim: Is. 22:20; Isaiah: Is. 20:3; the prophets: Jer. 33(26):5, 42(35):15, 51(44):4; cf. Baruch 2:20, 24. Note also Wisdom 2:13, where the righteous man calls himself παῖδα κυρίου.

53 in particular. It is very improbable that the ἀμνός of John 1:29, 36 is derived from Is. 53:7. It is much more natural to locate this designation in an early Christian tradition which saw Jesus as τὸ πάσχα ἡμῶν (I Cor. 5:7; cf. John 13:1, 19:31, 36).

5. Miscellaneous Texts. There are other NT passages which O. Cullman (op. cit., pp. 73, 76) and B. Lindars (op. cit., pp. 79-85), for example, think contain clear allusions to Isaiah 53. I must disagree with their judgment at several points because I believe they begin with the untenable assumption-- untenable especially since Miss Hooker's book appeared--that the Suffering Servant of the Lord and Isaiah 53 exercized consider- able influence in the primitive church. Thus, they can find clear allusions to the "idea" of the vicarious suffering of the Servant of God (cf. e.g., Cullmann, p. 76) even when the texts concerned do not of themselves support such an interpretation by linguistic or precise conceptual parallels. Rejecting their basic assumption, I find no allusion to Isaiah 53 in Rom. 5: 12ff.; 8:3, 32, 34; II Cor. 5:21; Mark 10:34 and John 19:1.

If, for the moment, one assumes with Lindars that allusions to Isaiah 53 are present in Acts 3:13-14 (cf. 3:26; 4:27, 30; 7:52), Phil. 2:5-12, Mark 9:12, and even in Luke 11: 21-22, it is striking that in these texts the point is Jesus' suffering and (or) exaltation; no mention is made of the vicar- ious or expiatory character of that suffering. This situation corresponds precisely with the understanding of Isaiah 53 in Wisdom of Solomon 2-5, where the reader is told about God's vindication of the suffering righteous man!

6. Hebrews. I cannot agree with Lindars (p. 83) that the author of Hebrews takes Isaiah 53 for granted "and builds his own work upon it." Also questionable is his assertion that Heb. 10:12 "briefly summarizes the Christian interpretation of Isaiah 53 . . . ." After all, the crucial words προσφέρειν and θυσία are not found in Isaiah 53 LXX; moreover, in 53:10 LXX it is said of "you," not the servant, ἐὰν δῶτε περὶ ἁμαρτίας.

More likely, only 9:28 reflects a conscious reference to Isaiah 53. If so, this adoption of Isaianic language is obviously a secondary development. The author of Hebrews does not begin with Isaiah 53 in explaining the expiatory character of Jesus' death, either as the source whence the initial

impetus for that interpretation or as an important scriptural
rationale. Rather, he begins with an interpretation of Jesus'
death that was already formulated before Paul. He develops
that interpretation by employing above all the categories of
the Levitical priesthood and its function. He alludes to Isaiah
53 only in passing.

7. I Peter. The only other NT writing in which quotations from or allusions to Isaiah 53 occur, with reference to
the meaning of Jesus' death as expiatory, is I Peter. In 2:22-
25 the following phrases, corresponding closely with the language of Isaiah 53 LXX, clearly attest dependence: "who
committed no sin, nor was deceit found in his mouth" (v. 22:
53:9); "he himself bore our sins" (v. 24: 53:12); "by his
wound you have been healed" (v. 24: 53:5); "for you were stray-
ing like sheep" (v. 25: 53:6). These semi-quotations, however,
are no clue to the origin or source of the concept of Jesus'
saving death. One need only note that the date of I Peter, ca.
90-95, precludes its usefulness for this purpose.[69]

The two texts which allude to or adopt phrases from
Isaiah 53 in connection with the meaning of Jesus' death for
the expiation of sins, Heb. 9:28 and I Peter 2:22-25, appear to
exhibit secondary appeals to the words of the prophet. The
only early text which could possibly demonstrate that this
concept was derived from or initially anchored in Isaiah 53 is
Rom. 4:25; but it can be argued (convincingly, in my view) that
this formulation represents a secondary stage of development.
In any case, this pre-Pauline statement by itself is a weak

---

[69]For this dating cf. P. Feine, J. Behm and W. G.
Kümmel, Introduction to the New Testament (New York and Nashville, 141966), p. 299. Even if one insists on Petrine author-
ship (1) I Peter 2:22-25 cannot be taken as a clue to the
origin of the concept of Jesus' expiatory death. The progres-
sion of thought in 2:18-25 indicates that Is. 53 is introduced
in order to describe Jesus' submission to undeserved suffering
with the language of a biblical prototype. But it is not the
initial reference to Is. 53 (in v. 22) which suggests the
concepts of v. 24. V. 21 shows clearly that the idea of
Christ's suffering for others was already such a familiar item
of belief that it intrudes into a statement where it is not
altogether appropriate. To present Christ's suffering as a
parallel experience and thus as a true example, the author
would have written, in v. 21, something like: " . . . because
Christ also suffered unjustly" (cf. v. 19). Instead he foregoes the parallel, appropriate and accurate though it would
have been, and writes: " . . . because Christ suffered for you,
leaving you an example."

foundation upon which to construct the theory that the concept of Jesus' death as saving event was "discovered" in the fifty-third chapter of Isaiah.

## C.  Other OT Texts and the Death of Jesus

With regard to other OT texts which played a part in NT passion apologetic--e.g., Ps. 22, 31, 34, 41, 69, 109; Zech. 9:9; 11:12, 13; 12:10; 13:7--one can say that most of them are quoted or referred to in order to show that the events of passion week were "according to the scriptures." The concepts of vicarious or expiatory death do not enter the picture.[70]

## D.  Conclusions

Isaiah 53 is the single OT text in which the idea of vicarious expiatory suffering is to be found (if, indeed, it is present there). Yet it is not until Hebrews and I Peter that one finds an assured allusion to that chapter or an adoption of its phrases in connection with the meaning of Jesus' death for sinful men. I Cor. 15:3 proves that already before Paul the idea of Jesus' death "for our sins" was thought to be grounded in scripture. That, however, does not demonstrate that it was first through searching the scriptures that this concept was "discovered." The absence of quotations or certain allusions in Paul and in the early strata of tradition in the Gospels and other writings, in fact, tends to suggest precisely the opposite--that is, that Christians appealed to Isaiah 53 as scriptural support for a "doctrine" already familiar to them.

---

[70] Reservations are appropriate at one point, however-- John 19:36: "For these things happened in order that the scripture might be fulfilled, 'Not a bone of him shall be broken.'" If the reference here is to LXX Ps. 34:21, the point of the quotation is God's protection of the righteous man! If, on the other hand, the reference is to LXX Ex. 12: 46/Num. 9:12 (cf. Ex. 12:10), that appeal to particular texts in relation to the idea that Jesus is the Christian Passover Lamb must be considered secondary in comparison with I Cor. 5:7. Moreover, it is likely a priori that the identification of a human being with the Passover lamb was a secondary connection, not the source of the concept of Jesus' saving death. (On John 19:36 and the other texts mentioned under C. cf. B. Lindars, op. cit., pp. 89-132.)

Part IV:   The Origin of the Concept of Jesus'

Death as Saving Event


A.  The Origin of the Concept:   An Hypothesis

On the basis of the available textual evidence, the
preceding three options afford improbable explanations for the
origin of the concept that Jesus' death had redemptive significance.  Another explanation is called for.

I suggest that the concept of Jesus' death as saving
event had as its creative source a tradition of beneficial,
effective human death for others.  Since I can find no evidence
of such a tradition in any Jewish writing not greatly influenced
by Greek ideas--that is, only in IV Maccabees (and possibly in
Josephus)--I must conclude that this concept originated among
Christians who not only spoke Greek but were also thoroughly at
home in the Greek-Hellenistic thought world.

Conclusive evidence in support of this hypothesis is
not available.  Nevertheless there is supporting evidence,
negative and positive.  On the negative side there is the
fundamental fact--popular scholarly opinion notwithstanding--
that a theologumenon of vicarious expiatory death was not current in pre-70 A.D. Judaism.  That concept can be documented
only in IV Maccabees.  If it were more widespread than this one
literary piece, one may assume that its currency was limited to
the martyrological tradition within Jewish circles dominated by
Greek-Hellenistic ideas.  Therefore, although such an impressive creative act is not absolutely inconceivable, it is a
priori improbable that either Jesus himself or a type of primitive Christianity not greatly influenced by Hellenism originated the concept of Jesus' death as saving event.

If one supposes that this interpretation of Jesus'
death arose in Aramaic-speaking Christianity as a response to
the problem of sin, he is faced with this question:  In light
of Jesus' own ministry and proclamation of the Kingdom[71] and

---

[71]I assume that Jesus proclaimed the eschatological
forgiveness of sins as a central aspect of God's inbreaking
rule.  In any case, that this message was at least implicit in

in view of the belief of the early (Palestinian?) church that
the Son of Man had power to forgive sins (Mark 2:3-12, especially v. 10), why would this step have been either necessary or
useful?  If, on the other hand, one supposes that this concept
arose in primitive Christianity as a response to the problem of
Jesus' scandalous death, he is faced with the question:  If
Jesus' death could be explained as a fulfillment of scripture
(e.g., Mt. 26:31, Lk. 22:37; 24:27, 44-45) and if the resurrection was understood as God's vindication of the crucified one,
why was it felt necessary to discover meaning for Jesus' death
elsewhere?  These questions imply that quite particular circumstances and needs were involved in the formulation of the
redemptive significance of Jesus' death.

The attempt to delineate those circumstances and needs
cannot avoid an element of conjecture.  Nevertheless, such an
attempt can serve a useful purpose in the present study if
conjecture is kept to a minimum and is supported by the available evidence.

Jesus' proclamation of the Kingdom of God was intended
for his fellow Jews.  Although he apparently exercized "messianic license"[72] with respect to the Law of Moses and was
especially apt to disagree openly with Pharisaic interpretations of the Law, he nevertheless lived and preached in the
theological context of covenant and Law.  It was those who
stood in this shared "realm of discourse" that he called to
readiness for the Kingdom.

But what happened when hellenized Jews begin to preach
the gospel to Gentiles as well as to other Diaspora Jews?  What
were the new factors which might have had a bearing on the
understanding of Jesus' death?  I suggest four probable aspects
of the new situation:  1) If Paul is any indication, Jesus' own
message played a very minor role in the early proclamation of
the gospel.  2) At the same time, as Gentiles began to respond
to the gospel, the question of sin and forgiveness outside a
covenant/Law context became significant.  3) The apologetic

_____

his ministry is suggested above all by Jesus' table fellowship
with sinners.

[72]Cf. K. Stendahl, "Messianic License" in Paul Peachey
(ed.), Biblical Realism Confronts the Nation ([New York],
1963), pp. 139-52.

need to "explain" the execution of the man confessed as Lord and Son of God was intensified. 4) These needs intensified precisely in an environment where suffering and death were viewed in a more positive way than in non-hellenized Judaism. Consequently, in the multi-faceted situation of the hellenized Jewish-Christian mission to Gentiles and fellow Jews, Jesus' crucifixion came to be understood as a death "for our sins."

This reconstruction, as well as my basic hypothesis, coincides with the view expressed by Werner Kramer in his discussion of I Cor. 15:3-5. Kramer argues that the Aramaic-speaking congregation formulated its Easter faith in these or similar terms: "God raised Jesus from the dead." At first no statement about the death was necessary since it was known to all members of the church. But

> The further the chain of missionary activity spread beyond the confines of the earliest and smallest circle, the less was Jesus' death generally known or tacitly presupposed. Thus it had to be expressly stated and justified together with the statement about the resurrection. This stage could not possibly have been reached until Greek-speaking Jewish Christians undertook the mission to the Gentiles.[73]

By way of support, Kramer observes that no interpretation of Jesus' death by the ὑπέρ phrase or similar expressions is present in the earliest strata of the Synoptic tradition; nor does it fit well with what can be established concerning the theology of Q.[74]

As I attempted to show in Chapter I, Rom. 3:25-26 is a pre-Pauline formulation which originated directly out of the situation created by the Gentile mission. It asserts that God regards the crucified Jesus as ἱλαστήριον for those whose sins He had heretofore "passed over." Thus He manifests his righteousness even to the Gentiles, who are now invited to share the πίστις Ἰησοῦ. If my interpretation of this important text is correct, Rom. 3:25-26 provides crucial support for the hypothesis proposed.

Additional corroboration is forthcoming, I believe, from the epistle to the Hebrews. This treatise reflects a thought world pervaded by Greek-Hellenistic ideas; at many

---

[73]W. Kramer, op. cit., p. 35 (7b).

[74]Ibid., p. 36 (7c).

points it is highly reminiscent of the hellenized Judaism represented above all by Philo. At the same time, the author of
Hebrews is the first Christian writer (and the only one in the
NT) to make the concept of Jesus' sacrificial death a constitu-
tive motif of his whole work. This could be nothing more than
a striking coincidence. But then again it might indicate
accurately what kind of early Christian thinker (i.e., one
imbued with Greek-Hellenistic ideas) could find the concept of
Jesus' saving death so significant that he made it, alongside
the humiliation/exaltation motif, one of the bases of his
Christology. In my view, then, Hebrews tells us a great deal
about the nature of the conceptual milieu in which the idea of
Jesus' vicarious expiatory death was at home in first century
Christianity.[75]

B. The Hypothesis Refined: Jesus' Saving Death and IV Maccabees

So far the proposed hypothesis has been formulated only
in very general terms. When one asks how ideas deriving from
"a tradition of beneficial, effective human death for others"
were mediated to early Christianity, the hypothesis may be
stated more precisely. Two alternative explanations appear
possible; not excluded is some combination of the two.

1) In a fashion parallel to IV Maccabees (but for different reasons) early hellenized Christianity was directly
influenced by the idea of effective vicarious death as it was
developed above all in the Greek funeral oration and in the
dramas of the tragic poets.

2) Early hellenized Christianity was familiar with this
concept as mediated and modified by IV Maccabees (or some
similar address, writing, or writings no longer extant).[76]

---

[75] See also Matt. 1:21: "You shall call his name Jesus,
for he will save his people from their sins." There is no
explicit reference to the death here, of course, but if one
can assume that the concept of Jesus' vicarious death underlies
this text, it is noteworthy that this sentence is embedded in
a legend which mirrors a Hellenistic milieu.

[76] Joseph Klausner is one of the few modern scholars who
have glimpsed the seminal importance of IV Mac. for the formulation of the Christian concept of Jesus' expiatory death. Cf.
From Jesus to Paul (New York, 1943), pp. 139-40.

The second alternative will strike many students of early Christianity as extremely unlikely. In my opinion, however, a surprisingly strong case can be developed in its support. In attempting to make such a case, I propose to begin with late and absolutely certain evidence that IV Maccabees was familiar to Christians and to work backwards to the first century.

## 1. IV Maccabees and Early Christianity

As several scholars have noted,[77] the widespread popularity of IV Maccabees in fourth century Christianity is attested by the fact that Ambrose, Gregory of Nazianzus, and John Chrysostom made extensive use of the work in their own orations in praise of the Maccabean martyrs. Although he considers it the work of Josephus, Eusebius (HE 3.10.6) is also familiar with this writing.

Since rabbinic sources give no indication of acquaintance with IV Maccabees,[78] I see no objection to the conclusion of Dupont-Sommer: "Il apparaît donc que c'est l'Église chrétienne qui a sauvé ce document du Judaïsme hellénistique."[79] This is certainly true from the fourth century onward. But what about the period from the first to the fourth century? Unless one assumes that the document lay out of sight for centuries and was suddenly discovered ca. 300 A.D., it is likely that also from at least ca. 70 or 135 A.D. to ca. 300 A.D. IV Maccabees was preserved among Christian circles. There is, in fact, literary evidence to support this probability.

a. The Martyrdom of Polycarp (ca. 155 A.D.). The description of the deaths of Polycarp, Germanicus, and the unnamed martyrs of chapter two exhibits numerous similarities with IV Maccabees.[80]

---

[77]Freudenthal, op. cit., pp. 29-34; Dupont-Sommer, Machabées, pp. 2-3; Townshend, AP, II, pp. 658-60; Hadas, op. cit., pp. 123-25.

[78]Dupont-Sommer, Machabées, p. 3; Hadas, op. cit., p. 128.

[79]Machabées, p. 3.

[80]In what follows, an asterisk marks those passages which von Campenhausen assigns to a later Euangelion-Redaktion. As for a date, he suggests tentatively the beginning of the fourth century. Cf. H. von Campenhausen, Bearbeitungen und Interpolationen des Polykarpmartyriums (Heidelberg, 1957), pp. 9-15; for the text, with interpolations presented schematically, cf. pp. 40-48.

Both writings emphasize the martyrs' endurance in suffering (MP 2:2, 3,* 4; 3:1; 13:3.   IV Mac. 1:11; 6:9; 7:9; 9:8; 15:30, 32; 16:19; 17:10, 17, 23).

The authorities attempt to dissuade the martyrs by appealing either to youth or to old age:

. . . λέγοντος, τὴν ἡλικίαν αὐτοῦ κατοικτείραι (MP 3:1)
κατελεήσατε οὖν ἑαυτούς,. . . καὶ τῆς ἡλικίας
. . . οἰκτίρομαι (IV 8:10; cf. 8:20)

αἰδέσθητί σου τὴν ἡλικίαν(MP 9:2)
αἰδοῦμαι γάρ σου τὴν ἡλικίαν (IV 5:7).

The martyrs endure horrible tortures:

οἳ μάστιξιν μὲν καταξανθέντες (MP 2:2)
ἀπεξαίνετο ταῖς μάστιξιν τὰς σάρκας (IV 6:6; cf. 6:3, 9:12; further compare MP 2:2 with IV 9:20, 28; 10:8)

τὰ πρὸς τὴν πυρὰν ἡρμοσμένα ὄργανα(MP 13:3)
διὰ κακοτέχνων ὀργάνων καταφλέγοντες αὐτόν (IV 6:25).

The attitude and bearing of the martyrs demonstrate their courage:

ἀλλὰ τί βραδύνεις; (MP 11:2)
τί μέλλετε; (IV 6:23) τί μέλλεις; (9:1)

τῶν κοσμικῶν κατεφρόνουν βασάνων (MP 2:3)*
τῶν μέχρι θανάτου βασάνων περιεφρόνει (IV 7:16; cf. 6:9, 13:9)

τοὺς δὲ καὶ εἰς τοσοῦτον γενναιότητος ἐλθεῖν,
ὥστε μήτε γρύξαι μήτε στενάξαι τινὰ αὐτῶν (MP 2:2)*
οὐκ ἐστέναξεν, ἀλλ'. . . ὑπέμεινεν εὐγενῶς τὰς στρέβλας (IV 9:21-22)

ἀναβλέψας εἰς τὸν οὐρανόν (MP 9:2, 14:1)
ἀνατείνας εἰς οὐρανὸν τοὺς ὀφθαλμούς (IV 6:6)

καὶ τὸ πῦρ ἦν αὐτοῖς ψυχρόν (MP 2:3)*
τὸ πῦρ σου ψυχρὸν ἡμῖν (IV 11:26)

βασανιζόμενοι τῆς σαρκὸς ἀπεδήμουν (MP 2:2)*
ὥσπερ ἐν ὀνείρῳ βασανιζόμενος (IV 6:5).

The ἀγών motif expresses the martyrs' struggle and their reward:

Polycarp's prize (βραβεῖον) is a "crown of immortality" (MP 17:1; cf. 19:2 below)

"Victory was immortality"/"God-piety was victorious and crowned her athletes" (IV 17:12, 15; cf. 9:8).

Cultic language is used in the prayers of Polycarp and Eleazar:

προσδεχθείην ἐνώπιόν σου σήμερον ἐν θυσίᾳ πίονι καὶ προσδεκτῇ (MP 14:2; cf. 14:1)

καθάρσιον αὐτῶν ποίησον τὸ ἐμὸν αἷμα καὶ ἀντίψυχον αὐτῶν λαβὲ τὴν ἐμὴν ψυχήν (IV 6:29).

The martyrs' deaths have remarkable effects:

διὰ τῆς μαρτυρίας αὐτοῦ κατέπαυσεν τὸν διωγμόν (MP 1:1)

διὰ τῆς ὑπομονῆς καταγωνισάμενος τὸν ἄδικον ἄρχοντα (MP 19:2)*

(For IV Mac. cf. supra, pp. 168-70).[81] The noteworthy similarities and the precise parallels between the Martyrdom of Polycarp and IV Maccabees argue for the probability that the author of the Martyrdom was acquainted with the book of IV Maccabees.

b. Ignatius, Bishop of Antioch. The epistles of Ignatius (110?) exhibit an attitude toward the value of martyrdom very reminiscent of IV Maccabees. In these letters one finds the same realism in the description of the suffering anticipated and the same enthusiasm to be sacrificed for the glory of one's religion.[82] These "psychological" similarities might be dismissed as coincidental were it not for definite terminological parallels between Ignatius and IV Maccabees. Taken alone, none of these parallels is significant; taken together, they point rather clearly to the probability that Ignatius was familiar with IV Maccabees.

It is to be recalled that in interpreting the martyrs' deaths IV Maccabees employs the phrases ἀντίψυχον αὐτῶν (6:29) and ἀντίψυχον . . . τῆς τοῦ ἔθνους ἁμαρτίας (17:21). Four times Ignatius uses an equivalent phrase: ἀντίψυχον ὑμῶν ἐγώ . . . (Eph. 21:1); ἀντίψυχον ὑμῶν τὸ πνεῦμά μου καὶ τὰ δεσμά μου (Smyr. 10:2); κατὰ πάντα σου ἀντίψυχον ἐγὼ καὶ τὰ δεσμά μου

---

[81]To these similarities can be added at least three others: eternal punishment by fire awaits the torturers (MP 11:2; IV 9:9, passim); death is described as a seal (MP 1:1; IV 7:15); and, more importantly, capitulation is unthinkable in light of a long life of devotion inspired by gratitude (MP 9:3; IV 5:34-36).

[82]See especially IgnRom. 4:1-2, 5:2-3 and Dupont-Sommer, Machabées, p. 84.

(Pol. 2:3); ἀντίψυχον ἐγὼ τῶν ὑποτασσομένων τῷ ἐπισκόπῳ (Pol. 6:1). To be sure, in these sentences Ignatius does not refer directly to his death, but he is on his way to die in Rome and he does, in fact, twice mention his chains. Yet, as he uses the term, ἀντίψυχον obviously does not bear the same theological weight that it does in IV Maccabees.[83] That observation, however, must be balanced by another, namely, that a word which appears twice in IV Maccabees and four times in Ignatius is found so rarely in Greek literature[84] and not at all in the LXX, the NT, or any other of the Apostolic Fathers. After Ignatius the word occurs again first in Eusebius.[85]

This noteworthy parallel invites attention to several descriptive terms and figures of speech that relate to the experience of suffering and its rewards.

The ὑπομένειν/ὑπομονή theme is encountered frequently in both works. That general similarity can be disregarded more easily than can these rather specific parallels:

ἕνεκεν θεοῦ πάντα ὑπομένειν ἡμᾶς δεῖ (Pol. 3:1)
δι'ὃν πάντα ὑπομένοντες . . . (Smyr. 9:2)
ὀφείλετε πάντα πόνον ὑπομένειν διὰ τὸν θεόν (IV 16:19).

It is surely of some import that the expression "to endure (something) on account of/for the sake of God" does not recur in the scriptures.

Again, common to both works is the designation of the faithful one as ἀθλητής:

νῆφε ὡς θεοῦ ἀθλητής (Pol. 2:3; cf. 1:3, 3:1)
οἱ τῆς θείας νομοθεσίας ἀθληταί (IV 17:16; cf. v. 15, 6:10).

At Pol. 3:1 Ignatius asserts that μεγάλου ἐστιν ἀθλητοῦ τὸ δέρεσθαι καὶ νικᾶν. With that statement should be compared IV Mac. 6:10: καθάπερ γενναῖος ἀθλητὴς τυπτόμενος ἐνίκα τοὺς βασανίζοντας ὁ γέρων.[86]

---

[83]The term may, in fact, be little more than an expression of devotion; compare περίψημα ὑμῶν and π. τοῦ σταυροῦ at IgnEph. 8:1 and 18:1.

[84]Liddell and Scott give only Lucian, Lexiphanes 10 and Dio Cassius 59.8.

[85]Cf. G. W. H. Lampe, A Patristic Greek Lexicon (Oxford, 1968), s. v.

[86]The motif of conquering through endurance in suffering is, of course, absolutely fundamental to IV Maccabees.

In the same context (Pol. 2:3) Ignatius writes that the reward (τὸ θέμα) for a "sober athlete" is ἀφθαρσία καὶ ζωὴ αἰώνιος. For the author of IV Maccabees also, τὸ νῖκος ἀφθαρσία ἐν ζωῇ πολυχρονίῳ (17:12; cf. also 9:22); he too can refer to life hereafter as αἰώνιος ζωή (15:3).

Another parallel in the letter to Polycarp is the figure of the pilot buffeted by tempests who safely returns his ship to harbor (Pol. 2:3; IV 7:1-3 and cf. 15:31-32).[87]

In another letter, Rom. 6:1, the metaphor of birth into immortality describes the end of suffering: ὁ δὲ τοκετός μοι ἐπίκειται. The same figure is found in IV Maccabees 16:13: εἰς ἀθανασίαν ἀνατίκτουσα.

Ignatius' description, in Rom. 5:3, of the suffering he anticipates provides yet another example of noteworthy similarity between his letters and IV Maccabees. Among the torments he expects are the following: πῦρ (cf. IV Mac. 5:32, 6:24-25, passim); συγκοπαὶ μελῶν (IV Mac. 9:17: τέμνετέ μου τὰ μέλη; cf. 10:19). Further, the image of the scattering of bones (σκορπισμοὶ ὀστέων: Rom. 5:3) bears some similarity to the frequent description of disjointing and dismemberment in IV Maccabees (e.g., 9:13, 17; 10:5, 8; 11:10).

These similarities are the more notable in light of a comment Ignatius makes at Rom. 4:2. Obviously he expects to be thrown to the lions in Rome (Rom. 4:1-2) and the descriptive figures mentioned above (except fire!) can be understood as referring to his body being torn apart by the wild beasts. Why, then, does he refer to them as "these instruments"? I call attention to two facts: 1) The word ὄργανον refers to an instrument of torture four (or five) times in IV Maccabees: 6:25; 9:20, 26; 10:5 (7?); otherwise this usage occurs in the Greek Bible only at II Maccabees 13:5. 2) Tortured διὰ κακοτέχνων ὀργάνων and near death, Eleazar prays that God will accept his death as purification and ransom for his people (IV 6:25, 29). In light of these two facts, Ignatius' request at Rom. 4:2 is particularly significant. He writes: λιτανεύσατε τὸν Χριστὸν ὑπὲρ ἐμοῦ, ἵνα διὰ τῶν ὀργάνων τούτων θεοῦ θυσία εὑρεθῶ.

---

[87]At Pol. 2:3 cf. κυβερνῆται--χειμαζόμενος--λιμένα; compare IV Mac. 7:1-3: κυβερνήτης--καταντλούμενος--λιμένα.

In view of the parallels noted earlier, the fact that Ignatius could refer to the wild beasts as τὰ ὄργανα and that he could ask that in death he might be regarded as a sacrifice points to the overwhelming probability that he was familiar with IV Maccabees (or some very similar document).

c. Hebrews. It is obvious from Heb. 11:35-38 that the author is familiar with traditions of suffering and martyrdom that go beyond anything suggested in the Hebrew Bible. Verse 35b has no closer parallel than II Mac. 6-7; ἐπρίσθησαν reminds one of the Ascension of Isaiah, but Isaiah himself is the only person sawed in two in that or any other extant writing. Verse 38 echoes certain passages in I and II Maccabees (e.g., I 2:29-32; II 6:11) and Josephus (Ant. 12.272-75). Mocking and scourging (v. 36) are especially suggestive of II and IV Maccabees. On the other hand, chains and prison, being stoned or clothed with sheep and goatskins strikes one as unfamiliar. One can say that in chapter 11 the author appears to be using a Jewish Vorlage,[88] but Heb. 11:35-38 is of little help in deciding whether he was acquainted with IV Maccabees.

Outside chapter 11, however, there is evidence upon which one can base a decision, namely, several parallels of motif and terminology. First there is the shared motif of τελειοῦσθαι through suffering and death. At IV Mac. 7:15 the author says with reference to Eleazar: ὃν πιστῇ θανάτου σφραγὶς ἐτελείωσεν. The author of Hebrews interprets the sufferings of Jesus in much the same way:

. . . διὰ παθημάτων τελειῶσαι ('Ιησοῦν) (2:10)

ἔμαθεν ἀφ'ὧν ἔπαθεν τὴν ὑπακοήν, καὶ τελειωθεὶς . . . (5:8-9)

. . . υἱὸν εἰς τὸν αἰῶνα τετελειωμένον (7:28).[89]

Again, in both writings the ὑπομένειν/ὑπομονή idea is of fundamental importance. According to Hebrews Jesus endured the hostility of sinners against him (12:3); likewise, Christians are called to endure (10:36; 12:1, 7), just as they have

---

[88]So H. Windisch, Der Hebräerbrief (Tübingen, ²1931), p. 98, who calls attention to Wisdom 9-10; Sir. 44-50; IV Mac. 16:16-23; Philo, virtut. 198ff. and de praem. et poen. 1ff. Cf. also O. Michel, Der Brief an die Hebräer (Göttingen, ¹¹1960), pp. 244-45.

[89]Note also 12:2. Christians are made perfect through Christ's sacrifice: 10:14, 12:23; cf. 11:40. The Law is unable to make perfect: 7:19, 9:9, 10:1.

240

in the past (10:32). One of the more noteworthy parallels, conceptual and terminological, between the two writings has to do with endurance in suffering:

ὑπέμεινεν σταυρὸν αἰσχύνης καταφρονήσας (Heb. 12:2)

ὁ δὲ ὑπέμενε τοὺς πόνους καὶ περιεφρόνει τῆς ἀνάγκης (IV 6:9).

As in IV Maccabees (cf. especially 17:11-16) the necessity of endurance is, in Hebrews, connected with the athletic motif: πολλὴν ἄθλησιν ὑπεμείνατε παθημάτων (10:32); δι'ὑπομονῆς τρέχωμεν τὸν . . . ἀγῶνα (12:1). Τοσοῦτον . . . νέφος μαρτύρων (12:1) easily recalls the statement of IV Mac. 17:14 that ὁ κόσμος καὶ ὁ τῶν ἀνθρώπων βίος ἐθεώρει.

Related to these shared motifs are other terminological parallels:[90]

οὔπω μέχρις αἵματος ἀντικατέστητε (Heb. 12:4)

μέχρι θανάτου τὰς βασάνους ὑπομείναντες (IV 17:10).[91]

πρὸς τὴν ἁμαρτίαν ἀνταγωνιζόμενοι (Heb. 12:4)

ὁ τύραννος ἀντηγωνίζετο (IV 17:14).[92]

A further example is even more striking. In Heb. 12:2 the race is to be run ἀφορῶντες εἰς . . . 'Ιησοῦν. At IV Mac. 17:10, in the author's proposed epitaph, it is said that the martyrs avenged their race, εἰς θεὸν ἀφορῶντες. Rendel Harris has recognized this expression from IV Maccabees as "peculiar."[93]

---

[90]Not directly related to these motifs (at least in IV Mac.) are the parallel expressions ἡμῖν συμπαθεῖ (IV 5:25, of God) and συμπαθῆσαι ταῖς ἀσθενείαις ἡμῶν (Heb. 4:15, of Jesus). Συμπαθής occurs at Job 29:25 and I Pet. 3:8. Otherwise συμπαθ-words are found only in IV Mac. (5:25; 6:13; 13:23; 14:13, 14, 18, 20; 15:4, 7, 11) and Hebrews (4:15, 10:34).

[91]Outside Hebrews, the equivalent phrase occurs only in the Christ hymn at Phil. 2:8 (ὑπήκοος μέχρι θανάτου) and in Phil 2:30. It does not occur in I Mac., but appears once in II Mac: Judas encouraged his men to fight until death (13:14). In conjunction with suffering the phrase is found nine other times in IV Mac. (5:37; 6:21; 7:8, 16; 13:1, 27; 15:10; 16:1; 17:7; cf. also 6:30).

[92]These are the only occurrences of this word in the LXX or NT. (The noun ἀνταγωνιστής appears only at IV 3:5 in the Greek Bible.)

[93]R. Harris, "Some Notes on 4 Maccabees," ET 32(1920-21), 184.

Indeed, ἀφορᾶν εἰς is unique in the Greek Bible.[94] The coincidence of expressions--and their respective contexts--cannot be
lightly dismissed. Along with the other parallels mentioned
previously, it is enough to justify the conclusion that the
author of Hebrews was acquainted with IV Maccabees.

In my view, this conclusion is confirmed by the most
important similarity of all. In IV Maccabees Eleazar exercizes
his priestly function by combatting the flames (7:9-12); he
prays that his own life be accepted for purification and ransom
(6:27-29). In Hebrews Jesus is the great and faithful high
priest who sacrifices his own life as an offering for sin once
for all (3:1-2, 4:14-15, 9:23-10:14). In both treatises the
one slain is both priest and offering. Since (to my knowledge)
no other Jewish or Christian writing which antedates Hebrews
makes a similar claim, this parallel can hardly be discounted
as a mere coincidence!

d. Paul. The evidence that Paul was familiar with IV
Maccabees is less certain than in the cases of Ignatius and
Hebrews. There are, however, attitudes, ideas, and particular
expressions which are more intelligible to the exegete if he
assumes this familiarity than if IV Maccabees is left out of
the picture.

Perhaps the most general of the similarities between
Paul and IV Maccabees is the idea of endurance in suffering.
By now the citation of passages in IV Maccabees illustrating
this emphasis is unnecessary, but special attention can be
drawn to the following texts in the epistles of Paul. In II
Cor. 6:4-6 the apostle writes: " . . . in every way we commend
ourselves as (and thus demonstrate that we are) servants of
God: through great endurance, . . . through purity, through
knowledge, through patience . . . ." The words ὑπομονή πολλῇ
are further modified by nine prepositional phrases--ἐν plus a
noun in each case. Each is a specific instance of suffering
or affliction. Thus, according to Paul, one way of demonstrating that he is a true servant of God, thereby "recommending"
himself as such, is through endurance in suffering (cf. 11:23-
29).

---

[94]The form ἀφορᾶν does not appear again at all. At
Jonah 4:5 and Phil. 2:23 ἀπιδεῖν/ἀφιδεῖν takes a direct acc.
object; III Mac. 6:8: ἀφιδών is textually uncertain; at IV
Mac. 17:23 occurs the expression ἀπιδών πρός.

242

In II Cor. 1:6 Paul speaks of "your consolation effected through endurance of the same sufferings which we also suffered." At Rom. 5:3-4 he can write that "we rejoice in the afflictions (we suffer) because we know that affliction brings about endurance, and endurance certifies that one is tested and approved, and being approved is the grounds of hope." If one recognizes that when Paul speaks of the hope that does not disappoint (v. 5) he is anticipating the joy of eschatological salvation (5:9-10), the importance to him of that endurance in suffering which earns divine approval becomes clearer.[95]

In Rom. 8:37 Paul writes: ἐν τούτοις πᾶσιν ὑπερνικῶμεν . . . . The verb, a hapax legommenon in the NT, is an intensified form of νικᾶν: we win extraordinary victories, we are super-conquerors.[96] Whatever the victories (or victory) that Paul has in mind, whether present/historical or future/eschatological, it comes about "ἐν all these," i.e., the experiences of suffering enumerated in v. 35. The proposition here may have the connotation "while suffering all these things." Also possible, however, is an instrumental or even a causal meaning: "by means of (or: on account of) all these sufferings." In either case, the idea of conquering through or in the midst of suffering is reminiscent of the fundamental motif of IV Maccabees that the martyrs conquer through suffering endured on behalf of their religion (cf. especially 1:11, 6:10, 7:4, 9:30, 16:14).

---

[95]See Rom. 8:25: Christians await the hoped-for salvation (vv. 19-23) δι'ὑπομονῆς. Taking account of "the sufferings of this age" in v. 18 and "our weakness" in v. 26, one might interpret this too as an allusion to endurance in suffering. Note that hope and endurance are also closely associated at I Cor. 13:7, Rom. 15:4, I Thess. 1:3, and Rom. 12:12. This last text, however, cannot even be considered as possible evidence for Paul's familiarity with IV Mac. since Rom. 12:9ff. represents a traditional unit of ethical instruction, Semitic (and Christian?) in origin, into which additional material (vv. 14, 15, 16c, 17b, 19b, 20) has been inserted, perhaps by Paul himself. This is the view argued persuasively by Charles H. Talbert, "Tradition and Redaction in Romans XII. 9-21," NTS 16 (1969-70), 83-93. But this situation with regard to Rom. 12:12 does not annul the potential import of the Pauline statements about endurance in suffering which have been discussed above.

[96]In view of the context, the meaning "we shall win an extraordinary victory (i.e., at the judgment)" is not excluded; cf. vv. 17c-18, 23, 32, and the language of the court in 33a.

Reading καυθήσομαι(or καυθήσωμαι) at I Cor. 13:3, Adolf
Deissman suggests that IV Maccabees, "which simply revels in
martyrdom by fire and its details," is a likely background for
Paul's remark about giving his body to be burned.[97]

Deissmann offers an explanation for the reading καυχήσωμαι in p[46] and the Egyptian MS tradition ("The variant from
καυθήσομαι may have arisen through the reflexion that Paul's
own martyrdom was not a martyrdom by fire.") but does not rebut
Harnack's "thorough defence" of the alternative.[98]

A point by point response to Harnack's argument cannot
be undertaken here either. I simply give several reasons for
rejecting his view and for reading καυθήσομαι with Deissmann
(and Nestle-Aland). (1) "Burn" has weightier MS support than
does "boast." Harnack himself (p. 396) has to admit that "burn"
is geographically more widespread since "boast" has almost none
but Egyptian testimony; (p[46], a subsequent discovery, simply
adds another Egyptian witness, albeit the earliest). He is
confident, however, that the witness of three of the Fathers
tip the scales for "boast." But two of those Fathers, Origen
and Clement of Alexandria, are, also Egyptian Christians, and it
is extremely doubtful that Clement of Rome read "boast" in his
text of I Cor. 13:3; Harnack's support of this view (398) is
an unacceptably speculative version of the argument from silence.
(2) At first glance Harnack's strongest argument is that a
future subjunctive (καυθήσωμαι: the Koine text type) in Paul
is unlikely whereas ἵνα with the future indicative does not
occur in Paul (401). This latter asseveration is simply incorrect. It is true that in the overwhelming majority of cases
Paul uses a subjunctive verb after ἵνα, but there are at least
two cases (in addition to I Cor. 13:3) where ἵνα is followed by
a future indicative: I Cor. 9:18 and Gal. 2:4. Thus at I Cor.
13:3 one is entirely justified in reading καυθήσομαι, although
it must be admitted that the resultant phrase is cumbersome.
(3) Harnack regards "burn" as a "very suspicious" reading
because martyrdom by fire for the good of others "had not yet
come within the Apostle's range of vision" (399). This dog-
matic pronouncement is completely vitiated by the fact that
Harnack does not once mention IV Maccabees, much less consider
the possibility that Paul was familiar with that work. Furthermore, the reading "If I give all my possessions piece by piece,
and if I give even my body," is not "stronger and more terse"
than the alternative (400) but more incongruous. Ψωμίζειν
means to distribute one's property bit by bit in order to benefit needy people; the idea of giving "even my body" is totally
incompatible with this image. (4) On the basis of meaning and
sense alone καυθήσομαι is to be preferred to καυχήσωμαι. a)
In v. 3 Paul apparently intends to call attention to the highest expressions of devotion to God and man; but "give one's
body" is too vague and general to be an impressive example of
the utmost in piety--unless, of course, one can point to
parallels which might suggest that Paul's meaning would have

[97]A. Deissmann, Paul (New York, 1957), p. 95, n. 9.

[98]A. Harnack, "The Apostle Paul's Hymn of Love (I Cor.
XIII.) and Its Religious-Historical Significance," The Expositor
3(1912), 395-404.

been obvious from that brief phrase alone. (This Harnack does
not do.) b) Nowhere in chapter 13 is there any mention of
attitudes toward the spiritual gifts or pious acts to which
Paul refers. To describe giving one's body as a cause for
boasting in v. 3, therefore, would be rather jolting; this
thought, in fact, is utterly out of place in the "hymn." c)
The only other modifying phrase which intrudes upon the basic
"if . . . but not . . . then" pattern of vv. 1-3 is ὥστε ὄρη
μεθιστάναι. The purpose of this phrase is to clarify and in-
tensify the immediately preceding clause; the same is true for
the ἵνα clause in v. 3. Here, as with the ὥστε phrase, the
purpose is to characterize further the idea involved in the
preceding clause: faith that could move mountains,.give up my
body and be burned. The point of the ἵνα clause is not reason
or motivation but end-to-which. d) If one reads "boast" and
if "give my body" refers to death (as it must in any case) then
the boasting would have to be one's boasting before God on the
last day. Although this is an idea found elsewhere in Paul
(e.g., I Thess. 2:19, Phil. 2:16), it is a discordant note in
I Cor. 13.

Deissmann's suggestion deserves careful consideration
and, in my view, assent. In I Cor. 13:1-2 Paul mentions those
gifts about which some Corinthian Christians had apparently
become arrogant and boastful: speaking in tongues (cf. 14:1-
27), prophecy (12:10; 14:6, 22), mysteries (14:2), knowledge
(8:1, 7, 11), faith (cf. miracle working at 12:10, 28). But to
the acts mentioned in v. 3 I Corinthians has no further allusions. Evidently, then, the source of the ideas involved here
was not the situation in the Corinthian church but traditions
known from elsewhere to which Paul turns for examples of ultimate expressions of one's piety. He speaks of the utmost in
devotion to one's fellow man, that is, giving away one's
possessions little by little to provide for the needy. He adds
a second example, evidence of the highest devotion to God:
giving up one's body to be burned (that is, as a witness to
one's faithfulness). It is unlikely in the extreme that Paul
created this example of devotion de novo. It could have suggested itself to him from Daniel 3:28 or even from Daniel 11:33.
More likely, however, the source of his example was a current
tradition of martyrdom by fire. No more impressive embodiment
of that tradition is known to modern scholarship than IV Maccabees.

The most persuasive support that can be marshalled for
the view that Paul was familiar with IV Maccabees is the concentration in Phil. 1:12-30 of attitudes, concepts and individual terms whose similarity with IV Maccabees reminds one forcefully of that work. With reference to the first of these

passages Ernst Lohmeyer has commented: " . . . in der Passivi-
tät seines Martyriums ist das Schicksal des Evangeliums mit
seinem persönlichen Schicksal unlöslich verknüpft."[99] If "Law"
or "religion of Israel" were substituted for "gospel" in this
statement, one has an affirmation that the author of IV Maccabees could have endorsed without question, for in his view
the destiny of true religion is bound closely with the martyrs'
faithfulness unto death. But the evidence goes beyond this
general similarity.

Phil. 1:20: The idea that Christ could be magnified
"in my body . . . through death" has, to my knowledge, no
closer parallel than the IV Maccabees motif that through their
death the martyrs upheld the Law (e.g., 5:33-34, 6:27, 11:12)
and so "fulfilled piety toward God" (12:14; cf. 13:13).

Phil. 1:21-23 reflects an attitude toward death--not
merely acceptance of its necessity but eager anticipation!--
which is not typically Jewish (cf. supra, Chapter III). It
does, however, recall the martyrs' eagerness to confront the
tortures and pass on to their heavenly reward.

Phil. 1:23: Paul expresses the desire to depart and
be σὺν Χριστῷ. Dibelius has observed that this expectation of
being with Christ immediately after death appears to be incompatible with I Thess. 4:16f. and I Cor. 15:51f., where Paul
asserts that first at the Parousia will deceased Christians be
joined with Christ.[100] Dibelius (p. 69) concludes that one
simply must reckon with a juxtaposition of an eschatological
awaiting of the Parousia and an individual hope for the period
right after death as the individuality (Eigenart) of the Pauline belief. Perhaps this is adequate, but the idea of dying
and being with Christ immediately, appearing as it does in this
particular passage about suffering, suggests that this component of Paul's ideas on the afterlife may have intruded from a
particular source. A likely candidate for such a source would
be IV Maccabees; in that work the martyrs die for their faith,
comforted by the hope that they will enter directly into the
heavenly presence of the patriarchs (13:17).

---

[99] E. Lohmeyer, Die Briefe an die Philipper, an die
Kolosser und an Philemon (Göttingen, 13 1964), p. 38.

[100] M. Dibelius, An die Thessalonicher I II. An die
Phillipper (Tübingen, 3 1937), pp. 68-69.

In Phil. 1:27 Paul enjoins the Philippians to conduct themselves worthily of the gospel of Christ. The verb used, πολιτεύεσθαι, occurs only once more in the NT (Acts 23:1) and only eight times in the LXX (outside the books of Maccabees, only once: Es. 8:13). Half of the LXX occurrences are in IV Maccabees: 2:8 (τῷ νόμῳ πολιτευόμενος), 2:23 (καθ'ὃν [the Law] πολιτευόμενος), 4:23 (τῷ πατρίῳ π. νόμῳ), 5:16 (θείῳ . . . νόμῳ πολιτεύεσθαι). If πολιτεύεσθαι is equivalent to περιπατεῖν,[101] a word which Paul uses frequently, it is all the more striking that in this particular context he chooses a word which he never used again in his extant letters. The use of this term in Phil. 1:27 may be a noteworthy coincidence. More likely, in view of the following verses, it points to Paul's familiarity with IV Maccabees.

In v. 27 Paul also exhorts the Philippians to "stand in one spirit, with one soul (ψυχῇ) contending together (συναθλοῦντες) for the faith of the gospel." Compare the following in IV Maccabees: εἱστήκεις (16:15, of the mother); the athlete/ἀγών motif (especially 17:11-16); "all together with one voice, as though from the same ψυχῆς . . ." (8:29; cf. also 14:7-8).

Paul continues: "Do not allow yourselves to be frightened[102] in any way by your opponents." Compare the emphasis of IV Maccabees on the martyrs' utter lack of fear, their courage and endurance; note in particular 16:20, where Isaac's unflinching courage is mentioned as an example: οὐκ ἔπτηξεν.[103]

Phil. 1:28: "This [ἥτις, i.e. not being frightened by their opponents] is for them a sign of (their) destruction, but of your salvation" (cf. II Thess. 1:4-8). Here the refusal to be intimidated is an omen which points to a turning of the

---

[101]Ibid., p. 70, calling attention particularly to I Thess. 2:12, Col. 1:10, Eph. 4:1.

[102]Πτύρεσθαι--the word is used especially of the shying or starting of horses when frightened. It is not used again in the NT, not at all in the LXX.

[103]Πτήσσειν: to crouch or cower in fear; cf. also ἐκφοβεῖν at 9:5.

tables in the future. In IV Maccabees the endurance of the martyrs is the grounds of their heavenly reward and the "salvation" of the nation. Likewise, as the martyr prayers and speeches make clear, their endurance unto death and God's response to it was considered the cause of the opponent's destruction and post-mortem punishment (9:8-9, 24, 30-32; 10: 11, 21; 11:3, 23-25; 12:12, 14, 18).

Phil. 1:29: "To you it has been granted (ἐχαρίσθη) for the sake of Christ to--not only to believe in him but also to suffer for his sake." In Chapter III it was noted that the idea of fighting, suffering or dying for God or Israel is, to say the least, not typical for the OT and other Jewish literature (but cf. Ps. 44:22!). Suffering "for the sake of" or "on account of" God, the Law, or religion, however, is a fundamental theme of IV Maccabees. In IV Mac. 11:12 one finds a rather specific parallel to Paul's statement. To Antiochus the fifth son cries out: "Glorious . . . are the favors you are granting (χαρίζη) us by allowing us to demonstrate our steadfastness toward the Law through noble sufferings (πόνων)." One is justified in calling this a parallel because, in the whole of the LXX and the NT, Phil. 1:29 and IV Mac. 11:12 are the only two texts in which suffering is described in terms of a gift, granted (χαρίζεσθαι) as an opportunity to demonstrate religious devotion![104]

In my judgment the expressions and ideas in Phil. 1:12-30 to which attention has been drawn can better be accounted for if one assumes that Paul was familiar with IV Maccabees than if one insists that such familiarity is out of the question.[105]

e. The Pre-Pauline Formulation at Romans 3:25-26. Does Rom. 3:25-26 give any indications of having originated

---

[104]Many of the similarities noted also hold true for Paul and II Mac., but however one decides the question of Pauline familiarity with II Mac. the ideas of suffering as a gift as well as victory in/through suffering (Rom. 8:37) point to IV Mac. exclusively.

[105]By "familiarity" I do not necessarily mean that Paul must have read the literary treatise that we call IV Maccabees. I only intend to suggest that he appears to have been acquainted with its contents--not only major themes but specific ideas and expressions as well.

in Christian circles either directly familiar with IV Maccabees or acquainted with particular ideas in that writing which may have been transmitted orally (and independently)? One cannot expect too much from such a relatively brief formulation; in spite of its brevity, however, this fragment seems to support such a possibility. No more probable background to ὃν προέθετο ὁ θεὸς ἱλαστήριον can be discovered in the extant pre-Christian literature than IV Mac. 17:21a read in the light of 6:29. (If πίστις refers to Jesus' faith, the phrase διὰ πίστεως ἐν τῷ αὐτοῦ αἵματι is illuminated by πιστὴ θανάτου σφραγίς--the faith-seal, death--by which Eleazar was "made perfect" [IV 7:15] and in view of which God is implored to regard his life as effective for ransom and purification.)

2.  IV Maccabees and Antioch

    The argument that IV Maccabees or some very similar work--either as oral address or as literary treatise--was the creative source for the Christian interpretation of Jesus' death as saving event would be enormously strengthened if IV Maccabees could be "located" at Antioch, a city with a thriving pre-Pauline Christian congregation. In my opinion, two con-verging lines of evidence provide an adequate basis for the position that Antioch was indeed the place where IV Maccabees was composed.

    a.  The first of these is the firm tradition, first clearly documented more than two centuries later, that the tomb of the Maccabean martyrs was located in Antioch.[106]

    In 1866 W. Wright published an ancient Syrian martyr list, a calendar of "the days on which they gained their crowns."[107] For the date August 1, it reads: "The confessors, who were of the number of those that were interred at Antioch, that is to say in . . .,[108] who were the sons of Shamuni,

---

[106]For a concise but cogent discussion of this tradition see Jeremias, Heiligengräber, pp. 20-23.

[107]W. Wright, "An Ancient Syrian Martyrology," The Journal of Sacred Literature and Biblical Record 8(1866), 44-56 (text), 423-32 (translation). Wright calculates that the MS of which this list is a part was transcribed in A.D. 412; thus he is inclined to date the martyrology "towards the end of the fourth century" (45). Further, cf. Obermann, op. cit., 252, n. 8.

[108]At the ellipses Wright gives the Syriac word and adds: "'in Krtia,' (Carteia?), probably the name of a place at

mentioned in (the book of) the Maccabees." Here one finds conclusive evidence that at least by <u>ca</u>. 400 there flourished a
Christian tradition that the Maccabean martyrs were entombed
in Antioch.

That tradition is further substantiated by an Arabic MS
which gives a topographical description of Antioch.[109] According to this MS,[110] there was to be found in the Kerateion
quarter of the city a large building which those of the populace
who had adopted Christianity had converted into the Church of
Saint Ashmunit; (by the Jews it was called <u>Proseuche</u>). Under
the Church, one is informed, there was a kind of crypt with
graves, to which one could descend by steps. Here were to be
found the grave of the priest Ezra (Eleazar) and the graves of
Ashmunit and her seven sons, whom King Agappius (Antiochus)
had had executed on account of their beliefs.

Vatican Arabic MS 286 clearly shows that by the sixth
century there was in Antioch a Christian sanctuary built over
the alleged burial site of the Maccabean martyrs and named in
honor of the mother of the seven brothers. Most probably this
sanctuary had originally been a Jewish synagogue and had subsequently been appropriated by Christians--former Jews, perhaps,
who brought to their new religion their veneration of the
Maccabean martyrs.[111]

A couple of remarks by Augustine can be understood as
support for the conclusion that the Church of Saint Ashmunit
had originally been a Jewish synagogue:

---

or near Antioch" (428). There can be little doubt that this is
a reference to the Kerateion section of the city.

[109]Vatican Arabic MS 286, described by Rampolla del
Tindaro, "Martyre et sépulture des Machabées," <u>Revue de l'Art
Chrétien</u> (1899), 390. The document is to be dated in the sixth
century; cf. M. Simon, "La polémique anti-juive de S. Jean
Chrysostome et le mouvement judaïsant d'Antioche," in <u>Mélanges
Franz Cumont</u> (Brussels, 1936), p. 414.

[110]I am following the translation of Max Maas, "Die
Maccabäer als christlicher Heilige," <u>Monatsschrift für
Geschichte und Wissenschaft des Judenthums</u> 44(1900), 153.

[111]Cf. Jeremias, Heiligengräber, pp. 22-23; Dupont-
Sommer, Machabées, p. 72; E. Bammel, "Zum jüdischen Märtyr-
kult," TLZ 78(1953), 119-26; Obermann, <u>op. cit.</u>, 253.

Sanctorum Machabaeorum basilica esse in Antiochia
praedicatur . . . et memoria martyrii eorum in
Antiochia celebratur . . . . Haec basilica a Christianis
tenetur, a Christianis aedificata est.[112]

M. Simon takes the first clause of the last sentence as an indication that the building had been in Jewish hands until very
recently.[113] He does not quote or refer to the last clause; I
assume, however, that "aedificata est" means that the Christians
had repaired or remodeled the synagogue in some way after taking
possession of it.

Simon observes further that the Christian appropriation
of this synagogue has to have occurred before John Chrysostom
delivered his homilies in praise of the Maccabean martyrs--in
the very basilica which stood over their graves! These pane-
gyrics were given ca. 385-390. Assuming a popular surge of
anti-Semitism in reaction to the reign of Julian the Apostate,
Simon thus calculates that the Christians of Antioch took over
the Kerateion synagogue between A.D. 363 and 386. By ca. 375,
then, they had appropriated not only a Jewish martyr tradition
but also the very building which had apparently been its focal
point.

How old is this Jewish tradition in which the graves of
the Maccabean martyrs are associated with a synagogue in the
Kerateion quarter of Antioch? One cannot say with absolute
certainty, but the evidence of a medieval Arabic document
suggests that it goes back to a period not very long after the
fall of Jerusalem in A.D. 70. The document is known as the
Faraq-Book of Nissim Ibn Shahin.[114] Regarding the Maccabean
martyrs this work contains mostly an adaptation of rabbinic
material, but with an important additional detail: "There was
built upon them the synagogue of Hashmonith, and it was the
first synagogue built after the Second Temple" (following
Obermann's translation).

In Obermann's view this statement implies that the
synagogue mentioned was built in Jerusalem.[115] However, this

---

[112] Sermo CCC: MPL 38.1379.

[113] M. Simon, op. cit., p. 414.

[114] Obermann, op. cit., 253-60, where the pertinent
statement is discussed.

[115] Ibid., 260-61. N. 37: ". . . unless the Synagogue

is by no means an inference demanded by the text; it has, in fact, been expressly rejected by E. Bammel and J. Jeremias.[116] "Hasmonith" corresponds closely with the names "Shamuni" and "Ashmunit" in the documents previously discussed; this similarity allows one to take the statement of Nissim Ibn Shahin as evidence that a synagogue was associated with the burial site of the martyrs in <u>Antioch</u>. Furthermore, since this synagogue is said to be the first one built after A.D. 70, one can reasonably infer a construction date <u>ca.</u> 100.[117]

To summarize, the first type of evidence supporting Antioch as the city where IV Maccabees was composed consists of: a persistent Christian tradition--centering in Antioch, probably Jewish in origin--of veneration of the Maccabean martyrs; an ancient belief that the martyrs were buried in the Kerateion section of Antioch; a Jewish synagogue, later a Christian basilica, located in Antioch and named in honor of the mother and the seven brothers.

b. The second type of evidence that IV Maccabees originated at Antioch is the testimony of IV Maccabees itself-- more precisely, a particular internal inconsistency. Although he never says so explicitly, it is clearly the author's intent to give the impression that the martyrdoms he recounts occurred in Jerusalem (cf. 4:22-26, 18:5). This is entirely in accord with his claim that "through them the <u>fatherland</u> was purified" (1:11; cf. 17:21-22: nation, Israel; 18:4: nation, fatherland). Thus any reader is certainly justified in inferring that the martyrs were citizens of Jerusalem or lived in its vicinity. But when the author asserts that Eleazar was "known (or recognized: γνώριμος) by many of those in the tyrant's court" (5:4) and when he later (6:13) refers to their sympathy based on

---

of Ḥasmônîth was built in Jerusalem, the tradition combining it with the Second Temple could hardly have been formed."

[116]Bammel, <u>op. cit.</u>, 122; Jeremias, <u>Heiligengräber</u>, p. 22, n. 4.

[117]Further literary evidence for the close association between the tomb of the martyrs and a Jewish synagogue in the Kerateion quarter of Antioch is provided by John Malalas (sixth century) in his <u>Chronographia</u>. For the pertinent text and an evaluation thereof cf. Jeremias, <u>Heiligengräber</u>, p. 20.

intimate acquaintance (συνήθεια), he implies just as certainly
that the old priest was a citizen of Antioch, the Seleucid
capital. It is difficult to perceive how these references to
the courtiers' acquaintance with Eleazar in any way serves the
author's purposes of panegyric, exhortation, philosophical
discourse or theological affirmation. They can best be explained as peripheral remarks, due to the author's novelistic
style, perhaps, but also betraying his geographical setting!
In these inadvertent allusions to Antioch he provides a clue to
the locale of that tradition upon which he draws and to which
he contributes mightily.

IV Maccabees has to have been composed (delivered or
written) somewhere! It is likely a priori that this somewhere
was a major city with a sizable population of loyal, hellenized
Jews. Alexandria was certainly such a city in the first century, but only very general features of IV Maccabees (primarily
its Hellenistic character and certain similarities with Philo)
give one the slightest reason to consider Alexandria as the
place of origin. Much weightier than such general features is
the fact that there is no trace of an Alexandrian tradition of
the Maccabean martyrs corresponding to the one centering in
Antioch. The fact that neither Philo, Clement of Alexandria
nor Origen cites IV Maccabees provides an additional reason for
dismissing the great Egyptian city from further consideration.[118]
On the other hand, Antioch, another of the most important cities
in the early Empire, harbored a large hellenized Jewish population in the first century.[119] In the subsequent centuries it
was the locale of a firm tradition, first Jewish and then
Christian, of veneration for the Maccabean martyrs--a tradition
which had as its focal point their alleged graves. To Antioch
also point several homilies of John Chrysostom, a native of
that city and its most eloquent churchman before he became
bishop of Constantinople. Nor should one overlook the fact
that early in the second century Ignatius, Bishop of Antioch,
was apparently acquainted with IV Maccabees. Finally, the
casual remarks in the treatise itself that Eleazar was known

---

[118]Cf. Freudenthal, op. cit., p. 112.

[119]Josephus, War 7.43-45. Cf. Carl H. Kraeling, "The
Jewish Community at Antioch," JBL 51(1932), 130-52.

to many in the court of Antiochus points to Antioch as the city
where IV Maccabees was delivered and where its novel ideas first
took hold.[120]

## C. Conclusion

If it can be agreed that IV Maccabees was composed at
Antioch[121] ca. 35 or 40 A.D., then the student of early Christianity can consider it extremely probable that at least one
early Christian congregation, consisting of hellenized Jews and
Gentiles, was familiar with that work and its noteworthy ideas.
The most striking of those ideas was that a human death could
be beneficial for others because it was regarded by God as
effective for the ransom of their lives, the expiation of their
sins. Whatever the correct explanation for the dynamics underlying the formulation of this concept (cf. Chapter V), having
once been formulated it was there, a given conceptual entity
with its own autonomous existence--incorporated in an address
or embedded in a literary treatise, but nevertheless free to
exert its powerful influence among Jews and Christians as an
exciting new "doctrine." Thus did the author of IV Maccabees
make available to early Christians, probably in Antioch, a
concept in terms of which it was natural and meaningful for
them to interpret the death of another man faithful unto death,
Jesus of Nazareth.

The inherent similarities between the death of Jesus
and the death of the martyrs, rather striking in themselves,
very likely played some role in this development. Like the
martyrs Jesus was innocent of any crime against his fellows or

---

[120]To argue thus is not to insist either that IV Mac.
was delivered at the site of the martyrs' alleged graves or
that a Jewish tradition locating those graves in Antioch ante-
dated IV Mac. The development might have been in the opposite
direction. That is, the address/writing (IV Mac.) could have
spurred a movement of religious sentiment which culminated in
the dedication of a memorial to the martyrs. Cf. Obermann,
op. cit., 263.

[121]Some of the scholars who do agree with this place of
origin are: Kraeling, op. cit., 148; Dupont-Sommer, Machabées,
pp. 69-73; Bammel, op. cit., 122-23; Hadas, op. cit., 109-13;
and Jeremias, Heiligengräber, pp. 19-21.

the state; like them he was put to death by hostile government authorities who were abetted by his fellow Jews. Like them he was killed for reasons which the government viewed as political and pragmatic but which he seems to have considered the unavoidable outcome of unswerving faithfulness to God. Furthermore, as in the case of the martyrs, it was believed that Jesus had been vindicated by God; his death was not the final datum but rather a prelude to exaltation and glory. For hellenized Christians familiar with IV Maccabees (or its contents), beset by the problem of sin and the scandal of Jesus' execution, these fundamental similarities can hardly have gone unnoticed.

The idea that the precipitous and undeserved death of an exceptionally worthy person can effect expiation for the sins of others served as the lens through which the crucifixion of Jesus could be viewed and understood. When that happened Christians could affirm not only that God raised Jesus from the dead but also that his death was meaningful in itself. Because God regarded Christ crucified as a means of expiation for all men (Rom. 3:25), Gentile as well as Jew could now confess: "Christ died for our sins" (I Cor. 15:3).

BIBLIOGRAPHY

I.   Texts and Translations*

Anthologia Lyrica Graeca edidit Ernestus Diehl.  Fasc. 1:
    Poetae Elegiaci.  3rd ed.  Leipzig:  In aedibus B. G.
    Teubneri, 1949.

Antiphontis Orationes et Fragmenta adiuntis Gorgiae Antisthenis
    Alcidamantis edidit Fridericus Blass.  Leipzig:  In aedibus
    B. G. Teubneri, 1871.

Die Apostolischen Väter.  Neubearbeitung der Funkschen Ausgabe
    von Karl Bihlmeyer.  2nd ed., with a Supplement by Wilhelm
    Schneemelcher.  Tübingen:  Verlag von J. C. B. Mohr (Paul
    Siebeck), 1956.

Biblia Hebraica edidit Rud. Kittel . . . . 9th ed.  Stuttgart:
    Privileg. Württ. Bibelanstalt, 1954.

Corpus Hermeticum.  Texte établi par A. D. Nock et traduit par
    A. J. Festugière.  Paris:  Société d'Édition "Les Belles
    Lettres," 1945.

The Dead Sea Scrolls of St. Mark's Monastery.  II/2:  Plates
    and Transcription of the Manual of Discipline.  Edited by
    Millar Burrows, with John C. Trever and William H. Brownlee.
    New Haven:  The American Schools of Oriental Research, 1951.

Flavii Iosephi Opera edidit et apparatu critico instruxit
    Benedictus Niese.  6 vols.  Berlin:  Apud Weidmannos,
    1887-94.

The Greek Versions of the Testaments of the Twelve Patriarchs.
    Edited by Robert Henry Charles.  Oxford:  At the Clarendon
    Press, 1908.

Joseph et Aséneth.  Introduction, texte critique, traduction et
    notes par Marc Philonenko.  Leiden:  E. J. Brill, 1968.

Lycurgi Oratio in Leocratem cum ceterarum Lycurgi orationum
    fragmentis post C. Scheibe et F. Blass curavit Nicos C.
    Conomis.  Leipzig:  BSB B. G. Teubner Verlagsgesellschaft,
    1970.

Midrash Rabbah.  Edited by H. Freedman and Maurice Simon.  Vol.
    III:  Exodus, translated by S. M. Lehrman.  London:
    Soncino Press, 1939.

*The LCL edition was used for Greek and Latin texts cited in
the thesis which are not listed here.

Novum Testamentum Graece cum apparatu critico curavit Eberhard Nestle, novis curis elaboraverunt Erwin Nestle et Kurt Aland. 25th ed. Stuttgart: Württembergische Bibelanstalt, 1963.

The Old Testament in Greek. Edited by Alan E. Brooke, Norman McLean, and Henry St. John Thackery. 3 vols. (incomplete). Cambridge: At the University Press, 1906-40.

Philonis Alexandrini opera quae supersunt ediderunt Leopoldus Cohn et Paulus Wendland. 6 vols. Berlin: Typis et Impensis Georgii Reimeri, 1896-1915.

Poetae Lyrici Graeci. Quartis curis recensuit Theodorus Bergk. Pars II: Poetae Elegiaci et Iambographi. Leipzig: In aedibus B. G. Teubneri, 1915.

Pseudo-Philo's Liber Antiquitatum Biblicarum. By Guido Kisch. Publications in Medieval Studies. Notre Dame, Ind.: The University of Notre Dame, 1949.

Qumran Cave I (Discoveries in the Judean Desert, vol. I). By D. Barthélemy and J. T. Milik. Oxford: At the Clarendon Press, 1955 (reprinted 1964).

Septuaginta. Id est Vetus Testamentum graece iuxta LXX interpretes edidit Alfred Rahlfs. Vol. I. 8th ed. Stuttgart: Württembergische Bibelanstalt, 1935 (reprinted 1965).

Septuaginta. Vetus Testamentum Graecum. Auctoritate Academie Litterarum Gottingensis editum. Göttingen: Vandenhoeck & Ruprecht.

IX/1:   Maccabaeorum liber I (1967, 2nd ed.)
IX/2:   Maccabaeorum liber II (1959)
XII/1:  Sapientia Salomonis (1962)
XIV:    Isaias (1967, 2nd ed.)
XVI/2:  Susanna, Daniel, Bel et Draco (1954).

## II.   Works Cited

Abel, Félix M. Les livres des Maccabées. Études bibliques. Paris: Librairie Lecoffre, 1949.

Adam, James. "Ancient Greek Views of Suffering and Evil." The Vitality of Platonism and Other Essays. Cambridge: At the University Press, 1911. Pp. 190-212.

Ball, Charles J. "Had the Fourth Gospel an Aramaic Archetype?" ET 21 (1909-10), 91-93.

Bammel, Ernst. "Zum jüdischen Märtyrerkult." TLZ 78 (1953), 119-26.

Barrett, Charles Kingsley. "The Background of Mark 10:45." New Testament Essays. Studies in Memory of Thomas Walter Manson. Edited by A. J. B. Higgins. Manchester: Manchester University Press, 1959. Pp. 1-18.

Bauer, Walter. A Greek-English Lexicon of the New Testament and Other Early Christian Literature. Translated and adapted by William F. Arndt and F. Wilbur Gingrich from the 4th ed. (1952). Chicago: The University of Chicago Press, 1957.

_____. Griechisch-Deutsches Wörterbuch zu den Schriften des Neuen Testaments und der übrigen urchristlichen Literatur. 5th ed. Berlin: Verlag Alfred Töpelmann, 1958.

Beck, Norman A. "The Last Supper as an Efficacious Symbolic Act." JBL 89 (1970), 192-98.

Bevan, Anthony Ashley. A Short Commentary on the Book of Daniel for the Use of Students. Cambridge: Cambridge University Press, 1892.

Bickerman, Elias. "The Date of Fourth Maccabees." Louis Ginzberg Jubilee Volume (English Section). New York: The American Academy for Jewish Research, 1945. Pp. 105-12.

Black, Matthew. An Aramaic Approach to the Gospels and Acts. 2nd ed. Oxford: At the Clarendon Press, 1954.

Blass, Friedrich, and Debrunner, Albert. A Greek Grammar of the New Testament and Other Early Christian Literature. Translated and revised by Robert W. Funk from the 9th-10th German ed. Chicago: The University of Chicago Press, 1961.

Bornkamm, Günther. "Lord's Supper and Church in Paul." Early Christian Experience. Translated by Paul L. Hammer. New York: Harper and Row, 1969. Pp. 123-60.

Brandenburger, Egon. Adam und Christus. Exegetisch-Religionsgeschichtliche Untersuchung zu Rom. 5 12-21 (1. Kor. 15). WMANT 7. Neukirchen: Verlag der Buchhandlung des Erziehungsvereins, 1962.

Brownlee, William H. The Meaning of the Qumran Scrolls for the Bible. New York: Oxford University Press, 1964.

_____. "The Servant of the Lord in the Qumran Scrolls." BASOR 132 (1953), 8-15; 135 (1954), 33-38.

Büchler, A. Studies in Sin and Atonement in the Rabbinic Literature of the First Century. Prolegomenon to the reprinted ed. by F. C. Grant. Library of Biblical Studies. New York: KTAV Publishing House Inc., 1967; first published 1927.

Bultmann, Rudolf. "ΔΙΚΑΙΟΣΥΝΗ ΘΕΟΥ." JBL 83 (1964), 12-16.

_____. "Glossen im Römerbrief." TLZ 72 (1947), 197-202.

_____. "πιστεύω κτλ.: C. Faith in Judaism. D. The πίστις Group in the New Testament." TDNT, VI, pp. 197-228.

_____. Theology of the New Testament. 2 vols. Translated by Kendrick Grobel. New York: Charles Scribner's Sons, 1951 and 1955.

.

Campenhausen, Hans Freiherr von. Bearbeitungen und Inter-
polationen des Polykarpmartyriums. Sitzungsberichte der
Heidelberger Adademie der Wissenschaften, Philosophisch-
Historische Klasse, 1957, 3. Abh. Heidelberg: Carl
Winter, Universitätsverlag, 1957. Reprinted in: Aus der
Frühzeit des Christentums. Tübingen: J. C. B. Mohr (Paul
Siebeck), 1963.

Charles, Robert Henry. The Assumption of Moses. Edited with
Introduction, Notes, and Indices. London: Adam and
Charles Black, 1897.

_____. A Critical and Exegetical Commentary on the Book
of Daniel. With Introduction, Indexes and a New English
Translation. Oxford: At the Clarendon Press, 1929.

Conzelmann, Hans. "Jesus Christus." RGG, III, 619-53.

_____. "Die Rechtfertigungslehre des Paulus: Theologie
oder Anthropologie?" EvTh 28 (1968), 389-404.

_____. "On the Analysis of the Confessional Formula in I
Corinthians 15:3-5." Translated by Mathias Rissi. Interpretation 20 (1966), 15-25.

Craig, Clarence T. "From the Last Supper to the Lord's Supper."
Religion in Life 9 (1940), 163-73.

Creed, John Martin. "ΠΑΡΕΣΙΣ in Dionysius of Halicarnassus
and in St. Paul." JTS 41 (1940), 28-30.

Cullmann, Oscar. The Christology of the New Testament. Translated by Shirley C. Guthrie and Charles A. M. Hall.
Philadelphia: The Westminster Press, 1959.

Davies, W. D. Paul and Rabbinic Judaism. Some Rabbinic
Elements in Pauline Theology. 2nd ed. London: S P C K,
1955.

Debrunner, Albert. "Grundsätzliches über Kolometrie im Neuen
Testament." ThBl 5 (1926), 231-33.

Deissmann, Adolf. "ΙΛΑΣΤΗΡΙΟΣ und ΙΛΑΣΤΗΡΙΟΝ. Eine lexi-
kalische Studie." ZNW 4 (1903), 193-212.

_____. Light From the Ancient East. 2nd ed. Translated
by Lionel R. M. Strachan. New York: Hodder and Stoughton,
1911.

_____. Paul: A Study in Social and Religious History.
Translated by William E. Wilson from the revised German ed.
of 1925. A Harper Torchbook. New York: Harper & Row,
Publishers, 1957.

Dibelius, Martin. An die Thessalonicher I II. An die Philipper. 3rd ed. HNT. Tübingen: J. C. B. Mohr (Paul Siebeck), 1937.

_____. From Tradition to Gospel. Translated by Bertram
Lee Woolf. New York: Charles Scribner's Sons, [1965].

Dodd, Charles Harold. "ΙΛΑΣΚΕΣΘΑΙ, Its Cognates, Derivatives, and Synonyms, in the Septuagint." JTS 32 (1931), 352-60.

Dörrie, Heinrich. Leid und Erfahrung. Die Wort- und Sinn-Verbindung παθεῖν-μαθεῖν im griechischen Denken. Abhandlungen der Adademie der Wissenschaften und der Literatur, Geistes- und socialwissenschaftlichen Klasse, 1956 (Nr. 5). Mainz, 1956.

Downing, John. "Jesus and Martyrdom." JTS 14 (1963), 279-93.

Driver, Samuel R., and Neubauer, Adolf. The Fifty-Third Chapter of Isaiah According to the Jewish Interpreters. Vol. II: Translations. Library of Biblical Studies. New York: KTAV Publishing House, Inc., 1969; first published 1877.

Dupont-Sommer, André. The Essene Writings from Qumran. Translated by G. Vermes from the 2nd revised ed. Meridian Books. Cleveland and New York: The World Publishing Company, [1962].

_____. Le Quatrième Livre des Machabées. Introduction, Traduction et Notes. Bibliothèque de l'École des Hautes Études 274. Paris: Librairie Ancienne Honoré Champion, 1939.

Eichrodt, Walther. Theology of the Old Testament. 2 vols. Translated by J. A. Baker from the 6th (vol. 1) and 5th (vol. 2) German eds. Old Testament Library. London: SCM Press, 1961 and 1967.

Ellis, Edward Earle. Paul's Use of the Old Testament. Edinburgh: Oliver and Boyd, 1957.

Euler, Karl Friedrich. Die Verkündigung vom leidenden Gottesknecht aus Jes. 53 in der griechischen Bibel. Beiträge zur Wissenchaft vom Alten und Neuen Testament 66. Stuttgart-Berlin: W. Kohlhammer Verlag, 1934.

Evaristus, Mary. The Consolations of Death in Ancient Greek Literature. Published Ph.D. Dissertation, Catholic University of America, n.d.

Feine, Paul; Behm, Johannes; and Kümmel, Werner Georg. Introduction to the New Testament. 14th revised ed. Translated by A. J. Mattill, Jr. Nashville: Abingdon Press, 1966.

Fitzer, Gottfried. "Der Ort der Versöhnung nach Paulus. Zu der Frage des 'Sühnopfers Jesu.'" TZ 22 (1966), 161-83.

Freudenthal, Jacob. Die Flavius Josephus beigelegte Schrift Ueber die Herrschaft der Vernunft (IV Makkabäerbuch), eine Predigt aus dem ersten nachchristlichen Jahrhundert. Breslau: Schletter'sche Buchhandlung (H. Skutsch), 1869.

Ginsberg, Harold L. "The Oldest Interpretation of the Suffering Servant." VT 3 (1953), 400-404.

Goodenough, Erwin R. Jewish Symbols in the Greco-Roman Period. 12 vols. Bollingen Series 37. New York: Bollingen Foundation, 1953-65.

Greene, William C. Moira: Fate, Good, and Evil in Greek Thought. Cambridge, Mass.: Harvard University Press, 1944.

Güttgemanns, Erhardt. "Χριστός in 1. Kor. 15, 3b--Titel oder Eigenname?" EvTh 28 (1968), 533-54.

Hadas, Moses. The Third and Fourth Books of Maccabees. Dropsie College Edition: Jewish Apocryphal Literature. New York: Harper & Brothers (for The Dropsie College for Hebrew and Cognate Learning), 1953.

_____, and Smith, Morton. Heroes and Gods. Spiritual Biographies in Antiquity. Religious Perspectives (Ruth Nanda Anshen, ed.), vol. 13. New York: Harper & Row, Publishers, 1965.

Hahn, Ferdinand. The Titles of Jesus in Christology. Translated by Harold Knight and George Ogg. New York and Cleveland: The World Publishing Company, 1969.

Hanson, Paul D. Studies in the Origins of Jewish Apocalyptic. Unpublished Ph.D. Dissertation, Harvard University, 1969.

Harnack, Adolf. "The Apostle Paul's Hymn of Love (I Cor. XIII.) and Its Religious-Historical Significance." Translated by Helena Ramsay. The Expositor 3 (1912), 385-408, 481-503.

Harris, Rendel. "Some Notes on 4 Maccabees." ET 32 (1920-21), 183-85.

Höistad, Ragnar. Cynic Hero and Cynic King. Studies in the Cynic Conception of Man. Uppsala: [C. Bloms Boktr.], 1948.

Hooker, Morna D. Jesus and the Servant. The Influence of the Servant Concept of Deutero-Isaiah in the New Testament. London: S P C K, 1959.

Hunkin, Joseph W. "The Origin of Eucharistic Doctrine." The Evangelical Doctrine of Holy Communion. Edited by A. J. MacDonald. Cambridge: W. Heffer & Sons Limited, 1930. Pp. 1-39.

Hunter, Archibald M. Paul and his Predecessors. Revised ed. London: SCM Press Ltd., 1961.

Jaeger, Werner. Paideia: The Ideals of Greek Culture. 3 vols. Translated by Gilbert Highet. New York: Oxford University Press, 1939-44.

Jeremias, Joachim. "ἀμνός, ἀρήν, ἀρνίον." TDNT, I, pp. 338-41.

_____. "Artikelloses Χριστός. Zur Ursprache von I Cor 15 3b-5." ZNW 57 (1966), 211-15.

Jeremias, Joachim. "Erlöser und Erlösung im Spätjudentum und Urchristentum." Deutsche Theologie II: Der Erlösungsgedanke (Bericht über den 2. deutschen Theologentag in Frankfurt a.M., Herbst 1928). Edited by D. E. Pfenningsdorf. Göttingen: Vandenhoeck & Ruprecht, 1929. Pp. 106-19.

_____. The Eucharistic Words of Jesus. Translated by Norman Perrin from the 3rd German ed. (1960). New York: Charles Scribner's Sons, 1966.

_____. Heiligengräber in Jesu Umwelt (Mt. 23,29; Lk. 11, 47). Eine Untersuchung zur Volksreligion der Zeit Jesu. Göttingen: Vandenhoeck & Ruprecht, 1958.

_____. "Das Lamm, das aus der Jungfrau hervorging (Test. Jos. 19,8)." ZNW 57 (1966), 216-19.

_____. "Das Lösegeld für Viele (Mk. 10,45)." Abba: Studien zur neutestamentlichen Theologie und Zeitgeschichte. Göttingen: Vandenhoeck & Ruprecht, 1966. Pp. 216-29.

_____. The Parables of Jesus. Revised ed. Translated by S. H. Hooke. New York: Charles Scribner's Sons, 1963.

_____. "Zum Problem der Deutung von Jes. 53 im palästinischen Spätjudentum." Aux Sources de la Tradition Chrétienne: Mélanges offerts à M. Maurice Goguel. Bibliothèque Théologique. Neuchatel and Paris: Delachaus & Niestlé S. A., 1950. Pp. 113-19.

Jervell, Jacob. "Ein Interpolator interpretiert. Zu der christlichen Bearbeitung der Testamente der Zwölf Patriarchen." Studien zu den Testamenten der Zwölf Patriarchen. Beiheft zur ZNW 36. Berlin: Verlag Alfred Töpelmann, 1969. Pp. 30-61.

Käsemann, Ernst. "God's Righteousness in Paul." Translated by Wilfred F. Bunge. Journal for Theology and the Church, vol. 1. Tübingen: J. C. B. Mohr (Paul Siebeck); New York: Harper & Row, Publishers, Inc., 1965. Pp. 100-10.

_____. "Zum Verständnis von Römer 3 24-26." ZNW 43 (1950-51), 150-54.

Kjellberg. "Iphigeneia." Pauly-Wissowa's Real-Encyclopädie der klassichen Altertumswissenschaft, IX, 2588-2622.

Klappert, Berthold. "Zur Frage des semitischen oder griechischen Urtextes von 1 Kor 15, 3-5." NTS 13 (1966), 168-73.

Klausner, Joseph. From Jesus to Paul. Translated by William F. Stinespring from the Hebrew. New York: The Macmillan Company, 1943.

_____. Jesus of Nazareth. His Life, Times, and Teaching. Translated by Herbert Danby from the Hebrew. New York: The Macmillan Company, 1925.

Koester, Helmut. "One Jesus and Four Primitive Gospels." HTR 61 (1968), 203-47.

Kraeling, Carl H. "The Jewish Community at Antioch." JBL 51 (1932), 130-60.

Kramer, Werner. Christ, Lord, Son of God. Translated by Brian Hardy. Studies in Biblical Theology 50. Naperville, Ill.: Alec R. Allenson, Inc., 1966.

Kümmel, Werner Georg. "Πάρεσις and ἔνδειξις. A Contribution to the Understanding of the Pauline Doctrine of Justification." Translated by James E. Crouch. Journal for Theology and the Church, vol. 3. Tübingen: J. C. B. Mohr (Paul Siebeck); New York: Harper & Row, Publishers, Inc., 1967.

Kuhn, Karl Georg . Konkordanz zu den Qumrantexten. Göttingen: Vandenhoeck & Ruprecht, 1960.

_____. "The Lord's Supper and the Communal Meal at Qumran." The Scrolls and the New Testament. Edited by Krister Stendahl. New York: Harper and Brothers, 1957. Pp. 65-93.

Kuss, Otto. Der Römerbrief (Erste Lieferung). 2nd unaltered ed. Regensburg: Verlag Friedrich Pustet, 1963.

Lampe, Geoffrey W. H. A Patristic Greek Lexicon. Oxford: At the Clarendon Press, 1968 (first published 1961).

Leipoldt, Johannes. Der Tod bei Griechen und Juden. Beiheft zu Germanentum, Christentum und Judentum. Leipzig: Verlag Georg Wigand, 1942.

Licht, Jacob. "Taxo, or the Apocalyptic Doctrine of Vengeance." JJS 12 (1961), 95-103.

Liddell, Henry G., and Scott, Robert. A Greek-English Lexicon. 9th ed., revised by Henry Stuart Jones, with Roderick McKenzie. Oxford: At the Clarendon Press, 1940.

Lietzmann, Hans. An die Römer. 4th ed. HNT 8. Tübingen: Verlag von J. C. B. Mohr (Paul Siebeck), 1933.

_____. Mass and Lord's Supper: A Study in the History of the Liturgy. Translated by Dorothea H. G. Reeve. Introduction and Supplementary Essay by Robert D. Richardson. Leiden: E. J. Brill, 1953-69 (fascicles 1-7).

Lindars, Barnabas. New Testament Apologetic. The Doctrinal Significance of the Old Testament Quotations. Philadelphia: The Westminster Press, 1961.

Lindblom, Johannes. The Servant Songs in Deutero-Isaiah. Lund: C. W. K. Gleerup, 1951.

Lohmeyer, Ernst. Die Briefe an die Philipper, an die Kolosser und an Philemon. 13th ed. Meyer 9. Göttingen: Vandenhoeck & Ruprecht, 1964.

Lohse, Eduard. Märtyrer und Gottesknecht. Untersuchungen zur urchristlichen Verkündigen von Sühntod Jesu Christi. FRLANT 64. Göttingen: Vandenhoeck & Ruprecht, 1955.

Luck, U. "Makkabäerbücher (4. Viertes M.)." RGG, IV, 622-23.

Lührmann, Dieter. "Rechtfertigung und Versöhnung. Zur Geschichte der paulinischen Tradition." ZTK 67 (1970), 437-52.

Maas, Max. "Die Maccabäer als christlicher Heilige. (Sancti Maccabaei.)." Monatschrift für Geschichte und Wissenschaft des Judenthums 44 (1900), 145-56.

McCarthy, Dennis J. Treaty and Covenant: A Study in Form in the Ancient Oriental Documents and in the Old Testament. Analecta Biblica 21. Rome: Pontifical Biblical Institute, 1963.

MacGregor, George H. C. Eucharistic Origins. A Survey of the New Testament Evidence. London: James Clarke & Co., Limited, 1928.

Manson, Thomas Walter. "ΙΛΑΣΤΗΡΙΟΝ." JTS 46 (1945), 1-10.

Manson, William. Jesus the Messiah. Philadelphia: The Westminster Press, 1946.

Meecham, Henry G. "Romans iii. 25f., iv. 25--the meaning of διά c. acc." ET 50 (1938-39), 564.

Michel, Otto. Der Brief an die Hebräer. 11th ed. Meyer 13. Göttingen: Vandenhoeck & Ruprecht, 1960.

_____. Der Brief an die Römer. 12th ed. Meyer 4. Göttingen, Vandenhoeck & Ruprecht, 1963.

Montefiore, Claude G. The Synoptic Gospels. Edited with an Introduction and a Commentary. 2 vols. 2nd revised ed. London: Macmillan and Co., Limited, 1927.

Morris, Leon. "The Meaning of 'ΙΛΑΣΤΗΡΙΟΝ in Romans III. 25." NTS 2 (1955-56), 33-43.

_____. "The Use of ἱλάσκεσθαι etc. in Biblical Greek." ET 62 (1950-51), 227-33.

Murray, Gilbert. Aeschylus: The Creator of Tragedy. Oxford: At the Clarendon Press, 1940.

Neusner, Jacob. "Jewish Use of Pagan Symbols after 70 C.E." Journal of Religion 43 (1963), 285-94.

Nickelsburg, George W. E., Jr. Resurrection, Immortality, and Eternal Life in Intertestamental Judaism. Unpublished Th.D. Dissertation, Harvard University, 1967.

Norden, Eduard. Die Antike Kunstprosa. Vom VI Jahrhundert v. Chr. bis in die Zeit der Renaissance. 2 vols. Leipzig: Druck und Verlag von B. G. Teubner, 1898.

Nygren, Anders. "Christus, der Gnadenstuhl." In Memoriam Ernst Lohmeyer. Edited by Werner Schmauch. Stuttgart: Evangelisches Verlagswerk GmbH., 1951. Pp. 89-93.

Obermann, Julian. "The Sepulchre of the Maccabean Martyrs." JBL 50 (1931), 250-65.

Oepke, Albrecht. "ΔΙΚΑΙΟΣΥΝΗ ΘΕΟΥ bei Paulus in neuer Beleuchtung." TLZ 78 (1953), 257-64.

Orlinsky, Harry M. "The So-Called 'Servant of the Lord' and 'Suffering Servant' in Second Isaiah." Studies on the Second Part of the Book of Isaiah (with Norman H. Snaith). Supplements to VT 14. Leiden: E. J. Brill, 1967.

_____. "The So-Called 'Suffering Servant' in Isaiah 53." Interpreting the Prophetic Tradition (The Goldenson Lectures 1955-66). The Library of Biblical Studies. Cincinnati: The Hebrew Union College Press; New York: KTAV Publishing House, Inc., 1969.

Otto, Rudolf. The Kingdom of God and the Son of Man. Revised ed. Translated by Floyd V. Filson and Bertram Lee Woolf. London: Lutterworth Press, 1943.

Percy, Ernst. Die Probleme der Kolosser- und Epheserbriefe. Lund: C. W. K. Gleerup, 1946.

Pfitzner, Victor C. Paul and the Agon Motif. Traditional Athletic Imagery in the Pauline Literature. Supplements to Novum Testamentum 16. Leiden: E. J. Brill, 1967.

Plöger, Otto. Das Buch Daniel. Kommentar zum Alten Testament 18. Gütersloh: Gütersloher Verlagshaus Gerd Mohn, 1965.

Pluta, Alfons. Gottes Bundestreue. Ein Schlüsselbegriff in Röm. 3,25a. Stuttgarter Bibelstudien 34. Stuttgart: Verlag Katholisches Bibelwerk, 1969.

Rad, Gerhard von. Old Testament Theology. 2 vols. Translated by D. M. G. Stalker. New York and Evanston: Harper & Row, Publishers, 1962 (vol. 1) and 1965 (vol. 2).

Rampolla del Tindaro, Mariano. "Martyre et sépulture des Machabées." Revue de l'Art Chrétien (1899), 290-305, 377-92, 457-65.

Reider, Joseph. "On MŠḤTY in the Qumran Scrolls." BASOR 134 (1954), 27, 28.

Rese, Martin. "Überprufung einiger Thesen von Joachim Jeremias zum Thema des Gottesknechtes im Judentum." ZTK 60 (1963), 21-41.

Reumann, John. "The Gospel of the Righteousness of God. Pauline Reinterpretation in Romans 3:21-31." Interpretation 20 (1966), 432-52.

Robertson, Jerry. "Ezekiel the Tragedian: Scholia." Unpublished paper submitted for the Graduate New Testament Seminar at Harvard Divinity School, May 8, 1970.

Robinson, Henry Wheeler. The Cross in the Old Testament. London: SCM Press Ltd., 1955.

Robinson, Henry Wheeler. Suffering Human and Divine. Great
Issues of Life Series. New York: The Macmillan Company,
1939.

Rohde, Erwin. Psyche: The Cult of Souls and Belief in Immortality among the Greeks. Translated by W. B. Hillis from
the 8th ed. New York: Harcourt, Brace & Company, Inc.,
1925.

Rose, Herbert J. "Iphigenia." The Oxford Classical Dictionary.
Oxford: At the Clarendon Press, 1949. Pp. 457-58.

Sanday, William, and Headlam, Arthur C. A Critical and
Exegetical Commentary on the Epistle to the Romans. 5th
ed. International Critical Commentary. Edinburgh: T. & T.
Clark, 1902 (reprinted 1960).

Sanders, Jim Alvin. Suffering as Divine Discipline in the Old
Testament and Post-Biblical Judaism. Rochester, N. Y.:
Colgate Rochester Divinity School, 1955.

Scharbert, Josef. "Stellvertretendes Sühneleiden in den Ebed-
Jahwe-Liedern und in altorientalischen Ritualtexten."
BZ 2 (1958), 190-213.

Schattenmann, Johannes. Studien zum neutestamentlichen
Prosahymnus. Munich: C. H. Beck'sche Verlagsbuchhandlung,
1965.

Schmid, Hans H. Gerechtigkeit als Weltordnung. Hintergrund
und Geschichte des alttestamentlichen Gerechtigkeits-
begriffes. Beiträge zur Historischen Theologie 40.
Tübingen: J. C. B. Mohr (Paul Siebeck), 1968.

Schmid, Wilhelm and Stählin, Otto. Geschichte der griechischen
Literatur. Erster Teil: Die klassische Periode der griech-
ischen Literatur. Vol. III. Munich: C. H. Beck'sche
Verlagsbuchhandlung, 1940.

Schmitt, Johanna. Freiwilliger Opfertod bei Euripides. Ein
Beitrag zu seiner dramatischen Technik. Religionsgeschicht-
liche Versuche und Vorarbeiten 17 Nr. 2. Giessen: Verlag
von Alfred Töpelmann, 1921.

Schrenk, Gottlob. "δίκη κτλ." TDNT, II, 178-225.

Schutz, Roland. "Die Bedeutung der Kolometrie für das Neue
Testament." ZNW 21 (1922), 161-84.

Schweizer, Eduard. Lordship and Discipleship. Translated,
with revisions, by the author. Studies in Biblical
Theology 28. London: SCM Press Ltd., 1960.

Simon, Marcel. "La polémique anti-juive de S. Jean Chrysostome et le mouvement judaïsant d'Antioche." Mélanges
Franz Cumont. Annuaire de l'Institut de philologie et
d'histoire orientales et slaves, IV/1. Brussels:
Secrétariat de l'Institut, 1936.

Smith, J. M. Powis. The Prophets and Their Times. 2nd ed.
revised by William A. Irwin. Chicago: The University of
Chicago Press, 1941.

268

Smith, Morton. "A Comparison of Early Christian and Early Rabbinic Tradition." JBL 82 (1963), 169-76.

Smyth, Herbert W. Greek Grammar. Revised by Gordon M. Messing. Cambridge, Mass.: Harvard University Press, 1963.

Snaith, Norman H. "Isaiah 40-66. A Study of the Teaching of the Second Isaiah and its Consequences." Studies on the Second Part of the Book of Isaiah (with Harry M. Orlinsky). Supplements to VT 14. Leiden: E. J. Brill, 1967.

Snaith, Norman H. "The Servant of the Lord in Deutero-Isaiah." Studies in Old Testament Prophecy. Edited by H. H. Rowley. Edinburgh: T. & T. Clark, 1950. Pp. 187-200.

Stamm, Johann Jakob. Erlösen und Vergeben im Alten Testament. Eine begriffsgeschichtliche Untersuchung. Bern: Verlag A. Francke A.-G., 1940.

_____. Das Leiden des Unschuldigen in Babylon und Israel. Abhandlungen zur Theologie des Alten und Neuen Testaments 10. Zurich: Zwingli-Verlag, 1946.

Stendahl, Krister. "Hate, Non-retaliation, and Love. IQS x, 17-20 and Rom. 12:19-21." HTR 55 (1962), 343-55.

_____. "Messianic License." Biblical Realism Confronts the Nation. Edited by Paul Peachey. [New York]: Fellowship Publications, 1963.

_____. The School of St. Matthew and Its Use of the Old Testament. Philadelphia: Fortress Press, 1968.

Strack, Herman L., and Billerbeck, Paul. Kommentar zum Neuen Testament aus Talmud und Midrash. 4 vols. 2nd ed. Munich: C. H. Beck'sche Verlagsbuchhandlung, 1956.

Strugnell, John. "Notes on 1QS 1,17-18; 8,3-4 and IQM 17, 8-9." CBQ 29 (1967), 580-82.

Stuhlmacher, Peter. Gerechtigkeit Gottes bei Paulus. FRLANT 87. Göttingen: Vandenhoeck & Ruprecht, 1965.

Suhl, Alfred. Die Funktion der alttestamentlichen Zitate und Anspielungen im Markusevangelium. Gütersloh: Gütersloher Verlagshaus Gerd Mohn, 1965.

Surkau, Hans-Werner. Martyrien in jüdischer und frühchrist-licher Zeit. FRLANT 54. Göttingen: Vandenhoeck & Ruprecht, 1938.

Talbert, Charles H. "A Non-Pauline Fragment at Romans 3 24-26?" JBL 85 (1966), 287-96.

_____. "Tradition and Redaction in Romans XII. 9-21." NTS 16 (1969-70), 83-93.

Taylor, Vincent. Jesus and His Sacrifice. A Study of the Passion-Sayings in the Gospels. London: Macmillan and Co., Limited, 1937.

Tedesche, Sidney (Translation), and Zeitlin, Solomon (Intro-
duction and Commentary). The First Book of Maccabees.
Dropsie College Edition: Jewish Apocryphal Literature.
New York: Harper & Brothers (for The Dropsie College for
Hebrew and Cognate Learning), 1950.

Thyen, Hartwig. Studien zur Sündenvergebung im Neuen Testament
und seinen alttestamentlichen und jüdischen Voraussetzungen.
FRLANT 96. Göttingen: Vandenhoeck & Ruprecht, 1970.

Titus, Eric L. "Did Paul Write I Corinthians 13?" JBR 27
(1959), 299-302.

Torrey, Charles Cutler. The Apocryphal Literature. A Brief
Introduction. New Haven: Yale University Press, 1945.

Turner, Nigel. Syntax. Vol. III of A Grammar of New Testament
Greek, by James Hope Moulton. Edinburgh: T. & T. Clark,
1963.

Vaux, Roland de. Studies in Old Testament Sacrifice. Cardiff:
University of Wales Press, 1964.

Vielhauer, Philipp. "Gottesreich und Menschensohn in der
Verkündigung Jesu." Festschrift für Günther Dehn. Neukir-
chen: Verlag der Buchhandlung des Erziehungsvereins, 1957.
Pp. 51-79.

_____. "Jesus und der Menschensohn." ZTK 60 (1963),
133-77.

_____. "Ein Weg zur neutestamentlichen Christologie?"
EvTh 25 (1965), 24-72.

Waterman, LeRoy. "The Martyred Servant Motif of Is. 53." JBL
56 (1937), 27-34.

Wenschkewitz, Hans. Die Spiritualisierung der Kultusbegriffe.
Tempel, Priester und Opfer im Neuen Testament. Angelos-
Beiheft 4. Leipzig: Verlag von Eduard Pfeiffer, 1932.

Wichmann, Wolfgang. Die Leidenstheologie: Eine Form der
Leidensdeutung im Spätjudentum. Beiträge zur Wissenschaft
vom Alten und Neuen Testament 53. Stuttgart: W. Kohlhammer
Verlag, 1930.

Wiencke, Gustav. Paulus über Jesu Tod. Die Deutung des Todes
Jesu bei Paulus und ihre Herkunft. Beiträge zur Förderung
christlicher Theologie II/42. Gütersloh: Verlag C.
Bertelsmann, 1939.

Windisch, Hans. Der Hebräerbrief. 2nd ed. HNT. Tübingen:
J. C. B. Mohr (Paul Siebeck), 1931.

Wolff, Hans Walter. Jesaia 53 im Urchristentum. 2nd ed.
Berlin: Evangelische Verlagsanstalt, 1950.

Wright, W. "An Ancient Syrian Martyrology." The Journal of
Sacred Literature and Biblical Record 8 (1866), 45-56 (text),
423-32 (translation).

Zeitlin: See Tedesche.

Zeller, Dieter. "Sühne und Langmut. Zur Traditions-
geschichte von Röm 3,24-26." Theologie und Philosophie
43 (1968), 51-75.